Advance praise for *A Nice Tuesday*

"*A Nice Tuesday* is tight, true, and lingers in the mind and heart. His is a wonderful prose. There is not an ounce of fat anywhere in this narrative. This is a valuable book for the library of any family who admires the written word."
—Harry Crews, author of *A Childhood* and *Celebration*

"Everybody has a 'what if' fantasy. Pat Jordan actually got to live his—with surprising results. A funny, moving, and insightful story about baseball, middle age, and manhood, by a gifted writer."
—Robert Ward, author of *Grace* and *Red Baker*

Praise for *A False Spring*

"Jordan is a major league writer and has written an unforgettable book."
—*Los Angeles Times*

"One of the most fabulous failure stories of our times . . . as unsparingly accurate and perceptive in his portrayal of himself as he is in his treatment of the often sad people and towns that make up the mostly bleak landscape of minor league America."
—*Kansas City Star*

"*A False Spring*, by turns rueful, amused, nostalgic, and disgusted, is just fascinating, probably the best book imaginable about baseball's under-pinnings."
—*The Boston Globe*

"Jordan's insight, intensity, and relentless honesty should earn it an honored place among the serious nonfiction of recent years."
—*The Baltimore Sun*

"Beautifully written . . . always pleasurably stimulating, often poignant."
—*The Philadelphia Inquirer*

"Affecting . . . elegiac . . . often comedic."
—*Houston Chronicle*

"Arguably the best baseball autobiography of all time."
—*SABR Review of Books*

A NICE TUESDAY

A NICE TUESDAY

A MEMOIR

PAT JORDAN

Golden Books
NEW YORK

Golden Books®

888 Seventh Avenue
New York, NY 10106

Copyright © 1999 by Pat Jordan
All rights reserved, including the right of reproduction
in whole or in part in any form.
Golden Books® and colophon
are trademarks of Golden Books Publishing Co., Inc.

Designed by [tk]

Manufactured in the United States of America

10   9   8   7   6   5   4   3   2   1

Library of Congress Cataloging-in-Publication Data

Jordan, Pat.
  A nice Tuesday: a memoir / Pat Jordan.
    p.   cm.
  ISBN 1-58238-028-7 (alk. paper)
  1. Jordan, Pat.   2. Baseball players—United States—Biography.   3. Minor
league baseball—United States.   I. Title.
GV865.J67A3   1999
796.357'092—dc21
[B]
                                                              98-48779
                                                                  CIP

For Hoshi, Kiri, Stella, Nero, Bubba,
Blue, Sweetness, Francis, and the Usual Suspects.
For Brian LaBasco, without whom this book
couldn't have been written.
For my brother and his wife, and my mother and father.
And finally, as always, for Susan,
and her mother, Peg, whom I've never met
but who is always there for us.

"The mind is its own place, and in itself can make a heaven of hell, a hell of heaven."

—John Milton, *Paradise Lost*,
Book 1, lines 254–5.

"I am such an egotist that if I were to write about a chair I would find some way to write about myself."

—*paraphrased from French dilettante*

"What would I be without baseball? I could think of nothing."

—Pat Jordan, A False Spring

"He cannot be a gentleman which loveth not a dog."

—*John Northbrooke, Against Dicing* (1577)

ONE

I SEE MYSELF AS I AM NOW, sitting at the head of the dining-room table at my most recent birthday party. My wife and my friends are sitting around me. They are drinking, smoking, laughing, gesturing with their hands, shouting to be heard. I am silent, smiling at my friends. A beautiful girl is sitting on each knee. One is blonde, thirty, with a languid touch. She rests her hand lightly on the nape of my neck and strokes my short hair. The other is a redhead, twenty-seven, with perfectly shaped breasts half exposed beneath her flimsy T-shirt. She is whispering in my ear, her breast pressed against my shoulder. I laugh. The two girls look down at me. They smile, dreamily, at me . . . a rough, good-looking man with curly hair, tall, trim, muscular.

Ronnie stands, weaving unsteadily, and aims a Polaroid camera at me and the two young girls. I put one hand on the naked thigh of the blonde and the other on the firm right breast of the redhead. The girls squeal with mock outrage, but do not push my hands away. My friends hoot at me with derision. Peter rolls his eyes to the ceiling. George and Al grin like elves. Sol smirks in disgust and turns his face from me. Phil throws up his hands, as if pleading. My wife shakes her head in weary resignation.

I smile seductively into the camera. Ronnie snaps our photograph. He hands me the developing snapshot. It's blurry gray, then grows darker as images form before my eyes. Colors appear. The two young girls appear. *I* appear! An old man! With a white beard! I am wearing a ridiculous-looking aqua-blue Hawaiian shirt dotted with pink flamingoes. I am leering like an old fool, with a cigar clenched between my teeth and two beautiful girls sitting on my knees, smiling at me—not dreamily, but with the condescending affection young girls reserve for belovedly lecherous, harmless old men.

I stare at the photograph. Finally it registers. I mutter to myself, "Jeez, I look like an old man."

My friends hear me. They shout in unison, "You *are* an old man!"

My wife smiles at me, with pity.

The two young girls hug me. The blonde says, "But we love you, Patty."

The redhead takes my hand and places it over her breast. "There," she says. "Feel better?"

It's funny how we see ourselves. It bears no relation to how others see us. It doesn't matter how others see us. It matters only how we see ourselves, frozen at those points in time that most truly defined us. It doesn't matter that our self-perception is a delusion. It matters only that to us it's real, that in *our* mind's eye we will always be what we were at those points in time that *we* decided most truly defined *us*.

* * *

I see myself at another birthday party almost fifty years ago. I am helping my mother set the kitchen table for my eighth birthday, in our new house in an old, Waspy, New England town.

"Put the Cassatta in the center of the table," she says. She is stirring the spaghetti sauce at the stove.

I slide the big heavy cake off the counter and carry it to the table. It has a plain yellowish frosting on top that tastes of butter and heavy cream. Its sides are coated with slivers of faintly bitter, toasted almonds. The filling is a semisweet custard flecked with bits of bittersweet, dark chocolate. The cake itself is as dense as peasant bread, chewy and moist and soaked with rum.

"Ma, why can't I have a cake like my friends?" My new friends in the suburbs always have birthday cakes as light as air, with sugary, whipped cream frosting as white as snow, and strawberry preserve filling, and hard, pastel-colored, sugar flowers on top that surround the words "Happy Birthday," scripted in hard blue sugar.

"Your aunts and uncles like Cassatta," she says. She tastes the sauce from a wooden spoon. She means my Uncle Ken, the judge, and his wife, Josephine. My Uncle Pat, the stockbroker, and his wife, Marie. My Uncle Ben, the draftsman, and his wife, Ada. Aunt Jo and Aunt Marie are my mother's sisters. Uncle Ben is her brother. My father has no relatives. He was an orphan who never knew his parents. His only relatives, he says, are my aunts and uncles, who will be my only guests at my eighth birthday party.

"Now get the antipast'," says my mother.

I take out the huge round silver tray of antipasto from the refrigerator and lay it next to the cake. It looks like a big flower with its petals of sweet red roasted peppers, sardines, calamari, artichoke hearts, black and green olives, thinly sliced, tightly rolled Genoa salami and prosciutto, chunks of Asiago and Pecorino, and, in the center, the heart of the flower: a round of tuna fish.

"The vino," she says.

I get the plain gallon jug of red wine from the floor of the pantry and struggle with it to the table. I put it down with a thunk. My mother turns and glares at me, then goes back to her sauce. I know enough not to ask her why I can't have hot dogs and Coke and colored balloons and my new friends at my birthday party. Balloons are a waste of money, she says. My new friends are a bother, she says. And my aunts and uncles, she says, certainly can't be expected to eat that "Irisher food."

She calls my new friends "Irishers" with a dismissive toss of her hand. But my new friends are not all Irish. They are English and German and Swedish and Jewish and Russian too. But that is all the same to my mother. "They're white," she says, and expects me to know what that means.

We are the first Italian family to move into this Waspy suburb, and we are certainly the only family here whose breadwinner sleeps all day because he supports his family by gambling all night. That's the real reason I can't have my new friends to my house. My mother is afraid they will tell their parents my father sleeps all day. Or, worse, that when he finally rises at three o'clock, he sits at the kitchen table drinking espresso with a lemon peel while he holds up pair after pair of red Lucite dice to the light, turns them over and over until he's satisfied, and then puts each pair in a meticulously numbered box.

"If they ever ask," my mother tells me, "say your father works the night shift at the Brass factory."

So I go to my new friends' houses instead. My mother doesn't mind. "Good," she says. "You'll be out of my hair."

I love going to my new friends' houses. It's a strange, new, exotic world for me. My new friends have dogs and cats and little sisters and freckled moms and smiling dads, who never speak loudly, in Italian, or gesture with their hands. Their dads are never too busy to go outside in the street and toss a baseball to them and their friends. Their moms are never too busy to make peanut butter and jelly sandwiches and a glass of milk for them and their friends. Peanut butter and jelly is so exotic to me. For lunch? My lunch is always pizza frite—dough fried in olive oil and then sprinkled with confectionary sugar. Or eggs scrambled in olive oil with sweet red peppers and crusty Italian bread. I never knew scrambled eggs were supposed to be yellow until I went to my new friends' houses and saw their mothers cook them in butter. My eggs, scrambled in olive oil, were always a dirty brown.

My new friends play wildly in their houses. They throw things, break things, then shout and laugh. I watch in horror, then glance over my shoulder at their parents. Amazing! Their moms and dads are shaking their heads and smiling at their rambunctious children. Then they bend down and sweep up the glass vase their children have just broken. I did not know that such things existed: children my age who never worry about pleasing adults, and adults who worry only about pleasing children.

When I talk too much in my house, or laugh out loud, my mother turns on me. "Shoosh!" she says, with a finger to her lips. "Your father's sleeping." When my father wakes up in a foul mood after last night's gambling losses, my mother tosses me a look. She gestures with her head toward my room upstairs. "Take some comic books," she says, "like a good boy."

My aunts and uncles arrive for my birthday party at eight o'clock. (My older brother, George, twenty-two, is still away at law school.)

They all bend down to kiss me on the lips, pinch my cheeks in a way that hurts, then tell my mother how beautiful I am, almost a man already, and wish me happy birthday. My uncles fish in their pockets for some bills and hand them to me as a present. Five dollars, three, six, whatever they find. My father has already given me my present, a wrinkled twenty-dollar bill he won last night shooting craps with shaved dice.

I finger all the bills in my hand.

"What do you say?" my mother says.

"Thanks, Uncle Ben, Uncle Pat, Uncle Ken." They pat me on the head, absentmindedly, like a pet, and sit down at the kitchen table for a moment. The women pour the men glasses of red wine, and me too, a little red wine mixed with water. I am, after all, a man too, in the eyes of my mother and my aunts. My aunts and my mother pour scotch for themselves, and then my aunts go to the stove to help my mother with the sauce. The men and women are talking now, sometimes in Italian, sometimes in English, and I have been forgotten.

Their conversation is always about Italians. Local Italians who have become doctors and lawyers, or famous Italians like Joe DiMaggio, who have become American heroes. Joe D is a credit to Italians because he has mastered the American pastime and American ways. He plays baseball and moves through his life with a style and grace and silent dignity that Italians can be proud of. He gives a lie to the image of Italians as small, dark, loud, coarse immigrants. He has assimilated American ways, yet he has done it without losing his Italianness.

"Joe D," my mother says at the stove. "He's a white Italian."

My aunts and uncles nod. "Not like that other one," says my Uncle Ben.

"Sinatra," says Uncle Pat.

"He might as well be a *melanzana*," says Uncle Ken.

"A real guinea," says my father, with disgust.

I speak up. "What's a guinea, Dad?" Everyone looks at me for a moment, then they smile.

"Don't worry," my mother says. "You'll know one when you meet one." Everyone laughs.

My father and my uncles get up and go into the living room to watch a Yankee game on our tall mahogany Motorola television set with the tiny round black-and-white screen. They light up Chesterfield cigarettes, while, in the kitchen, the women hover over pots of spaghetti sauce. They sip scotch and smoke Chesterfields too, while they fantasize about the handsome DiMaggio.

"Sooo handsome!" says Aunt Marie with a dreamy smile.

"He needs a good Italian wife," says Aunt Jo, ever practical.

"If only your daughters were old enough," my mother says to Aunt Jo.

Aunt Marie holds up a huge sausage link she is about to drop into the sauce. She says something in Italian. Her sisters laugh.

My mother holds her hands twelve inches apart and rolls her eyes to the ceiling.

"Mama mia!" says Aunt Jo. "What a big bat!" The women squeal with laughter.

"Your poor daughters," my mother says.

"He'll probably marry some Irisher," says Aunt Marie.

My mother and Aunt Jo turn on her. "Never!" they say in unison. "Not Joe D."

I go into the living room, where the men are hunched forward in their easy chairs, watching Yogi Berra at bat. Berra is squat, homely, taciturn, hardworking. The men love him but the women have little interest in him. They have interest only in the handsome DiMaggio. They are short, dark, mannish women with big noses and hair like Brillo. They are not unattractive women, with their strong faces, but they do not think of themselves as attractive in their adopted country of the Andrews Sisters. It would be years before Sophia Loren redefined beauty in America, and the world.

"That Yogi," says Uncle Ben. "He's a tough one. A clutch batter."

"Not as good as Campanella," says Uncle Ken. The two men begin to argue over the relative merits of Berra and Roy Campanella, the Brooklyn Dodgers catcher. Finally my father intervenes.

"What difference does it make?" he says. "They're both Italians."
The men all nod.

Finally Uncle Pat says, "What about that time Campanella struck out? Berra would never have done that."

"Campanella wasn't Italian then," says Uncle Ken. "He was a *melanzana* then." The men laugh. *Melanzana* is the Italian word for "eggplant." It's slang for "black." Campanella has a black mother and an Italian father. When he hits a home run, he's a *paisano* to Italians. When he strikes out he's a *melanzana*.

The women call the men into the kitchen to eat. First the antipasto. Then the spaghetti with sausage. Finally my birthday cake. My mother lights the candles.

"Turn the lights out, Ma," I say.

"Why?" she says.

I blow out the candles and make a wish, while, around me, my parents and my aunts and uncles are talking. I smell the espresso boiling on the stove. My mother puts the first piece of cake in front of me and says, "Hurry up. Eat. It's time for bed."

I finish my piece of cake before the others have even touched theirs.

"To bed," my mother says. I look at her. "You heard me," she says.

I go around the table and kiss everyone good night and go upstairs to bed as Aunt Marie begins to pour the espresso and Aunt Jo puts the bottle of scotch on the table and everyone lights up Chesterfield cigarettes.

But I don't go to bed. I sneak back to the top of the stairs and sit down. I can see my aunts and uncles and parents as shadows illuminated on the living-room wall below. I hear their voices. They speak mostly in Italian now. I can hear their laughter. The sound of their voices and their laughter sends chills down my spine. I hug myself and begin to rock gently in the darkness at the top of the stairs. I think of my new friends. How different I am from them. The loss of their privileged childhoods will be so painful for them someday. But not for me. I understand it all at that moment. My parents are not raising me to be a child. They are raising me to be an adult. This realization makes my body tingle with an almost sexual thrill. I cannot wait for that moment when I will step out of the shadows of my silent childhood to assume my rightful place at the head of the table among adults. It is what I wished for when I blew out the candles

*   *   *

I toss the photograph of the old man and the young girls on the table, which is littered with bottles of Jim Beam, Smirnoff vodka, Santa Carolina merlot, and Heineken beer. My friends have no interest in the picture. They see me every day. They go back to their talking and laughing. I pour some Jim Beam into my yellow tin cup and light another cigar. My wife gets up to clear off the empty bottles. The two young girls get off my knees to help her. They have to step around my six dogs, who are sprawled around the dining room and kitchen, sleeping.

I stare at my friends through a haze of cigar smoke. The Usual Suspects. Sol, the Jew, a retired marijuana smuggler from Brooklyn. Phil, the owner of the Booby Trap, "Home of Stylish Nude Entertainment," from Detroit. "Stylish" was Phil's idea. He wanted to elevate his club from the sleazier strip clubs in town. "Like the broads in the Trap flash their bush more ladylike," says Sol. Chelsea, the redhead, is Phil's girlfriend. She's a bartender at the Trap and a criminal justice student from Miami. Peter is a litigation lawyer from Miami. Ronnie is a photographer from a little town in Wisconsin that Sol calls East Bumfuck. Mary Beth, the blonde, is his wife. She's a struggling writer from Virginia whom I've been helping with her career. George is a retired drama teacher from a small town in Nebraska. Alberto, George's lover for twenty-five years, is from Cali, Colombia. My wife, Susan, is a retired actress from our hometown of Fairfield, Connecticut.

Sol is bald and fat with a Vandyke beard which he thinks is sinister, and three beepers on his hip. Peter is tall and rumpled, with shaggy hair, a droopy mustache, and the sad eyes of a young Marcello Mastroianni. Phil is handsome and sleek, with his bleached blond hair pulled back tight into a ponytail. Alberto is tiny, dark, plump and bald, like a Latin elf. George is also small and bald, with an austere gray beard and a child's mischievous blue eyes. Ronnie, with his Prince Valiant haircut and aviator sunglasses, looks like John Denver. Mary Beth, with her perfect, bold features, looks like Linda Kozlowski from the movie *Crocodile Dundee.* Chelsea, with her burgundy-red hair, vivid blue eyes and perfect breasts, looks like a young Ann-Margret. Susan is tall and tan and lightly muscled at fifty-eight. She has three-dimensional blue eyes, like a doe, and short, ash-blond hair that sticks up like spring grass. She resembles her daughter, Meg Ryan.

That's how I see my friends. I know now how they see me.

Sol is telling George about his trip to Paris.

"Did you go to the Louvre?" George asks.

"Naw. I went to get laid," Sol says. "French broads love American gangsters."

George nods, seriously. "Of course."

"All I had to do was tell 'em I was in the slam." George looks confused. Sol says, "Prison, George."

George slaps his hand against his knee like an excited child who has just made a discovery. "Of course!" he says. Then he says, "Did you like it?"

"Like what?"

"Prison."

Sol looks at him. Then he says, "What's to like? I couldn't even get laid. I spent two years sleeping on my stomach and no one would fuck me."

George looks at Sol's big stomach, then says, "Of course." Then he says, sweetly, "I wouldn't fuck you either, Sol."

Phil hands an empty bottle to Susan. "Here, Ma." He always calls Susan and me "Ma" and "Pa." Phil lights a cigar. He leans back in his chair, his hands clasped behind his head, and exhales a puff of smoke.

Chelsea bends over Peter's shoulder to pick up some beer bottles. Peter glances sideways at her half-exposed breasts. He raises his eyebrows like Groucho Marx, wiggles the cigar clenched between his teeth, and says, "Here they are! Chelsea!" She smacks him in the side of the head with her left breast.

Ronnie and Alberto are swapping recipes. Ronnie says the secret to peanut butter pie is not to use too much sugar.

Alberto nods, then tells Ronnie in his heavily accented English that the secret to crispy fried plantains is the smooth stone he uses to flatten the little slices of plantain before he double fries them in hot oil.

Mary Beth is drifting through the house, admiring Susan's colorful tin Haitian sculptures. She stops at the fireplace and picks up a photograph from the mantel. She studies it.

"God!" she says with lust. "Who is *this?*"

"That's me," I say, grinning.

She looks at me, then at the photograph of the lean, tanned, shirtless young man with a halo of curly black hair, like a Greek god. The young man has folded his arms across his chest to underline his luxuriant black chest hair. His brown eyes are seductively half lidded.

Mary Beth looks at me again, then the photograph again. She shakes her head of long, ash-blond hair as fine as corn silk. "God!" she says, "you were *hot* when you were young."

I resist the urge to tell her, But I'm *still* hot! It's true. When I look out of my eyes at people looking at me I assume they see what I see: that young man who is having his picture taken by a still-naked twenty-three-year-old girl he has just had sex with. But that's not what they see. My friends are all younger than I. They see me only as they have known me these past ten years in Fort Lauderdale. An old man, now fifty-six, a writer, with six dogs, a parakeet he talks to, and a wife of infinite patience. An old man who rises before the sun each morning, the way old men do, as if anxious to snatch from every remaining day as much of life as possible. An old man rooted to his routine.

My friends never saw me as I see myself.

My friends are smiling now, looking over my shoulders. I turn to see Susan carrying, like an offering, my birthday cake ablaze with candles. Mary Beth and Chelsea are passing out plates and forks and napkins. My dogs, in various states of sprawl around the room, look up with interest but do not approach the table. Susan sets the cake down in the center of the table.

"What a *lovely* cake!" says George.

"Did you bake it, Sue-sahn?" asks Alberto.

Everyone groans. "Let's hope not," says Peter. Susan smiles.

"Pa," Phil says to me, "what kind is it?"

Sol looks at Phil. "You kiddin'?" he says. "You're supposta be a guinea, Phil."

"It's a Cassatta cake," I say.

Two

THE USUAL SUSPECTS leave after midnight. Susan and I wash the dishes at the sink and then go to bed. The dogs have already retired. The four oldest dogs are sleeping on their rugs around the bed. The two youngest dogs have already staked out their place on the bed. Susan and I contort ourselves around them, trying not to disturb them, and click on the TV. We watch a movie for a few minutes. Susan rolls over onto her side and is asleep. I try to watch the movie. I begin to drift off. I force my eyes open. But it is no use. I am too tired. I sleep. And then I dream. Always the same dream. Every night of my life since 1962.

*　　*　　*

I see myself from a distance, in shadow. I am standing on a pitcher's mound in a Milwaukee Braves baseball uniform. Sometimes I see myself as a young man, sometimes as a man of forty, and sometimes as I am now, an old man of fifty-six, with a white beard. The stadium around me is always deserted, except for a catcher crouching behind home plate and, behind him, behind the home-plate screen, a dozen major league scouts. They are leathery old men with big bellies and tufts of white hair. They sit in a cluster with their notebooks and radar guns. Their eyes are on me as I prepare to throw my first pitch, which will redeem me, *finally*, from that failure of my youth that has informed my adult life. I take a deep breath, toe the rubber, and begin my delivery. I pump, kick, rear back, feel the fear rising in my breast, and wake up at 4 A.M. to prepare my coffee for yet another day.

My friends have never seen me in a baseball uniform, except for the yellowed photographs on my office wall. Me as a boy of twelve, very serious, with big ears, in a baggy Little League uniform, posed stiffly in my follow through. Me as a young man of seventeen, still serious, with dark, brooding eyebrows, in a trimmer high-school uniform, posed again in my follow through, only less stiffly. And finally, me as an older young man of twenty-one, not serious now, bewildered, a frightened look in my eyes as I stand on a pitcher's mound in my Braves uniform, frozen.

That last photograph was taken in 1962, the year I left baseball. That is the phrase I always use, even though it is not quite accurate. Baseball left me.

I had been a baseball protégé since the age of ten. The Mozart of my day. Gifted, obsessed, destined, worshiped. Parents pointed me out to their children as an inspiration. I was interviewed on television at the age of twelve. Newspaper columnists from around the country wrote stories about me. By fifteen, I was pitching against thirty-year-old men with such easy, almost careless success that even I felt sorry for those grown men being embarrassed by a boy. Old men of distant baseball fame fawned over me. They stuttered in my presence, could barely speak. By eighteen, I was wealthy beyond the dreams of any boy my age. Except me. I accepted wealth as my birthright. I had more money than my father, at fifty, or my brother, at thirty-two, who had been a lawyer for eleven years. The year was 1959, the year I graduated from high school and immediately signed a $50,000 bonus contract with the then Milwaukee Braves.

The Braves sent me to the minor leagues to have a few seasons of blinding success. Then they would call me up to the major leagues at twenty. After a year or two of modest success, I would settle into a long, sustained career of such brilliance that I would be elected into the Hall of Fame after I retired. But my career did not happen the way the Braves and I envisioned. I struggled in the minor leagues for three years of diminishing success, and then outright failure. Finally, blessedly, the Braves released me in spring training of 1962.

I returned to my hometown of Fairfield with my young wife. We lived with my parents at first, in the house in the suburbs where I had been raised. My mother said we could stay as long as it took "Patty to get back on his feet."

But I couldn't get back on my feet. I spent each day lying on my back in our bedroom, *my* old bedroom, staring at the sunlight slanting in through the window. It illuminated in a dusty haze the mementos of my career arranged on the dresser. Bronze trophies from Little League with cheap plastic bases. Scuffed baseballs on which were printed in ink the coded details of my past successes. 19 Ks. 4 BB. 2 HITS. Prep vs. Tech, 1957. The three photographs of me, now on my office wall, were then on my bedroom wall.

I lay in bed, staring at those mementos for hours. They drained me of will. I could not muster the energy to get dressed each morning, to go down to breakfast, to sit and talk with my young wife.

From my bed, I could hear whispering voices in the kitchen below me.

"What's wrong with him?" said my mother's voice.

"I don't *know!*" said my wife's voice.

"What is he gonna do?"

I heard my wife's sobs. "I don't know."

Finally, I got out of bed. I got a job as a laborer for a stonemason.

The mason did not like athletes, he said. Not even ex-athletes. They were too soft. Compared to him, I was. He was forty-eight, with the smooth, tanned, muscular body of a man who'd worked hard all his life. He was a small man with not an ounce of fat on him. His leathery skin had gone slack with age so that he looked, not like a man growing soft with age, but rather a man growing smaller, shrinking inside his skin until one day it would be empty.

He built fireplaces and chimneys for expensive homes in Fairfield County, Connecticut. He alternated different shades of used brick so that his chimneys and fireplaces would be aesthetically pleasing. He considered himself an artist, not a craftsman. By extension, he considered his laborer an artist too. He told me stories about some Italian or Slovak immigrant who had kept him supplied with bricks and mortar as he worked up the side of the house building his chimney.

"He never fell behind me," he said. "And he always left the job spotless."

I thought he was crazy. That all a mason laborer could do was work and sweat like a mule.

It took me only two days to realize I was a lousy mason laborer. We were building a chimney on a $300,000 colonial house. With each passing hour, I fell farther and farther behind with bricks and mortar. I had no enthusiasm for this job. It was too physically demanding. It was mind-numbingly dull. But mostly it was terrifying. I hated to climb the maze of rusted pipes and brackets he called his scaffold. He never took care in building that scaffold. He settled it on uneven ground so that it wobbled.

Often it toppled over, with the mason flung to the ground. He liked telling me about these "trips," as if they were proof of his courage. His most recent trip shattered most of the bones in his right leg, which was now encased in a knee-to-hip cast. Which was why he had to hire a laborer as worthless as myself.

On this day he had built his scaffold to the second floor on a breezeless morning. By midafternoon a strong breeze had come up. From the ground I could see the top of the scaffold swaying left and right and back again past the half-completed chimney. The mason stood on the rotted planks with a brick in one hand and a trowel of mud in the other. He waited for the wind to blow him past the chimney so he could slap down his mud and brick before he was blown too far past to reach it. Then he waited for the wind to blow him back so he could level the brick with a tap of his trowel. He worked steadily like this, taking on the rhythm of the wind.

I looked up, terrified. When I climbed the ladder resting against the scaffold I wrapped my arms around it like a lover. I carried a bucket of mud or some bricks in one hand as I worked my way up, a step at a time. When I reached the top, I dumped the mud or bricks in a heap and hurried back to earth.

It wasn't only the dull, physically demanding work, or my fear, that caused me to fall behind the mason those first few days. I couldn't concentrate. I would be mixing mud in the tub and my thoughts would drift. I would lean motionless on my shovel, lost on some distant pitcher's mound in Palatka or McCook or Waycross, trying to discover where and how I had misplaced my career. I would rummage through my past reliving each season, each game, each pitch, as if expecting to come to a point, like a point on a graph, where I could say "There! Right there! That's where I lost it!" Then I could trace my failure along a succession of downhill points that had brought me to where I was now. A mason laborer. A failed one at that. Once I discovered that point I could begin retracing my career again, back up that graph. I could make a comeback, even now, if only I could discover that point where it had begun to slide away. But I never could.

In the midst of my reveries, the mason would bring me back to the present with his trowel. Whenever he slashed his trowel into the tub beside him and it was empty, it made a clanking noise. He would keep making that clanking noise until I rushed up the scaffold with more mud. How I hated the clank of that trowel! At first I just cursed him silently and took my sweet time bringing him mud. But soon that sound infuriated me. It was a reminder that I could not even handle a job as menial as this.

I decided one day to silence that trowel by mixing mortar faster than the mason could use it. But no matter how hard I worked that day I couldn't still his trowel. I was exhausted and defeated, standing at the foot of the scaffold, listening to the clank, clank, clank of his trowel. I was too exhausted even to take that first step up the scaffold. Suddenly it dawned on me that what was now happening to me—this frustration and failure—was to be the new pattern of my life. Baseball was not the one great failure of my life, as I had thought. It was just the first.

The following morning I arrived an hour early for work. It was 7 A.M. on a chill, sunny morning that would grow hot by noon. The house we were working on was tucked back among trees and wild undergrowth that had not yet been landscaped. I made my way across a grassless front yard strewn with boulders, planks, shingles, and empty paint cans, until I came to the side of the house where we kept our materials alongside the chimney. I flipped over the tarpaulin covering the sand and bags of lime and cement. I pulled the long, rowboatlike mortar tub into the open. I shoveled sand into it. I slit open a bag each of lime and cement with my shovel and shoveled part of each on top of the sand. The white lime billowed back into my face and burned my eyes. After a week of breathing lime the membranes of my nose were inflamed. I woke each morning with my throat dry and scratchy from having breathed through my mouth all night because my nose was clogged with dried lime and cement.

I raked through the sand and lime and cement until it was blended into a grainy, grayish substance flecked with white. Then I added water and hoed through the mix until it turned into mud. I pushed and pulled the hoe through the mud to make sure there were no pockets of lime or cement or sand.

I had been working for about thirty minutes. The morning chill was gone. The sun was hot. Sweat ran down my cheeks and the middle of my back. I was wearing a gray flannel baseball undershirt with blue sleeves cut off at the elbow. The sweat and the flannel itched my back but I paid no attention. I reached forward with my hoe, bending at the waist, and pulled the hoe toward me. It dawned on me that this motion—bending, reaching, straining—was the same I'd used when I pitched. I was using the same muscles too. When I'd first begun to work, my muscles were stiff and heavy, just as they were when I began to warm up to pitch a game. But after I stretched them out, after my sweat had loosened them, the heaviness was gone. I was now in a rhythm as smooth and effortless as any I'd ever had as a pitcher.

When I finished mixing the mortar I shoveled it into an old paint bucket and carried it up the ladder. I had partially overcome my fear of the scaffold and I needed to hold on with only one hand now, while I gripped the wire handle of the bucket with the other. The bucket and mud weighed almost thirty pounds. The wire handle dug into the underside of my fingers as I climbed the ladder. By the end of the day my fingers would be cramped into a claw and I would be unable to straighten them until the next morning.

I made six trips up the scaffold before the tub was filled. Then I began to carry up the bricks. On the first day I'd worked for him, the mason had taught me to carry the bricks in a row running from the underside of my wrist to the underside of my elbow. In this way I could bend my wrist in and the row of bricks would be locked between my wrist and my bicep. By the end of that first day, the jagged bricks had scraped away all the skin on the underside of my arm and it had begun to bleed. The next day I wore long gloves to work. When the mason saw them he said, "I never had a laborer worth a damn who used gloves." I took them off. Now as I carried the bricks up the ladder in the crook of my arm I could feel them scraping at the dried scabs until by the third trip my arms had begun to bleed as they always did. The sweat and the lime ran together with the blood until my arms began to burn.

I stacked the bricks until he had enough to keep him going for hours. Then, exhausted, I sat down in the shade of the house. I washed my arms with water from the tap and waited.

When the mason arrived in his battered old flatbed truck and saw what I had done he never said a word. He just climbed to the top of his scaffold, turned on his radio to some polka music, and began laying brick. He never again had to clank his trowel for more mud. After a few days I no longer had to arrive early to stay ahead of him. At the end of the week, just to show him up, I mixed so much mud so quickly that, as darkness came, he had to dump it down the chimney when he thought I wasn't looking. I felt the first sweet satisfaction I had felt since I left baseball.

One afternoon, a few weeks later, the mason and I sat against the side of a house eating lunch (we always ate in silence). He said, "You know, kid, if you work at it, some day you might make a half-decent mason." It was the highest compliment he could pay me, I thought, but at the same time it filled me with a despair so utter and complete that I could not finish my lunch. It was as if he had just forecast for me a life of stoic weariness equal to his own. I stared at him. He sat hunched over, his eyes glazed and riveted to the sandwich he held in his gnarled hands and chewed so methodically that the act seemed to require all his concentration. He was a dulled, uncomprehending, little man whose body and spirit seemed to shrink daily under the weight of his oppressive work. His life was like the brick and stone with which he worked. There was no softness, no lightness about it anywhere, not even in the long hours he spent drinking shots and beers at the Free

Eagle Hall. Was this what life held for me too? I wondered. Was this all those thirty-five-year-old minor league veterans meant when they said they'd take any job in baseball rather than return to "that lunch-bucket brigade" that awaited them back home?

Later that afternoon as I worked, I began to feel faint, light-headed, as if from hunger or too much sun. I had experienced this feeling frequently over my last year in the minor leagues. There would be two men on base. I would be standing on the pitcher's mound, helpless, my fastball gone, knowing I had nothing left. No fastball, no curveball, no control. Nothing.

For the first time in over a month I fell behind with bricks and mortar. I heard again that trowel clanking against the side of the mortar tub. Two days later, I quit the mason.

I was so disheartened by my failure at such a menial job that I couldn't bear to look for another one. I could think of nothing to do now, nothing that mattered, except to pitch. I would make a comeback. It wasn't too late. I was only twenty-one. It would be easy. I'd throw on my own for a few weeks, then I'd call up some high-school catcher who'd be only too happy to catch an ex-minor leaguer like me. Then after a few more weeks of throwing, watching his eyes light up when I cut loose a fastball, I'd call up some manager in the Senior City League, where at fifteen I had pitched a no-hitter in my first game and struck out fourteen. He'd jump at the chance to pitch me a few games. He'd probably offer me some money. A hundred dollars a game. Maybe fifty. Then after a few nice games, four-hitters, maybe ten strikeouts, the scouts would begin to come around again. I'd know them this time. We'd swap stories before a game, minor league stories, players they'd signed and I knew, inside stuff—who was drinking too much, was hurt—and then we'd get down to it. You're throwing good yourself, they'd say. Not bad, I'd say. Then one or more of them would make me an offer. Not a bonus like before. Not a big bonus, anyway. Maybe just a few thousand, to show good faith. And I'd be back where I belonged in the minor leagues, fulfilling my destiny.

But first I had to muster the courage to even go *see* a Senior City League game. I had been so ashamed of my failure that I couldn't bear to show my face at any of the parks in town where I'd had my youthful successes. I feared the inevitable question: "What happened?" I still didn't know. I knew only that I had left to play minor league baseball on a cloud of expectations and then, three years later, I was dumped, unceremoniously, in the dust. Dazed. Uncomprehending.

Finally, one weekday evening, I drove to Seaside Park in Bridgeport, near Long Island Sound. I stood behind a huge tree along the first base line. Hid behind it, really. Watching the players arrive. Most SCL games were played at twilight. The players rushed to the park from their real jobs as carpenters, masons, factory machinists, only minutes before the games began. They changed into their uniforms in their cars and took the field without warming up——they had no careers to protect—looking so odd with their chalky white hands dusted with lime.

SCL games were not like the Babe Ruth and high-school games of my youth. Young boys with high-stirrupped stockings playing in cool green suburbs before polite crowds of their parents and teen-age girls on ten-speed bikes. These were city games, played after work in the heat, before a crowd of blacks and Puerto Ricans and old men drinking out of paper bags, and even older men, ex-players, who now stood only a few feet away from me. These old-timers were tough on the players on the field, who, no matter how gritty a game they played, were never as tough, in those men's minds, as the players they remembered from their youth. Each generation, it seemed, was weaker than the last.

The players in those SCL games were in their late twenties, thirties, forties, even. They had once been prospects, had maybe even gone away to the minor leagues before getting released. Some were even in their fifties, like big Al Bike, a mean-looking, barrel-chested catcher; and Rufus Baker, a lean, trim black man with gray hair. Some of the players had even made the major leagues for a brief spell, like Tom Casagrande. Tommy "Big House," 6' 3", 235 pounds. A huge, redheaded, freckle-faced, southpaw pitcher with a smooth, effortless motion. His meaty arms were freckled and dusted with orange hair, like down. Tom was my idol when I was a kid. He had pitched a few years with the Phillies and Robin Roberts before he drifted back to the SCL, where he still threw good, good enough to get those batters out anyway.

Some of the players, like Bill Onuska, a catcher, had come so close to the major leagues they could almost taste it, but never did. Bill caught in AAA for years without being called up to the majors and finally, in his thirties, quit and returned to the SCL. I was a senior in high school when I heard he had returned home. It was midwinter. I called him up, introduced myself. He said he'd heard of me. I asked him if he'd catch me at the Boys Club gym, teach me a few things. He agreed. I said I'd pay him ten dollars a workout. We met there one cold night. I began to throw to him on the side of the court while kids played basketball. After about five minutes I cut loose with a fastball. Bill caught it and bounced out of his crouch. He walked toward me. He reached into his back pocket for the ten-dollar bill I'd given him. He handed it to me.

"Here, kid," he said. "You don't need me."

I was only a kid when I pitched in the SCL. A fifteen-year-old sophomore in high school. I struck out SCL batters at will then. I struck out thirty-year-old ex-minor leaguers like Nicky Vancho and Vinny Corda and Ronnie "The Globe" DelBianco. They didn't like it much. They shouted at me on the mound after they swung through their third strike. "You bastard! I'll get you next time." But they didn't.

I'd walk off the field at the end of the inning and my first baseman would meet me as we crossed the foul line. "Nice throwing, son," he'd say. He was a meticulous man with neat, short hair and a placid nature. Whitey McCall. He never swore like the other players. Whitey McCall. Father John McCall, a Catholic parish priest.

As I stood under that big tree, watching the game unfold, I grew excited at the thought of being a part of it again. How, now, all the other guys on the field would treat me as an equal, not a kid, because I had taken my lumps, like they had, in the minor leagues. Maybe, too, I would bring my young wife to my games now, like they did. The wives standing off together, chattering absentmindedly, rocking baby carriages, glad to be out of their third-floor, unair-conditioned walk-up apartment in the city for even a few hours.

Suddenly I heard my name. It came from the old-timers standing only a few feet in front of me. I caught a breath. They stood there, a cluster of wizened magpies, bachelors all, little old ladies, really, with nothing to do in their lives except carp about young players.

"Jordan's back," one of them said.

"Figures," said another. There was a clucking of tongues and a shaking of heads.

"I knew he'd never make it," said a third.

"He didn't have the guts," said still another.

I felt weak-kneed, light-headed again, as I had with the mason. I waited a few minutes before I walked back to my car. I hoped no one saw me. I got in and drove off. I put baseball out of my life that day. It was an illusion to think baseball would always be a part of my life. I never picked up a ball or glove again. It was years before I could even watch a game on TV.

I began my ordinary life. I had children. I went back to college. I worked odd jobs at night to support my growing family. I pumped gas. I was a soda jerk. I sold ties at a men's clothing store. I worked the 6 P.M. to 2 A.M. shift for the sports section of our local newspaper. My job, at first, was simply to read the horse-race results to a local bookie named Clyde. I knew him only as a gravelly, disembodied voice over the phone. "Dis is Clyde. You got da toid at Hialeah?" At the end of my first week, I found a box of Connecticut Topstone cigars on my desk. I showed them to my editor. "A gift from Clyde," he said. It was the beginning of my thirty-five-year cigar habit. I have never smoked a cigarette.

After a few weeks my editor entrusted me with the job of writing all the headlines for the local high-school baseball, basketball, and football stories. It took me hours. I hunted and pecked across the keys of a tall, old, black Underwood typewriter. After a year, I was allowed to write the two-paragraph stories of those games. When I finished, at midnight, I laid out my college textbooks and studied until 2 A.M. for my next day's exam. The only other reporter left in the office was an old-timer named John Johannsen. He'd been writing sports stories for the paper for over forty years. Now he was just an old drunk, hunched over his desk, a cigarette dangling from his lips, the ashes burning holes in his filthy white shirt as he banged away at his old Underwood, stopping every few words to sip bourbon from a white Styrofoam cup.

One night, after I finished one of my two-paragraph stories, I walked over to Johnny's desk. He was typing furiously, meaningless words that would never see print. I looked down at his greasy, swept-back, yellowish-white hair and waited for him to notice me, smoking my cigar.

Finally I said, "Johnny, can I bother you a minute?"

"Sure, kid." He kept typing furiously.

"You know, I'm beginning to like this sportswriting stuff, Johnny. I think I might like to do it for a career."

He stopped typing and looked up at me with his bleary, red-rimmed eyes. "It's a good job, kid," he said. "I owe everything I am in life to this job."

I quit the newspaper that year when I finally got my college degree. I had three children now and I needed a real job that paid more than sixty-five dollars a week. I began to teach English at an all-girls' parochial high school run by nuns. I corrected papers at night in my attic room, and then I tried to write stories. I wrote a short story about one of my students and sold it to *Ingenue,* the teenage girls' magazine. They sent me a $375 check made out to "Miss Pat Jordan," which pleased me. Then I sold a story to *True* magazine about one of my old teammates, Phil Niekro, who was now a star pitcher for the Atlanta Braves. I got a check for $1500. The editor, Norman Lewis Smith, called me and asked me to come to New York to meet him. I went to his office and he offered me a contract to write four stories a year for *True* for $6000, the same salary I was making as a teacher. So I quit my teaching job that May of 1970 and returned to Norm's office in June to sign my contract. Another man was sitting at his desk.

"Where's Norm?" I said.

"He got fired."

"But I'm Pat Jordan," I said. "He offered me a contract."

"That was his deal. Not mine."

I returned home and told my wife what had happened. I tried to get my teaching job back, but the diocese had already hired someone to replace me. I had a wife and five children by then, and three thousand dollars in a savings account. I told my wife I would write stories every day and try to sell them until that three thousand was gone. Then I'd get a job.

I sold a story that summer to Ray Cave at *Sports Illustrated.* Then I sold another. And another.

I am still writing. I have been a freelance writer since 1970. I have never worked on the staff of any magazine. I have never gotten a salary check, stock options, paid health care. I work from story to story, check to check, just as I did when I began my career as a freelance writer almost thirty years ago. I have written hundreds of magazine articles, short stories, two novels, and seven nonfiction books. One of those nonfiction books was a memoir about my minor league baseball years. I called it *A False Spring,* from a quote I found in Ernest Hemingway's *A Moveable Feast.* My memoir ended with these words: "What would I be without baseball? I could think of nothing."

I have been writing every day of my life since 1965. I have not thrown a pitch in a game since 1962. My second wife, Susan, my children, the Usual Suspects, have never seen me pitch. Only my first wife, Carol, my brother, now seventy, and my parents, of all the people who know me, have ever seen me pitch. But I don't see them much. The people I do see now in my life see me only as a writer. Except me, of course. I still see myself as a pitcher, with a 95 mph fastball, and infinite promise, who happens to be writing just now. Writing is what I do. Pitching is what I am. In my mind's eye, writing has always been just a temporary respite for me from that day when I will take the mound again and pitch. The fantasy of an old man of fifty-six. An old man who leads a sedentary life. An old man so rooted to the mundane order of his life that he is the butt of his friends' jokes.

THREE

PHIL CLOSES THE BOOBY TRAP at 4 A.M. He waits until all the dancers have left the darkened parking lot, then he drives home in his Porsche Turbo with the "Doin O K" license plate, changes into his skin-tight, day-glo-orange, spandex bicycle shorts and goes for a run along the dark streets of Fort Lauderdale. He runs south along Federal Highway until he reaches Sunrise Boulevard, then he turns east toward the Intracoastal Bridge and the beach beyond.

One morning, Phil turns west on Sunrise, rather than east. He jogs into Victoria Park, an old Fort Lauderdale neighborhood of one- and two-story mom-and-pop apartments and 1920s, wood-frame, Key West style bungalows. When he comes to a pink bungalow with white trim and a rusting tin roof on N.E. 17th Avenue, he stops, breathing heavily, in front of a white picket fence. He bends over to catch his breath, then opens the white gate and goes up to the front door. He knocks at 4:45 A.M. Dogs bark inside.

I open the front door in my shorts and T-shirt. My dogs, behind a gate in the hallway, stand on their hind legs to see who it is. Bubba barks impressively.

"Philip," I say, smiling. "What a nice surprise!" I am holding a mug of Cuban coffee and smoking my first cigar of the morning.

Phil just smiles at me and shakes his head. "Pa," he says. "I had to see for myself." Then he turns and runs off.

*   *   *

I *am* an old man rooted to his routine.

I wake in darkness at 4 A.M., every morning. Susan is still asleep, one arm thrown around Bubba nestled against her chest like a lover. Blue is curled in a ball at my feet. The older dogs, Hoshi, Kiri, and Stella, are sleeping on their rugs around the bed. Nero is sleeping on my wingchair in the Florida room. Francis, the parakeet, is sleeping in his cage, under his dark blue sheet dotted with stars, in my office.

I get out of bed slowly, in stages, full of aches and pains. I can't turn my neck to the left. My legs are cramped from having to contort them around Blue all night. My lower back is sore from yesterday's squats at the gym. I stand up and try to put on my shorts. I hobble on one leg, unable to bend over because of my stiff back. My toes get caught in my shorts and I lurch forward, crashing into the closet. Susan grumbles in bed and slaps a pillow over her head. The older dogs look up at me with malevolent eyes and turn away. Bubba and Blue wake. They stretch sensuously on the bed, the way dogs do, their front legs straining in front of them, their asses high in the air. Then they stretch each of their back legs behind them. I envy them, their youth. They are three-year-old brothers, the sons of Stella and Nero. They torment our older dogs, Hoshi, ten, Kiri, nine, and Stella, eight, in the way prepubescent boys torment teenage sisters. They crouch behind potted plants and leap out at the older dogs when they walk by. The older dogs snarl and chase them around the house, but they can't catch them. Before the puppies were born, our older dogs slept much of the day. They started to get fat. Even Nero, five, seemed to be getting old before his time. Now Nero runs with his sons, who have made all our dogs younger, even if it has been against their wills.

Hoshi, Stella, and Bubba have reddish-orange fur with white markings on their faces, chests, and tails. Kiri, Nero, and Blue are black, with tan and white markings. They all look like a cross between a fox and a wolf with their pointy noses, pricked ears, and tails that curve over their backs, like scythes.

I sit on the edge of the bed to pull on my shorts. Bubba and Blue jump off the bed, wagging their tails, ready to start the day with me as I do every morning.

I turn on my pot of Cuban coffee, always Cafe Bustelo, never Pilon, and retrieve the newspapers from the front porch. When the newspapers are late, I sit on the front porch and wait for the deliveryman in his truck, a Haitian named Jerome. He pulls up, flings me the papers, and says, "Sorry, mon. Be late."

I go back into the house and turn on the backyard lights to warn the possums who like to walk on top of our privacy fence. I flick the lights on and off, then leave them on and wait for the possum to get the hint. Bubba has already killed one possum who ventured into our backyard. He's a great hunter. He's killed a squirrel too, and a mouse. The mouse was behind our refrigerator when I woke one morning to the sound of all our dogs barking at the refrigerator. I pulled it away from the wall and there was a terrified mouse. The other dogs just looked at it, but Bubba caught it in his mouth in a flash, shook his head, breaking the mouse's neck, and then dropped it, without interest. Blue picked it up and ran outside with it. I chased him outside, forgetting I was naked.

Susan heard me screaming. "Blue! Blue! Drop it!" She ran outside naked too. We finally got the mouse away from Blue and swept it into a paper bag. Then we realized we were both naked in our backyard. Susan covered her breasts with her hands in case the neighbors were looking.

"What are *you* worrying about?" I said. Most of our neighbors are gay men, like George and Alberto.

Bubba and Blue are leaping wildly at the Florida room screen door. Finally I let them out. They race furiously to the wooden fence that surrounds our backyard and begin tracking the possum's scent along the perimeter of the fence. They race around the yard, then back again, two, three, four times, until they realize there is no possum this morning. They remember to piss.

I slide the deadbolt behind the screen door so it will stay open a few inches. Nero hops off the armchair where he has slept the night. He stretches luxuriantly, sticks his nose through the door opening, flings the door open with a toss of his head, and goes outside to see what his sons are up to. He sits on the deck and watches them race around the yard, just as all the older dogs do when they're awake. They don't understand what the fuss is for Bubba. They are all Shiba Inus, Japanese hunting dogs, but only Bubba hunts. Blue just follows him. My dogs are a pack, just like wolves, from whom they are descended. But they are a pack of individuals. None of them wants to lead, except for Bubba. When Bubba was a year old he began to attack his father, Nero, for no apparent reason. Nero, half Bubba's size, was confused at first. Then he began to fight back. They had vicious battles, both dogs rearing up on their hind legs, slashing their teeth at each other's throat. Susan and I flung ourselves between them. We got bit and bloody ourselves. I beat Bubba unmercifully with sticks, brooms, anything handy. I picked him up by the rough of his neck and flung him against the wall, almost cracking his ribs. But he wouldn't stop. Finally we realized Bubba was trying to leap above his father in the pack order. Nero must have realized it too, the way human fathers do. His son had to prove his manhood at his father's expense. So, like a good father, Nero stopped fighting back. He withdrew and gave up his pack position to his son. Bubba never fought the two females—Stella, his mother, and Kiri, his aunt—because they were no threat to his position. Bubba never fought Blue either, because he knew Blue was small and weak. Blue has a heart murmur. Bubba is no bully. So finally Bubba became the leader of a pack that does not follow him, except for Blue. The others watch Bubba hunt, amused. They let him push ahead to get to the water bowl first. They hold back, waiting, while Bubba slurps water, until he's finished. Bubba pushes everyone around except for Hoshi. He gives Hoshi a wide berth, not out of fear but out of the respect one gives to a shaman. Even Bubba knows Hoshi has a nobility he can never hope to have. Susan and I know we can never have his spare nobility. When the dogs' water bowl is empty, Bubba noses it into the air so that it lands with a loud clatter, and we fill it. When the bowl is empty and Hoshi wants a drink, he sits in front of it and stares at it with his brown, almond-shaped eyes. He'll stare for as long as it takes for us to notice. "I'm sorry, Hosh," I say, and fill the bowl. When I put it in front of him, he looks up at me and nods before he drinks. He is an inspiration to me. I wish I could live my life, and write, with his spare dignity. Susan says he's a higher being who's come back to earth to teach us patience and dignity and forgiveness and unconditional love. When I snap at Bubba for some doglike indiscretion, his ears go back and he throws himself at me with abject apology. When I do the same to Hoshi, he just looks at me, turns his back, and goes into my office to lie under my desk. "Apologize," Susan says to me. I go into the office and pet Hoshi. "I'm sorry, Hosh." He licks my hand.

I light my first cigar of the morning, get my mug of coffee—one tablespoon Coffeemate, one packet of Equal, a half teaspoon of raw sugar—and go into my office to take the cover off Francis's cage. "Good morning, Francis," I say. He responds in his guttural, little bird's voice, "Fuck you!" I look at him, a yellow parakeet with splashes of green on his wings. "Nice talk, you little shit." Francis says, *"Shit!"* I bring his cage to the coffee table in the Florida room. I dislodge Nero, who's returned to my wingchair. He grumbles, stretches, and goes back outside with his sons to hunt the possum. I sit down and begin to read the *Miami Herald*, always the sports section first, then the rest of the paper. The *Herald* warms me up, sharpens my mind. I begin to read the *New York Times* now, while Francis shakes his bell with one foot and masturbates against it.

Outside, I hear Bubba, Blue, and Nero thrashing through the lariope after a possum on the fence. When the possum freezes on top of the fence, the three dogs throw themselves against the fence to shake it and dislodge the possum. That's how Bubba killed the last one. He ripped open its stomach, spilling its guts at Nero's feet. Nero cringed, horrified. He'd thought it was a game, not a life-and-death battle. He was so upset he had one of his fits. Nero has epilepsy. He stiffens and his eyes roll back into his head. I hold him in my lap, whispering to him, stroking his forehead, until he comes out of it and begins to pant heavily.

I hear the fence rattling and look out the window. I see the three dogs leaping against the fence. The terrified possum is gripping the top of the fence with his claws, swaying back and forth, like a sailor on a mast in a storm. I whistle for the dogs. Nero and Blue come running. They leap against the screen door with their front paws, rattling it open, and run to their water dish.

Bubba stays outside. He is sitting now, perfectly still, staring up at the possum, waiting. Bubba has no patience. The other dogs sit and wait their turn when I give them their afternoon biscuits. Bubba salivates uncontrollably and leaps on me to get his first. But when it comes to the possum, Bubba will sit there for hours, until the possum leaves.

Susan wakes at 6 A.M. and staggers out of the bedroom naked, followed by the older dogs. She puts on a T-shirt and then tries to put on her panties. She can't bend over either. She balances herself with one hand on a chair and stabs a foot at her panties. She misses, points her toe like a ballerina, and stabs again. She misses again, begins to wobble, grips the chair more firmly, and makes a third stab at her panties.

"Yessss!" she cries, pulling up her panties. "The first score of the day!" Susan's first husband was a New York Knicks fan. "I still hear Marv Albert's voice in my sleep," she says.

Susan gets her mug of coffee and comes to sit with me to read the papers. The older dogs stretch lazily in the living room, not vigorously like Bubba and Blue. We know how they feel. Finally, they nose open the screen door and wander outside to piss. They have no interest in the possum, a fruitless quest.

We dress into our workout clothes at 7 A.M. to go lift weights at our gym, the same gym we have been going to since 1979. I wear my Tobias the Pig T-shirt.

Susan wears her T-shirt with the words "It's not pretty being easy" written across the chest.

We return home at 8 A.M. to feed the dogs and have our protein shakes. Coffee shakes Monday, Wednesday, and Friday, fruit-juice shakes Tuesday, Thursday, and Saturday. We drink our shakes at the dining-room table and talk about the day. Then we go to our respective offices to work, me to write a story, Susan to edit a book. Nero follows Susan and sleeps under her desk. Hoshi sleeps under my desk. The other dogs flop down around the house or outside, sunbathing, on our deck.

We quit work at 2 P.M. to go shopping. Susan goes to thrift shops to look for bargains. Brass lamps that don't work. Ladderback cane chairs with no cane. Coffee tables with three legs. She buys them all for three dollars. It's always three dollars, and fifty dollars to repair them. I go to Winn Dixie for groceries. I weigh myself at the big scale by the check-out counters, then shop the way old people do, buying just enough for this night's dinner: two chicken breasts, four ears of corn, one cantaloupe. I stop at Blockbuster on the way home to pick up the night's movie.

I fix our afternoon drinks at three. Always the same drinks, *every* afternoon: vodka on the rocks for Susan, with a squeeze of lime from our Key Lime tree, and for me, Jim Beam, rocks, with a splash of water in my yellow tin cup. When the dogs hear the ice cubes tinkle in my tin cup they come running from all parts of the house and backyard. Francis begins squawking madly in his cage on the dining-room table. The dogs sit down in front of me and wait patiently for their biscuits, except for Bubba, who leaps on me, and Francis, who squawks even louder and rings his bell. I make Bubba sit down like the other dogs. I feed Francis his millet first, since he's putting up such a racket. I clip the spray of millet to a clothespin inside his cage. Francis bites the hand that feeds him. "You little shit!"

I feed each dog their biscuits in turn, starting with the oldest dog, Hoshi, and then working my way down the age ladder to Blue and Bubba. Blue was born two hours before Bubba so Bubba gets his biscuit last. He tries to keep his ass on the hardwood floor while he waits, like the other dogs, but he can't stop himself from sliding his ass from dog to dog until finally he gets his biscuit, which he wolfs down. Then he looks around to see if any of the other dogs left any crumbs. He tries so hard to get out of himself, to fight his nature, that sometimes, looking at him, my heart breaks. I know how he feels. At war with what God made him. God's cruel joke. He gives us our natures and then expects us to fight them.

We eat dinner at four, talk about the day, read the mail, and then clear the dishes and put them in the sink. Susan takes Francis out of his cage and puts him on her shoulder while she washes the dishes. He nibbles her ear and coos to her. Me, he bites. Francis's wings are clipped so he can't fly away. But sometimes he'll fly off Susan's shoulder and drop to the floor next to the dogs. The dogs tolerate Francis because they know he's part of our family. They'll just nose him around the floor a bit to make him squawk until he fights back and pecks them on the nose. One time he flew onto Blue's nose when Blue was a puppy.

Blue thought he was a toy. He put his mouth around Francis's little body, very gently, and began tossing him up into the air and catching him, as if Francis was a Nerf ball. Feathers flew everywhere while Francis bleated "Help! Help!" until we got to him. Francis refused to talk for a week after that.

We never take Francis out of his cage unless Bubba's outside. Bubba can't help himself. Bubba was sleeping on the bed with Susan one night when Susan took Francis out of his cage and let him walk on her chest while she watched TV. Suddenly Francis tried to fly off. He landed on Bubba's nose. Bubba woke and instinctively slashed his teeth at Francis, ripping out his tail feather. The yellow feather hung from Bubba's lips as he bared his teeth and prepared to slash again. Susan screamed "No! Bubba! No! No!" and scooped up Francis in her hands. Instantly, Bubba realized what he'd done. He looked abjectly at Susan, his brow wrinkled, his tail wagging for forgiveness. I bought Susan a card for Mother's Day once and signed it "Love, Bubba," followed by "I'm sorry! I'm sorry! I'm sorry!"

Susan works in the backyard after dinner. She trims the avocado and mango and grapefruit trees. She plants a male Key Lime tree next to the female tree to pollinate it. She plants orange jasmine and carrotwood trees and lariope. The dogs follow her, fascinated. Everything she plants, they dig up, furiously. She screams at them and replants.

I make some telephone calls inside. Editors. Eliot Kaplan at *Philadelphia Magazine* asks me if I want to do a cigar story in the Dominican Republic. Certainly, I say, and convince him to have Ron take the pictures. Jon Black, the managing editor of *Playboy,* tells me about his twin newborn sons. Jon is fifty-one. Eric Copage, an editor at the *New York Times Magazine,* talks about his recent divorce. I tell him, "Hang in there, Eric. Don't let it get you down." Alice Turner, the fiction editor at *Playboy,* tells me one of my stories she published has just been chosen for a Houghton Mifflin anthology, *The Best American Mystery Stories.*

I call my parents. My mother, ninety, tries her best to sound weak and pitiful. "Oh, Patty," she says. "It's terrible. I don't feel like I used to." I say, "Ma, I don't feel like I used to." She laughs. My father, eighty-eight, gets on and wants to know why I haven't called my older brother in months. I tell him I've been busy. "Too busy to call your brother?" he snaps. "Call him!" I tell him, "Sure, Dad," but when I hang up I don't call my brother. It's too depressing. I call the Usual Suspects instead.

Peter says he can't talk now, he has a case in court. I tell him to call me after it's over. He says, "It may not be over until late." I say, "Well, just lose it early, Peter." Nothing is sacred among the Usual Suspects. Sol is a bungling smuggler who got caught. Susan is a lousy cook. George and Al are two fags. Ronnie's a dumb Pollack. Phil is Silas Marner. Sol calls him "a fucking Jew." When Phil drives past his club and sees the parking lot filled, he goes, "Ka-ching! Ka-ching!" the sound of a cash register. Chelsea is nothing more than a pair of perfect tits. I'm a foolish old man. Peter's a lousy lawyer. "When Ronnie and I get a divorce," Mary Beth told him once, "I want you to be Ronnie's lawyer." She paused a beat, then added, "That way I'll be sure to get everything."

Mary Beth is a BIG girl. I call her "the little woman," and then say, "a misnomer." She's 5′ 8″, sturdily built, like an athlete. Her mother once excused her daughter's size to a friend, saying "Her bigness is not her fault." Mary Beth made the mistake of telling that story to the Usual Suspects.

I call Sol. He asks me if I read the story in the *Herald* about the thirteen-year-old boy who won a science award for studying dust mites. I tell him yes. Sol says, with genuine disgust, "Fucking kid. He should be in his room whacking off." Then he tells me he's used me as a reference for a car loan he has no intention of repaying. "When they start calling you," he says, "tell 'em I'm in Belize."

I make the mistake of telling Sol that Susan and I went to a Miami Herald party last night. "Susan was talking to this writer," I tell Sol, "and in mid-sentence, the guy walks away. She turned to me and said, 'Am I *that* boring!?' "

Sol asks to talk to Susan. She gets on the phone. Sol asks her what happened last night at the party. Susan begins to tell him. Sol hangs up on her.

I call Phil. He tells me he's just bought another club in Hollywood. "Booby Trap II," he says. I say, "Like a chain, Phil. The McDonald's of strip joints."

Mary Beth calls me in tears. She's just had a story rejected by Arthur Frommer, the travel-guide publisher. "He said it was a rancid, indigestible hash," she says, between tears. I reassure her she's too good a writer for travel guides. She's too hip, funny, and ironic for such service pieces. She stops crying. I tell her how it was for me when I was trying to become a writer at twenty-eight. I was teaching English at an all-girls parochial high school. After I corrected papers at night, I tried to write a book about my baseball experiences. I had written one-hundred pages when I finally got up the courage to send them in to an editor at Random House. A week later the editor called and asked me to come to New York. I walked through the streets of New York in my new tweed sports jacket from J. Press Clothiers in New Haven and my new oxblood, wing-tip cordovan shoes, my heart literally bursting in my breast. This would be the beginning of my new career as a writer.

I sat in the editor's outer office for an hour, waiting. Finally he summoned me into his office. It was lined, floor to ceiling, with books. He sat behind his desk and began asking me questions about the players I had played with in the minor leagues. Joe Torre. Ron Hunt. Phil Niekro. They were all major leaguers now. I told him what they were like when we were kids together. After an hour of such baseball talk, I couldn't control myself any longer. I asked him about the manuscript I'd sent him.

"What makes you think a jock like you can become a writer?" he said.

I stuttered. "I dunno . . . I thought . . . maybe . . ."

"You'll never be a writer."

I walked back to Grand Central Station with tears in my eyes. I saw everything, the people, the tall buildings, the train station, swimming through my tears.

"I had no one to reassure me," I tell Mary Beth. "At least you've got me."

"I know," she says. "I've got to take rejection better." Then, cheering up, she says, "Why don't you and Sue-Bee come over for dinner tomorrow night?"

"What are you having?"

"Rancid, indigestible hash."

Ronnie gets on the phone and thanks me for cheering up Mary Beth.

I call George and Al. Al answers. He tells me he has some bananas and papayas for me from his backyard. I tell him I'll pick them up when I drop off the *New York Times* for him and George later. They live only two houses over from us. One of our neighbors is a lesbian. She just adopted a stray dog with a broken leg. The dog was living on the streets when she found him, hit by a car, in pain by the side of the road. She took him to the animal hospital down the street. The vet told her the leg would mend on its own. Then he extracted over a thousand ticks embedded in the dog's flesh. After she paid the bill, the vet told her the dog would need about sixty dollars in shots within the month. She didn't have the money, she said. The vet just shook his head. "It's up to you," he said.

When I found out from Susan about the shots, I waited until I saw the neighbor leaving for school one morning. I hurried outside and stopped her before she got into her car. I gave her the sixty dollars for the shots. She resisted at first. "It's not for you," I said. "It's for Barney." Finally she took the money.

"How can I ever repay you?" she said.

"You can give me a blowjob."

She looked defeated. "I don't think I know how," she said, very seriously. "My whole life has been driven by pussy."

"Mine too."

After I get through talking to Al, George gets on the phone. He asks me if Susan and I want to go to a gay wedding with him and Al. The couple getting "married" think Susan and I are gay-friendly because of our friendship with George and Al. I tell George I'm neither gay-friendly nor homophobic.

"I just happen to like you and Al," I say. "You just happen to be fags." I decline the invitation. "It'll be too confusing," I say. "I won't know who the bride is to kiss."

After my calls, I write out some checks to pay bills. I glance through Susan's Victoria's Secret catalog. I study my J and R Tobacco Company catalog, then call their 800 number and order some cigars. I hang a new Haitian print Susan bought in Delray. I rehang it, then rehang it until it's just right. Susan comes in from the backyard covered with dirt, which somehow makes her sublimely happy. "It must be my English side," she says. She goes into the bathroom to take her bubble bath in our old cast-iron tub with the lion's paw feet. She languishes in bubbles up to her chin, sipping from a glass of white wine. Then I take my bath like a Roman emperor, sipping from my tin cup and smoking a cigar.

At dusk I prepare tomorrow morning's coffee in the pot so I won't have to do it in the morning when I'm half asleep. Susan takes Francis's cage into my office. She sings him his lullaby, the same lullaby she has sung to him every night since we got him five years ago. When Susan takes a trip with me, she leaves Francis with George and Al. She gives them a tape recording of her singing Francis' lullaby for them to play for Francis at night. Susan lays Francis's sheet over his cage now as she whispers, "Under your stars, Francis. Sweet dreams."

Hoshi is sitting at the bedroom doorway, staring at the bare bedroom floors. He won't go to sleep until his rug is on the floor. Like me, he is an old man rooted to his routine. I put down all the dog's rugs around the bed. Hoshi nods, thank you, and lays down on his rug. He is such a courtly being, with an uncanny instinct for the appropriate. The definition of a gentleman. But Hoshi is so much more than just a gentleman. He has no base emotions. He forgives me my anger. He surrenders his bones to the others. He licks the other dogs at night to clean them. Except Bubba. He gives Bubba as wide a berth as Bubba gives him. Hoshi came upon a copperhead snake in a bush once. He nosed the snake to introduce himself and it bit him. Hoshi pulled his head back, stunned by such anger. It was beyond his comprehension. So he nosed the snake again, gently, to reassure it he meant no harm. The snake bit him again. Hoshi would have died if Susan had not gotten him to the vet in time. When I got home that afternoon, she told me what had happened. I grabbed the shotgun in a blind fury and ran outside, looking for that snake. When I found it, it reared up its head and bared its fangs at me. I blew its head off. I pumped the shotgun and fired again, and again, until the snake was nothing but crimson mangled meat.

Sol loves Hoshi. He has ever since we first met ten years ago. Susan and I were living in an apartment complex next door to Sol at the time. Whenever I took Hoshi for a walk, I often stopped at Sol's to talk about his latest scam. One day Hoshi was annoyed that Sol was delaying his walk, so he raised a leg and pissed on the chair Sol was sitting on.

Sol was very amused. It appealed to his perverse sense of humor. He began to take a liking to Hoshi.

When Sol went away on his "sabbatical" to a prison in Georgia, we often visited him with Hoshi. Hoshi had to stay in the car while we talked to Sol in the prisoners' visiting room. When we returned to the car, Sol would already be walking across a field to his dormitory, so we let Hoshi out of the car. Hoshi would smell Sol's scent off in the distance and begin to howl pitifully while Sol waved to him.

After Sol returned from his "sabbatical," he would often go with me to Hoshi's obedience classes. One day Hoshi's trainer tried to introduce him to an 130-pound Rottweiler. Hoshi took a distinct dislike to that Rotty, the only time I've ever seen him be aggressive with any living thing. He leapt at the Rotty with a great gnashing of teeth. The trainer yanked back the stunned Rotty before he could attack back. The trainer just looked at my forty-pound Hoshi in disbelief. Sol looked at Hoshi too, with a smile.

"Heh, you should make that little fella look in the mirror," the trainer said. "Let him see what a little dog he is."

Sol, not smiling now, snapped at him. "Heh, Slick. Don't ever call him a dog. The Hosh is my man. He's beyond dog."

He's beyond me too. He is what he is without a thought. God's perfect creature. I tell Susan I wish I could be as noble a creature as Hoshi is. She says, not kidding, "Maybe in your next life."

The other dogs drift into the bedroom and flop down on their rugs. Bubba and Blue hop up onto the bed, make little nervous digging circles, and then finally flop down too. Susan and I get into bed. We try to arrange ourselves around Bubba and Blue. We put on the movie I got from Blockbuster and begin to watch it. Very sexy. *Bound,* with Jennifer Tilly and Gina Gershon playing two lesbians. The sex scenes are hot. I get an idea. I roll over on top of Susan. She says, "Careful, Baby, your wrists. You did bench presses today." I ignore her warning and push myself above her with my palms planted on the bed. But my wrists *are* sore from doing those bench presses. I try to hold myself above her with my elbows planted on the bed. Suddenly I get a charley horse in one leg. I begin kicking it behind me to stop the pain. Bubba and Blue grumble at my intrusion into their sleep. Susan begins to laugh. I spill off her onto my back.

"An aged man is a paltry thing," Susan says.

"Yeah, well, it ain't easy fucking a broad with an AARP card," I say. We both laugh.

We lay there with our dogs, and watch the movie. It lulls me to sleep before we ever see the end of it.

And then I dream.

FOUR

I AM STANDING on a pitcher's mound, squinting into the early evening sun setting behind the home-plate stands. But the dream is different. The stands are filled with cheering fans. Vendors are hawking beer through the stands. Children are playing in the aisles. My brother and his wife, my father, my wife, Susan, and Mary Beth and Ronnie are sitting together behind the home team's first-base dugout. They are shouting out my name. But I do not hear them. I hear nothing. I am conscious of nothing, except, at the end of a long dark narrow tunnel, the umpire, the batter, my catcher. I see them only as dark shadows shooting off slivers of light that are painful to my eyes yet, curiously, hypnotizing. I see it all in slow motion. The umpire signaling. Play ball! My catcher's arm moving back, then forward. The ball coming toward me, moving in and out of shadows like a shooting star. I turn my face away at the last instant, reach with my glove, and miraculously catch the ball before it hits me in the face.

The right-handed batter steps into the batter's box. My catcher crouches behind the plate. The umpire bends over until his facemask is almost resting on my catcher's left shoulder. A perfect tableau, except for the shadows and the painful light. My catcher sticks one finger down between his spread legs. I squint to make it out, then nod. He sticks up his big round mitt like a bull's-eye shooting sparks. I grip the ball in my glove with my two fingers slightly spread across the seams. I feel the pinpoint of pain in my right shoulder, the dull ache in my left knee encased in a brace with a metal hinge. I remind myself not to kick my leg too high. And then, as I have done thousands of times in my dream, I begin my motion. I pump, kick, feel the ache in my knee, rear back, feel the fear rising in my breast as it has so many times in my dream until I wake, mercifully, at 4 A.M., to prepare my Cuban coffee.

Only I don't wake. I see my right arm with the ball in my hand passing my head, feel the pinpoint of pain in my shoulder, hear myself grunting with the effort, see my arm extended in front of me now, the ball leaving my fingertips, spinning through the long narrow dark tunnel.

I see it all. . . . I see myself, as I am now, in a white baseball uniform trimmed with lavender. I see an old man with a white beard, throwing the first pitch I have ever thrown in a baseball game since that day I left baseball, the phrase I always use, over thirty-five years ago.

*　*　*

In late August of 1996, I flew to St. Paul, Minnesota, to research a story I was contracted to write for *Men's Journal* on the St. Paul Saints minor league baseball team. The Saints played in the Independent Northern League, none of whose teams was affiliated with a major league club. It was, in a sense, an outlaw league whose teams had great license in conducting their affairs. NL teams signed ex-major and minor league players who could no longer find a home in organized baseball for various reasons that had little to do with their talent, or lack of it. Their organized careers had come to an end because of an injury or advancing age or because they had reputations as troublemakers. They were lame, halt, sore armed, scarred from one too many operations. They were aging, wrinkled, arthritic, with a faded fastball that was only a memory, and a slow bat that had once been quick. They were drinkers, drug abusers, wife beaters, pussy hounds, lockerroom thieves, and uncontrollable "red asses" who had broken one too many bats over their dugout roof or an opposing player's head. They were a defeated army of miscreants and malcontents. Men with a past but not much of a future, playing out their string in a sanitarium for troubled players. Some of them even thought they could put their troubled pasts behind them and return to organized ball. A few did. Darryl Strawberry made amends for his past as a wife beater and drug abuser. He learned to enjoy the game again, to sign autographs for his fans, to stay sober, and, in the process, to recapture his home-run swing. The Yankees signed him out of the NL in the summer of '95, and he is still with the Yankees today.

The Saints were the most creative of the NL teams. They didn't stop at signing ex-major leaguers like Strawberry and Jack Morris to draw fans. They signed novelties, like the catcher with no legs. They held outlandish promotions every night. Flying Elvises dropped out of the sky. Abe Lincoln threw out the first pitch. Opposing managers in rubber Sumo wrestling suits grappled in the dirt at home plate. The Saints had a 350-pound pig, Tobias, for their mascot. Tobias brought out baseballs to the home-plate umpire every inning, except one. That was the night the Saints' opposition, the Madison Black Wolf, brought their mascot to the stadium. A wild gray wolf. The wolf sniffed the grass around the pitcher's mound and caught Tobias's scent. Tobias emerged from his little opening underneath the home-plate stands and stopped dead in his tracks. He stared at the wolf with his tiny red pig eyes. The wolf stared back with his unreadable yellow eyes. Tobias turned and scurried on his tiny pig feet back underneath the stands.

The man behind these promotions was the team's forty-year-old owner, Mike Veeck. He is one of those men who hides his extreme shyness behind outrageous humor. He has a social outlaw's view of life, which he inherited from his deceased father, Bill Veeck, a former major league club owner. Bill was called the ''P.T. Barnum of Baseball'' because of his innovative and outlandish exploits. He invented the exploding scoreboard to keep fans amused. He once sent a three-foot-tall midget up to bat under the assumption his strike zone would be so small the opposing pitcher would walk him. He did.

I stayed in St. Paul for ten days. I interviewed players, coaches, fans, Tobias, even the wolf, and during that time I became friendly with Mike. He'd already heard of me from his father's book, in which Bill referred to my book, *A False Spring,* as one of the best books ever written about baseball. Mike and I vowed to keep in touch after I left.

I began to write the story in the fall of '96. Often, during the writing, I'd laugh to myself at some of the things I'd witnessed at Saints games. The massaging nun. The naked fans in a hot tub. The face painter, Saint Carol, an attractive woman in Kabuki makeup who dressed like Elvira,

Queen of the Night. In the middle of writing a scene that made me laugh, I'd pick up the phone and call Mike. We'd talk, about nothing really, just two ex-jocks bantering back and forth, and then hang up.

One morning I read a story in the *Miami Herald* that claimed that Charlie Sheen, the actor, had signed a contract to pitch for the Saints in the summer of '97. Charlie was perfect for the Saints. A real actor with a troubled past. His name in Heidi Fleiss's little black book. A porno actress girlfriend. Drug and alcohol abuse. A fancied past as a high-school pitcher. The closest Charlie had come to playing professional baseball was when he starred in John Sayles's movie of the 1919 Black Sox scandal, *Eight Men Out*. He played centerfield like an actor trying to look like a baseball player. There's a story in this for me, I thought, as I picked up the phone and dialed Mike's number. I approached my story idea obliquely, the way wise-guy ex-jocks always do, with a smartass comment.

"So," I said. "I hear Charlie Sheen's gonna pitch for you."

"Yeh."

"A fucking actor! Jesus, Mike! If that fucking actor thinks he can pitch, so can I."

"You serious?"

I couldn't stop myself. "Shit, yes, I'm serious."

"Then get in shape. I'll pitch you this summer."

"You're on."

After I hung up, my wife looked at me. "What's wrong?" she said.

"Nothing."

"Your face is as white as a sheet." So I told her. She shook her head. "It serves you right."

I didn't do anything for days. I tried to think of excuses I could use to call Mike back and tell him I couldn't pitch for him. I was too busy traveling on assignments. I had deadlines. I could never find the time to get in pitching shape. I had to make a living, for chrissakes! I had a mortgage to pay, a wife, six dogs, and a parakeet to feed. I had no glove, no spikes, no catcher, only an old baseball from my youth that had written on it "7 inn., 19 Ks, 2 hits, 1959." I was an old man, for chrissakes! I hadn't pitched a game since 1962. I was afraid.

Finally, on a whim, I got the old baseball out of the attic and decided to make a feeble attempt at practicing my motion in pantomime in the living room. I made sure Susan was in the kitchen, ironing clothes, where she couldn't see me.

The ball felt strange in my hand. Light, slippery, elusive. An odd feeling for such a simple object. A ball. I cradled the ball in both hands as I would before I began my motion. I faced the full-length mirror. I saw an old man with a white beard holding a baseball. I turned away from the mirror and faced the Florida room. The dogs stared at me through the screen door the ways dogs do, their heads tilted, when their master is doing something strange to them. I began my motion. I pumped, my two hands rising over my head. The dogs burst through the screen door. They came at me, barking and growling and leaping on me.

"Get down! *Down,* for chrissakes! What the hell's a matter with you?" I tried to push them away, but they kept leaping at the ball in my hand. I held it above my head, like the Statue of Liberty. Susan peeked her head into the living room.

"They think the ball's for throw and fetch," she said.

"Well, it isn't." The dogs kept leaping at the ball as I carried it into the kitchen and put it on the counter. They lost interest in it now, except for Bubba. He sat down and stared at it as if it was the possum.

"It's no use," I said. "I can't practice here."

"Then go to the park," Susan said. She meant Holiday Park, a few blocks from our house. The park has two soccer fields, two Little League diamonds, tennis courts, and a big league diamond that is rarely used. It is also home to a legion of homeless vagabonds and cruising homosexuals. The bums sprawl around the park during the day, drinking together out of paper bags. At night they sleep under trees in little groups, like cowboys around a campfire. The homosexuals cruise the park in their cars day and night. They try to make eye contact with male joggers and bikers and the young male prostitutes who loiter near the parking lot next to the big league diamond. They are all gaunt-looking youths, shirtless and dirty. They stuff their T-shirt into their back pants pocket so that half the shirt hangs down to their ass, a sign.

"I don't wanna go there," I whined. "It's depressing."

Susan stopped ironing and looked at me. "You'll have to go sooner or later," she said.

"Why?"

"You're going to pitch, aren't you?" I didn't say anything. "Aren't you?"

"Yeh, yeh, yeh."

She went back to her ironing. "You pitch at a baseball park, don't you? So go to the park and pitch." Again, I said nothing. She narrowed her eyes at me. "What are you afraid of?"

"I'm not afraid of anything!" I thought quickly. "I don't have a catcher."

"You don't need a catcher right now. Throw into the home-plate screen for a while, just to start out."

"That's a pain. I'll have to walk after each pitch and then walk back to the mound."

"So? It'll be good for your legs. You'll get in shape that way." I narrowed my eyes at *her* now. She could be merciless at times. "All right," she said. "*I'll* catch you."

"You?" I laughed. "You can't catch me. You don't even have a glove."

"I won't need one."

"Thanks." I went to the counter to get the ball again, but it was gone. "Jeez," I said. "Where'd the ball go?"

She pointed to the living room. Bubba was lying on the rug, chewing the ball like a bone. I snatched it out of his jaws. He instinctively growled at me. When he realized what he'd done, he threw himself at me, ears pinned back, tail wagging, in abject apology.

"That's all right, Bub. You were doing me a favor." The ball was chewed up but still in good enough shape to throw at a home-plate screen. I glanced toward the kitchen. Susan was ironing with her head down. I looked back at Bubba and tried to hand him the ball. "Take it, Bub. Go on." But he wouldn't touch it now. "Traitor."

For a month, I found one excuse after another to keep me from going to the park. I had to finish a story. Then I had to leave town on an assignment. When I got back I had to write the story. And so it went until the first week of January, when I found myself between assignments. I took the dogs for walks three times a day. I threw out the garbage before it was half full. I repaired the hinge on the screen door in the Florida room. I laid down mulch in the backyard. I spent my afternoons at George and Al's, drinking beer on their back deck overlooking the tropical rain forest Al had grown in the backyard. Banana trees and papaya trees and orange trees and grapefruit trees and orchids everywhere.

"Why so depressed, Niño?" Al said to me.

I told him about the pitching.

"Oh, that's wonderful!" George said, with his little boy's enthusiasm that now infuriated me. "What fun! Can Al and I be your cheerleaders?"

"Yeh. Only if you wear the little short skirts and no underwear."

"Of course!" George said. "A man should always get in touch with his feminine side by wearing a dress." I glanced sideways at him with malevolent eyes. "Oh, Patty," he said. "You straight guys are so uptight. Lighten up. Get in touch with your feminine side. Wear a dress, for chrissakes."

"Yeh. Right, George. Just what I need. A fucking dress."

"Oh, it'll do wonders for you," George said. "It does for me."

I looked at him. "Trust me, George. I'll do anything once. Remember what Voltaire said? 'Once, a philosopher. Twice, a pervert.' But I'll never wear a fucking dress."

"Suit yourself."

The next afternoon, bored, with nothing to do, I put on one of Susan's summer dresses and a big straw hat with a flowing pink ribbon. I looked like a deranged, 200-pound, cross-dressing, L'il Bo Peep. With a white beard and a cigar clenched between my teeth, spilling out of a too small summer dress the color of robins' eggs—which, it occurred to me, insanely, did not go with my coloring. I peeked out the front door—the coast was clear—and ran up the street holding up my skirt with one hand and holding down my straw hat with the other. The pink ribbon fluttered behind me. In my mind's eye, I saw a police car rounding the corner, saw myself handcuffed in its backseat, finger-printed, booked, then tossed into a holding cell with felons.

When I got to their house, I knocked on the door. George opened it. "Patty!" he said, beaming. "You look *wonderful!* See? Now don't you feel better?"

I looked down at myself, appraisingly, then up at George. "I would, George, if it was, you know, a little more stylish. Susan's taste isn't mine."

Two days later, I offered to pick up Susan's panties on layaway at Marshall's. "Enough already!" she snapped. "You're losing it. Go to the damned park and pitch."

I drove the two blocks to Holiday Park on a hot sunny afternoon in early January. I parked in the lot alongside of the big league diamond. The diamond was deserted, but there were dozens of cars parked in the lot. Homosexuals sat shirtless on the trunks of their cars in languid poses. They eyeballed passing cars, puckered their lips, and blew kisses. When I got out of the car in my T-shirt, shorts, and sneakers, they stared at me. Six-one, 190 pounds. I weighed the same as I had in high school, only now I was more muscular from twenty-five years of lifting weights. It was the one thing I had going for me in my comeback. At least I hadn't gotten fat over the years. I didn't have to lose weight before I even threw a pitch. My muscles were in shape from years of squats and shoulder presses and bicep curls. Suddenly it occurred to me. Comeback? Was that what this was? A comeback to what? A second career, at age fifty-six, of pitching in the minor leagues? Or was this just an aging old man's attempt to recapture his youth? Or was this just an attempt to put to rest the demons of my failure, to bury, once and for all, that dream?

Another thought occurred to me. Maybe I was just trying to recapture the love I'd once had for pitching? I used to love to throw a baseball. I used to marvel at the flight of the ball, the tight rotation of the seams, the way the ball would rise or sink on my whim. I loved throwing a baseball as much, as I did defeating a batter. I remember one year in the minor leagues when I was walking to the mound to start a game. I heard a fellow pitcher in the dugout call out, "Pat, you can't give Jim Hicks fastballs. He murders fastballs.'' I glanced back over my shoulder and said, "He murders *your* fastball, maybe, but the sunuvabitch won't murder *my* fastball.'' I struck out Jim Hicks on nothing but fastballs three times that game. After each swing, he fell to his knee and had to push himself up with his bat like an old man. Was that what I pitched for? The sight of Jim Hicks on one knee after another futile swing at my elusive fastball. Was it as simple as that? Did I just want to get batters out again? I was, after all, a pitcher.

The homosexuals were still starting at me as I stripped off my T-shirt and tossed it into the car. I glared at them. They looked up at my face, the face of an old man with a white beard, and lost interest. They turned their attention back to the passing cars.

I walked to the pitcher's mound and stared down at home plate with the chewed ball in my hand and a cigar clenched between my teeth. Behind the home-plate screen, I saw, not scouts, but a group of homeless men sprawled on a grassy mound, drinking out of a paper bag they passed around. They turned their attention toward me. I began my motion. I pumped, my two hands, cradling the ball like a precious object, rose above my head. I twisted my right foot clockwise and slid it off the rubber into the dirt parallel to the rubber and pointing toward third base. I held this pose a moment, a ballet dancer's first position, and then began to bring my arms back down in front of my face. Simultaneously, I raised my left leg and turned it toward third base. My two hands, still joined, were settled at my waist now. My left leg was bent like an inverted L, my entire body facing third base. I tried to hold this one-legged pose, like a flamingo in a swamp, the way I used to, for that split second when I drew in all my concentration and strength and then reared back, my right arm reaching behind me, before I pushed off the side of the rubber with my right foot and my entire body swiveled back toward the plate as I exploded at the batter.

But I couldn't hold the pose. My right leg wobbled unsteadily. My sneaker slipped in the dirt. I felt my body lurching forward too soon, my right arm still reaching back. I fell forward to my left, my knees hitting the dirt as my right arm came around, too late. I flung the ball into the dirt, twenty feet in front of home plate.

I got up and dusted off my knees. I saw, through the home-plate screen, one of the homeless men stand up and raise his paper bag over his head in salute. He shouted, "Nice pitch, bro!"

It wasn't like riding a bicycle. I couldn't just jump on and it would all come back to me. This was the most difficult thing I'd ever tried to master in my life. I'd mastered it in my youth, without thought. And then I'd failed at it, at twenty-one, when I was in my athletic prime. What made me think I could recapture even a semblance of my talent now, at fifty-six, much less *master* it? I felt defeated already, weak in the stomach, filled with the same fear I'd felt in the minor leagues when I saw it all slipping away. So what if I quit now? I'm a fifty-six-year-old writer. Nobody really expects me to do this thing.

Except me. This realization stunned me. I *did* want to pitch again. I liked it here, elevated above everyone else on a pitcher's mound. This is where I'd always felt at home, natural, myself. When I pitched I felt in touch with the purest part of my nature, God's gift, that made me unique. The rest of my nature was common, even base. I had once pitched as innocently as a Thoroughbred colt runs in a field of tall grass. Without thought, or effort. He just runs. Everything else I'd ever done in my life was an exhausting mental and physical struggle against the rest of my nature. I felt like a dray horse, matted with flies, eternally pulling a heavy wagon up an endless hill. I forced myself to *like* to sit in an empty room, hour after hour, and write. I forced myself to be considerate of others before myself. I forced myself *not* to lash out in a blind fury at those who crossed me. I forced myself to be the kind of man I admired but knew I wasn't. It did not matter that the things I forced myself to become were honorable and good, and that the thing I was most purely, a pitcher, was trivial. It mattered only that, like us all, I could not deny the trivial thing that defined me. To do so, as I had done all these years, was an act of self-betrayal.

So I would pitch. It would be my last chance to return to my self. To prove that I was a pitcher who happened to be writing just now. That was the persona I had created for myself, the ex-pitcher who had turned to writing. The ex-pitcher who had pitched to Hank Aaron (I walked him on four pitches), the ex-pitcher whose catcher was Joe Torre, the ex-pitcher whose first minor league roommate was Phil Niekro. Aaron and Niekro are in the Hall of Fame now. Torre is the Yankee manager. I wrote a profile of Joe for the *New York Times Magazine* in 1996. The day I was supposed to interview him my press credentials were two hours late. I fumed and cursed in the runway of Yankee Stadium while waiting for those credentials. When I finally got them I stormed into Joe's office, furious, cursing, red-faced. Joe stood up behind his desk, extended his arms, his palms facing me as if to fend off a blazing light, and said, "Calm down, Pat. Don't worry. I'll give you all the time you need." It was the same gesture he used to use with me when he walked out to the mound where I was kicking dirt and cursing after yet another walk when we were both twenty years old.

When Phil was elected into the Hall of Fame two years ago, I decided to call him to congratulate him. I remembered how he had struggled that first year in McCook in 1959. He was afraid to throw his knuckleball with men on base. The batters ripped his fastball and slow curve and he was one outing from being released. Our manager, Bill Steineke, told him, "Either throw that knuckler or go home." So Phil overcame his fear and became the best pitcher in the league. When I lost my career because of fear I realized how hard it must have been for him to surrender himself to that capricious pitch. And then it took him ten more years to reach the major leagues because the Braves were afraid to take a chance on a knuckleball pitcher as a starter. Finally Phil forced them to realize they had to. I have always admired Phil as much as anyone in the game for the qualities of his character. His refusal to quit in the face of undoutable obstacles. He went on to win over 300 games and he never changed from that amiable, considerate, self-effacing yet dogged pitcher I knew when he was twenty. I remember the time I flew with him to Tucson when he had been traded from the Yankees to the Indians during spring training. I was interviewing him for a piece for *People* magazine. I sat in coach with my wife while Phil sat in first class. After the plane took off, Phil walked back to coach. He offered my wife his seat in first class and then sat down with me to drink beer and eat a cheese sandwich while my wife drank champagne and ate filet mignon.

After Phil retired, he became the Braves AAA manager at Richmond, Virginia. I was assigned a story by *Sports Illustrated* on the Richmond Braves flaky pitcher Turk Wendell. Turk was high strung, emotional, and a bundle of ticks on the mound that his fans called "Turk's quirks." When I walked into the Richmond clubhouse I went straight to the manager's office where Phil was writing out that night's lineup card. He looked up at me and laughed.

"You don't even have to tell me," he said. "There's only one guy who'd bring you here. He's as flaky as you were."

Years later I called him at his home outside of Atlanta to congratulate him on being elected to the Hall of Fame. Phil answered the phone.

"It's me," I said. "Pat. I just had to call, Phil, to tell you how happy I am for you."

"Thanks, Pat. I appreciate it."

"No one deserves it more than you, Phil."

"Thanks," he said, "but we both know it should have been you."

It was such a gentlemanly thing to say, but I knew even then it was false. Mentioning my name in the same breath as Phil's and Joe's was implying that, in some way, I was like them. But that was a lie. They had something I never had. They had something that had brought them to major league stardom. They had the courage and the character to stay themselves. They were still themselves. I wasn't. It was shameful of me, this deceit. It was a delusion to think of myself as a pitcher who happens to be writing just now. But, still, that's how *I* saw myself. If I was to make that delusion real I had to do this thing now that I feared. I had to prove I was always a pitcher, not merely in my mind's eye but in my self.

The one thing I had going for me in this quest was the one part of my nature I admired. I had never quit at anything in my life. I had never quit baseball. Baseball had quit me. But I had let it quit me without fighting back. I'd just slunk off, shamefaced, into my ordinary life. Fuck it! I'd fight back now. What was there to be afraid of? It was just a fucking *game!* It didn't matter that now I had a fifty-six-year-old body. I also had a fifty-six-year-old brain. Whatever physical ability I had lost I could make up for with the brains I didn't have at twenty-one. It would be an interesting intellectual exercise. If I couldn't master pitching with the physical talent of a twenty-one-year-old, then maybe I could master it with the brains of a fifty-six-year-old. *Maybe,* my ass! I *would* do it!

I walked to the home-plate screen, picked up the ball, and walked back about twenty feet. I spit the cigar out of my mouth. I faced the screen and tossed the ball at it without my elaborate pitcher's motion. Like a child learning to walk, I'd begin from the beginning. Rethink my way back to that innocent, young pitcher I once was. I'd break pitching down to its simplest parts. Just raise my arm to the side of my head and toss the ball forward. I did this for about ten minutes. I tossed, walked after the ball, walked back, tossed. When I had worked up a sweat I remembered something. The next time I tossed the ball I lowered my left shoulder, which raised my right arm higher over my head. The classic fastball pitcher's overhand motion. I tossed the ball. It went straighter, with less of an arc on it. I smiled to myself. A small accomplishment, to be sure. Still so far to go.

But I had learned to live a life of small satisfactions as a writer. To take pleasure in a perceptive nuance, or a nicely turned phrase, in a boring story I was writing just for money. So what if my editors cut out that nuance, that phrase? They could never take away my pleasure in having written them. My entire life as an old man was filled with small satisfactions personal only to me. I set up little challenges for myself. I went to the gym at 7 A.M. on mornings when I had a hangover. I dieted after the Christmas holidays. I weighed myself every afternoon on the Winn Dixie scale until I had lost the five pounds I had gained. I drove my 1989 Taurus SHO with a leaking exhaust for months until I had saved the *extra* two hundred dollars it would cost for the racing exhaust system that would give my '89 SHO ten extra horsepower. Imagine! All those months of rattling smoke for just TEN extra horsepower.

I learned the exquisite pleasure of delayed gratification, how, the longer that gratification was delayed, the greater the pleasure when fulfilled. I could never wait for anything as a young man. I bought a four-thousand-dollar Chrysler 300 on the day I received my baseball bonus. I drove it to my first spring training in 1960. When I saw that other bonus babies had bought new Corvettes, I immediately lost interest in my Chrysler. I made plans to trade it for a new Corvette. When I pitched a shutout in my first minor league season, I didn't savor that moment because my mind had already leaped ahead to the possibility that the Braves would now call me up to the major leagues. When they didn't, I was crushed.

As a young pitcher, I missed every nuance, every small satisfaction, every significant moment that makes life worth living, because I so lusted after the biggest ones. Success, fame, recognition, certitude. I had to prove I was the best. I had to get a $100,000 bonus when I graduated from high school because that was the biggest bonus ever paid an amateur at the time. Anything less would be a failure. When the Braves offered me $50,000, I could barely keep back my tears. I did not see that money for what it was. More money than my father and brother had ever seen. It allowed me to buy a four-thousand-dollar Chrysler at eighteen, while my brother, a struggling lawyer at thirty-two, with a wife and five children, was driving a Volkswagen Beetle. It would allow me to buy my wife and children a house in the suburbs one day that other young men my age could only dream about. I never saw the gifts I was given. I only saw the gifts I wanted. When I didn't get what I wanted, I felt betrayed. Life was unfair to me. I wanted that $100,000, my gold star, to prove I was the best. Fifty-thousand dollars. What was that? Nothing.

But I have learned my lesson over the years. Now, as an old man, I delight in nuances, small moments, delayed gratifications, unrealized expectations. I have taught myself to get my satisfactions from the smallest gifts, the most distant possibilities. I no longer have to sit down immediately to write the story I am excited about. I wait until the excitement has passed. I think the story through. Search for the nuances and subtle details. Then I write it. I don't have to write the novel I want to write *now*. I enjoy waiting until I finish my *TV Guide* piece on a 25-year-old millionaire racecar driver who has yet to have his first thought. I don't hate writing that *TV Guide* story. It's a good discipline. It pays the rent. Besides, I've found a place in it where I can do a little writer's dance.

I have turned into satisfactions things that, as a young pitcher, I'd have seen as deprivations. A pound less on the Winn Dixie scale. A nice phrase, edited out. A novel that existed only in my head. A wife with one breast.

*   *   *

We had our first date on Fairfield Beach almost twenty years ago. We sat far out at the end at the end of a jetty of rocks and talked for hours. Then, at twilight, we walked back to shore to have a drink at the Nautilus Bar. We sat down at the bar filled with rough workingmen nursing their shots and beers. Susan was wearing her old-fashioned, high-waisted bikini out of an Annette Funicello movie. Her bra, with metal wires, was too big for her shriveled breasts. The men at the bar glanced at her for an instant, then turned back to their shots and beers. A few of them watched a Yankees–Red Sox game on the television over the bar. They weren't used to women in the Nautilus Cafe and Rest.

Billy, the bartender, nodded hello. I nodded back. He was a beefy one-eyed ex–Marine. He lifted weights at the YMCA and punched the heavy bag. Every day, he said, he envisioned a different face on that bag. "It keeps me going," he said.

I introduced Susan to Billy. He bowed his head in the courtly way of a confirmed bachelor. I ordered Bloody Marys. Billy made them from scratch.

He told me he was redecorating the house he had inherited from his mother. He turned to Susan and asked her advice about curtains. They discussed chintz. One of the men at the bar called out, "Heh Billy, how 'bout a fucking drink?"

Billy glared at him with his milky bad eye. The man fell silent and stared into his empty glass. "What color chintz?" he said to Susan.

"Baby blue would be nice," Susan said. He nodded, then got the man his drink.

Leo came out of the kitchen. He was still wearing the muddy hip boots he had worn hours earlier when he had dug up clams from the beach. He was making clams and linguine for dinner. He had worked up a sweat in the hot kitchen making the sauce. He never used salt. He just mopped the sweat from his brow with his hand and flung the sweat into the sauce.

"Dinner will be ready in a few minutes," Leo announced to the bar. Someone called out, "About fucking time."

Leo returned to the kitchen. He had once been a high-school football star. Now, at thirty-six, he was a traveling pencil salesman built like a Sumo wrestler.

I ordered another round of Bloody Marys. While Billy mixed them, I pointed out Bernie Reynolds to Susan. He was standing at the far end of the bar. He sipped delicately, his pinkie raised, from a shot glass of Calvert's whiskey. He puffed on a Top Stone cigar.

"He looks like John Barrymore," Susan said. He had a pencil-thin mustache, and he wore a Hawaiian shirt with neatly pressed brown slacks and polished hard-soled shoes like the kind advertised in the back pages of Sunday magazine supplements. "Who is he?"

"He's a former heavyweight fighter," I said. "Too light for his class. He once fought Rocky Marciano. He stunned Rocky with a right hand in the first round."

"Did he win?"

"No. Rocky knocked him out a few rounds later. Years later, when a reporter asked Rocky if he was ever scared in the ring, he said, 'Only once. When I got hit by Bernie Reynolds.' "

Bernie stood at the end of the bar, muttering to himself. No one stood near him. Every so often he'd throw a punch in the air. One night he threw a punch from his dreams and knocked a college kid off his barstool. Bernie looked down at the kid, blinked, and said, "Learn to drink like a man."

When I had returned from my failed minor league career, I got a job digging ditches for a construction company. I worked with Bernie. He taught me how to dig a ditch. Not with the arms, he said, as I stabbed the shovel into the dirt. With the legs. He pushed the shovel into the dirt with his feet. He worked for hours in the heat without stopping. His mind was always somewhere else. Someone had to tap him on the shoulder to break for lunch.

"He dug perfect holes," I said to Susan. "Even on all sides."

Leo came back out of the kitchen and sat down at the bar next to Jimmy Flannigan. They began to argue, as they always did, about the game on the TV. I told Susan about the time Jimmy was arguing with Leo about Tom Seaver's pitching. In midsentence, Jimmy clutched his chest. He told Leo to call an ambulance. Jimmy was rushed to the hospital, where he was told he'd had a heart attack. He was sedated. When he woke the next morning he saw a nurse standing over his bed. "Make mine a scotch and soda, honey," he said. They tried to keep him in the hospital for a few days, but he refused. He snuck out one night in his Johnnycoat and took a taxi to the Naut. He sat down beside Leo and said, "As I was saying . . ."

Damian Castle came through the front door. He went up and down the bar talking to the men. They slipped him money. He came back our way and sat down next to Susan. I introduced them. Damian shook the tips of her fingers very gently. He was a huge, soft, amiable man famous for his eating habits. We called him the Rocky Marciano of the knife and fork. Whenever he went out to eat at a restaurant he ordered three entrées. After he finished his T-bone steak, four-pound lobster, and linguine with marinara sauce, the chef and waiters came out of the kitchen. They gave him a standing ovation. He waved in appreciation and pushed himself up from the table.

"And what do you do?" Susan asked Damian.

"I make book," he said.

Susan smiled. "Really! Pat writes books too."

Damian looked at her to see if she was kidding. "No, honey. I *make* book."

"Oh, I see." But she didn't see. I had to explain to her that Damian Castle, not his real name, was a bookie, vaguely connected.

Susan excused herself and went to the ladies' room. Damian said, "She's very funny."

"She doesn't mean to be," I said. Out of the corner of my eye, I saw the Babe get up off his barstool. He began to stagger up the bar toward the door. I hunched over my drink, but it was no use. He stopped behind me.

"How's the big fucking bonus baby?" he said.

"Fine, Babe."

"Big goddamned bonus baby. I woulda made a livin' hittin' you."

"Sure you would, Babe."

"You think I'm kiddin?" I shook my head no. "You never had the guts to stick it out." I just nodded. He smiled at me, a nasty, impish smile. "Nobody said it was gonna be easy, kid. You don't want me to let up on ya, do ya?"

"No, Babe. Don't let up." He slapped me on the back and roared with laughter. I watched him stagger outside and begin walking up Beach Road. A big, barrel-chested man pushing fifty. He'd been a minor league third baseman in the Yankees' farm system for years. He set a fielding record one year in AAA. The Babe had been a solid .280 hitter who never got the call up to the Yankees. He stayed in AAA for years, waiting for the Yankees' Clete Boyer to retire. By the time he did, Babe had retired too.

I had never seen Babe play. I had always assumed he was just another washed-up ballplayer whose former talents resided mostly in a boozy corner of his mind. Then, one day, I did see him play for the Naut's slow-pitch softball team. A lazy Sunday afternoon. A lot of guys with big bellies drinking beer during infield practice. Grounders bounced off fat stomachs. Throws sailed over the first baseman's head into the trees. A lot of puffing, cursing, beet-red faces. Babe, hung over, was hunched over at shortstop. His long arms dangled to the ground. A ground ball rolled to his right. He moved sideways, as light and graceful as a figure skater. His hands snapped up the ball on the short hop in a blink. An unforgettable instinct. Those hands.

Susan returned from the ladies' room, smiling. "Some interesting graffiti on the wall," she said. "Who's Jeff?" I told her. "Well," she said, "according to one of his ladies, he's the best lay in Fairfield."

We got up to leave. Billy came down to the bar to shake Susan's hand. "Thank you for the drinks," she said. "It was an interesting experience." She looked around at the dark, dirty, smoky bar filled with men. "This was not one of my usual stops."

"Come back again," he said. "I could use the company."

"You seem to have a lot of company here," she said.

Billy's face clouded over. "Those fucking guys," he said. "They get to you after a while."

*   *   *

We had only been going together for a month, back in Fairfield, in 1979, when I felt the lump in her right breast. It was the size of a small pea that had turned to stone and rooted to her chest muscles inside the liquidy sack of her breast.

"What's the matter?" Susan said.

"Nothing."

She smiled at me as if I was a child. "I know," she said. "I felt it myself. I didn't want to worry you. I'm seeing a gynecologist tomorrow."

The doctor's reception room was deserted, except for an old couple sitting across from us and a receptionist behind a sliding-glass partition that was closed. Susan got up and went over to the receptionist. Her high heels clattered against the linoleum floor. She was wearing nylons and a tweed suit. I had watched her dress that morning. Panties. Bra. Garter belt. Nylons. Slip. The suit. I had never seen her like that before. She looked older, severe, a middle-aged woman of forty, preparing for a long journey, alone. I had only known her in jeans, shorts, a bikini, naked.

Susan returned from the receptionist and sat down. We leafed through magazines for what seemed like an eternity, not speaking. A nurse entered the room and called Susan's name. She got up, smoothed her skirt with the flat of her hand, and went away with the nurse. I waited. An hour passed. Suddenly Susan burst through a door and walked quickly to me.

"Hurry!" she said. "Let's get out of here."

Driving home, she told me. "I've got it," she said. "I have to go in for a mastectomy next week."

She was released from the hospital ten days after her mastectomy. She wore a loose-fitting blue sweater over layers of gauze bandages around her chest when I picked her up. She looked down at herself, her chin tucked into her neck, like a fat person trying to see over their belly.

"I can't see much difference," she said. "Maybe with the bandages off." Then she looked at me and said, "Poor baby! You'll be so deprived."

"Don't remind me. A tit man all my life. Jesus, what a sense of humor He has." We both laughed, but she had to stop laughing because of the pain.

That night, she asked me to change her bandages. She knew how much I hated the sight of blood—not because of the blood but because of the pain that blood implied.

"Are you sure you can do it?" she said.

"I got to get used to it."

She sat on the edge of the bed. I knelt on the floor in front of her and began unwrapping the bandages. Susan turned her head away. A thin dark purple scar ran down the front of her right shoulder. It passed through the center of where her breast and nipple had been and stopped at the bottom of her rib cage. The scar was rimmed on either side with dried blood and inflamed skin. It was laced with fine black stitches that stuck up like hairs.

"Lay down," I said. I put my hand on the small of her back and eased her down on the bed. Then I took off her skirt and panties and we made love. I held myself over her with my palms planted in the bed so my chest wouldn't touch hers. We made love like that for a year, never touching chest to chest, until it had healed. She had only one breast for almost two years before she got an implant. During that time, I taught myself to appreciate the curve of her lower back until it aroused me. It was a good discipline.

Now that I am an old man, my satisfactions have gotten smaller. They still keep getting smaller and smaller and smaller until I expect to wake one morning to discover that what now pleases me is not even a small satisfaction but a deprivation. The secret to life. It was a secret my Uncle Ben tried to impart to me when I was a boy.

* * *

My uncle was a squarish-built man with dark skin and a hooked nose like an Arab. He had wiry gray hair cut short and parted to one side in a Princeton cut. He dressed in a preppy way too—navy blazer, Gant shirt, gray flannel slacks—but always with a distinctive touch his own that would have looked ludicrous on anyone else but on him seemed so obviously appropriate. A knit wheat-colored tie that matched his suede wheat-colored Italian loafers. Although he was not a particularly handsome man, his three sisters called him an Italian Cary Grant. He was a lot like Cary Grant. He had that deep, rich voice and sensually methodical gestures that were mesmerizing. He seemed to move a beat or two more slowly than the rest of us. He was a courtly man with his own elegant style. Like Cary Grant, who always seemed boyish beyond his years.

My uncle lived down the street from us in the suburbs of Fairfield, Connecticut, when I was a boy of seven. I walked to his house for breakfast every morning. I left early, before my parents began their daily argument over my father's gambling. Our volatile house made me, a child of seven, quake with fear each morning until I could escape to my uncle's childless house, which was always as quiet as a church. He met me at the front door dressed in pajamas and a bathrobe. ("A smoking jacket," he called it. "But you don't smoke!" I said, and he laughed.) He raised a finger to his lips. "Sssshhh! Aunt Ada's sleeping." Aunt Ada always slept late, it seemed.

I would sit quietly at the dining-room table while Uncle Ben made our breakfast. I was surrounded by my aunt's doilies and knickknacks and little boxes of violets. She had a tiny, aqua-blue porcelain Buddha in a glass breakfront. After breakfast my uncle would take it out and let me rub its belly for good luck. From the kitchen he talked softly about our breakfast. It was always the same. Orange juice. Two pieces of buttered toast. One soft-boiled egg. A cup of coffee, mine mostly milk. It was an old man's breakfast, a meager breakfast, certainly not the breakfast of a child. But from the kitchen Uncle Ben made it sound like a king's feast. He explained how he always squeezed the oranges by hand in a cut-glass juicer. How he never ground them too hard or else there'd be too much pulp in the juice. The toast had to be a perfect shade of tan, he said. He held out a slice in the doorway for me to see. I nodded. He laid a pat of warm butter on top of the toast until it melted. Then he spread it evenly over the toast. (My mother would take a cold pat of butter and mash it into the toast until it was a doughy pulp that always made me sick to my stomach.) He cooked the egg for exactly three minutes and brought it to me in an egg cup. He showed me how to tap around the egg's circumference with the side of my spoon to take the top half off. Our breakfast each morning was a ritual. A very elaborate ritual for a child. The egg, the coffee, the juice, the toast. That toast! The most perfect buttered toast I have ever eaten!

While we ate, Uncle Ben read out loud the major league baseball scores from the night before from the newspaper. I clapped my hands softly at his mention of the Yankees' every success. I dreamed some day of being part of them.

After breakfast I helped him wash and dry the dishes so Aunt Ada wouldn't have to do them when she woke. Then we'd go upstairs to his office, where he had his drawing board and all his draftsman's tools. He let me sit at his huge slanted pine board where he tried to teach me his draftsman's trade. His immaculate drawings on tissue-thin paper always looked like scientific works of art to me. The pencil-line corners of a triangle never overlapped. His numbers and letters in the margins looked as if they had been printed by a machine. I envisioned him, in my mind's eye, hunched over his board like some modern-day monk, copying a technological manuscript for a future age. It was the perfect job for him, draftsman. He had a clear, logical mind and an aesthetic sense to go along with his almost fanatical obsession for detail. He worked for the same company all his adult life. My mother used to tell me that his work was so perfect that his bosses would hang it up on the bulletin boards for the other draftsmen to see. Often his boss would come by to compliment him on work in progress. But later, dissatisfied, because he worked from some higher sense of accomplishment, my uncle would crumple up that work and begin again.

After my draftsman's practice, we went outside to have a catch in his narrow driveway hemmed in by his house and his neighbor's shrubs. He got down stiffly into his catcher's crouch. He pinched the knee of each pants leg and laid a piece of folded cloth on the pavement as a plate. Then I pitched to him. We made believe I faced the mighty Yankees. After each pitch, he would bounce out of his crouch like a boy and fire the ball back. "Atta boy, Paddy!" he'd say. "You got him now!" Like many childless adults, he didn't have to feign having fun with a child. He was as fascinated by children, especially boys, as my parents were oblivious to them.

Uncle Ben called balls and strikes as I pitched. He was always tough on me until I got behind in the count on Joltin' Joe and he saw my face flush with panic. Then he'd give me a break on a pitch even I knew was off the plate. "Strike three!" he'd call, and fire the ball back to me so that it stung my hand. I always pitched a perfect game with Uncle Ben. He was more my cheerleader than my coach. He didn't know enough about pitching to teach me anything. That came later, with my brother, who began to coach me in pitching in earnest after I exhibited my first flashes of talent in Little League.

Every Sunday morning Uncle Ben took me to church with him. He didn't go to the big, stone, darkly wooded Gothic church down the street from us in the suburbs that was always stiflingly hot in the summer and dark inside. He went instead to the small, whitewashed, airy shrine near the Italian ghetto where he was born and raised and where the pastor still spoke his sermons in Italian. Uncle Ben and I stood with the other ushers at the back of the church. They were holding their long-handled wicker baskets they used to collect money. I felt special among those men, especially my uncle. Always at the last minute, one of the ushers would duck outside for one last puff of his cigarette.

Mass unfolded in the summer heat with an insistent breeze blowing across the pews from the open windows. In the slanting sunlight, women's dresses billowed like the wings of birds until they laid their hands on them. Every so often one of their straw hats would blow off. It went skittering down the aisle. My uncle snared it with his long-handled basket and gallantly returned it, with a little bow, to its owner.

After Mass, Uncle Ben came back to my house, where my mother had a shot glass of whiskey waiting for him. He sat at the kitchen table with my parents, who never went to church. They talked. My mother, the oldest sister, always babied my uncle, as she did most good-looking men. My hot-tempered father always tried to hide his jealousy, but it must have showed. He always made Uncle Ben nervous. He would begin to clear his throat, a nervous gesture, before he answered my father.

As I watched my Uncle Ben sitting there, it dawned on me, even as a child, that he was not comfortable with adults. Adults, with all their neuroses and duplicities, always made him nervous. Children, in their innocence, always calmed him. Which was why he jumped at the opportunity to become our town's Little League baseball coach when it was offered to him. Even though Uncle Ben had no kids, it was assumed by the townspeople that he'd coach for the two years I was eligible to play, then quit when I graduated. But he was still our town's Little League coach twenty years later when I was married, with children of my own.

As my Little League coach, my uncle was hard on me, harder that he was on the other players, all of whom he treated, not like children, but like small adults. We both knew his "hardness" was a ruse to hide his obvious affection for me, his nephew. He called me "Jordan" now, not "Paddy." At practices, he made me carry the heavy canvas bat bag from his car to the field. When he pitched batting practice he always made me hit last, even though I was leading the team in home runs, in addition to being its star pitcher. He threw batting practice wearing his chino slacks and a crewneck Shetland sweater. He threw stiffly, like a man who had come to baseball late in life. (There was no Little League in the Italian ghetto where he was raised. I'm sure he didn't become aware of baseball until he became Americanized in his adult years.) Whenever I faced him in batting practice he always grunted a little harder when he threw his fastball. He always tried to fool me with his curve by not telling me it was coming, as he did for the other players. It wasn't much of a curve, just a little lopsided spin and a last-second wrinkle. I made a point of bailing out of the batter's box on his curve every once in a while to make him feel good. He'd growl at me. "Come on, Jordan! Hang in there like a man!"

No matter how hard on me he tried to be, my uncle could never hide his pleasure in me when I pitched. I would be on the mound in the final inning of a one-run game, with a runner on third base and two outs. He would be pacing back and forth in the dugout, yelling out encouragement. "Come on, Paddy! You can do it!" (I wasn't "Jordan" then.) I would get two strikes on the batter. Before I delivered, I'd give my uncle a wink, and then strike out the batter. He would leap out of the dugout and come running toward me. He was always the first one to shake my hand. Then he shook the hand of every other player on our team.

Despite my uncle's superficial sternness—"Jordan, take those bags!"—he was not really a stern man. However, he could not abide "silliness" in his ballplayers, even if we were children. He ran herd on us to act like little men. I remember one time in particular. It was the only time he ever really spoke harshly to me. It was before a game I was not scheduled to pitch. I was fooling around, showing off behind the dugout with a few other players for the benefit of some twelve-year-old girls who had come to flirt with us. I put my cap on backward. My spikes were unlaced in a deliberately sloppy manner to elicit laughter from those girls. My uncle looked over the dugout roof and snapped at me. "Fix your hat and spikes, Jordan! Look like a ballplayer!"

I sulked for the entire game. My face was flushed and I felt humiliated. After the game, my uncle drove me home. I sat in glum silence in the front seat beside him. He tried to explain why he had snapped at me over such an inconsequential matter as my uniform.

"It's important how you look, Paddy," he said. "Those little details, like wearing your uniform just so, add up. They count. If you do all the little things right, then when the big things come along, it'll be easier to handle them. That's why you've got to pay attention to the details. Sometimes the little details are all you have in life. You can take a great satisfaction from those details. It makes things worthwhile."

As a child of twelve, I only vaguely understood what my uncle was talking about. I understand now, of course. He was talking about pride in one's self. He was talking about his own life. All those details he mastered because there was no big thing in his life—a son—to make him happy.

People came from all over the state to see me pitch that year. Newspaper reporters interviewed my uncle. He discoursed on baseball and kids and managing and his star pitcher. He became an unofficial expert on the raising of young boys into manhood. Reporters wrote about him as if he was the Casey Stengel of Little League managers.

He was a little eccentric, like Casey, but not a knowledgable baseball man like Casey. He didn't know enough about baseball to really manage our team, so he kept things simple and orderly, his secret to success. He knew the limits of his boys. He never pushed them beyond those limits. The other managers overextended their players by concocting elaborate pickoff plays at second base, which always backfired, humiliating those boys in front of their parents. Those managers managed, not for their boys, but for themselves. To show the fans how much *they* knew. My uncle always managed in a way that kept the attention on us, not him. He readily acknowledged that he knew little about the intricacies of the game. So he just drilled us long and hard in the basics and let us play our game. He ran practices by his stopwatch. Batting practice 6:15 to 7:05 P.M. Infield 7:05 to 7:30 P.M.

Before our games, he hit fungoes to us during infield practice, firmly, but not with all his might. The other managers showed off by blasting the ball past their poor befuddled third baseman. And then, in embarrassment, they let up on the next one, hitting a little dribbler that barely reached third, which humiliated their third baseman even worse. Uncle Ben made us look good by extending us precisely to, but never beyond, our limits. And each game, those limits progressed. People came early to our games to watch us take infield practice in a crisp, professional way. They applauded us when we ran off the field.

We were the best drilled team in the state and a heavy favorite to win the state championship on our way to the Little League World Series at

Williamsport, Pennsylvania. But we lost our final game, 1–0, and were eliminated. I pitched a one-hitter that day before three thousand fans. I threw wildly on a bunt attempt early in the game, which let in the winning run. After the game, we were presented with our trophies at home plate. When my name was announced, the crowd rose in their seats and gave me a standing ovation. My uncle walked out to home plate with his arm around my shoulder. I began to cry. He was crying too.

I still have a yellowed newspaper photograph of my uncle and me taken at that winter's Little League awards dinner. We look a lot alike. We both had crewcuts. We were both wearing tan suits. We both had innocent smiles too, which eventually I would lose, but which my uncle never did. He always remained childlike in a lot of ways. He was always best with children, and children were always best with him. To an adult, he seemed like a fussy spinster, so enmeshed in his myriad little details that he felt were so important. To an adult, his interests may have seemed trivial. That perfect buttered toast. The little blue Buddha. As I became an adult, I began to see my uncle in this way too. Like a lovable but childishly eccentric spinster, whose life had little meaning for me now. An adult, lost in my work, my family, my children.

I didn't see my uncle much when I became an adult. He stopped by my house only once in a while. He'd talk about his new team, his players, their strengths and weaknesses. I feigned interest. He began to make those nervous little coughs as he had with my father. Then, suddenly, he was gone. Retired to Florida. Two years later, he was dying of cancer. I called my Aunt Ada to tell her I was coming to visit Uncle Ben in the hospital.

"Oh, no, don't, Patty," she said. "He's not the Uncle Ben you knew. Just remember him the way he was."

I remember my uncle as a man who took a child's delight in small things. Like that perfect buttered toast. Those little things sustained him in the face of his one great disappointment. He never had a child of his own. He could have let that disappointment overwhelm him, make him bitter or, even worse, self-pitying. But he never did. He never found an excuse to be unhappy. My uncle was a happy man because he knew happiness was not a given. It was not something deserved. It was something to be worked at, created out of any little thing at hand. My uncle was a master at finding joy and wonder in life's minutest details that the rest of us so often overlook in our pursuit of grander pleasures. Like that toast. It was the most perfect buttered toast I have ever had.

FIVE

WHEN I RETURNED home from that first day of throwing at Holiday Park I was soaked with sweat. Susan said, "How'd it go?"

"Okay."

She looked at me. She must have seen something that pleased her. "Good," she said.

I put the baseball on top of the refrigerator so Bubba couldn't get at it. Late that night, I waited until Susan was asleep beside me. I eased myself out of bed. Bubba and Blue stirred. "Shhh! Go back to sleep." They lay back down. I went to the refrigerator, got the ball, and went into the living room. I began to pantomime throwing the ball into the full-length, gilt-framed mirror. I didn't see an old man now. My white beard. My lined face. I saw a pitcher going through his motion, naked.

I changed my daily routine. I went to Holiday Park three times a week to throw in the afternoon. I had to do battle with the drunks and the fags and the crazies. The drunks saluted me with their paper bags as I threw pitch after pitch into the home-plate screen from twenty feet away under a winter sun that made me sweat. When I threw in the rain, the drunks took cover under a tree. They laughed at me now. An old man, grunting, sweating, drenched, mud-splattered. For what? To exorcise some private demons they had long ago surrendered to. I envied them. Their camaraderie. Their absence of will. Their bliss.

The fags, sprawling insouciantly on their cars in the lot, began to notice me, too. I must have looked younger to them now, more macho, my shirtless, muscular body glistening with sweat. They tried to make eye contact with me as I threw. I deliberately avoided looking at them. But once in a while, when I paused, doubled over, trying to catch a breath, I'd straighten up and catch their eye. They blew me kisses.

A young filthy-blond woman wandered behind the home-plate screen one sunny day. She was pushing a grocery cart filled with aluminum cans. Her two young sons followed her. One was blond, the other half black. The boys, maybe eight or nine, stopped behind the screen to watch me throw. Their mother began screaming at them insanely. The boys ignored her. She continued to scream at them. They paid her no attention.

I tried to block out the drunks, the crazies, the fags, from my mind. I tried to concentrate only on my throwing. But it was hard to do. I had never had the ability to concentrate only on my pitching when I was in the minor leagues. My concentration was diffused, like fractured light, shooting everywhere. I'd be standing on the mound in McCook or Kokomo or Palatka, staring down at the batter, *trying* to concentrate on only him. But I'd hear the fans screaming. "Take the bum out!" I'd see their faces contorted in such hatred. For me? I'd see a girl in a halter top and jeans walking up the home-plate stands with a tray of cokes. She had a blond ponytail that flounced behind her as she walked. I'd see farmers in bib overalls with their wives in cheap, summer dresses. I'd see little boys running through the aisles. I'd see my manager, out of the corner of my eye, call time as he hopped out of the dugout. I looked around me. The bases were loaded. How? My manager was coming closer now, his arm extended, his hand palm up, waiting for the ball.

I remembered how it had been in the minor leagues as I threw at Holiday Park. I used that memory. I tried to force myself to block out the drunks, the fags, the crazies. I did it for a pitch or two and then was distracted. Every day I tried harder and harder to blot out those distractions until I was conscious only of my throwing, as if in a vacuum.

When I returned home, I gave the dogs their biscuits, Francis his millet. I fixed Susan and me our drinks. Vodka rocks for her. Jim Beam rocks for me in my old tin cup. I helped her make dinner. We sat down to eat at the dining-room table. My mind wandered to that afternoon's throwing.

I had been throwing for two weeks now. My arm motion was becoming more consistent. But the ball still felt slippery, elusive in my hand, like a bird that wanted to take flight. I was just releasing it to its own whim, not controlling it with mine. It sailed high into the home-plate screen. Why? I had been holding it the way I always had in the minor leagues, loosely, with my first two fingers close together across two seams. Then I remembered watching John Smoltz, the Atlanta Braves pitcher, throwing in the bullpen last spring training. I was standing behind him, marveling at his control of his 96-mph fastball. I remembered that he gripped the ball tightly, with his first two fingers slightly spread apart across two seams. His spread fingers gave him a broader, more controlled grip on the ball. I'd try that the next time I threw. My wife's voice intruded on my thoughts.

"What, babe?" I said.

She was staring at me. "How long is this going to go on?"

"What?"

"You not talking."

"Oh, I'm sorry. I was thinking."

"About what?"

"Nothing, really." She narrowed her eyes at me. "My throwing, that's all."

"What about your throwing?"

"Nothing. You don't want to hear it." Susan never liked sports. She equated sports with her first marriage. She was pregnant and scared at twenty. Her husband left her alone every night to play basketball. When I came along twenty years later, I was a writer, not an athlete. Susan had never known me as a baseball player. I never talked about sports with her or the Usual Suspects. Sports was just something from my past that floated around in my psyche at night or at odd moments during the day. I rarely watched sports events on TV, except for an occasional Miami Hurricanes football game. I'd be lying on the sofa in the Florida room, watching the Canes, when suddenly I'd be conscious of the French doors to the living room being slammed shut. I'd glance up and see Susan looking at me, then walking away. The next thing I'd hear was the sound of her music blasting through the house. Which was why I didn't think she'd want to hear about my pitching.

She put down her fork and said, "Yes, I do want to hear about it. *This* I want to share. It's the only thing about you I don't know."

Susan and I met in our late thirties in Fairfield. We courted in bars, on the beach, in restaurants, in my third-floor office in an old Victorian house in town. I was still married then. Susan and I made love on my office floor, in a car at midnight in a church parking lot, in the lavatory of a 727 flying over the Rocky Mountains. I got divorced in 1984. Susan and I moved to Fort Lauderdale to distance ourselves from the failures of our past lives. Failed marriages. Estranged children. We started anew. We got married in a bar by a redneck female justice of the peace who was already drunk before the ceremony. We found new friends. We got our dogs. Francis. A house. We made a new life in "Paradise." We tried not to talk about the failures of our adult lives. We had both gone through the same thing. Marriage at nineteen. Children. Her four, my five. Divorce. Guilt. Those things we shared. Those things we knew. What we'd never shared, the way young lovers do, was our youth. So we tried to fill in for each other the blank spaces of our youthful lives the other had never seen. It's the great loss of lovers who get together late in life. We wanted each other to know what we'd once been when we were young and innocent.

When Susan was eight, her father piled the family into a new Ford coupe and drove them across the country to California to find work. They lived in a garage apartment in Santa Monica. Susan remembered one sunny Christmas day. She was playing outside when she heard a noise overhead. She looked up into the sun and saw, above the palm trees, Santa Claus arriving in a helicopter.

In Santa Monica, Susan became nervous, high-strung, prone to stomach cramps a doctor could not explain, except to say "She misses her home." Her father dismissed her cramps as a spoiled child's pique. Her mother tried to calm her. Finally her father drove the family back to Fairfield. They settled in an old colonial house separated from the

Long Island Sound beach by a swamp of pussy willows and wild asparagus. Susan picked the wild asparagus and fished for crabs, both of which her mother refused to cook. She climbed an apple tree to inspect a robin's nest of tiny pale blue eggs. She was shocked one day when she discovered that out of those beautiful blue eggs had hatched ugly pink chicks. The mother squawked at Susan until she went away.

Her father bought her a new Schwinn bike with a basket on the handlebars when she was nine. She pedaled the bike furiously to the library in town, a long-legged, skinny girl built like a spider hunched forward over the handlebars, her black pigtails flying behind her. She loaded as many books into her basket as it could hold, then pedaled furiously back home to read them all as fast as she could.

On weekends, her three aunts visited. They had been Rockettes at Radio City Music Hall. They congregated in the kitchen while her mother cooked and often broke out into a spontaneous chorus line, high-kicking over the turkey.

"That's how I got interested in the theater," she said. "How did you get interested in baseball?" So I told her.

I told her about Joe DiMaggio and the Yankees and my father's gambling, and the day I learned their true order of importance.

I was a child of seven in short pants. I was standing under the shade of a leafy oak tree in the backyard of my new house in the suburbs of Fairfield on a bright, sunny, summer afternoon. My father was hunched over the big stone barbecue fireplace exposed to the sun. He was trying to light the charcoal briquettes for our cookout of sweet Italian sausages for my aunts and uncles.

My uncles were standing around him, watching, as they sipped from glasses of scotch. My aunts and my mother were sitting at a circular lawn table shaded by a fringed umbrella. They were sipping scotch too, and smoking cigarettes while they played poker—deuces and one-eyed jacks wild—for a penny a point.

I remembered that day, not only for the lesson I learned but because my father was not a cookout kind of dad, and my "aunts" and "uncles" were not my real aunts and uncles. They were my father's gambling cronies and their wives or mistresses. They still lived in the Italian ghetto of Bridgeport in three-family houses with asbestos siding and tiny backyards covered with tomato plants growing out of green, red, and yellow Medaglia D'Oro espresso cans. They still spoke Italian in those houses, and had names that ended in vowels. My father had changed his name from Giordano to Jordan when he was fifteen.

My uncles made nervous small talk, in English, while simultaneously listening to Mel Allen's mellifluous voice broadcast a Yankees–Red Sox game from the radio propped on the open kitchen windowsill. They watched my father sweating in the sun, lighting match after match, cursing the ancestry of those briquettes. My uncles laughed at his discomfort, then fell silent as a crucial play unfolded over the radio. They resumed their small talk. One of my uncles, with exaggerated politeness, asked my father for permission to light up a Toscano cigar. Of course, my father said, why not? My uncle, a gruff little man I rarely saw in the daylight but whose voice I heard often on the telephone at night—"Is Patsy dere, kid?"—gave my father a little shrug and a deferential smile. He made a delicate, sweeping gesture with the back of his hand to encompass our serene backyard and our new Dutch colonial house in these leafy, Wasp suburbs.

He was a bookie. My other uncles were a card cheat, a craps cheat, like my father, and a carnival shill. My father spent most of his nights and early mornings with them behind the heavy bolted door of the Venice Athletic Club back in the Italian ghetto. Outside that door, an old Sicilian with an elaborate mustache, sat on a milk crate reading *Il Progresso* and watching out for the *polizia*.

My uncles were not like the big gregarious blond uncles and fathers of my new friends in the suburbs. They had no interest in tossing a baseball to a child. They had no interest in children—in me, their "nephew"—except on rare occasions when they taught me how to palm the ace of spades and how to spot shaved dice. My uncles seldom smiled. They spoke in muffled, conspiratorial voices, as if their minds were always occupied with matters too weighty, and dangerous, for women and children. They were somber, dark, manicured little men in shimmering sharkskin suits. They had names like Chickie, Freddy the Welch, and Tommy the Blond. Chickie always had a blowzy "chick" on his arm. Freddy never paid his debts; he was a welcher. And Tommy, he was not really blond. He was just not so dark as the others.

I heard my mother's harsh voice offer scotch to my aunts. Heads nodded. She offered water. Hands went up, palms out, long red fingernails like daggers. There were imperceptible shakes of heads. A shrill voice said, "Just rocks, hon."

I went over to stand behind my aunts to follow their play of cards. The hot summer air was heavy with the odor of peroxide and cheap perfume. One of my aunts, a gaunt, nervous woman with bleached black hair, began to cough. A forced cough, it seemed to me, even then. She cleared her throat. "A summer cold," she said. The others commiserated. She reached into her patent-leather handbag and withdrew a bottle of Cheracol cough medicine. The others looked away, busied themselves with their cards. My aunt raised the bottle to her dark red lips. The back of her skeletal hand shook. She threw back her head and drained the bottle in one gulp.

I moved behind the aunt my mother called the Strasha, but never to her face. She was a big-boned, orange-haired Irisher. She had translucent white skin, like parchment, threaded with blue fibers. All the other women were dark-skinned. A cigarette hung loosely from the Strasha's cherry-red lips. She was wearing a low-cut summer dress of orange polka dots on a white background. I stood behind her, hypnotized by the heaving of her huge freckled breasts. She studied her cards through wisps of smoke, one eye flickering shut. She looked over her shoulder at me. "Whaddaya tink, kid?" she said. "Should I stick with kinks?" Caught in the cleavage of her breasts was a residue of talcum powder. "Well, kid?" she said.

I studied her cards, then nodded expertly. Her shrill laughter rang out through our quiet neighborhood. From the barbecue, her "husband," Chickie, looked up and glowered at her. But she did not see him. She turned back to her cards. When she won that hand she reached out both arms and hugged her winnings to her. The loose, freckled flesh under her arms quivered. She stubbed out her cigarette with little stabs, reached around, grabbed my face with both hands, and kissed me on the lips. She laughed again, then turned back to her cards. My mother, a small, dark, fierce, birdlike woman, dealt the next hand. The Strasha absentmindedly ran her tongue over her upper teeth and sucked off the excess lipstick.

I wiped her greasy lipstick off my face with the back of my hand and went over to the kitchen windowsill to listen to the Yankee game. The adults were oblivious to me now. My uncles, in a dark cluster, like crows, around the barbecue. My aunts, like gay magpies, chattering around the table. I lost myself in the game. The score was tied with Joe D at bat. He hit a home run to put the Yankees ahead. I shouted out, "Yeah!" and clapped my hands, the first sounds I had made this afternoon. Suddenly I was aware that everyone was looking at me. My uncles muffled voices and my aunts gay chatter was stilled. My father's face was flushed. I caught my mother's eye. Her lips were pursed in a threatening smile.

She called out, sweetly, "We mustn't root for the Yankees today, sweetheart. Uncle Freddy is down on the Red Sox."

"I was only seven," I said to Susan. "But my mother already expected me to know what 'down on the Red Sox' meant. I was a gambler's son."

"What was the lesson?" she said.

"Until then I'd thought that Italians, the Yankees, and baseball were the most important things in our lives. That day I realized it was gambling."

All our lives were subordinated to my father's gambling. His wins and losses were all our wins and losses. His gambling was a living, breathing thing that had to be nurtured. It was a petulant child whose every whim had to be appeased. It was as if gambling was a spoiled stepbrother, who got all the attention I didn't. My parents expected me to understand that I couldn't listen to *The Shadow* on the radio because my father had to listen to *Harvey Pack at the Track*. They expected me to understand that I couldn't play with matches, not because I might start a fire but because I might burn up a matchbook on which my father had written that night's betting line on the inside cover. They expected me to know I couldn't go into their dresser drawer because that's where my father kept his boxes of numbered and shaved dice. They expected me to know I was being selfish when I asked my father to have a catch with me on the sidewalk in front of our house. He had to deal cards that night at the Venice A.C. His soft pink fingers were our livelihood, like Vic Raschi's arm.

I hated that spoiled brat that ruled our lives, even when he was generous and let my father win at craps so he could buy me an expensive toy. He was just teasing us. Most of the time, he delighted in depriving us of the most basic needs, like security. He made me a fearful child when my mother whispered, "Shhh! Your father's on a losing streak. We might have to sell the house."

That night, I knelt down beside my bed. I prayed to the Blessed Mother to let the Celtics win tonight by at least a point and a half.

My father's gambling became an embarrassment to my mother in our new house. Sometimes he didn't come home in the morning. My mother would scan the newspaper until she came to a story buried on the back page. "Police Raid Gambling Den at Venice A.C." The last paragraph of that story listed the names of the men arrested. My mother had to explain to our neighbors, the Browns, that the "Patsy Jordan" arrested was no relation to her husband, even if he did have the same address. Ironically, the Browns, an Irish family, had their own spoiled brat that ruled their family. Mr. Brown was a drunk, an Irish vice my parents couldn't countenance.

My mother began to nag my father to quit gambling and get a "decent" job so we could lead a "respectable" life. She waited for him to come home in the morning from a night of gambling. She pounced on him in the kitchen. The sounds of my parents savaging each other in the kitchen woke me from my sleep. I went downstairs in my pajamas. They were raging back and forth at one another across the white linoleum floor. I sat down, shivering, and wedged myself in the narrow space between the refrigerator and the wall. I hugged my knees to my chest and rocked back and forth. I whimpered and pleaded with them to stop. But they couldn't hear me above the sounds of their own voices.

Terrible curses! Whore! Bastard! My father cocked his fist low to his side and lunged at my mother. My tiny mother, hands on hips, did not flinch. I screamed. No! Daddy! No!

He never hit her. She knew he would never hit her. His feigned attack and her mock defiance were merely the theatrical gestures of a couple who, no matter how often they played this scene, had a tacit understanding of how it would end. There would be no climax. Only a denouement. A punch never thrown. More curses. Threats to leave. My pleas. A slammed door. Silence. My mother would not even be crying. But I would, wedged into the corner between the refrigerator and the wall. My hysterical sobs now seemed deafening in our silent kitchen. My mother was aware of me now for the first time. She would look at me sternly. Stop behaving like a baby, she would say. Over nothing. She'd begin to clear the breakfast dishes off the table. "Go upstairs and wash your face with cold water!"

No matter how many times this little drama was played out in our kitchen, I never intuited its ending. I never understood that it was a drama. Theatrics. I thought that what was unfolding before my terrified eyes was real. It was real to *me!* I *waited* for the punch. For my father to leave and never return. But he always did return, that very night. They have been married now over sixty years. Despite all those curses. I realize now, of course, as an adult, that those curses were only words. They meant nothing. By morning they had been forgotten. By my parents. But not by me. Nor have I ever forgotten how those terrible fights were resolved.

For as long as I can remember, my father has always slept in the tiny guest room between my mother's bedroom and mine in our house. Late at night, after one of their arguments, my father would get out of bed and come to my bedroom door.

"Are you asleep, Patty?" he would ask. Huddled under the covers strewn with my comic books, I feigned sleep. He asked again. My heart began to pound. When I did not answer, he went down the long hallway into my mother's bedroom.

"What do you want!" she said in a voice that gave me chills. He whispered something I could not hear. "What?" she said. "It was your birthday last month!" He whispered again. "Why should I?" she said. "Besides, you'll wake the kid."

My father began to whisper again. There was a moment of silence. Finally, his barely audible voice broke the silence. "Please, Florence."

"All right!" my mother said. "But this is the last time this month, do you hear?"

I heard the dresser drawer open, the sound of aluminum foil being unwrapped. My father, amid soft curses, began to struggle with the contents of that aluminum foil.

"Hurry up!" my mother said. "I want to get some sleep."

Then I heard them fumbling on the bed, and suddenly my mother's brief, inward gasp of pain. My father began to grunt softly, in rhythm with the creak of the bedsprings. My mother began to grunt too, but less with pleasure than with discomfort, as she did when climbing our cellar stairway with a load of wash.

My father's breathing began to come faster now. For a brief moment, my mother's breathing seemed to be in union with his. Then she caught herself. "Well!" she said. "Are you gonna take all night!"

My father let out a high-pitched sigh of surrender. The springs stopped squeaking. I could hear only their labored breathing now, then my mother's voice. "Get off me!" She grunted with great emphasis as my father rolled off her and sat up on the edge of the bed. He sat there for a long moment, catching his breath. Then I heard the snap of rubber, and the springs creaked one last time.

"And don't flush it down the toilet!" my mother said, as my father left her bedroom and went into the bathroom. A few moments later my father came back down the hall, paused a moment at my bedroom door, and then got back into his bed in the guest room.

Years later, I bought that house from my parents. When I was in my midthirties I had stopped sleeping with my wife too. I slept in that guest room. It was a dark little room fit only for a child. Often I had trouble sleeping there. When I did, and was on the verge of getting out of bed and walking down the hallway to my mother's bedroom—my wife's bedroom now—I would remember how it had been with my parents, late at night, after an argument, when I was a child.

* * *

As soon as I was old enough, I fled my parents' house. I pedaled my bike to the baseball park near our house. I was eight. My dog, Lady, a collie, would run alongside my bike. She stood panting beside me, in rightfield on the Little League diamond whenever I was lucky enough to be chosen by one of the older boys for a game of pickup. They always sent me to rightfield where, they assumed, I could do the least damage. I always batted ninth. Even then they tried to bat around me when I wasn't paying attention.

"Heh! It's my bats!" I would shout at a twelve-year-old standing at the plate. He would drop his bat in disgust and shuffle back to the bench, kicking up clouds of dust.

I assumed my earnest stance at the plate, facing the pitcher, who looked so big to me then. My teammates shouted confusing instructions to me from the bench. "Hold the bat higher. Higher! Farther back! Spread your legs! Oh gee, not like *that!* Swing!" Invariably, I struck out on three pitches. My teammates grabbed their gloves in disgust and trotted out to the field.

"I told ya!" they hissed at me.

I ran to rightfield with tears in my eyes. I pounded my glove and assumed my outfielder's stance. Lady jumped and barked around me. I ignored her, lost in my shame. Lady grabbed the cuff of my jeans in her mouth and yanked. I tried to shake her off. I heard the crack of the bat against the ball and looked up to see the ball sailing over my head. Lady ran after the ball. I ran after her. She scooped it up in her mouth and ran to the pond behind the rightfield foul line. My teammates shouted behind me. "No! Stop her!" They came running too. But we were all too late. Lady waded out into the center of the pond, looked at us with the ball in her mouth, and dropped it into the water.

On my way home from the park, I always stopped at the drugstore for a chocolate malt and to read copies of *Sport* magazine about my favorite players. Whitey Ford. Vic Raschi. Allie Reynolds. The pharmacist made Lady wait outside for me. She stared through the glass door, looking pitiful, while I sat at the counter on a round swivel stool, spilling my milkshake over the magazines I never bought. The pharmacist just shook his head in despair but said nothing.

One day at the park, I was standing in rightfield when I saw a car pull up in the gravel parking lot behind the third base line. A man got out. He was tall and lean, with sandy-colored hair. The play on the field stopped. All eyes turned toward the man. He went to the back of his car, a station wagon, and opened the rear door. He pulled out a long canvas bag, hefted it onto his shoulders, and walked over to the third base bench. All the boys but me ran wildly toward him. I stood, confused, in rightfield. The man upended the bag, and its contents spilled out in the dust. Baseball bats. Balls. Catcher's shinguards. Chest protector. Plastic batting helmets with protective flaps, like earmuffs. One of the older boys began waving for me. He shouted, "Come on, stupid. It's the Little League coach."

I ran to him just as he was telling the boys he would call each position and that they should raise their hands for the one they wanted to try out for. I was still panting from my long run from rightfield and my heart was pounding with excitement. I couldn't control my enthusiasm at the thought of being on my first real team. I shot up my hand at the first position he called out.

"Pitcher!" Mr. McGregor said.

*   *   *

I loved being a part of that Little League team. The uniforms, the camaraderie, my teammates, even if, as an eight-year-old, I rarely played that first year. The games were played at twilight before a small crowd sitting on skeletal wooden slats for bleachers. The young mothers in Bermuda shorts chatted among themselves, stopping only to change their newest baby's diaper or glance down through the wooden slats to chastise their small sons fooling around under the stands.

The fathers, in loosened ties and rolled-up shirtsleeves, came directly from work. They stood around behind the home-plate screen, like Indian scouts surveying the horizon. They shaded their eyes with the flat of their hands as they tried to follow the unfolding action on the field under the harsh orange light of the sun setting behind a line of trees beyond rightfield.

A college boy sat at a folding card table behind the home-plate screen. He kept the official scorecard and worked the record player that played only the National Anthem to begin games and, between innings, choruses of "They Call the Wind Mariah," by Frankie Laine. He was surrounded by boys and girls my age on bicycles. The boys leaned against the home-plate screen, gripping it with their fingers, heedless of the umpire's warning that a foul tip could smash their fingers. The umpires were gnarled, unshaven, ex-ballplayers of local repute who had once starred in the Senior City League for the White Eagles A.C. or the Rosebuds or the Savoy A.C. Now, in their fifties, they still liked to keep their hand in the game.

They parked their cars in the rightfield lot and waited, sipping coffee, until game time before beginning their long, heavy-bellied, pigeon-toed walk to home plate. Some of them worked as stonemasons. Their skin was coated with a fine white powder. Some were carpenters with gnarled hands criss-crossed with cuts and purple bruises. When they reached home plate they acknowledged, with a nod, the respectful greetings of those fathers who remembered them from their playing days.

Before the game was more than a few innings old, a dozen girls, high-school cheerleaders, would assemble underneath the maple tree beyond the leftfield fence. They formed a chorus line and, led by their blond captain in jeans rolled up to her knees, they began practicing their cheers for the upcoming football season. I never noticed them when I was eight and nine, but when I turned eleven, and had become a Little League star pitcher, they suddenly seemed so exotic to me, like colorful, tropical birds. They kicked their tanned legs high, in unison, and their voices rang out with incongruous football cheers amid the sounds of the Little League game in progress.

When I was ten, I became my team's star pitcher. It separated me for the first time from my peers. It was my first distinction in life. The first thing I could do well others my age couldn't. People came from surrounding towns to see me pitch. They pointed me out, called out my name, applauded my strikeouts. Old men of distant local repute followed my pitching with interest. I saw them nod to one another after I struck out a batter. A sign. But of what? Parents looked at me with big eyes and introduced me to their younger sons and daughters as if I was someone special. Sometimes their daughters were older, thirteen and fourteen, and had no interest in me, a boy of ten. But I was beginning to have an interest in them. When I turned eleven, then twelve, a big boy for my age, those girls began to reciprocate my interest. I could see them behind the home-plate screen, hanging back a bit but watching me through narrowed eyes, wondering when I would catch up to them. It excited me. All the attention. The old men nodding to me as I passed in my uniform after another no-hitter. The parents smiling at me. Their daughters staring. They confused me. I averted my eyes and blushed at their brazen, appraising smiles.

I lost myself in the order and discipline of the game, and my small stardom. It was an escape from my parents' disorderly house. Ironically, my baseball seemed briefly to bring my parents closer together. They united around my pitching. My father bought me a $50 Herb Score model glove and kangaroo-skin baseball spikes. My mother never made me do chores on days I was to pitch. After supper, I rode my bicycle to the park in my uniform. Lady no longer went with me. She had to be locked up in the cellar because at the park during my games she would run onto the field to the pitcher's mound to be with me. She didn't understand that these games were now organized, were now *serious*, not like the pickup games when I was eight. The fans would laugh at her, and me, as I dragged her off the field in embarrassment. On days I was to pitch, I'd drag Lady, whimpering, to the cellar and leave her there. Soon, whenever she saw me in my uniform, she would put her head down and slink down to the cellar of her own accord, her tail between her legs. Now she would not even follow me to the park when I didn't have an organized game no matter how hard I tried to coax her out of the cellar. I missed her at the park on those days.

My parents went to all my games. They sat high in the skeletal wooden bleachers along the third base line. A couple. Respectable now. My father, not a gambler now, but *my* father, his new found distinction. Other parents pointed them out, acknowledged them with respectful, hellos. Doctors, lawyers, judges. They all complimented my parents on my pitching. "A fine boy," they'd say. "You should be proud." It was as if, to those parents, my talent on the mound implied some qualities of inner character that other boys my age lacked because they could not throw a baseball as fast as I could.

My mother beamed at these compliments, at this respectability my pitching brought her. She cheered my every pitch. When I got two strikes on a batter I would hear her shrill voice call out, "Strike him out, Patty!" And when I did I looked back and saw my mother clapping her hands with glee, while my father leapt down behind the stands and half walked, half ran toward the pay telephone near the tennis courts to call his bookie.

*   *   *

He stood on the pitchers' mound with a baseball in his hand—a tall, gangling boy of twelve in a Little League uniform that was so small on him, the pants barely reaching his knees, that he resembled a stick figure.

He didn't look like a pitcher, not even a Little League pitcher. He had to pause a second before each pitch to remind himself how to put his foot on the rubber, and then how to pump, kick, and lunge, and follow through so that he was squared to the batter now only a few feet away.

He had been recruited to pitch by his coach, the produce manager at a local supermarket, because he was so much taller than the other boys his age. His coach felt his size alone would frighten batters in a way his talent—or, rather, lack of talent—would not. But he frightened no one. On this clear summer day, in full view of his parents, the fans, other boys and girls his age, and myself, seated in the stands along the third base line, he could not retire even the tiniest of batters. The fans laughed at him at first. "Imagine! A boy his size!" And then they began to feel sorry for him. "He's trying so hard," said a mother seated beside me.

With each succeeding base hit, the pitcher took more and more time between pitches, until he was almost immobile on the mound, unable to deliver another pitch. He looked toward the dugout for his coach with pleading eyes, but his coach was bent over, his hands cupped around a match, lighting a cigarette. The pitcher's shoulders sagged and he forced himself to begin his mechanical delivery once again. The batter hit a ground ball toward the mound. The pitcher followed it with his eyes, but he could not make himself reach down for it. The ball passed close to his right foot and continued on into centerfield. The pitcher remained frozen in his follow through for a split second as an idea trudged across his brow, and then he fell to the ground, clutching his left foot, then, remembering, clutching his right foot as he writhed in the dirt. His coach and teammates rushed toward him as the umpire called "Time!" They hovered over him for a few minutes—his coach down on one knee, massaging his pitcher's foot—and then he struggled to his feet. He draped his arms over the shoulders of two smaller teammates—his arms like an eagle's wings over his chicks—and hobbled off the mound to applause from sympathetic fans.

That applause seemed to me then, as it does now, so false. It stemmed not only from the fans' sense of relief that the pitcher was not seriously hurt but also from their sense of relief that they would no longer have to watch his humiliation. The fans' sympathetic applause began to build as he crossed the third base line. Only I was not so sympathetic. I yelled out, loud enough for everyone to hear, "That's one way of gettin' off the mound!" The fans booed and hissed at me. Somebody shoved me in the back. "You should be ashamed!" But I wasn't. Even as my face reddened under the fans' abuse, I knew I was right. He was a quitter. He didn't take it seriously. Like I did. At eleven. Already a Little League star. My name in headlines every week in the local newspaper. More strikeouts. Another one-hitter. Sports was a serious business for me even then, and I did not harbor much sympathy for anyone who did not take it as seriously as I did. I ran windsprints at twelve to stay in shape. Imagine!

*   *   *

I showed Susan the photographs of me in Little League and high school and the minor leagues.

"You were so serious then," she said. "Didn't you enjoy it?"

"The pitching," I said. "I enjoyed that. It was the pressure I couldn't handle."

"What pressure?"

I went to my desk and pulled out old newspaper clippings. Headlines in the *Bridgeport Post-Telegram*. Jordan pitches no-hitter. Jordan pitches fourth no-hitter. Jordan strikes out nineteen. Jordan gets $50,000 bonus. Jordan expected to be Braves' new Warren Spahn. Jordan finishes first season 3–3. Jordan sent down to Class D. Jordan released by the Braves. Reject of the diamond returns home.

Susan read them all. When she was finished, she looked at me. I said, "The pressure to be me."

"At least you had the chance to be you," she said.

She had wanted to be an actress as a child. At fifteen, she was acting in summer stock with John Cassavetes and Gena Rowlands and Martin Balsam. She was offered a scholarship to the American Theater Wing in New York City. But her father wouldn't let her accept it. He was afraid that in New York, his high-strung daughter would fall under bad influences. So she stayed in Fairfield, went a year to college, met her future husband, got pregnant, and had to get married. She stopped acting for a few years when she had her first two children. At twenty-three, she realized her marriage had gone bad. She began to act again in theaters around Fairfield County.

She showed me a photograph of herself in a gauzy dress, with a fragile smile, when she played Laura in *The Glass Menagerie*, and another of herself in a low-cut slip, with a defiant smile, when she played Maggie in *Cat on a Hot Tin Roof.* I stared at her in the slip, kneeling on a bed, pressing her crotch against a bedpost.

"Jesus!" I said. "You must have been a horny thing."

"I wasn't getting much at home." I couldn't stop staring at her in the slip. "You and I had gifts we both associate with failure," she said. "When I returned to acting during my marriage I knew it was a sign my marriage was over."

"I wish I'd known you then. I'd have given anything to have seen you act."

So she did. Act. One last time for me. She got the lead in Neil Simon's *The Gingerbread Lady* at a theater in a strip shopping mall in Boca Raton. She played a self-destructive woman deteriorating into alcohol. I sat in the audience on opening night, on a metal folding chair. I watched her fall apart on stage. She made me cry. When the play was over, I went backstage. Susan was sitting in front of a mirror taking off her makeup. Before I could say anything, she turned to me with her big expressive smile. "Wasn't that fun?" she said.

It was a strange word to use, I thought. I had never used such a word to describe my pitching.

Susan had a gift that touched people. My talent merely amused people. But I didn't pitch for that. I pitched for me. I never thought of my pitching as a gift I was sharing with others, as Susan thought of her acting. Watching her that night, I felt shamed. My talent was trivial, and my selfish attitude toward it was impure. It was *my* talent. I hoarded it. So it became my failure. Which frustrated me for thirty-five years. Susan's gift freed her from frustration because she never thought of it as hers alone. She was just a conduit between her gift and others. Her gift flowed through her to enrich others, and, in the process, herself too. We were alike in so many ways, except this one. I look at the world through a mirror and see reflected only my self. She looks at the world through a window and sees everything but her self. Now she wanted to look through that window into my past to see the me she'd never known.

"I want you to tell me everything," she said that afternoon at dinner. "Everything."

So I told her what I'd been thinking, about my grip on a baseball. I felt foolish talking so passionately about such a trivial thing. But I couldn't stop myself. "I have to have a tighter grip," I said. "Look!" I showed her my new spread-finger grip on a ball. "See! I can control the ball instead of it having a will of its own."

She nodded. "Makes sense." I looked at her, nodding seriously about something she knew nothing, and once cared even less.

"Makes sense?" I said.

"To me." We both laughed.

Six

WE TALKED ABOUT my throwing every day over dinner. I told her how intricate a pitcher's motion was, all those little parts that were so much more than the sum of those parts. They all had to fit together seamlessly so you couldn't see they were parts of a whole.

"Like a well-made play," she said.

"I guess. But before a pitcher's motion can be a whole you've got to break it down into parts, understand each part, master them separately, and then put them all back together again. And still they're not a whole. You just keep doing it over and over until at some point those parts are no longer parts but one fluid motion. *Then* you can concentrate on your fastball and curveball and slider."

"Like learning your lines," she said. "It's not enough to know them and say them onstage. You've got to feel them."

"Yeh. But I don't feel it yet. They're still just parts to me. And even as parts they're so hard to master physically. Like standing on one leg, facing third base." I stood up and assumed my one-legged flamingo pose. My right leg began to wobble. "See!" I snapped. "It's not because my leg is weak, 'cause it isn't. I can squat two-fifty. It's just that I don't feel the balance, like a tightrope walker."

"You'll get it," she said. "You've got plenty of time." It was late January. The Northern League season wouldn't begin until June.

One afternoon I told her how hard it was to keep myself from flinging the ball from the side of my head. I had to remind myself to drop my left shoulder so that my right arm would rise above my head in that classic fastball pitcher's motion. Then I had to do it! It took all my strength to do it, *when* I reminded myself to do it.

"The hardest part," I said, "is that they're all the hardest part. You've got to know the right way to throw first. Thank God I haven't forgotten that. Then you've got to remind yourself to do what you know. And finally, you've got to muster all your strength to make yourself do physically what's in your head. All of it. Every little part. You forget one piece, it's like a house of cards, it all falls apart. And the joke is, you've got to do it all without thinking about doing it because you're supposed to be thinking about the batter. He's got a say in this too. You can't be thinking about your motion. You've got to be thinking about putting that fastball in on his hands, and then the curve low and away. That's the whole fucking point!"

She smiled at my passion. I rarely talked about writing like this. Talking about writing was boring. Writing was something I did privately, not publicly. Readers care about the result, not the process. The story was good or bad. Who cared why except me? But pitching was a public thing, like acting. The fans saw the process, pitch after pitch, inning after inning, that resulted in a shutout. They felt a part of the process. That was part of their enjoyment. They worked along with a pitcher, batter after batter. They saw, right there, a mistake, a hanging curveball. They talked about it in the stands. Why did he throw a curveball there? Why did it hang? Pitchers talked about pitching constantly too. It's a mystery they're all trying to unravel. Why did *that* curveball break and not the other one? They can't stop themselves. They go over every pitch of a game in their minds, with fellow pitchers, their coaches, manager, roommates, anyone who'll listen.

Now Susan was all of those people for me. She listened patiently every day as I talked about what was becoming, again, an obsession. To throw the ball right, once and for all. I thought about it every waking minute. I'd be doing squats at the gym when suddenly I'd stop, put the bar on the rack, face the mirror, and begin my motion. I pushed off an imaginary rubber and forced my left leg to pull hard to my left to force my body to swivel toward the batter. I'd be pushing my grocery cart through Winn Dixie and I would suddenly stop in the aisle. I'd make a little overhand throwing motion, forcing my upper body low to the floor on my follow through. That was hard, I thought. I did it again. The young mother behind me, with her baby in her shopping cart, watched for an instant. Then she backed up her cart, turned it around, and fled.

I thought about pitching when I was writing and giving the dogs their biscuits and taking my bath. I'd be lying there in the tub, smoking a cigar, sipping from my tin cup, my flesh puckering up like a pink prune, when Susan's voice would intrude on my thoughts.

"Babe! What the hell are you doing in there?"

Annoyed, I snapped, "Whacking off! What the hell do you care?"

She stuck her head into the bathroom. "Was that necessary?"

"I'm sorry."

One night in bed, Susan pushed my face away from between her legs. I looked up, startled. "What? What'sa matter?"

She shook her head. "This isn't working."

"Why?"

"I can't compete with your fastball." She pulled the covers up to her chin and flicked on the TV.

"I'm sorry," I said.

"It's all right. I understand." She tossed her hand toward the kitchen. "Go ahead."

"Go ahead, what?"

"The ball's on the refrigerator. I'll wait until you're through."

But she was already asleep by the time I finished throwing into the mirror.

I was thinking about pitching more than I was pitching because I couldn't pitch every minute of every day. It bothered me, at first, until I remembered what I'd told Mary Beth when she told me she wanted to become a writer.

"The problem with most beginning writers," I said, "is they think they're not working unless they're physically writing. Sometimes it's more important to think than to write. The older I get, the more I find myself thinking more and writing less. Once I get it right in my head the writing's easy." I was doing the same thing with pitching. I was mastering it intellectually first, which made it easier to master it physically.

I'd been throwing for almost a month now. Not hard. Just easily into the screen, trying to get my motion right. I felt more comfortable with it. But it wasn't there yet. The odd thing was, my arm felt great. I'd expected some soreness in my bicep or elbow or shoulder, but there was none. Why should there be? I had a twenty-one-year-old arm. It's not like I'd been throwing for thirty-five years, wearing it out. Besides, all the weightlifting I'd done must have strengthened all the muscles and tendons. Even the shoulder. I'd been warned that throwing at my age was almost a guarantee of a rotator cuff injury, which ended most pitchers' careers.

I was in Minneapolis, researching a story on Kobe Bryant, the rookie basketball player with the Los Angeles Lakers. I was staying in a hotel with the Lakers. I spent most of my time in the lobby bar, talking to the coaches when they passed by. One day, I ended up drinking late into the night with the team's trainer. He was a short muscular Italian with a neat little mustache. When I told him I was trying to pitch again, he laughed.

"You'll never do it," he said. He tapped my right shoulder with his finger. "Rotator cuff. I guarantee it." He seemed to enjoy telling me this. He was in his early forties. Maybe he didn't like the idea that a man much older than himself was trying to compete again? Maybe that threatened him? The little prick!

Now, after a month of throwing, there was no hint of rotator cuff pain, or any pain in my arm. Still, I had a lot of little nagging injuries I hadn't counted on. A pinched nerve in my right calf. It made me limp, stiff-legged, but didn't stop me from throwing. Then one rainy day my sneaker slipped in the mud and I felt a pull in my groin. When I got home, in pain, Susan asked what had happened. I told her.

"Why were you throwing in the rain?" she said.

"It was my day to throw."

"Of course." She knew I had set up my pitching routine just as I had my writing for the last thirty-five years. It paid, sometimes, being an old man rooted to his routine.

I had to stop throwing for a week until my groin injury healed. I spent the time thinking.

Over dinner one afternoon, I told Susan, "It's time to get on the mound again." She nodded. "But first I've got to buy a pair of spikes so I won't slip anymore." She nodded again. "And maybe a glove and a decent baseball." She stopped eating.

"What are you trying to say?" she said.

"I need a catcher."

"Well, get one."

"Everyone works. Who's free on a weekday afternoon to catch me?"

"Ronnie." She was right. I felt the old fear again. It had been easy throwing by myself. My little intellectual game. Thinking, talking, throwing in private. With a catcher I'd be going public. Someone would see me. They'd find me lacking.

Susan misunderstood my hesitation. She said, "Ronnie caught Goose Gossage once, didn't he? Goose Gossage was a major league pitcher."

That was the point. Gossage had been a major league pitcher with a 99-mph fastball. What was I? An old man deluding himself. A dilettante playing at being a pitcher. George Plimpton. Susan saw the look on my face.

"Baby, what's to worry about?" she said. "Ronnie's your friend. Just go and have some fun. Have a catch with your friend."

Ronnie *was* my friend, and so was his wife, Mary Beth. She called me her "best girlfriend." We talked almost every day on the phone, mostly about her writing. I called her "Her Bee-ness." She called me "His Pee-ness." After her rejection by Arthur Frommer, I began calling her "Hash." She called me "Re-Hash." She called Susan, "Sue-Bee." They went shopping together, a thirty-two-year-old blonde and a fifty-eight-year-old grandmother.

Mary Beth helped me pick up Susan's fifty-eighth birthday present. I had stopped at Hollywood Ford with Susan one day under the pretext of buying a part for my SHO. She wandered through the showroom, admiring the new Explorers. A salesman eyed her up and down, a tall, tanned, leanly muscled blonde in a tight T-shirt that had written across the chest: "Beyond Bitch."

"Can I help you?" the salesman said.

"No, thank you. I'm just waiting for my husband." I saw her eyeing the Explorers dreamily when I returned from the parts department.

"Forget it," I said. "Too expensive."

"I know."

On the day of Susan's birthday, Mary Beth picked me up in the old red Hyundai we had given her. She drove me to Hollywood Ford to pick up the black Explorer I had bought for Susan. The salesman eyed the young beautiful blonde with me. He remembered my wife. He smiled, a salesman's knowing smile.

"Oh, no," said Mary Beth, wide-eyed. "You've got it all wrong." She smiled. "*I'm* his wife. The other one, *she's* his mistress."

Ronnie was forty-nine. He had been an award-winning photographer at *Sports Illustrated* for twenty-five years. Before that he was an army scout in Vietnam. He went out, alone, far from the front line, deep into the jungle in darkness. He was born and raised in a small, northern Wisconsin town. As a boy, he hunted and fished with his father. Then he was drafted into the army and sent to Vietnam like so many other small-town country boys who knew how to handle a rifle in the forests. When he came back from Vietnam he was in his twenties, a high-school graduate. He had no idea what he wanted to be in life. I asked him once how he became a photographer. "It was the only thing I knew how to do," he said. "I'm a shooter."

Ronnie spends most of his life on the road for SI. I spend most of my life at home, in my office, working. When Ronnie's home, he doesn't work. He *could* catch me. I called him one day and asked him. He said sure. But he didn't have a catcher's mitt. I told him I'd buy one, and a ball, and a glove for myself.

"Don't bother," he said. "I have a pitcher's glove. I got it from Goose Gossage."

*   *   *

I went to the Sports Authority and picked out a catcher's mitt and a ball. I was trying on a pair of spikes when a young salesman came over to me.

"I see you're a soccer player, sir."

I smiled. "No. Baseball." I felt foolish saying this, at my age.

The kid grinned at me, then said with the infinite patience of smartass kids dealing with old people, "But those are soccer spikes you're trying on. Sir."

"Oh." I looked at them as he put them back in the box.

"Let me get you the right spikes."

"Sure." I was beginning to sweat.

He brought back another pair of spikes. They looked the same to me. "What's the difference?" I said.

"The cleats, sir."

Jesus! I didn't even bother to try them on. As I was paying for them at the checkout counter, I saw the kid laughing with another salesman. He gestured with his head toward me. I hurried out of the store with my new glove and National League baseball and spikes I hadn't even tried on. When I got home and tried them on, I discovered they were too tight.

"Then take them back," my wife said.

"They'll break in," I said.

*   *   *

"Paddy Wagon! You ready to throw?" Ronnie was smiling at me as he stood in the parking lot next to the big league diamond.

I tossed him the brand new catcher's mitt. He pounded his fist in it. "Stiff," he said.

"I'll break it in quick."

"Yeh. Sure." He tossed me Goose Gossage's glove. It felt strange on my hand after thirty-five years. To calm myself, I lit a cigar.

We walked toward the mound on a hot, sunny, humid afternoon. My feet hurt in my new spikes. Ronnie glanced over his shoulder at the men sitting on the trunks of their cars in the parking lot.

"What's with all the fags?" he said.

"My fans." It was the first time in weeks I was conscious of them. I had been so lost in my throwing that I no longer noticed them until now. I was conscious too, for the first time in weeks, of the homeless men drinking on the grassy mound behind the home-plate screen. I remembered that first day when one of them saluted my first feeble pitch with his paper bag. Jeez, it was hot! I stripped off my T-shirt and tossed it on the dirt as I stepped on the mound. Ronnie stood halfway to home plate, waiting. I tossed him the ball. It bounced out of the stiff mitt.

"This thing is *stiff*," he said. He bent over like an old man to pick it up.

"Put your free hand over the ball when it hits the glove," I said, exhaling cigar smoke. I tossed him the ball again. My new cleats caught in the dirt. I lurched to my left and flung the ball to Ronnie's right. He lunged at it. The ball hit the mitt and bounced out.

"Jesus, Ron! You a dumb Polack, or what?"

"Better than a dumb guinea," he said. "Pitching with a cigar in his mouth."

I yanked the cigar out of my mouth and flung it in the dirt. "Just catch the fucking ball," I said.

"You try catching with this thing." He fired the ball back at me. It sailed over my head into centerfield. My shoulders slumped in the heat. I trotted after the ball. At second base, the nerve in my calf cramped. I limped to the ball and then back to the mound.

"What's wrong with your leg?"

"Just a cramp."

"You wanna quit?"

"We just started, for chrissakes! No, I don't wanna quit!"

We tossed the ball back and forth for a few minutes. I aimed it at his mitt so he wouldn't have to lunge for it. Still, the ball kept bouncing out of the mitt. He had to bend over stiffly to pick it up. Jesus, he was thick! He moved like a fucking old man. I threw the next ball harder so it would stick in the mitt. It sailed over Ronnie's head, rattled the home-plate screen, and dropped to the dirt.

"Nice pitch," he said. He walked back to get the ball.

"Stay there," I said. "I'm loose."

"You sure?"

"Yes, I'm sure." Ronnie positioned himself behind home plate. "Get down in a crouch," I said.

"I can't. My knees." I remembered Ronnie had bad knees from years of lugging around heavy camera equipment. He stood there, smiling at me. I toed the rubber, reminding myself of all the parts of my motion. I raised my joined hands over my head and turned my right foot clockwise and slipped it into the dirt parallel to the rubber. My feet hurt. I saw Ronnie smiling. Jeez, don't make him chase it! I swiveled toward third base, tried to balance myself on one leg, saw, over my left shoulder, the big round mitt, felt my leg wobbling, the heat, hoped the ball wouldn't bounce out of the mitt, *again,* make poor Ronnie bend for it with his bad knees. I began to lose my balance, felt the pain in my calf, and swiveled back toward Ronnie too quickly. Instead of my arm exploding toward the plate in unison with my body, my right arm stayed behind me as my body lunged forward. My left foot landed in the dirt, all my body momentum spent, when finally my right arm trailed behind. I flung the ball into the dirt at Ronnie's feet. He skipped away from it without trying to catch it.

"At least make a stab at it!" I said.

"And catch it in the nuts? I'm not wearing a cup."

"Oh, for chrissakes!"

Ronnie retrieved the ball and threw it back to me. I toed the rubber again. I tried to force myself to remember all the parts of my motion I had worked on for a month. I remembered them all. I began my motion, tried to remember, *forced* myself to remember, saw Ronnie standing there, the mitt, the homeless men behind the screen, sweat dripping into my eyes, the pain in my calf, the fags on their cars, my toes cramped into too-tight spikes, the sound of a car horn far off in the distance, the ball sailing over Ronnie's head, Ronnie leaping for it, too late, as the ball hit the home-plate screen and dropped to the dirt.

I threw for five more minutes. Every pitch was the same. I remembered everything I had worked on until I began my motion and then it all flew out of my head like a bird loosed from its cage and I became conscious, not of my motion, but of every single detail around me. It was the first time my writing betrayed my pitching. I had a writer's consciousness now, not a pitcher's. I had spent thirty-five years learning to be conscious of every nuance of life. Now I had to be conscious of only one nuance, my pitching, if I was to be successful. My writing betrayed me, just as it had helped me get this far. It had taught me routine; to be conscious of every detail; to analyze everything; to break things down to their simplest parts; to intellectualize physical acts so that when I had mastered them in my mind it would be only a simple step to mastering them physically. But now, my writer's consciousness was too diffused. I needed an athlete's ocular bloc, the ability of every great athlete to concentrate all his thoughts and energy on the one simple activity that was most important to his life. But pitching wasn't the most important thing in my life. My wife and my dogs and my parakeet and my friends and my writing, *they* were the most important things in my life. Pitching was a trivial thing.

It had always been merely a trivial pursuit even if I had let my failure at it inform my adult life. That was my fault. What kind of man could devote his life to such a trivial pursuit? I wasn't that man anymore. I had made myself a different man, with a different life. I had done it by rethinking my life, by rethinking myself, by rethinking what I wanted to be as a man. When I was a young man, I was so self-absorbed I never noticed the people who passed through my life. I never noticed their kindnesses. I never noticed Sally, the girl in McCook, who said she loved me. It never dawned on me that she might love me because *I* didn't love her. I never noticed the Salvation Army major in Davenport, Iowa, a kindly old man in whose house I rented a room. He sat in his easy chair in his den and watched me come and go, a sullen youth, until he took pity on me. He invited me into his study for a beer. I declined without thought. Why would I want to have a beer with a fat old man? It never dawned on me that he might be lonely too.

Twenty-five years ago, I wrote the following lines in *A False Spring*: "And as I go about my ordinary day, I'll wonder, now, what people are passing unseen, through my life, only to be remembered years later with a warmth I never felt at their moment of passing.'' I was thirty-two then. Still self-absorbed. But with a difference. At thirty-two I had assumed a persona: the abused, sensitive writer. I stayed aloof from people by a great effort of will. I sat at a darkened corner table in crowded bars. I watched others my age laughing and drinking together. I suppressed my desire to get up from that table and go join those laughing people, because it would have intruded on the exquisite pleasure of my self-pity. The older I have gotten, the less I like that man. He was such a fraud. At least that young pitcher, in his arrogance, was being true to his nature. So I taught myself not to be either of those men. I am conscious today of every living thing that passes through my life.

I noticed Nero was limping one day. He seemed to be favoring his left hind leg. I took him to the vet. The vet examined him and then told me he had a slight inflammation in his hip. He gave me some pills for Nero. As I paid for the pills at the front desk, the girl who took my money asked me what I'd been writing recently. I told her I'd just come back from the Dominican Republic, where I'd researched a story on the Arturo Fuente cigar company.

Out of the corner of my eye, I noticed a surly-looking shar-pei sitting with his owner. The shar-pei was eyeing Nero in a threatening way. I felt Nero tense on his lead. The girl was still talking. She was telling me she takes empty cigar boxes, hand-paints tropical scenes on them, and sells them as jewelry boxes. I smiled, nodded, waited for my change.

''Want to see one?'' she said.

''Sure. Yeh.'' She went to the back room. I heard Nero growling low in his throat at the shar-pei. I walked toward the door with him. I made sure I walked between him and the shar-pei. Just as I got to the door, the girl came back with her beautifully hand-painted cigar box. She held it out for me to see.

''Very nice,'' I said. ''Really nice. I've got to go.'' I left her standing there, holding out the box for me.

I didn't realize what I'd done until I got home. I felt such a fool. I went to my office, emptied the cigars out of all my cedar cigar boxes, carried them to the car, and drove back to the vet. When I gave them to the girl, she was thrilled. She began to tell me how she was going to decorate them.

I listened. When she finished, I said, "Let me see that box you showed me again? My wife could use a jewelry box."

I noticed the elaborately painted fingernails of the homely black girl who checked out my groceries at Winn Dixie. "Honey," I said. "I love your nails." She smiled. I added, "Honey, you ever go out with old men?"

She flapped her long nails at me. "Hush, baby," she said. "You ain't old."

I noticed the four black guys at our gym who stayed conspicuously to themselves. I tried to draw them out, into the camaraderie of the gym. "Yo, Melvin," I said. "Where'd you get them gold teeth?" Melvin eyed me suspiciously. I tried another tack. "Melvin, it true all you brothers got big dicks?"

Melvin glowered. "Yeh, and all you rednecks got little dicks."

I stared at his crotch, shook my head, and said, "I don't know, Melvin. You ain't got any rhythm, you probably can't jump, and it looks like you ain't got much of a dick." Now Melvin and all the brothers were glowering at me. I added, "Heh, Melvin. You might as well be white." They all laughed.

I noticed the big fat motorcycle mechanic who started coming to our gym to lose the fifty pounds he'd gained from years of drinking beer. He had grease under his fingernails and his body was covered with tattoos. He was almost fifty, with a ravaged, homely face and a lot of missing teeth. He reminded me of Tex Cobb in *Raising Arizona*, only Cobb, in that film, looked like Cary Grant compared to Joe.

Joe's heavy feet pounded away daily on the treadmill. He rarely looked up as he sweated off the pounds. He was a shy man who was embarrassed to be so out of shape among men his age who weren't. But he came every day, sweating silently. I tried to draw him out.

"Big Joe," I shouted across the gym. "You keep losing weight you'll be nothing but skin." He nodded. I added, "You know, Big Joe, most people die, they leave their organs to science." He looked up, confused. "You die, you can leave your skin to the Louvre." He smiled sheepishly.

I hold open every door. I surrender every parking space. I flirt with every waitress and then leave too big a tip. I ask everyone about their job, their girlfriend, their dog, their new baby, their life in a way I never did as a young man obsessed with *my* life. My pitching. I have become pathological about my concern for others out of fear I might regress. Imperfect contrition, I know, but the best I can offer. I hurt no one, am quick to forgive those who hurt me.

I *hated* myself for making poor Ronnie chase the ball! He was my friend. He was doing this for *me*. When I was a young pitcher, my catcher was just an object to me. It was his job to chase my wild pitches.

But if I was going to master pitching now, I had to stop being the man I had made myself all these years. I had to go back to being the young man I had been—No. The young man I was still now. I have never changed my true nature. I just learned to hide it under all the layers of the things I'd taught myself. I have always known this, even if all the people in my life now don't. If I was to succeed at pitching, I'd have to let free the man I was. This thought depressed me out of my mind. All those years of hard work, for what? Nothing? I didn't want to be that young man again. I *liked* the man I'd made myself into. I would give up pitching before I'd be that young man again. I would just have to learn one more thing, to live with my failure until the day I died. I had no other choice. Which wasn't quite true. I had two choices. One failure or the other. I couldn't be both men. Or could I? Both men had one thing in common. The old writer and the young pitcher both thought they could do anything they put their mind to. So I would be both. I would compartmentalize my life. I would be the man I had made myself into, every waking moment of my life, until I stepped on the mound and let myself be what I was, a pitcher.

I looked down at Ronnie sweating in the sun with his bad knees. He was still smiling. "Come on!" he yelled. "Gimme your best shot."

I wiped the sweat from my brow. He was my friend, not my catcher. I couldn't give him my best shot because I was more worried about his bad knees than I was my own pitching. If I was to succeed, I had to go back to being that obsessed young man again, at least for the few minutes a day when I was on the mound. I needed a real catcher. It wasn't Ronnie's fault. This was a joke to him. Two old friends having a catch. He didn't know how important this was for me.

"I've had it, Ronnie," I said. "Let's go get a cold one." I became the man I'd made. I released Ronnie from his purgatory.

"All *right!*" he said. "Some cold brewskis!"

Ronnie left town that week on an assignment. Before he left he gave me four old baseballs he had lying around the house. I went back to the park and began to throw alone again. I threw every Tuesday, Thursday, and Sunday afternoon. Susan and I always went to the beach on Sunday afternoon. She lay on a towel close to the ocean while I sat on the wall facing the street. I drank a light beer and watched the rollerbladers glide by. I eyed the beautiful girls in their g-string bikinis. Only now I wouldn't go with Susan on Sunday afternoon.

"Oh, baby," she said. "It's my only day to relax."

"Then you go." She looked at me strangely.

On days I was to throw, I didn't worry about Winn Dixie or Blockbuster or the dogs or Susan's afternoon drink. I became a selfish man again. I blocked everything out of my life for thirty minutes in the afternoon, except my pitching. I approached it with the total self-absorption I had as a young man when nothing came between me and my pitching. It felt good again to be me, if only for those thirty minutes three days a week. I felt powerful again, arrogant, with a real athlete's ocular bloc. It was a pleasure to simplify my life like that. I distilled it all down into the one simple thing *I* wanted to do. I became an elemental man, instead of that complex one who struggled through every day pathologically afraid he might miss a nuance.

It was easy to slide into the real me. It was intoxicating, like an addiction. I was throwing one day when one of the homeless men wandered down from his grassy mound out to the pitcher's mound. He stood beside me, weaving in the hot sun, swigging from his paper bag, watching me through his red-rimmed eyes. He was a skinny black man in filthy clothes that smelled. I ignored him and kept on throwing. He smiled at me, and said, "Hey, bro. You a pitcher or sumthin?"

"Fuck off, Sambo." He looked startled.

"Heh, man. You don't gotta be like that. I was just askin'."

I stopped and glared at him. "Fuck off, I said."

He backed away from me, still weaving, and staggered back to the grassy mound.

When I got home that afternoon, soaked with sweat, I got ice from the freezer, wrapped it in a towel, and iced my arm at the dining-room table. Susan was preparing dinner.

"Babe," she said, as she had a thousand times before. "Could you give the dogs their biscuits?"

"Christ! Can't you see I'm icing my arm!"

She looked at me, stunned. After a long moment, she went back to her cooking. I got up and got the dogs their biscuits. I gave Francis his millet.

"You want a drink, babe?" I said. She said nothing. I fixed her her afternoon drink, made myself a Jim Beam rocks, and sat down at the table with the ice wrapped around my elbow. I had to work harder to compartmentalize my life, I thought. I had to struggle to keep my hard self from obliterating my softer self, never the other way around, because that hard self had always been infinitely more powerful than the self I had made.

I had six baseballs now, so I didn't have to walk after every pitch. I warmed up from half the distance to the plate, then moved back to the mound. I forced myself not to think about my motion. I just threw pitch after pitch as hard as I could. I had been thinking too much about pitching in the same way I sometimes thought too much about a story I was afraid, for some reason, to simply sit down and write. I had been thinking about every detail of my pitching for over six weeks now, every waking minute. It was all implanted in my mind. Now I just had to do it, over and over, until what was in my mind filtered down by osmosis into my body, and it all became a natural activity. I remembered as a minor leaguer I had been taught that thinking was an athlete's curse when he competed. My coaches used to say "Don't think. React." Thinking was for practice, not a game.

I equated what I knew in my head about pitching with the subtext of a story. As long as I had every detail of that story in my head I didn't have to think about it when I sat down to write. The subtext showed through, even when I didn't put it down on paper. What I knew about pitching would show through then, even if I didn't think about it as I went through my motion. And it did. I could feel my motion smoothing out every day, becoming more and more natural, a unified piece instead of distinct parts.

One morning in late February, I woke up with a sore arm. A dull ache in my elbow and a tenderness in my bicep. It scared me, at first, until I remembered this was how my arm had felt when I threw full speed for the first time in spring training. A spring training sore arm, we called it. A sign a pitcher was throwing hard again. Jesus! I *was* throwing hard again! I must have passed some invisible threshold. My pitching had ceased to be an intellectual exercise and had become a purely physical act. I *was* a pitcher again. My fastball was probably in the 80-mph range, a far cry from the 95-mph fastball I had as a young man, but still respectable for spring training. I could probably be throwing in the mid-80s by June. The average speed of most major league pitchers.

I didn't throw for a few days so my arm could heal. I was nervous, distracted around the house. Finally, Susan said, "Babe, why don't you just go to the park? Do some exercises, run or something. Anything to calm yourself down."

"Good idea, coach."

"Take Hoshi. He could use the exercise."

I got out of the car at the park with Hoshi on his leash. He sniffed the grass, looking for a scent. I jerked his chain tight on his neck. He looked up, confused. "No fucking around, Hosh. This is business." I led him to the rightfield foul line and faced centerfield. He sat down. I jerked his chain again. He stood up. "Let's go," I said. I began to trot toward centerfield. Hoshi walked beside me. He fell behind me as I picked up the pace. I jerked his chain again. "For chrissakes, Hosh!

Keep up!'' He began to trot too, until he was beside me. When we reached centerfield I stopped, turned around, and walked back to the rightfield line. Hoshi walked beside me. When we got to the foul line, I pivoted and began jogging back to centerfield. Hoshi sat down, jerking me to a stop. "Hosh, for chrissakes! Come on!" He trotted half-heartedly after me.

We jogged to centerfield and walked back ten times until we were both panting heavily. Hoshi's tongue was hanging out. I stood along the rightfield line, doubled over, trying to catch a breath. Hoshi sat beside me, looking up at me, his head tilted in that dog's way when they're confused. He didn't understand what the point was. Chasing things, possums, squirrels, rabbits, that he understood. Running after nothing was a human thing. It made no sense in his dog mind. He looked at me, this part of me Hoshi did not know, my past, and tried to understand.

When my arm finally healed, I went back to the park, excited. I wanted to see what I'd missed in my throwing that caused that sore arm. I wanted to see if I really was throwing hard again.

I warmed up quickly and moved back to the mound. After ten pitches, I was ready to throw full speed. I pumped, kicked, reared back, and swiveled toward the plate. I forced my left shoulder down so that my right arm was straight over my head. I could hear myself grunting with the effort. I forced my upper body low to the ground and to my left as I released the ball. It cut through the air with a hissing sound. I saw the red seams revolving so swiftly they were a blur. God, that was always a beautiful sight! The ball crossed the left corner of the plate, knee high, and rattled the screen. A perfect pitch! I shook my head as if to clear it. Then I laughed out loud.

For the next twenty minutes I just threw fastball after fastball until I was exhausted, panting in the heat. After my last pitch, I stood on the mound staring at home plate. I was breathing heavily, like my dogs chasing that possum. I had to wait a few seconds before I could walk to the screen to pick up the balls and go home.

Two days later, I began throwing curveballs. I had once had a devastating overhand curveball that approached the plate like a fastball and then dropped straight down, like a duck shot on the wing. My first minor league manager, a tough old man named Bill Steineke, used to call my curve the Unfair One. Whenever I got two strikes on a batter, he'd stand on the top of the dugout steps and yell out, "Jordan! Give this cocksucker the Unfair One." I'd nod and throw it. The batter would begin his swing as the ball approached the plate, an optical illusion. When I threw my overhand fastball the seams of the ball rotated upward. When I threw my overhand curveball the seams rotated downward. In either case, the ball was spinning so rapidly it always looked to the batter as if the seams were spinning in the same direction.

Just as the batter was halfway through his swing at what he thought was a fastball, my curveball would drop as if it had hit an air pocket. The batter would try to adjust his swing, too late, and end up lunging wildly at the ball. His ass stuck out behind him so that he looked like a 1950s housewife demonstrating a vacuum cleaner. Strike three! Steineke would cackle like a dirty old man and yell to the batter, "Fucking unfair, ain't it, sonny?"

But I didn't have the Unfair One anymore. Age had taken away that vicious snap in my wrist at that instant just before I released the ball. It was like reaching for a string to a light and yanking it down. But now my wrist just rolled lazily over the ball. It approached the plate in a big, sloppy arc. Not a bad changeup, I thought, but not the strikeout pitch I once had. I needed a sharper breaking pitch if I expected to fool twenty-five-year-old minor league hitters. I began to experiment with a slider, a pitch I never needed when I had a 95-mph fastball and the Unfair One. I adjusted to the dictates of my age, instead of fighting them.

A slider is half a curve, half a fastball. It doesn't have the speed of a fastball or the pronounced break of a curve. It approaches the plate like a poor fastball and then breaks sharply right to left (in my case, as a righthander) at the last second. A slider only breaks six to eight inches instead of the eighteen inches and more of a good curveball. But a slider is deceptive because the batter can't pick up that point when the ball begins to break as he can with most curveballs. He begins his swing at a half-assed fastball and ends it missing a sharp slider.

I held the ball slightly off-center so that two thirds of the ball showed between my thumb and forefinger. Then I just threw it as hard as I could, without rolling my wrist over at the last second. The ball slipped out of my hand with its off-center spin, approached the plate like a fastball, and then darted left at the last instant. As a young pitcher with the Unfair One, I'd always equated a slider with pitchers who didn't have good enough stuff to win with a fastball and curve. It was a poor man's curveball.

I worked on my slider for weeks, until I could throw it on the outside corner to righthanded hitters at will. Not a bad pitch, I thought one afternoon, standing on the mound. I could see now what kind of pitcher I was becoming at fifty-six. A decent fastball. A mediocre slow curve. A good slider. I worried only about my ability to throw my pitches over the plate. I didn't have control as a young pitcher, so what made me think I could find it now? One of the reasons I walked so many batters as a young pitcher was that I had to throw so many pitches to each. They never popped up my first fastball or hit a routine grounder to shortstop. They missed it. And the next one. And fouled off the next three. I'd end up throwing ten to twelve pitches to each batter, eventually walking many of them. The fastball I now had was hittable. Batters would hit my first fastball instead of missing it. Maybe they'd pop it up, and maybe they'd hit it off the outfield wall. In either case, I wouldn't walk them. Less was more for me now. I would have better control. If I did, I was positive I could get minor league batters out.

I didn't expect to strike out Jim Hicks anymore. The sight of him on one knee was gone forever for me. But I could pitch respectably, not embarrass myself, pitch maybe two or three innings, give up a run or two, and then retire myself from baseball and that dream from my nights. If I couldn't at least do that, I wouldn't take the mound. I would not embarrass myself. I was no George Plimpton, nor was I meant to be. This was not some preordained exhibition in which my opponents would lay down for me, the fifty-six-year-old writer, who wanted to see what it felt like to be a pitcher, a quarterback, a goalie, a prizefighter. I knew what it felt like to be an athlete. I knew what it felt like to pitch to a batter, to sit in the dugout, to hang with my teammates in the locker room. Those things held no interest for me. I didn't want to pitch to a batter who wasn't going to try to rip my fastball over the fence, who was going to take an easy swing at my fifty-six-year-old pitches because it was understood I was only doing this as a journalist to write a book. Paper pitcher. I wasn't *really* a pitcher. I was an old writer. A dilettante sniffing jocks. But *I* wasn't doing this as a writer. I had no intention of writing a book. I kept no notes. When I was pitching, I no longer thought of myself as a writer. It was probably the only time in my last thirty years when I forgot that I was a writer. I wanted the batters who faced me to see me as a pitcher too. I wanted them to be angry at me, an old man daring to step onto their turf. I wanted precisely the kind of ill will that exists between athletic opponents in a real competition. I wanted them to try to rip my pitches off the wall to drive me off the mound as quickly as possible. This would be a real game for them. And for me. Neither of us wanted to look foolish.

I came home from throwing one afternoon in late March and met the woman who lives across the street, Betsy, coming home from school. She was a teacher at St. Thomas High School. She saw me soaked with sweat, carrying my glove, still wearing my spikes.

"Patrick!" she said. "What *are* you doing?" Betsy was sixteen years younger than I but always the schoolmarm.

I told her about my pitching. The St. Paul Saints. Holiday Park. Throwing baseballs at the home-plate screen.

"Why don't you get a catcher, Patrick?"

"Because everyone I know works in the afternoon."

She smiled. "I can get you a catcher. One of my students is on the baseball team." St. Thomas had the best high-school baseball team in the country in 1996. Its shortstop was drafted in the first round by the Atlanta Braves. They regularly played against teams with pitchers who threw over 90 mph and beat them.

Betsy wrote the name and a telephone number on a scrap of paper and handed it to me. "Call him," she said. "He's a great kid."

I looked at the name and number. Brian LaBasco. I remembered his name from the *Fort Lauderdale Sun-Sentinel* sports section. He was the St. Thomas third baseman who'd hit .476 as a junior.

"Thanks, Betsy."

As I was about to open my front door, she called out, "Don't forget. He'll love to catch you."

I put the scrap of paper on my desk and stared at it. I was afraid to call. I stared at it every day for weeks, that accusing name of the boy who would change my life. Then the Japanese came.

SEVEN

THEY CALLED FIRST. A strange Japanese voice over the phone I could barely understand. He said he was the producer for a Japanese TV program called *Pets Around the World*. He'd heard I had six Shiba Inus, a breed so revered in Japan that they had been declared a national treasure. The Emperor's children were always photographed with Shibas at their side. For centuries, Shibas could not be exported out of Japan. Then, after World War II, American GIs began bringing Shibas to the States. Most of them were brought to the West Coast. Shibas were almost unknown on the East Coast until the mid-1980s. We had never heard of them until we bought our first one, Hoshi, ten years ago. It was purely by accident. I had been allergic to dogs ever since I broke my nose at nineteen. Then I discovered, ten years ago, that the only breed I wasn't allergic to was Shiba Inus. It was a great relief to me. I missed dogs in my life. Dogs had always had an important place in my life. They had helped me to overcome great loss.

*   *   *

I bought my wife and children a puppy on the night I left them. I stood in the kitchen doorway and watched my children play on the floor with the puppy. My wife washed dishes at the sink. It was a cold night in January. I could hear the wind whistling through the trees and rattling the shutters of our old Connecticut house.

"It's to replace me," I said with a smile. My wife looked up from the dishes. She glanced sideways at me in that unblinking, accusatory way of hers that always sent me rummaging through my memory for some real or imagined transgression. This time, it was real. She knew I really did buy that puppy to replace me.

I went upstairs to our bedroom—my wife's bedroom now—and packed my things. I carried my bags downstairs, through the kitchen, outside to my car. I scraped the ice off the windows of my rusted-out '74 Alfa Romeo. I held a lit match to the door lock, until the ice melted. I opened the door, loaded all my clothes and books and my typewriter into the backseat, then just stood there, shivering in my windbreaker. I looked around one last time at the house and neighborhood where I had lived with my parents as a boy, and then my wife and children as a man. The light was on in my old bedroom—my son's bedroom now—where, as a boy, I lay huddled under blankets, listening to the Green Hornet and the Shadow on the radio. My old bedroom looked down over a Japanese maple tree in the front yard close to the sidewalk. I used to pitch to my brother on that sidewalk when I was a boy. My mother and father sat on the porch steps and applauded my pitches.

My parents bought me a puppy when I was eight. Lady was a high-strung, twitchy collie, with a silky sable and white coat. She used to run wildly with me in the woods across the street when I played imaginary games of cowboys and Indians. She trotted beside my bike when I went to the park to play baseball. One afternoon, when I was ten, I was pedaling home from the park with Lady beside me when a boxer came running out from behind a house. He chased Lady down the street. I pedaled after them furiously, screaming "No! No!" My bike skidded against the curb and I tumbled off it onto the sidewalk. My knees were skinned and bleeding. I looked up to see that the boxer had turned from Lady and was running toward me now. He was snarling and foaming at the mouth. I was so frightened that I didn't see Lady come running back. Without breaking stride, she leapt at the boxer when he was only a few feet from me. They fought viciously while I screamed and cried and looked around for an adult.

The fight was over quickly. Lady was covered with blood. The boxer's blood. The boxer lay in the grass, his tongue hanging out, his throat ripped open. He gasped for breath through a mouth filled with blood. Then his eyes rolled back into his head and he was still.

When I was sixteen, and my parents weren't home, I took a girl up to my bedroom to show her my baseball trophies. Lady trotted up behind us. The girl and I sat on the bed admiring my trophies. Then we started kissing. Lady sat in the doorway, looking at us, with her head tilted. I thought she was reproaching me. I got up and chased her downstairs.

By then I didn't spend much time with Lady anymore. I was outgrowing her. I had other interests. Girls. Baseball. A driver's license. A part-time job at the drugstore. I left her care to my parents. They fed Lady, took her for walks, brushed out her fur, while I went out on dates and pitched no-hitters.

When I left home to play in the minor leagues, I didn't think much about Lady. I was too busy with my career. I returned home from my first year in the minor leagues in September. I didn't even notice that Lady didn't come running to greet me at the door. I kissed my parents in the kitchen, then I looked around.

"Where's Lady?" I said.

"She died, Patty," my mother said. "Of a broken heart. When you went away, she stopped eating. She waited for you to come home, and when you didn't, she went down into the cellar. She wouldn't come out. Then one day she didn't get up."

Lady was only ten years old when she died. Young for a dog. But that didn't dawn on me then. I could only think of my loss. She had been such a part of my life as a boy. She comforted me during my parents' furious arguments. She tried to teach me how to love something other than myself. I worried about her when she was sick, or when she didn't come home at night. I stood in the doorway, yelling "Lady! Lady! Come home!" I feared she was lost, or hit by a car. Then I'd see her running toward me, her fur covered with brambles from the woods.

I broke my nose playing basketball that winter after Lady's death. Ever since, I have been allergic to dogs. My eyes water and grow puffy until they're almost closed. I have to struggle for breath. A doctor told me, "Under the wrong circumstances, a dog could kill you."

My allergy didn't bother me at the time because I had no interest in ever getting another dog. It was a blessing in disguise when I got married and had children. Whenever my children pleaded with their mother for a dog, she'd just look at them sternly. "Don't be ridiculous," she'd say. "You know how allergic your father is."

Until I was forty, I was one of those men who see in dogs—or cats, or any pets—only a nuisance to be brushed aside. I'd smile at a dog's owner as I pushed their leaping dog away from me. "I'm sorry," I'd say. "I'm allergic to dogs."

So I waited until I left them to buy my wife and children a dog. I went back into the house this one last time. My wife was still drying dishes at the sink. My kids were playing with the puppy on the floor. I bent down and kissed each of my five children goodbye. They barely noticed. Then I stood behind my wife, drying dishes at the sink. I waited for her to turn around so I could kiss her on the cheek one last time. But she didn't turn around.

"I'm going now," I said. She didn't look up. I laid the house key on the sink beside her. She looked at it. I moved toward the door. I looked back one last time. My wife was staring at me in that unblinking way of hers, and then I noticed that my oldest daughter, twenty, was looking up at me too, with a wide-eyed look of terror, and then, gradually, that same unblinking look of her mother's.

I fled in a snowstorm. I outran it. I drove south through the night, the speedometer of my Alfa quivering between 103 and 105 mph. I stopped only for gas and coffee until I arrived in Fort Lauderdale, twenty-three hours later, on the afternoon of January 3, 1984.

Fled is the only word to use. No one *moves* to Fort Lauderdale. People flee to it, on the run from a bad check, a bad rap, a bad marriage, a bad life that is driving them mad. Fort Lauderdale residents, only half sarcastically, refer to their city as Paradise. It *is* paradise, if paradise is a place where people go to be born again. People flee to Fort Lauderdale to reinvent themselves in a city in the sun where everyone is new and no one passes judgment. People who flee to paradise aren't running away from themselves the way people do who flee to Los Angeles, so they can take on new names, new looks, new personas that have nothing in common with what they once were. People who flee to paradise are running *to* themselves. The selves they always thought they could have been when they were suffocating in the still, dead air of conventional society.

I waited out the divorce in a small apartment on the Intracoastal. Then Susan joined me. We got married. The years passed. Our children grew up, got married, had children of their own. We waited for them to visit us in Florida but they seldom did. We both grew estranged from our children over the long distance. It confused us. We spent hours asking each other, why? Maybe it was because their other parents, Susan's ex-husband and my ex-wife, were unmarried, alone? Maybe it was because we were so obviously happy together? Maybe they felt guilty visiting us in the riches of our affection toward one another? Maybe they thought we didn't need them, that we had each other? Finally we just threw up our hands. Who knows what goes on in the minds of those you love?

The loss of our children brought us even closer together. We lavished on each other all that parental affection we couldn't lavish on our children. It was excessive. Unnatural. A surfeit of "I love you,"s and sex and solitary Christmases devoted to each other. We had few friends those first few years in Fort Lauderdale, but to those few we must have seemed like a cloying couple. But we had so much affection to give! Susan suggested we get a pet.

"Maybe a bird?" she said. "You aren't allergic to them."

"A bird. Babe, that's nothing but a framed print."

"What about a dog then? Maybe there's a breed you aren't allergic to."

I called an allergist. He told me there was no such thing as a nonallergenic dog. But for everyone who's allergic to a dog, there's a breed that that person isn't allergic to. The breed differs from person to person. "You'll just have to hunt around," he said.

So we haunted the pet shop at the Galleria mall. We went every night so I could pet a poodle, a spaniel, a keeshond, a Lab. Whatever. And each night I went home wheezing, with puffy eyes.

One night I petted a small red aloof puppy. I went home and forgot about him. I woke the next morning and realized I hadn't had an allergic reaction to the puppy. Susan and I hurried to the pet store, only to be told the puppy had been sold. "What kind was it?" I asked. The owner said, "A Shiba Inu." We went to the library to read everything we could find on Shibas. We discovered they had a short, double coat of fur, which probably kept my allergic reaction to a minimum. They were also said to be intelligent, proud, stubborn, courageous, aloof with humans, and hunters of game, like bears and wild boar. The latter was their only drawback, as far as we were concerned.

"They're runners," said a breeder we found in Bradenton. "You've always got to walk them on a lead. They get on the scent of game, they're gone." She suggested we get a male because, as she put it, "they don't call females bitches for nothing." We picked up our little red puppy that we called Hoshi-O, which means "Little Star" in Japanese, seven weeks later.

In all the years we've had Hoshi he never hurt us, except once. He was three years old. We had just bought our cabin in the Blue Ridge Mountains of western North Carolina. Each morning I would take Hoshi for a walk up the mountain on his leash. And each morning I passed an old mountain man in bib overalls who chided me for leashing my dog.

"But he's a runner," I said. "I'm afraid I'll lose him."

The old man laughed. "You cain't lose a *dawg*."

I felt foolish, like those little old blue-haired ladies in Miami Beach who smother their little Shih Tzu-mops with an unnatural affection. In their need to make their dogs human, to replace a human they've lost, they deprive them of their true nature.

So I began to walk Hoshi unleashed. It was torment for me. He roamed in the woods until he was almost out of sight. I called him back. He returned indifferently, at his own pace. One morning, a rabbit crossed our path. Hoshi stiffened, then bolted after the rabbit and was gone over the mountain. I ran after him, screaming his name, but he never looked back.

Susan and I were still crying on our front porch hours later. "That sunuvabitch!'' I said. "After all we've done for him. I will *never* get another living thing." And there was Hoshi, wagging his tail, panting, with his dog smile. He bounded up the steps and ran to us. He smelled of something dead he had rolled in.

That night in the cabin I heard a bear roaming through the woods. His bear grunting sounded like an angry old man laboring at a task at 2 A.M. I opened the door to the front porch and went outside. Hoshi followed me. He ran to the end of the porch where the bear's grunting was coming from, far up the mountain. Hoshi stood up on his hind legs, his front paws against the porch railing, and threw back his head. His nose pointed up to the black sky, his eyes rolled back into his head until only the whites showed. He howled like a wolf at the moon. It was so otherworldly, that sound from my domesticated dog, that it momentarily frightened me. It was a part of Hoshi I didn't know. Maybe even he didn't know?

I watched him in his trancelike state as he howled his unearthly howl. He was lost in his nature. I tried to understand it. But it was too much of a mystery for me. There was something in him I would never know. Who can ever know the nature of the ones we love?

*   *   *

The breeder who sold us Hoshi tried to warn us. "Once you get a Shiba," she said, "you can't have just one." She was right. Two years later, we got Hoshi's sister, Kiri. She charged into our apartment at six weeks old and bullied Hoshi out of his toys and bones. She growled at him when he went near what was once his. He let her have his things. I called the breeder, furious.

"He's acting like a pussy," I said. "He doesn't even put up a fight."

"Don't worry," she said. "A good male dog always defers to a bitch."

When I told Susan, she said, "Take a lesson."

"Okay, bitch."

Hoshi raised Kiri, but when we got his and Kiri's sister, a year and a half later, he would have no part of Stella. When she growled at him over his bones, he stuck his nose under her belly and flipped her in the air. It was Kiri who now took over Stella's raising. Then, two years later, we got Nero from a different breeder so we could eventually mate him with Stella. Kiri bit him the first day he was in our new house. Stella mothered him.

When Nero was a year and a half, Stella went into heat. We tried to keep the two separated, but Nero was a dog possessed. He followed Stella everywhere, his nose up her ass, his eyes glazed over like a rapist's. We were successful in keeping them apart until a bird flew into the house one afternoon. The dogs went wild. They leapt onto chairs, the sofa. They knocked over lamps trying to get at the bird. The terrified bird fluttered close to the overhead fan in the Florida room. I was afraid the fan would kill him, so I got a broom and tried to sweep him out of the house. When I finally succeeded, I heard Susan's voice from the kitchen.

"Are you watching Nero and Stella?"

I looked around, but they were gone. Then I saw Nero walking jauntily around the corner of the house toward the Florida room. He was smoking a cigarette. Stella followed him. She was leaping into the air with joyful abandon, as if to say "I'm a woman now." Eight weeks later we prepared for the birth of their puppies.

We had set up a little birthing area for Stella in the tiny hallway that led from our bedroom to our bathroom. We put down newspapers and padded the walls with blankets. At three o'clock one morning, Stella started to whimper. She began walking nervously in circles on the newspaper. Susan and I sat up in bed and watched. We had already been prepared by our veterinarian for the possibility that Stella wouldn't know how to cut open each baby's birth sack so it could breathe. We had a scissors ready to cut open the sack, and a string to tie off the baby's umbilical cord.

Stella circled and whimpered for almost an hour. She kept getting more and more agitated until suddenly, in midcircle, she let out a "Yip!" and a silvery sack dropped out from behind her. She immediately nibbled off the silvery sack to expose a tiny black puppy that looked exactly like its father, Nero. Stella then devoured the umbilical cord and, within seconds, the puppy was crying until it found Stella's nipple and began slurping milk. We watched in amazement as Stella lay there, licking the afterbirth off her son.

Two hours later, Stella began to whimper and circle again. This time the silvery sack that popped out contained a brownish-looking puppy almost twice the size of the black one. Stella chewed off the sack and the umbilical cord again, and again, within seconds, the new puppy was slurping her milk alongside his black brother.

When the big brownish puppy was full, he scuttled away from his mother to a far corner of the birthing area and went to sleep. The smaller black puppy wouldn't leave his mother's side. If he didn't feel her up against his body, he'd begin to cry.

Stella had a third puppy inside her. It was so large it couldn't get through Stella's birth canal. When the puppy wasn't born after three hours, Susan had to take Stella to the vet's. First she had to drop me off at the airport. I had to be in St. Louis by noon on an assignment. When I got to St. Louis two hours later, I called Susan from the airport. She told me it was a female, we'd planned to call Rose.

"Rose didn't make it," Susan said. "She was too big."

I walked through the airport in a daze, my tears blurring my vision.

We raised the puppies for eight weeks with the understanding that we would sell one. When it came time, I asked Susan which one she wanted to let go.

"Sophie's choice," she said. "But I'm not Sophie." We kept them both under the assumption that a couple with six dogs isn't any crazier to their friends than a couple with five. We called the big brownish puppy Bubba, and the little black one Blue. They are three years old now. Bubba's fur has turned red, like it was supposed to. He is still almost twice the size of Blue. He's a big, tough, aloof dog who likes to hunt. Blue, who looks just like his black and tan father, Nero, is a small, timid, almost neurotically loving house dog. They have not changed their natures since the moment they were born.

*   *   *

The Japanese producer, whose name I had deciphered as Yoshi, asked if he could film us and our dogs for his program. He explained that it was part travelogue, part pet documentary, and part biography of the pets' owners. It would be shown only in Japan, but he'd make sure to give us a tape shortly after the filming. We agreed.

Four little Japanese men came bowing into our house a few days later. They bowed to me and Susan, and then to each of our six dogs, who leapt on them and licked them.

"Ah, so. So many Shiba," said Yoshi. His crew was already setting up their cameras in the living room.

"First, we do breakfast shot," Yoshi said. "Then we do beach shot. Then writing shot." He nodded.

He directed Susan in the kitchen for the breakfast shot. "Suzie make breakfast for Pat," Yoshi said. "Then Suzie call Pat from office." Yoshi assumed what he thought to be Susan's voice: "Breakfast ready, honey!" He looked at me. "Pat come out of office with Shiba and sit down for breakfast."

I tried to explain to him that Susan and I might take direction pretty well, but my dogs didn't. "No plobrem," he said. "Shiba smart."

"Yes," I said. "Stubborn too." It was beginning to dawn on me that Yoshi didn't know much about Shibas—or any dogs, for that matter. Dumb dogs, like Labs and retrievers, were obedient *because* they were dumb. Smart dogs had a will of their own.

I went into my office as I was told. I called the dogs. They ran outside through the screen door. I called them again. They ignored me. I went to the porch and saw them sitting by the fence, staring up at a squirrel. I dragged them all inside by their collars. They stiffened, their feet sliding across the hardwood.

Once I had them in my office, I snapped, "Now sit, goddamn it!" They sat around my desk.

Yoshi called out from the living room. "We film now." Then he said to Susan, "Suzie call Pat." He assumed Susan's voice. "Breakfast ready, honey!"

A few seconds later Susan called out in a strange falsetto, "Breakfast ready, honey!"

Yoshi called out, "Now Pat come with Shiba." He made his voice sound deep. "Coming, honey!"

I got up and went into the dining room. "Coming, honey," I said. The dogs stayed in my office. The crew filmed me sitting down at the table. Susan put a glass of orange juice in front of me.

"This is breakfast?" I said.

"Shut up and drink it."

"Yes, honey."

"Where Shiba?" Yoshi said. "Cut! We do again."

I went back to my office and waited for my cue. Then I pushed all the dogs through the door before I walked after them and sat at the dining-room table. The dogs ran outside.

"Cut!" Yoshi said. "We get Shiba."

I dragged the dogs back into the house and made them sit around me at the table while I had breakfast. I drank my orange juice, smiled up at Susan, hovering over me, the dutiful wife, a role she was not used to. "Honey," I said, sweetly. "Where are my pancakes and eggs?" She glared at me.

"Cut!" Yoshi said. "Good. We have breakfast shot. Now we do beach shot."

We only took two dogs to the beach, Hoshi and Nero. It was a blisteringly hot St. Patrick's Day. The sidewalk along the beach and the beach itself were packed with tourists. Many of them were already drunk. The air smelled of sickly sweet coconut oil and spilled St. Patty's Day beer that was staining the sidewalk green.

Yoshi made me and Susan sit on the beach wall alongside the sidewalk. Hoshi and Nero, panting in the heat, flopped down at our feet. The crew set up their camera. People stopped and stared. A skinny guy with a dirty blond ponytail and inflamed skin weaved in front of us. "What's with all the slopes and the dogs?" he said.

Yoshi said, "Now Pat and Suzie talk." Pat and Susan talked.

"Cut! Now for walking shot. Pat and Suzie walk Shiba down sidewalk."

The camera crew went up ahead of us and we walked toward them with the two dogs panting and straining at their leashes. We had to repeat the shot a few times because the dogs kept pulling away out of the camera shot.

By the time we got back home, Hoshi and Nero were in a foul mood. When the other dogs greeted them at the front door, Hoshi and Nero growled at them. The other dogs backed off, confused. Hoshi and Nero went straight to their water bowl, slurped water for almost a minute, · and then slunk off to my office with their tails wilted. But Yoshi was merciless.

"Now we do writing shot," he said. The crew jammed into my tiny office and filmed me sitting at my desk, typing. After that, they filmed my office. Yoshi saw all the old photographs of me in baseball uniforms. I told him I had once pitched in the minor leagues, and then made the mistake of telling him I was going to pitch again, this summer.

"Oh, Japanese love basaboo," he said. "We must get basaboo shot. Pat pitching with Suzie and Shiba."

I looked down at Hoshi and Nero. They growled at me. So we took Bubba and Blue to Holiday Park instead. Susan sat on the infield grass with Bubba and Blue and watched me pitch off the mound while the crew filmed me. I threw for about ten minutes in the heat until I was panting as badly as Hoshi and Nero had been. Finally Yoshi yelled, "Cut! We have a basaboo shot."

After Yoshi and his crew left, I caught Susan looking at me strangely, as if I was somehow different now.

"What?" I said. "What'd I do?"

"You know, that was the first time I'd ever seen you pitch."

"So?"

"You were so graceful. Pitching is so graceful. I'd never thought of it like that." She smiled. "I never thought of you like that."

"My lost youth. What'd you think? I was always a creaky old man?"

She didn't laugh. She looked very seriously at me now. "It has nothing to do with youth," she said. "You just looked so . . . how can I put it? Natural. Like pitching was the most natural thing you'd ever done in your life."

"It was."

"You looked transported too. You were lost in it, weren't you?" I nodded. "It was beautiful to watch, babe."

"It's a beautiful thing when it's done right."

"I have to be honest. I thought it was just something you had to do, for yourself. Even if it seemed foolish to me, I had to support you."

"Maybe it is foolish?"

"No. It isn't. I can see that now."

A week after Yoshi and crew—I mean, Yoshi and *the* crew—left, we got the video in the mail. Susan wasn't home, so I went into the Florida room and slipped the tape into the VCR. I watched Susan serving me breakfast. I watched Susan and me and the dogs at the beach. I watched me typing at my desk. I watched Susan sitting in the grass with Bubba and Blue, watching me pitch. I watched me pitch, the first time I had ever seen myself pitch. An old man with a white beard dressed in a T-shirt and shorts. Old, maybe, but still in good shape. Throwing the ball nicely. Smoothly. Effortlessly. I replayed the tape. I watched myself. I looked like a pitcher. I threw like one.

That night I called Brian LaBasco.

EIGHT

I **WAS SITTING** on the pitcher's mound of St. Thomas High School's baseball diamond, lacing up my spikes, when I heard the school bell ring. Students rushed out of their classes at the end of the day. I watched them, laughing, jostling one another, as they hurried to their cars. They were like young, innocent animals freed from their cages. I had never been one of those laughing kids in high school. Baseball was a serious business for me by then. I was plodding so seriously toward my destiny. Little League. National Junior League. High school. Senior City League. I was a humorless youth obsessed with my "career." That's what we all called it in my family. My "career." But in truth, it was my family's career. Part of my baseball bonus would pay off the mortgage on my parents' house. They would lose that house because of my father's gambling debts, if not for me.

"You can't only think of yourself," my brother, George, said. "You've got to think of Ma and Dad too."

George had been my pitching coach ever since I was twelve. I pitched four consecutive no-hitters and two one-hitters (bunts) in my last year of Little League. I struck out every batter I faced that year, except two. Mel Allen invited me and my parents to appear on a Yankees' pregame TV show. I wore a tan suit and tie and I brought my glove in a brown paper bag. I expected Allen to turn to me at some point and ask me to throw a few pitches for the fans. Then I would step onto the field and dazzle all the fans, and the Yankees, with my blazing fastball in my tan suit. When I finished, the Yankees would offer me a contract, right then and there. In their next game I would be on the mound, pitching for the Yankees at the age of twelve.

But Allen never did ask me to throw a few. He talked about me, and around me, to my parents, and then the interview was over.

By twelve, baseball had already ceased to be fun for me. I ran windsprints under the watchful eye of my brother so that I wouldn't "get out of shape." He ran me like a Thoroughbred until I was exhausted. Then he ran me some more. When I stopped to gasp for a breath, he shouted, "What are you, a quitter? Don't you want it? Show me." So I showed him. I ran again from home plate to first base and back again on the big league diamond near my house. My Little League teammates were on the Little League diamond beyond centerfield. They were playing pickup games and flirting with the girls who'd come to watch. They looked over at me and laughed. They thought me strange. I couldn't understand why.

"What do they know?" my brother said. "They play for fun. They don't have your talent." So I ran. It did not occur to me until years later that twelve-year-old boys did not get "out of shape."

My Little League games were so important to me when I was twelve that I often couldn't sleep the night before one. I'd read comic books in my bed. Listen to *The Shadow* and *The Green Hornet* and *The Lone Ranger* on radio, until finally I fell asleep. It is a habit I have yet to break. I can only go to sleep at night while watching TV. When I doze, fitfully, and my wife clicks off the TV, I instantly wake.

On the days of my games, I was a nervous wreck. My parents and my brother refused to let me go to the park to blow off steam in games of Wiffleball with my teammates. It would tire me before the game, they said. So my father would give me five dollars and I'd take two buses to downtown Bridgeport to buy stamps for my collection. I'd begun to collect stamps at ten, like my friends did. But they stopped a year or two later, bored with such a phlegmatic hobby. I didn't. I liked the order of collecting stamps. It appealed to something foreign in my nature as a boy. I would sit for hours with my album spread open and study my stamps. The order of a complete set. The aesthetic beauty of miniature works of art. The history they revealed. Franklin at the Continental Congress. Icelandic bardic poetry. Garibaldi uniting Italy. I knew where Zululand was and Zanzibar, and the Ivory Coast. I bought blank album pages and made my own arrangement of stamps on the pages. I fiddled with the various aesthetic and logical order of those stamps on a page for hours at a time, until I found the one that pleased me the most. Then I hinged them to a page. I contemplated the one stamp I needed to complete a set. It would take me weeks to earn the money to buy it. I wanted it *now*, my nature, but tried desperately to delay my need for instant gratification.

I went first to buy new issues at the Plaza Stamp Shop from Freddie. Glatz, a stooped, ferretlike little man. He wore thick-lensed eyeglasses and always seemed to be eating a tunafish sandwich with too much mayonnaise. He talked and chewed with his mouth wide open, the mayonnaise oozing through his teeth and dripping onto the stamps he was trying to sell me. Freddie didn't know much about stamps. I always stopped at his shop first in the hope I would find a bargain.

After Freddie's, I would go uptown to Harold Turner's Yankee Stamp Shop, near the bus stop across from Morrow's Nut House, ("Nuts from all over the World.") Hal was a gaunt man in his forties, with thinning, close-cropped hair and a protruding Adam's apple that was always underlined by a bow tie. He always greeted me with a smile that was more a baring of teeth. Then he tried to sell me defective old U.S. stamps he had acquired from the estate of some deceased Yankee whose relatives would rather be short-changed by Hal than have to deal with either of the two Jewish dealers in town, Freddie Glatz or Gene Goldman.

I saved Mr. Goldman for last. His seventh-floor office was in a tall building occupied mostly by lawyers and CPAs. My heart began to race the moment I stepped off the elevator and saw his frosted glass door with the sign "New England Stamp Shop."

"Ak, da little goy!" he would say as I stepped inside. "I suppose you want me to teach you stamps again, ah? All right! All right! Sit down!"

I would sit enthralled for hours by this strange old man. He combed his hands through his thick shock of white hair as he lectured me on stamps and girls and sports and his native country, Austria. He was very excitable, in his sixties, and he could not sit still for long. He was always jumping up, pulling up his trousers, pacing around his tiny office, waving his arms to punctuate a point.

"That fukink Turner," he would say. "He is a fukink anti-Semite."

(Hal Turner, smiling through bared teeth, referred to Mr. Goldman simply as "The Jew.") When he saw the look of ignorance on my face, Mr. Goldman would lecture me on anti-Semitism, on the Holocaust, and the state of Israel. I never told Mr. Goldman I patronized Hal's shop, but he always knew. This knowledge made me feel guilty. It was as if those canceled old U.S. stamps in my pocket were a mark of my betrayal.

Mr. Goldman never minded that I patronized Freddie's shop and not simply because they were both Jews. Mr. Goldman delighted in knowing that what he taught me about stamps one day, I would use the next to outsmart Freddie. Grinning, I would hold out in my palm my latest bargain from Freddie Glatz.

"That fukink putz!" Mr. Goldman would roar with a backhand swipe at my stamps. "He wipes his ass with his elbows!" Then, planting his hands on his hips, he would learn toward me and say, "I suppose you spent all your gelt there, huh?" I shook my head, no, and produced some bills from my pocket. "Good!" he would say, going over to his old black safe. "Now, let's see what we have for the little goy today."

He made a great production of examining his stock books before bringing one over to his glass counter where I sat. Under the glass, he had arranged cheap topical stamps—birds, flowers, rocket ships—from a host of Third World countries. The stamps were curled at the edges and yellow with age. "Rocket ships!" he would say, with a shake of his head. "Rocket ships from a country of fukink Zulus who can't read or write." Mr. Goldman never expected to sell those stamps. He kept them only to amuse the mothers of his clients, boys like me, who studiously poured over his stock books while their mothers exclaimed over the pretty stamps under glass. Mr. Goldman, a widower, was not averse to flirting with those mothers. More than once I heard him tell a woman ("Goirl," he called her) standing before him that she could not possibly be old enough to be the mother of this little man.

"Oh, Mr. Goldman!" the woman would say, smiling, blushing, as she led her son out the door. As soon as she was gone, Mr. Goldman, eyes wide, tongue protruding, would grab his genitals and make an obscene thrusting gesture with his hips toward the door.

Now he took a pair of stamp tongs from the breast pocket of his shirt. Like a surgeon making a first incision, he slipped a stamp from his stock book and laid it on a piece of black paper. He slapped the back of the paper with his knuckles. "Superp!" he said. "Look at the centering!"

I took the tongs from him and turned the stamp over to examine the gum. "Hinged," I said.

"Hinged?" he shouted. "What do you mean, hinged?" He took out his magnifying glass, hunched low to the stamp, and examined it. "A gum imperfection," he said. "From printing."

I reached for his magnifying glass but he pulled it away from me. I took out my own magnifying glass and examined the gum.

"Don't buy it!" he said, leaping to his feet. He shot his fingers through his swept-back white hair. "Go to that putz friend of yours, Freddie Glatz! See if he has such a stamp at any price!"

"It's definitely hinged," I said. He withdrew a soiled handkerchief from his pants and mopped his brow.

"Hinged, shminged!" he said. "Who cares? You are a collector, not an investor. I taught you."

"You taught me unhinged," I said, confused. The old man shook his head. "You *did!*"

He threw up his hands in surrender. "Take it, for chrissakes!" he said. "I'm an old man." He clutched his breast as if having heart palpitations, then quoted me a price for that stamp that was much less than was worth. I took his tongs and slipped the stamp, *my* stamp now, into a glassine envelope. He pointed an ominous finger at me. "You'll be the death of me yet," he said. Then, with a grin spreading across his big-featured face, he added, "You out-Jew a Jew." I smiled.

When I was thirteen, Mr. Goldman insisted I buy a cheap collection of Italian stamps. "But they're not worth anything!" I said. "You taught me to spend wisely."

He glared at me. "They are your history!" he bellowed. "Such things you can't put a price on!" So I bought it.

When I was fourteen, Mr. Goldman insisted I buy a four-dollar, carmine-rose, U.S. Columbian issue, costing two hundred dollars. That was more money than I had spent in months at his shop. "Give me what you have," he said, "and then pay me ten dollars a week." He kept that stamp for me for months until I paid it off. He would bring it out every time I stopped in his shop. He laid it on a black paper and we looked at it as if it was a beloved child. "The color!" he exclaimed. "Superp!" Then he smiled at me. "Any real collector would be proud to own such a stamp!"

My heart swelled at the knowledge that I, a mere boy, was appreciative enough to own such a stamp. That *I* had the patience to wait six months. Other boys my age wanted only to buy as many cheap stamps as possible in a day so they could spend hours hinging them into their albums. When I finally brought that four-dollar Columbian stamp home, I put it in my album and stared at it for hours. "Those other boys," Mr. Goldman said. "When they go to sell their cheap stamps they will discover they are only good to wipe their ass. You, you will have a valuable collection some day." He was right. I bought our cabin in North Carolina with the money I made when I sold my stamp collection. Fifty thousand dollars.

I grew up in Mr. Goldman's shop. I went from a boy to a teenager to a young man, and as I did my relationship with him began to change, imperceptibly at first. It was as if one of us was losing his innocence, and I am not sure that one was me. I was no longer merely an empty vessel for his teaching. Oh, I never questioned his teaching about stamps, only about other things. He seemed to be growing cynical with age. When he told me I was a fool ever to have children, I told him he was wrong. "I want to have lots of kids," I said. He waved the back of his hand hard at me. "Bah! You know nothing!" he snapped. He seemed increasingly envious that my adult life was spread out before me with its infinite possibilities, while he, an old man who had suffered two heart attacks, had nothing in life but his stamp shop and his impending death. He took out his bitterness on me. He had always seemed proud of the stamp knowledge I learned from him, even when I used it against him. It had been a game we played. He taught me how to spot a regummed stamp and then tested me the next day by offering me a regummed four-cent U.S. Trans-Miss. When I caught him, his outrage was both feigned and gregarious. In my late teens, that outrage grew bitter. I fled his shop almost in tears. When I returned again he goaded me by offering me expensive stamps he knew I couldn't afford. Then he berated me for not buying them like "a serious collector would." I grew red-faced and silent in my chair. What had I done? I could think of nothing. I fled again.

After one especially long absence before I turned eighteen, I returned to the old man's shop with a hundred dollars in my pocket. He knew I never spent more than twenty dollars in a visit, so he immediately offered me a "superp" mint set of Graf Zeppelins for the ridiculously low price of ninety-five dollars. He knew I couldn't afford such a set. "Take it for ninety," he snapped. "If you can." He laughed a bitter laugh.

I stood, dug into my jeans pocket, and withdrew my hundred dollars. I counted out that money on the glass table where I had sat for so many years. When I reached ninety, I tossed another ten dollars on the table and said, "Keep the change, Mr. Goldman." His features seemed to collapse like melted wax. The blood was drained from his face as he stared at those bills. When he looked up at me, in sorrow and pain, I turned away. I picked up my three stamps and left his shop, never to return.

*   *   *

I finished lacing my spikes and lit a cigar. The St. Thomas students were gone now. I was alone, waiting for Brian LaBasco. Maybe he wouldn't come? He'd forget, the way kids do. That possibility didn't bother me. It calmed me, actually. It would almost be a relief if he didn't come. I stood up, ready to leave, when I saw a boy climbing over the centerfield fence. He began walking toward me. He was wearing a white T-shirt and shorts. A wiry, muscular teenager, about 5′ 9″ tall. He waved to me. Then he did the strangest thing. He began to run toward me as if I was a long-lost friend. When he reached the mound he was breathing heavily. A handsome, dark-haired boy with a buzzcut, like a Marine, that made his ears look big. He had a big, guileless smile. I had a buzz-cut like that when I was his age. It made my ears look big too. I wondered: Did I ever have such a smile? And if I did, when did I lose it?

"Mr. Jordan," he said. "I'm Brian LaBasco." He stuck out his hand to shake mine.

I glared at him with mock anger. "*Mister,* my ass! It's Pat."

He laughed. "Okay, Pat. You ready to throw?"

I tossed him the catcher's mitt and we began to soft toss. He looked at me as if confused.

"What?" I said. "What's the problem?"

"You always pitch smoking a cigar?"

"Always. You want one?"

He smiled. "No thanks. I don't smoke."

"A good boy, heh?"

"Not always. Not *that* good."

I asked him questions as we threw, the way adults do, to draw kids out. He told me he played three musical instruments. He liked to draw and write in his diary.

"Brian!" I said. "A sensitive kid. I never would have guessed."

He blushed. "Writers are sensitive, aren't they?"

"Not this one. I'm just a dumb jock."

"Yeh, sure."

"What do your friends think about your 'sensitive' interests?"

"I don't tell them."

"Who do you tell?"

"No one. I don't really have anyone I can talk to."

"What about your baseball? Do you want to go to college or the minor leagues?"

"I don't know," he said. "I don't know if I'm good enough for the minors. Maybe college first."

"You a good student?"

"I'm okay. I'm not real smart, but I'm not dumb either."

"Any scholarship offers?"

"Notre Dame. Florida. Florida Atlantic University. Tulane."

"Tulane's a good school. My wife's son went there. He loved New Orleans."

"Yeh. They've got a good baseball team too. But my mom"—he lowered his eyes—"she wants me to stay close to home."

"Well, you can't live your life for your parents. Sooner or later you've got to make your own choices."

"I know. But she's gonna miss me."

We'd been throwing for almost ten minutes. I hadn't noticed that he'd moved back behind home plate. I began my motion and threw the ball in the dirt at his feet. He snapped it up with the quick hands of an infielder and tossed the ball back to me.

"Everybody has to hurt their parents eventually, Brian."

"I know," he said. "But I have to think of my mom."

We threw for a while without talking. I concentrated on my motion until I was throwing full speed. Without my asking, Brian got down in a catcher's crouch behind the plate. He gave me a big round target. I pumped, kicked, and threw a fastball on the outside corner of the plate.

"Awright!" He smiled. "Nice pitch."

"How fast, you think, Brian?"

"Low eighties."

"You're not bullshitting an old man now, Brian, are you?"

I thought he'd laugh, but his smile vanished. He looked at me with pleading eyes. "Oh no! I'd never do that! I'm serious. I faced enough good pitchers to know how hard you're throwing."

I threw more fastballs for the next ten minutes. I grunted hard on each pitch. It was another hot day. My T-shirt was soaked with sweat. I was beginning to breathe heavily. But I felt good, throwing hard, pitch after pitch, without thinking. I'd throw one or two good fastballs in a row, then a flier, a wild pitch in the dirt or over Brian's head. He seemed not to notice. He snapped up my fliers like he was swatting a fly, without interest, and tossed the ball back to me. I forgot about the fliers and just threw hard.

"A little slider now, Bri."

"Okay."

I threw a hard slider that started for the middle of the plate, then broke sharply right to left at the last instant. Brian snapped at it, almost too late, but caught it. He leapt out of his crouch, grinning.

"Holy shit! That was the best slider I ever saw!" He saw me looking suspiciously at him. "No, Mr.—I mean, Pat. It was. I wouldn't bullshit you."

I threw him two more sliders that didn't break as sharply as the first one. "Not so hot," he said after each one. Then, "Maybe you're tired?"

"You mean because I'm an old man?"

"Heh, you're not old. You're not throwing like an old man. I got to give you credit. I admire you. When my teacher asked me to catch you I thought you'd be some fat, out of shape, old guy." He caught himself. He looked anxiously at me to see if he'd hurt my feelings.

"Well, I am old, Brian. I'm a fucking exhausted old man."

"Maybe it's the cigar. You ever try pitching without it?"

"What are you, my father?"

"Heh, old people need someone to watch over them too."

"That's it, Brian. Let's call it a day."

"You sure?" I nodded. He came out to the mound and sat in the grass beside me as I took off my spikes.

"That's a cool T-shirt," he said.

I looked down at my T-shirt. Navy blue with the words "Navy Rum" scripted across the chest. "You like it?" He nodded. I stripped it off and tossed it to him.

"I didn't mean that!" he said. "You don't have to—"

"Brian. It's rude not to accept a gift."

He smiled and stripped off his T-shirt and put on mine.

"Fits you like a fucking dress," I said. "What are you, about five-two?"

"Heh. I'm a little under six foot." He shrugged. "Maybe a little more than 'a little.'" We both laughed.

"You think you can catch me again?" I asked.

"Any time you want."

"Three days a week after school?"

"No problem."

"What, you don't have a girlfriend?"

He smiled. "Three of them."

"Jeez," I said. "Throw one my way."

"Sure. I'll tell 'em you're my older brother." We both laughed.

"You don't have anything to do after school?" I said.

"Naw. I'm just gonna lift some weights now. Then I got two games tonight."

"*Two* games!"

"I got two games every night."

"You sure this won't be too much for you?"

"You kiddin? I love it. Heh, I'm only a kid."

When I got home that afternoon, Susan said, "How'd it go?"

"Good," I said. "I was throwing pretty good." I fixed our drinks, got some ice for my arm, and sat down at the dining-room table.

"What was the boy like?" she said.

I didn't answer right away.

"What's the matter?" she said. "Wasn't he a nice boy?"

"He was nice."

"Then what?"

I looked down at the ice wrapped in a towel around my elbow. I was embarrassed to tell her what I felt.

"Babe! What is it?" She looked worried.

"He reminded me of me, Susan." Finally I looked at her. "Not the me I ever was. But the me I might have been."

"Oh." She nodded but said nothing.

The following afternoon, I was walking to my car when Betsy, Brian's teacher, came home from school. I waited until she got out of her car.

"Thanks for Brian," I said. "He's a sweet boy."

"I knew you'd like him, Patrick. He liked you too. Do you know what he called you to me?" I shook my head, no. She waited a beat, then smiled and said, "The Old Man and the Sea!"

"That little prick! Wait'll I see him again."

I couldn't wait to throw with Brian again. I called him that night to remind him he said he'd catch me tomorrow after school. When he answered the phone, I said, "Brian, it's me. The Old Man and the Sea."

He laughed. "She told you, huh?"

"You got no secrets from me now, Brian. Don't forget. I'm a reporter. It's my job to know things."

His voice got low over the phone, as if to make sure no one would hear him. "She didn't tell you what happened, did she?"

"Now, what do you think, Brian?"

"Jeez, she told you I got suspended from school?"

"Of course," I lied. "She didn't tell me why, though."

"Me and a couple of guys skipped class. We got caught drinking beer in a car."

"How the hell did you get caught?"

"I threw a beer bottle out the window and it hit a passing cop car."

I had to laugh. "Jesus, Brian. You may be sensitive but you aren't too bright, are you?"

"I know. I know. I already heard it from my parents. They grounded me."

Instinctively, I thought about myself. Who would catch me? "You mean you can't catch me anymore?"

"Oh, no. I told them I'd promised you. They said okay."

I felt relieved, and ashamed that my first thought was about myself, not Brian. "You sure it's all right?"

"Yeh."

"I was just calling to remind you."

"Aw, Pat," he said. "You don't have to call me. I won't forget."

I felt foolish. I stopped calling him. He was there every afternoon, smiling. I looked forward to those moments with him in a way I had never looked forward to pitching. It had always been work for me. That's the word my brother used to use. "Time to go to work," he'd say as I took the mound to pitch to him. It wasn't work with Brian. It was fun. We were just two kids having a catch. We talked between pitches.

"Great slider, Pat," he said, bouncing out of his crouch. "I could barely pick up the spin."

I waved him toward me. "You'd better learn to pick it up if you expect to hit good pitching," I said. I held the ball up for him to see.

"See this white dot?" I said. "Whenever you see that white dot on the ball when it leaves a pitcher's hand, it's a slider." He nodded. "The better the slider, the smaller the dot, the harder it is to pick up."

"Yours is real small," he said.

"Good."

We went back to our throwing. He started to talk about one of his girlfriends. "She plays mind games," he said. "It pisses me off."

"They all do," I said. "Women don't talk like us. They don't say what they mean." We stopped throwing. "A woman says yes, she means no. She says maybe, she means no. She says whatever you want, dear, she means I don't want to." Brian was smiling now. I went on. "She says the kitchen's too small, she means she wants a new house. That's why men and women don't understand each other. We talk different languages. A guy says I'm hungry, he means he's hungry. A guy says I'm tired, he means he's tired. He says what's wrong, honey, he means what meaningless self-inflicted psychological trauma are you going through now."

Brian started laughing. I said, "You know what a guy means when he says honey, I love you?"

"Let's have sex," Brian said.

I put my hands on my hips and stared at him. "Now what the hell do you know about sex? You're a fucking kid."

"I may be a kid, but I get my share." He shrugged. "Maybe not my full share." We both laughed. Then he said, "Pat, you won't believe what happened the other night. I've been dying to tell someone, but I couldn't think of anyone but you."

"What?"

He looked around the deserted field to make sure no one would hear him. Then he walked close to me on the mound. "I went out to Hooter's the other night by myself," he said. "These two girls kept staring at me. They were in their twenties. Gorgeous. I mean, *gorgeous*. The way they were looking at me made me embarrassed. Finally, they came over to me and asked if I wanted to go to their house in Miami."

"They wanted you to do them *both?*"

"Yep. At the same time. I couldn't believe it."

"So what did you do?"

"I chickened out. I had to be home by eleven, and it was already ten." I shook my head. "I know. That'll never happen to me again, will it?"

"Trust me, Brian. Never in your lifetime."

"Did it ever happen to you?"

"Are you kidding? Look at me, for chrissakes."

"Yeh, you're right. Who'd want The Old Man and the Sea?"

"Fuck you, Brian. Just remember: I turned down more pussy in my life than you'll ever see."

"Yeh. But that's because you're so friggin' old."

"I may be old but I can still throw a fastball by a little shit like you."

"Little! I'm almost six foot. I'd rip that shit of yours."

"So. You've been lying to me?"

His smile vanished. "No, no, Pat. I was only kidding. You're throwing good."

"I know, Brian. I don't need you to tell me." But I did.

His smile returned. He walked back to home plate and got in his crouch. He gave me a big target, then said, "Come on. Throw me that shit of yours I'd rip all over the park."

One afternoon while we were throwing, Brian was distracted. I could see something was bothering him.

I stopped throwing. "You gonna tell me?" I said.

"I'm sorry," he said. "I wasn't concentrating."

"What is it?"

He told me his grandmother had just been diagnosed with breast cancer. "Not only that," he said. "But now my mom is worried that it's hereditary."

"It is," I said. Then I told him about Susan. How she overcame her breast cancer by an act of will. "It's not a death sentence, Brian, unless you let it be."

He was quiet for a minute. Then he said, "Do you think my mom could call Mrs. Jordan sometime? To talk?"

"Of course." He nodded and went back to home plate. I stared at him for a long moment before I began my motion. What was I looking for? Something of myself in him? But I couldn't find it. What was in Brian wasn't in me, and never had been. So I just appreciated Brian for what he was. Someone who made me feel good about myself that had only partly to do with my pitching. I even thought that maybe something of Brian would rub off on me. I prayed that nothing of me would rub off on him.

After a month of throwing, we began to pitch to imaginary batters. Brian called balls and strikes. He always gave me a break on pitches just off the plate when he sensed I was getting tired or losing my temper in frustration.

One afternoon, I had a 3−2 count on an imaginary batter. I reared back and threw a fastball too high and inside.

"Strike three!" Brian said. "It was close, but a strike."

I glared down at him. "For chrissakes, Brian! That was not a fucking strike and you know it." He smiled weakly and shrugged.

"It was close," he said, without conviction.

"Brian!"

"Awright. Ball four. Next batter."

I threw from my stretch position to hold the imaginary runner at first base. I threw two more fastballs too high and inside. I kicked the dirt in disgust. "Goddamn it!"

"Heh, relax, Pat. You'll get there." Then he snapped at me, "Maybe if you got rid of the friggin' cigar you could concentrate."

I took the cigar out of my mouth and threw it at him. "Nice," he said. "Now act like a friggin' pitcher and relax."

"Relax? I gotta be able to throw a fucking fastball for a strike one of these days."

"Why?"

"Why?"

Brian walked halfway out to the mound, his hands on his hips, the way so many of my catchers had when they tried to calm me down as I stormed and kicked dirt around the mound.

"Why does your fastball have to be your strike pitch?" he said.

I reminded myself he was only a kid. I exhaled a deep breath and tried to explain. "Because, Brian, a fastball has to be your strike pitch. If I can't throw my fastball for a strike whenever I want, what the fuck am I gonna do?"

"Use your slider as your strike pitch. You can throw your slider over whenever you want. Use your fastball as your off pitch when you're ahead of a batter. You miss, so what? You've always got the slider."

I started to laugh. It made such obvious sense. "So, now you're teaching me how to pitch. A fucking infielder. What do you know?"

Brian flashed me a sheepish grin. "Not much," he said. "Heh, I'm only a kid, right?"

That afternoon, after we had finished throwing, we sat in the grass and talked for a while. I asked him if he was playing well for St. Thomas.

"Okay. I'm making good contact, but it's always right at some-body."

"Don't worry," I said. "They'll start to drop."

He nodded. "Last game I made three friggin' errors, though. Jeez, my father was pissed. He won't talk to me now."

"He sounds like my brother. I once struck out nineteen of twenty-one high-school batters as a sophomore, and you know what he said?"

"What?"

"I shoulda struck out the other two. 'You choked,' he said."

"Jeez. I thought my father was bad."

"When's your next game?"

"Tomorrow night at seven-thirty. at Nova High School. Do you wanna come?"

"Yeh. Maybe I will. It's about time I saw *you* play."

I got up to go. "You gonna lift weights now?" I said.

"Naw. I got nuthin' to do this afternoon."

"You wanna come over for lunch? Meet Susan?"

"Sure."

I called Susan from my car phone and told her I was bringing Brian home for lunch. "It's about time you met him," I said. Brian followed me in his car.

Susan me us at the front door. Brian said, "Hello, Mrs. Jordan."

"Hello, Brian. I've heard a lot about you."

He blushed and looked down. He was a boy in front of Susan, an older woman, in a way he wasn't with me. Or maybe he was, and I wasn't an old man with him. We were just two baseball players having a catch in the afternoon. I remembered when I was fifteen, and I pitched a game against thirty-year-old men in the Senior City League. I struck out sixteen, and after the game, all the players went to the White Eagle Hall to drink beer. I drank a beer too, with those men who had wives and children. We talked about the game. They didn't talk to me as if I was a boy but as an equal. My talent made me their equal on the diamond. It forced me to act grown up in front of those men before I was grown up. But Brian wasn't acting grown up in front of me. He was just being himself. He didn't think of me as an adult, or as a boy. He just thought of me as a fellow baseball player. Susan, now she was an adult. He became a boy with her.

Susan made us T-bone steaks on the grill, a salad, and for Brian, a big banana split for desert. He was bashful, like a boy, during lunch. After he ate everything, he looked at Susan and said, "That was great, Mrs. Jordan. I'm too stuffed to even eat dinner tonight." He smiled. "Almost."

We laughed. Susan said, "I haven't had a teenager around the house in years. It feels good."

Brian asked her about her kids. She told him about them, then asked about his colleges. They talked a bit, very politely, stiffly. He wasn't the Brian I knew.

Suddenly Brian blurted out, "My mother would love to meet you, Mrs. Jordan. She doesn't have any grown-up friends. She spends all her time with me and my younger brother."

"That would be nice, Brian. I'd love to meet her."

Before he left, Brian carried his dirty dishes to the sink. Then he thanked Susan again and went out to his car. I went with him. Susan stood in the doorway, watching. Brian whispered to me, so seriously, "Pat! Mrs. Jordan's sooooo nice. Wait'll I tell my mom."

"Yeh. Suzie's a good old girl. You can call her Suzie, Brian."

He winced and shook his head. "I dunno."

I let it go. "See you Thursday," I said.

"Don't forget my game tomorrow night."

"I won't."

I walked back to Susan at the front door. Brian, waving out the window, drove off. Susan said, "I see what you mean."

The following night I fell asleep watching TV at 7 P.M. I didn't wake until midnight, long after Brian's game was over. There would be other games, I told myself. But it bothered me. I stayed awake most of the night, watching TV, berating myself.

The next time Brian and I threw, I told him I was sorry I had missed his game. "I fell asleep," I said.

"That's all right," he said. "You're an old man. You need your sleep."

We threw in awkward silence for the first time since we'd begun throwing together two months ago.

NINE

I FINISHED A SHORT story at the end of April and sent it off to Alice Turner, the fiction editor at *Playboy*. Alice had been buying my short stories about the adventures of a small-time south Florida smuggler and his much older girlfriend for the past four years. She called me her AC-DC writer because I was one of a few nonfiction writers who could write nonfiction and fiction successfully. My only problem, she said, was that like all nonfiction writers, I tended to explain too much in my fiction. All those nuances I was terrified of missing. So Alice just cut the nuances and ran my stories as mysteries. She even suggested I expand them into a novel. This would be the fourth story I sent her. I knew she'd call me as soon as she read it, within a day or two after she received it, but I'd be in Venice Beach, California, by then, working on an assignment for a week. I told Susan to give Alice my cellphone number. "I'll have it on all day," I said.

It's funny. I get paid a lot less for my fiction than my nonfiction, but I love writing fiction so much more. All those characters doing what they want, surprising me. I always know what my nonfiction characters are going to do. They never surprise me. I leave nothing to chance, one of my failings as a nonfiction writer, according to my editor at *Sports Illustrated* years ago.

"Every time I get one of your stories, Jordan," said Pat Ryan, "I've gotta muss it up a little. They're always so neat. Everything tied together." Pat was the second editor I'd ever worked for. The first was her husband, Ray Cave, who started me on my writing career. I'd sent him some stories at *SI* that I'd written in my attic room late at night when I was still teaching English at an all-girls parochial high school. He read them and called me to New York. I thought, This was it. He was going to buy them all and I'd be able to quit teaching and write full time. But all he said to me when he called me into his office was "These don't quite work, Pat. But keep writing. You'll make it some day."

I was crushed. But still I managed to mutter, "How do you know?"

He smiled. "Because you see everything three degrees off-center."

That depressed me even more! I wanted to see things the way other writers saw them! Wasn't that the point?

I hated to interrupt my throwing with Brian to go to L.A., but I still had to make a living. So I flew to L.A. with my glove, spikes, and six baseballs in my bags. I rented a car at LAX and drove to Venice Beach to stay at Susan's son's apartment. Andrew was a rock and roll singer who was on the road a lot. His apartment was just a crash pad in a garage in the backyard of his manager's house. It was in the middle of gang territory. I went to bed that first night to the sound of gunfire on the streets.

I worked for two days and then got up early on the morning of the third day to throw. I had found a small scruffy park near the apartment. It was cold when I got out of my car at the park. Jeez, I missed the heat and humidity of Fort Lauderdale. I missed throwing to Brian.

I got my baseball gear and my shoulder bag out of the trunk. I saw a group of black kids standing on the corner eyeing me warily. Great! I had to slip sideways through a narrow opening in a wrought-iron fence to get into the park. The only other person in the park was a guy throwing a Frisbee to his pit bull. It was a mean-looking dog with clipped ears for fighting and dead yellow eyes. Well, at least the Bloods won't bother *him*, I thought as I walked to the pitcher's mound. The pit bull followed me with his mean eyes. The Bloods on the corner kept their eyes on me too. Great! The Bloods are gonna cut me up into little pieces and the pit bull's gonna eat my remains.

I laid my shoulder bag with my wallet and cellphone in it close to me at the mound and began throwing in the chill morning air. I warmed quickly. I forgot about the pit bull and the Bloods as I began to grunt fastball after fastball against the home-plate screen. Suddenly I felt something brush my leg. "Christ!" I saw the pit bull streaking after the baseball I'd just thrown. He clamped his jaws on it, gave it a vicious shake to kill it, and trotted off with it.

I heard a voice behind me. "Gee, dude, I'm sorry." I turned to see his owner, a surfer dude in baggy shorts and shades. "I'll get it back for you."

I smiled. "No, that's all right. Let him play with it. I got dogs of my own."

"Heh, cool, dude! Thanks."

Well, at least I got the dog off my back, I thought, as I glanced at the Bloods. They were still looking at me, shaking their heads at this crazy white guy throwing baseballs into a screen at eight o'clock in the morning. Probably scared them off too, I thought. Don't wanna mess with a lunatic.

I went back to my throwing, at ease now, and almost didn't hear my cellphone ringing inside my leather bag. It was Chris, Alice Turner's assistant, calling me from New York. I answered the phone out of breath.

"What'd I catch you, jogging or something?" Chris said.

"No. I was just throwing baseballs against a screen."

Pause. "Sure." Then he told me Alice had liked my story but she was out of town so she couldn't tell me herself. She had a few suggestions, however, on how to tighten up the plot. Chris read me her suggestions while I scribbled them down on a scrap of paper I'd found in my bag. When he finished, I told him I'd rewrite the story as soon as I got home, then send it back to him.

After I hung up, I went back to throwing. I thought about the changes I'd make in the story as I began to throw sliders. I thought about the changes and my slider as I threw for the next ten minutes until I was exhausted. It doesn't get any better than this, I thought, as I grabbed my stuff and walked to the car. Pitching and writing, the only two things I ever loved to do. And now I was doing them both, at the same time. Now they were truly interwoven, instead of separated by time. I was learning from each one about the other. Everything I had learned from my baseball failure I had applied to my writing so I wouldn't make the same mistake in the second career that God had given me. And now I was applying everything I had learned in thirty-five years of writing to my pitching. I couldn't believe how lucky I was.

As I drove off, I flashed the Bloods the thumbs-up sign. They gave me the finger.

I called Brian the minute I got home and made a date to begin throwing again at a park near his home in Hollywood. When I got there that Sunday morning I saw a man standing with him near the mound. His father. Shit! I wanted to throw with just me and Brian. I fidgeted around in my car for a few minutes, calming myself, before I got out. I walked toward them, smiling, hating myself for my selfishness.

Brian was smiling. "Pat, this is my father, Mark." His father looked at his son as if confused. Pat? This old guy?

I shook his hand and said, "It's good to meet you, Mark." I tossed a head fake toward his son. "I don't have to tell you what a bad kid he is." Brian's guileless smile got even bigger.

"Yeh, he's a good boy," Mark said, seriously. He was about forty, handsome like his son, but with styled hair and a neat, brush mustache.

Brian and I began to soft toss. Mark stood behind me, talking.

"That one was high," he said.

"I'm not loose yet," I said.

"Give him a break, Dad," Brian said. "He's old."

"Not too old to strike you out, you little shit," I said.

"In your dreams," Brian said.

Mark looked at us, confused. An old man and a teenager, bantering back and forth like equals. Like most adults, he expected me to assume an adult personae with his son. And he expected his son to be deferential to adults.

"You really think you're gonna be able to pitch against minor leaguers?" Mark said.

Before I could answer, Brian said, "You kiddin', Dad? Pat's throwin' good."

"How do you know?" Mark said. "Did you face any batters yet?"

"He doesn't have to," Brian said.

"If I'm throwing as good as Brian says," I said, "I'll get 'em out."

"I dunno," Mark said, and he shook his head.

Brian was crouched behind home plate now as I cut loose with my first fastball. Brian caught it in the web of the mitt so it didn't make a loud *pop*.

"How fast was that?" Mark said.

"Mid-eighties, Dad," Brian said. "Pat's throwin' eighty-five, eighty-six all the time now."

"You sure? How can you tell?"

Brian began to get annoyed. The first time I'd ever seen him annoyed. "I ought to know, Dad. I faced enough guys didn't throw as hard."

When I threw my first slider, Brian leapt out of his crouch with his big smile. "Awright! Unhittable!"

"That didn't look like a curveball," Mark said.

"It wasn't," Brian said. "It was a slider."

"It didn't break much."

"It doesn't have to, Dad. It's so darned sharp and late. I couldn't hit it."

Mark just shook his head. "You sure?"

When I finished throwing, Mark told Brian, "Okay, Bri, now it's time to work." He got some baseballs and a bat out of his car and went back to home plate. He told Brian to go out to short to field grounders. I stood on first base to catch Brian's throws.

Mark hit a grounder sharply to Brian's left over second base. Brian couldn't reach it before it went into centerfield. "We gotta move quicker than that, Brian." Brian walked sullenly after the ball, picked it up, and fired it to me at first base.

"We gotta watch our arm, Brian," Mark said. "Don't wanna throw out our arm in practice."

Brian walked back to his shortstop position. "My arm's fine," he snapped.

Mark hit a slow roller Brian had to charge. He scooped it up on the run and fired it underhand to me at first.

"Nice play, Brian!" I said.

"I told you, we gotta watch our arm, Bri," said Mark. "Just lob it over." Brian hung his head and went back to short. His face was flushed.

After Mark had finished hitting Brian grounders, Brian carried the bat and balls to the car while Mark and I talked at home plate. I asked him about Brian's colleges.

"We're thinking Notre Dame or Florida," he said. "But we can't concentrate just on baseball. We're playing football this season and maybe soccer."

"Isn't that maybe too much on Brian's plate?" I said.

Mark looked at me seriously. "We can do it."

I looked at Mark. So serious. It's usually kids who think they can do everything. Like in Sherwood Anderson's short story "Sophistication." They think the world is spread out before them with its infinite possibilities. Then they become adults and discover they're nothing more than a leaf blown by the wind. Usually their parents try to warn them. Rein them in. Tell them to concentrate only on the things that are most important in their lives. In Brian's case, he was already the father to his father. I think Brian already knew that. But as a seventeen-year-old he was powerless to act on what he knew. He had to be a kid in the face of his father's childishness and hold his own counsel.

It occurred to me as I drove home that it wasn't only Brian making it fun for me. I made it fun for him too. His father didn't know how to make it fun. It wasn't part of his nature. He was an Old World guinea, stubborn, plodding, without lightness in his life. He was more Italian than American. He was raised to be like his father, just as his father was raised to be like his father. It was a matter of pride for Old World guineas not to change from generation to generation. Now he was raising Brian to be like him. Only Brian wasn't like him. He was like me. He was an American.

I was raised by a certain kind of Italian-American parents. They understood that their generation was rooted to their past, but they insisted I not be. *They* might think of themselves as more Italian than American, but they insisted I think of myself as an American. They tried not to speak Italian in the house when I was there, except when they were arguing. When I filled out a form for school one day and they saw I had listed my nationality as Italian, they were furious.

"You're an American," my father snapped. "Born here. What's Italy but a country that couldn't feed us?"

When I got in a fight in the sixth grade one year, my father asked me what it was about. I told him a boy had insulted me. "I had to save face, Dad," I said.

My father threw up his hands. "Save face! The curse of Italians."

But I wanted desperately to *be* an Italian when I was a teenager. It seemed so exotic to me. It separated me from my phlegmatic WASP friends in the suburbs. I *liked* being called "the Guinea." When I went on to an Irish-Catholic prep school in the fifties, I deliberately dressed in the zoot-suit way of Old World Italians. Long, baggy, shoulder-padded sport jackets. Narrow black ties. Pants pegged so tightly at the ankle I could barely get them on over my feet. I wore black, pointy-toed shoes. I hung around only with the few other Italian boys at that school. Bobby Calabrese. Butch Barletto. Joe Troiano. We slicked back our long black hair with grease. When our Irish classmates taunted us—"What's the smallest book in the world? A book of Italian war heroes."—we responded with "You Micks were living in caves and painting your faces blue when our ancestors were painting the Mona Lisa."

But it was only a ruse. A pose. I learned that one summer when I met two Italian brothers who were not much like me.

*   *   *

Joey Furnari was in his thirties when he started cutting Susan's hair in Fanfield. He was short, dark, with a swarthy stubble of beard and a halo of black curls. He had the face of a Botticelli cherub who had misspent his youth on the back streets of Palermo, Sicily, where he was born.

Joe's clients were mostly wealthy suburban housewives in navy blazers, Greenwich-green wraparound skirts, and Papagallo flats. They insisted on the same short, parted, Princeton cuts that their husbands got from the barber down the street. Occasionally, though, he would get one of the tough city girls from Bridgeport, who chewed gum loudly as they leafed through his glossy Italian hair-fashion magazines. When they came to some spiky-punk creation they liked, they'd let out a squeal. They'd rush over to Joe, cutting some housewife's hair, and thrust the magazine under his nose. "There, Joey! That's the 'do I want."

Joe had infinite patience with those city girls he knew only too well from the discos, and with those housewives he was working very hard at knowing. They all loved him in turn. The city girls loved the rough way he handled their hair that brought tears to their eyes. ("Joey ain't no fag," they said). The housewives were so charmed by his "dees" and "dems" and "dose" as he cut their hair that they slipped into reveries from the more erotic scenes from *The Roman Spring of Mrs. Stone.*

Joe cut my hair too. I was his only male client. He didn't like men in his shop as a rule, he said. "Dey spoil da allusion for da broads." I was different. We went back a long way, he said. Besides, I was his only respite from all those women. He made me come in late in the day when most of the women were gone and we could talk. He could talk, actually. Joe spilled out long monologues to me while he took his sweet time cutting my hair. He complained about his landlady, who had been trying to raise his rent ever since her husband died because, as Joe put it, "She ain't got laid since." He complained about the pale, plump, and pampered owner of the massage parlor next door who was always barging into his shop when one of his clients parked in her space. "I got all I can do to keep from droppin' a dime on her," he said. He complained about the two FBI men in raincoats and hard-soled shoes who were always disrupting his shop just by their presence.

"Da way dey dress, Pat," he said. "No class." The FBI men were hounding Joe about his relationship with one of his former clients, a madam. She operated her business out of a restored colonial house in the historic district of town until it was raided and she was sent to the state prison. The state troopers who raided the house found the madam's little black book with the names of city detectives alongside the names of Mafia chieftains. The FBI was pressuring the madam and anyone who knew her for information that would help them connect those two sets of names. The police and the Mafia chieftains were pressuring the madam and her friends to remain silent about those names.

"It's a damned shame," said Joe. "She's caught in between. She's just a workin' girl, trying ta support her kids. Now she's ruined. Day got her readin' da Bible in da can!" He shook his head. "She don't even look da same." Joe went on to describe how, at forty, the madam had had the body of a college cheerleader, thanks to about $40,000 worth of plastic surgery. "She's like a walkin' picture, ya know what I mean, Pat? A Picasso. Da guy who worked on her, he's da best. He left his signature everywhere."

Joe stopped complaining only when he began to talk about his brother, Al. Al was doing well now, he said. He had a wife and two kids. His own business, a used-car lot. A new camper. A new speedboat. A new house in the country. Al, the country squire. I smiled.

"Al's come a long way since da old days, huh, Pat?" Joe said. He stopped cutting for a moment, looked around his chic salon, and then back to me. He smiled. "We all have, huh?"

* * *

It was in the midsixties. Al and Joe had only been in the States for a few years. They lived with their parents in the Italian ghetto of the city. Their parents were an Old World couple who spoke no English. The mother dressed always in black. She spent her days in the kitchen hovering over pots of sauce. The father, a trim, dapper little man, still saw himself as a Sicilian *padrone*. He spent his days playing bocci in the park across the street from their three-family tenement house, and his evenings shooting craps at the Venice Athletic Club downtown. Joe was fourteen, a skinny, undersized kid who rarely spoke. Al was twenty, a mechanic for a local Ford dealer. Al tuned cars by ear, not by the Ford service manual, because he could not read English. He could speak it, though. He had taught himself how. He insisted that his little brother learn too. Their father laughed at their attempts. Al argued with him in Italian. He threw up his hands and left the house.

I was twenty-three when I met them. I had just started teaching English at an all-girls parochial high school run by an order of Belgian nuns for the princely sum of $4,000 per year when I met Al and Joe. We seemed to have nothing in common, Al and Joe and me, except that I too was of Italian heritage, two generations back. My parents had lived in the same Italian ghetto that Al and Joe lived in now. But we had moved to the suburbs when I was four.

Al and Joe and I had one other thing in common. We were in love with fast cars. I had just bought one of the first new Mustangs in the state, a black fastback with a 289 high-performance engine, from the Ford dealer where Al worked. I met Al the first time I brought the car into the shop for a tune-up. He walked over to the car in that swaggering, puffed-up way of little men. He waved aside his service manager with the back of his hand. "I'll handle dis one," he told him, as if only he, of all the mechanics, could do justice to this high-performance engine. Al ordered me to pop the hood. It was the first time he ever spoke to me. It was the way he would always speak to me when it came to that Mustang. It was as if, at that moment, the car had become his, not mine. I did as I was ordered. He hitched up his pants with both hands and stuck his head into the engine compartment. I could see, from my driver's seat, that his eyes had lit up like a child's in a toy store. Unlike Joe, Al was not a handsome man. He had a long, pockmarked, hatchet face. A big nose. Small black eyes. Wavy black hair, not curly, which he always greased down and combed straight back in a very Old World Italian way.

When Al straightened up again, that childlike look was gone from his eyes. In its place was that cocky, heavy-lidded look of his I was to see only too often over the next few years. He hitched up his pants again and swaggered over to my window. He gave his shoulders a little tilt and said, "I can make dis ting go fast."

We struck up a deal that first day. Al would tune my Mustang and do all the mechanical work on it for nothing. I, as owner and driver, would pay for all the parts. We would race it every Sunday at Dover Drag Strip in Dover Plains, upstate New York. At first it seemed like the deal was weighted in my favor, since Al would do all the dirty work and I would get all the glory as the driver. But, in retrospect, I can see that we both got what we needed at the time. I had come home from baseball with a monumental ego that had lost its sole source of gratification. Drag racing my Mustang in front of large, cheering crowds would replenish it. And Al . . . well, Al didn't plan to be a Ford mechanic all his life. He wanted to strike out on his own as a race-car mechanic. My car could give him just the reputation he needed to do it. He had tried to build such a reputation with his own car, a rusted, 1955 Crown Victoria. But the drag strip fans only laughed when he smoked down the strip in his old clunker that George Bignotti himself could not turn into a trophy winner. We shook hands.

I returned to the Ford dealer's garage at six o'clock the following Sunday morning. Al and Joe were standing outside, waiting for me. Al had gotten permission from his boss to use the garage on Sundays to set up my car. If it won some trophies, it would sell that dealer a few more Mustangs. Everybody, it seems, was getting what they wanted. Al opened the garage door and I pulled the car inside. He shut the door. He didn't want anyone to see what he was doing to my Mustang. It was a new car, with unknown potential. Al wanted to keep all the secrets he would learn about making it go fast to himself. He swore me to secrecy that Sunday. "Don't tell no one what we done to the car in here, unnerstand?" he ordered. I nodded like a child. He showed me all the things he had gotten from his parts department for our drag car. Fat racing slicks. Traction bars. Exhaust headers. Rear axle gears. Assorted spark plugs, ignition wires, points. He presented me with the bill. I wrote him out a check. He pocketed it, hitched up his pants, and ordered me to pop the hood. He went to work while I stood around, reading to him from the Ford service manual whenever he needed some information. Joe watched it all silently, with his big black eyes. He was our "gofer." Al would snap at him, "Get me the five-sixteenth ratchet." Joe would run to Al's toolbox, get the ratchet, and hand it to him.

Throughout the morning and afternoon and late into the night, Al worked. Joe went across the street to a diner. He bought us all a coffee and danish (with my money), and then meatball grinders for lunch, and then hamburgers and french fries for supper. He loved his job, loved just being around the car with us. I tried to talk to him, but he responded only with a silent nod of his head. What I didn't see at the time, but which I see now, was that Joe was in awe of me. Not only did I let him be a part of my race car, but also I was the kind of guy his older brother had told him they could both become. I was an Italian-American who looked and talked and acted like an American, not an Italian. I had done American things in my life. I had played baseball. I had gone to college. I was a schoolteacher. I was what Al had told Joe they could both become someday if they studied me, which was precisely what Joe always seemed to be doing then, when he was fourteen. Throughout the day and night I would catch him staring at me, his eyes narrowed, his brow furrowed. And me? I studied them. Two tough, street-wise Italian kids. I saw in them something I had lost. I was an Italian-American with few vestiges of my Italian heritage, not even my name. Pat Jordan Jr., not Pasquale Giordano.

Al finished with the car near midnight. He cleaned up his tools, his work area, then he cleaned the grease from his hands with a gritty, Vaselinelike solvent he scooped out of a metal can. He changed into fresh navy-blue workclothes with a knifelike crease. He wiped a speck of dirt off the Ford emblem on his shirt pocket with the back of his fingers. He pinched the points of his shirt collar with both hands and adjusted the shirt. Al always began work on a car looking like a very Latinized version of those spotlessly pressed WASPish actors in an Amoco TV commercial. He always left it looking the same way. He once dismissed another mechanic's race car by saying, "Look at him! He looks like a pig! How could he make anything go fast?"

Al turned to me and Joe. "Awright, yous two," he said. "You ain't done nuthin' all night. Wash the car." Joe and I obeyed. I washed with a soapy sponge. Joe hosed it down with water. His eyes were bright with pleasure as he sprayed. He sprayed me accidentally. I threw the sponge at him. Joe smiled at me—a kid's big-faced smile—for the first time since we met that morning. We were both drenched and soapy by the time we finished. Al, hands on hips, looked at us. He forced back a grin and shook his head. Joe and I looked at each other with sheepish grins. Joey and me. Two kids.

Al wouldn't take our car to the strip until he tested it first on the city's streets. He was too proud ever to be embarrassed in front of a big crowd again. Nothing fancy, he said. Just a little street race. Maybe a Barracuda or a small-block Nova. Something in our class. There was no better time than now, he said, and no better place than the Greek's. I could feel the new surge of power in the engine the moment I fired it up and backed it out of the garage. Al closed the door, and he and Joe got in. "Jesus!" I said. "What the hell did you do to it, Al?" He smiled across at me. Joe, in the back, leaned forward and rested his elbows on the back of Al's seat.

Even past midnight, the Greek's parking lot was filled with every type of hopped-up drag car I could ever imagine. Novas. Barracudas. GTOs. Super Sports. Vettes. They entered the lot from the street, circled the tiny wood building that dispensed greasy hot dogs and french fries, and then settled into a parking space with one final blast of their exhaust. No one left The Greek's without laying a twenty-foot strip of burning rubber on the street. I parked near a streetlight. All around me in the darkness were guys and girls my own age who were nothing at all like me. They leaned insouciantly against their cars. They sat on the hoods, smoked cigarettes, looked tough. The guys wore white T-shirts with a pack of Camels rolled up in one sleeve and a Bic lighter rolled up in the other. The girls chewed gum and were not afraid to get grease under their fingernails. They were like a foreign army to me, a suburban kid, who had played baseball and gone to college. They had gone to trade school. The guys dropped out at sixteen because already they knew more about cars than their stodgy old shop teacher. The girls followed them out. They waitressed at the Comet Diner and went to hairdresser's school part-time. The guys worked in gas stations and speed-part shops, where they always parked their freshly waxed cars out front so they would be visible from far down the city street. Those cars were their distinction in life. Years later, settled with a wife and kids, driving a station wagon now, they would reminisce about those cars of their youth that had given them their only distinction. Tony Tempest. Kajewski's Comet. Vagnini's Vette.

A crowd drifted over to my new Mustang, the first ever seen at the Greek's. A voice called out, "Pop the hood." I reached for the hood latch. Al put his hand on my arm. He yelled out the window, "It'll cost ya." Someone flung the back of his hand at Al. "In your dreams," he said. The crowd drifted off again toward a brand new 427 Corvette that had just pulled into the lot. Al sent Joe for coffee. "We stay in the car until they come for us," Al ordered me. Joe returned and the three of us sat there, sipping what must have been our twentieth cup of coffee this long day.

The owner of the Vette popped his hood. The crowd "ooohed" and "aaahed" over his chrome-plated, 425-horsepower engine. Someone pointed toward our Mustang. The Vette's owner, a skinny guy with thick-lensed glasses, walked over to my side. He leaned down.

"Whatcha got in there?" he said. I told him. He laughed. His big-clock Chevy was almost twice the size of my Mustang engine and had over 200 more horsepower. At least it did on the day I bought it. He started to walk away. Al yelled after him. The guy came back to Al's side of the car.

"Wanna run that rat of yours?" Al said.

"You kiddin'?"

"My partner's got a hunnert bucks says we ain't kiddin'." Al gestured with his head toward me. I stared at him.

"You're on," the guy said.

"One thing," Al said. "We run open exhaust. Just to even tings up."

"Anything you want, sucker," the guy said, and he walked back to his car.

"Are you crazy or what?" I said. "I don't have a hundred bucks."

"You won't need it," Al said. "Open exhaust is good for thirty more horses."

I calculated in my head. My car came from the factory with 271 horsepower. Thirty more gave it 301. "That still leaves me 124 horses short of his Vette," I said.

Al smiled. "No it don't."

We drove side by side, the Vette and my Mustang, through the city streets toward the Merritt Parkway. A double line of cars from the Greek's followed us like a conga line. When we reached the parkway, Al told me to pull off into the grass. He got out in the darkness, slid under the car, and unbolted my exhaust headers. When I started the car again, the engine rumbled and growled like a race car. I was momentarily scared in the darkness. We lined up side by side on the parkway. All the other cars lined up behind us, stopping traffic for almost a mile back. The guys and girls got out of their cars and stood on the highway divider up ahead of the Mustang and the Vette. There must have been a hundred of them. A girl with a kerchief in her hand stood between the Mustang and the Vette a few feet in front of us. Another girl and a guy had sprinted up ahead in the grass until they had reached a big maple tree by the side of the highway that was exactly one quarter of a mile away. I could not see them up ahead in the darkness. The girl in front of us raised the kerchief over her head.

"Bring it up to five grand!" Al shouted. I depressed the clutch and pressed the accelerator pedal until the engine rpms reached 5000. The car shook and rattled as if the engine was trying to burst through the hood. The girl flung her kerchief to the road. I popped the clutch. The engine let out a high-pitched, animal-like whine as it shot to 7000 rpms. There was smoke everywhere, the smell of burning rubber from spinning tires. Then they caught. The rpms dipped back to 5000 and the body of the car seemed to rise off its frame like some wild animal rising off its haunches. Then it leapt forward with such force that I was pinned to my seat.

Suddenly, everything slowed down, grew silent, still, weightless in the darkness as it must be on the moon. I was vaguely conscious of Al screaming at me to shift into second gear, then third, then fourth, but I did not hear a sound. I shifted in a dream, from outside myself. I saw my arm move. I saw my face smile. I saw trees and people flashing by my

window as in one of those cheaply made old movies in which the
scenery moves but the car is still. Time passed. I watched everything
with a perfect, calm, effortless clarity: the trees, the people, the dotted
white line rushing silently toward me, Al gesturing beside me, Joe
slapping the back of Al's seat, the guy and the girl and the maple tree up
ahead, caught in the glare of my headlights. Then everything came back
again with the force of an explosion: the engine whining, the exhaust
growling, the car rattling, Al screaming, Joe pounding. I could feel
myself drenched in a cold sweat as the car hurtled past the maple tree at
120 mph. I became conscious, for the first time, that the Vette was no
longer beside me. I lifted my foot off the accelerator and the car slowed
with a jolt. The Vette sped past me, too late.

*　*　*

I got home at 3 A.M. My wife was sitting up in bed with tears of
worry in her eyes. When I told her what I had been doing with our new
Mustang, her tears of worry turned to tears of rage. Her last boyfriend
before me had dropped out of college to drag-race his car, which was
why she had broken up with him. Now she saw me, in her mind's eye,
dressed in dirty workclothes, my hands stained with grease. I tried to
reassure her that wouldn't happen. It's just a lark, I said. I need it now,
after my baseball failure. Trust me. She dried her tears. She didn't
understand, she said. But still, she would trust me. "If you think you
need it, all right," she said, "but don't ever expect me to be a part of
it."

*　*　*

The following Sunday, at six o'clock on a crisp, sunny, September
morning, Al and I were sitting in his old Crown Victoria, driving along
narrow, winding, country roads through upstate Connecticut on our
way to Dover Drag Strip. The black Mustang was hitched to a tow-bar
behind us. Every so often I would glance in the rearview mirror to see if
it was secured. Joe was sitting in the Mustang's driver's seat. His head

was barely visible above the steering wheel. He was making believe he was steering the car while making imaginary shifts. In *my* imagination, I could hear Joe making growling engine noises as he shifted.

It was a beautiful morning drive in the country. I would come to love these drives almost as much as I loved the races. We passed weathered old barns, and cows in a field, and old white colonial houses shaded by a maple tree. We passed pine forests and lakes and quaint little New England towns like Brookfield, New Milford, and Kent. We were not the only race car to make that country drive in the morning. Often there would be a daily chain of old cars towing exotic-looking race cars: '29 Willys with chrome superchargers protruding from their fiberglass hoods; '55 Chevy Nomads with huge racing slicks on their rear wheels. Top-fuel dragsters that were nothing more than a 600-horsepower Chrysler hemi mounted on an aluminum tubular frame. The people who lived in those colonial houses would sit in rocking chairs on their porches in the cool morning air and sip coffee from big mugs. Some of the racers, those with stock-bodied cars, drove their race cars to the strip rather than tow them. When they passed those farmers sitting on their porches, they would downshift into second gear, leaving a burning strip of rubber for a few hundred yards before backing off the accelerator to polite applause from the farmers.

Dover Drag Strip was a two-lane blacktop cut between two small hills in a pastoral setting. The paying fans sat on wooden bleachers on one hill looking down on the strip. The racers tuned their cars in the dusty pit area on the opposite hill. The races lasted all morning and all afternoon, with only a break for lunch. I loved the exploding sounds of engines echoing off the hills. The shouts of mechanics working in the pits to repair a blown gasket. The voice of the public-address announcer calling each class. "At this time I want all SuperStock/AStock/BStock/CStock/DStock cars in the staging lane." The announcer spoke so fast all classes ran into one another. He commented on each car as they staged. "Ladies and gentlemen, watch the little black rat in lane two, you *will* not believe it!" Then the crowd roared as two cars hurtled off the starting line down the quarter-mile track. The winning light flashed on and the winning driver stuck his arm out the window and raised a clenched fist. His mechanic, still at the starting line, leapt in the air and shouted out "Awright!" as he began sprinting toward the pits to greet the returning driver.

We won a trophy in our class, D Stock, that Sunday. We beat a girl driving a '62 Vette that had painted on its trunk, "If you can beat me, you can eat me." She had won that class every week for the last two months until Al and I showed up with our new Mustang. A crowd milled around our car in the pits after the race. The girl got out of her Vette farther down in the pit area and glared at us. Her husband, her mechanic, put his arm around her shoulders to console her. She shrugged him off. Al popped the hood on the Mustang. He made a great production of checking underneath to make sure everything was all right. Someone in the crowd asked if this was the Mustang that had beaten the 427 Vette. I nodded. Someone else asked what Al had done to the little Ford engine to make it go like hell. He hitched up his pants and smiled. "My secret," he said.

Another mechanic asked him if he'd take a look at his big-block Ford 390. "It ain't runnin' worth a shit," the mechanic said.

Al nodded seriously. "I'll give it a look," he said. He walked off in that puffed-up, little man's way of his with the mechanic. The crowd drifted away back to the final races of the day. It was dusk. Someone patted me on the back. I looked around. It was Joe. His street-wise urchin's face was beaming. "You drove a great race, Pat," he said. I thanked him and took a great breath of air.

We drove home in darkness. Al and I were silent, each of us savoring our own particular satisfaction of the day. I replayed, over and over in my mind's eye, the sounds of the crowd cheering as I pulled the Mustang up to the starting line. It was the first time a crowd had cheered for me in years. It felt good to get it back again.

We won a trophy and a little victory sticker every week for the last eight weeks of the season. So many Dover Drag Strip "kill" stickers dotted my rear window that I could barely see out of it by the time the season ended in November. That winter, I spent all my free time with Al at the Greek's. But we never had another street race. "We don't need it anymore," Al told me. Besides, the Mustang's reputation was so great no one would run us anyway. "The Mystery Mustang," they called it in awe. Al and I, like visiting dignitaries, spent a lot of cold winter nights, huddled in the Mustang at the Greek's. We greeted well-wishers, dispensed advice, and made plans for the spring season. Al wanted to rebuild the engine, but I told him it was too soon. We could get another season out of the engine just as it was. We argued. He wanted to flex his mechanical know-how. I was more cautious. I was afraid he was going to mess up a good thing just to show off. Besides, it was my car. I couldn't afford to have it tied up for months at a time while he rebuilt his engine. I told him I'd rather get his Ford dealer to sponsor us first, before we tackled anything as complex as rebuilding the engine. We would paint the Ford dealer's name on the side of the car in return for free parts. Al laughed at my idea. "He ain't interested," Al said. "I already asked him to sponsor my car and he said no."

I didn't want to hurt Al's feelings, so I didn't tell him what I was thinking. Why would any Ford dealer want to sponsor a rusted-out '55 Crown Victoria and become the laughingstock of every car dealer in the state? Instead, I simply said to Al, "You watch! This spring I'll get him to sponsor us."

Al asked me if he could have all the trophies we'd won. I said, "Sure, why not? My old lady's not too hot about propping them up on the fireplace mantel in our living room anyway." Al kept them on his tool bench in the Ford dealer's garage. When I stopped by for a visit one day I heard him explaining to a customer how he'd won all those trophies with "his Mustang."

In March, I asked Al if I could borrow those trophies for a day or two. "Why?" he said. I told him I had my reasons. Reluctantly, he let me have them. That Saturday morning, I dressed into a gray suit, a white button-down-collar shirt, a rep tie. I drove my freshly washed and waxed Mustang over to Al's Ford dealer. I parked in front of the showroom window. I arranged all the trophies on the inside rear deck so they'd be clearly visible through the rear window. I popped the hood and walked across the street to a diner. I sipped coffee and watched through the plate-glass window as a crowd began to form around the Mustang. People were leaving the dealer's showroom to inspect my chrome-plated engine and the racing trophies. Finally, I saw a gray-haired man in a dark suit come out of the showroom and stand on the sidewalk in front of my car. Hands on hips, he glared at the car. He looked around for its owner. I went over to him and introduced myself. He looked me up and down as I explained to him that I was an English teacher at a parochial high school, that I had a wife and a daughter, that I lived in the suburbs, and that I was going to offer my very successful drag Mustang for sponsorship to Ford dealers in the area.

"Since I bought the car from you," I said, "I thought it was only proper that I give you first chance to become my sponsor." Before he could speak, I added, "I think it could be a profitable business venture for the both of us." He invited me into his office, where we worked out a deal.

After I shook hands with the owner, I walked to the garage to tell Al. I told him how I had talked my way into a sponsorship, but he seemed not to hear me. He kept staring at my suit and tie, the first time he had ever seen me in a suit and tie, as if confused, as if he had never seen this person who was now standing before him. "Al, you don't understand!" I said. "Free parts! You can do anything you want to the car now." He kept staring at me. Then suddenly it dawned on him. He looked devastated. Now I was the one who was confused. "What's the matter?" I said.

He gave me a weak smile and a little nod of his head. "Dat's good, Pat," he said. "Dat's good. Listen. I got a lotta work, huh. I'll see yous."

"Sure, Al." I forced a smile and reached out my hand. "Partner," I said.

Al looked at his own hand, his palm, as if expecting an offering to appear in it, or maybe something to disappear from it. He turned it over and held it flat like women do when inspecting their nails. Al had long, neatly trimmed fingernails he always took great pains with at the end of a day spent working on my car. Joe and I would get fidgety waiting for him. "Come on, Al, for chrissakes!" I'd say. He'd shoot us a look. "Hold your horses," he'd say as he took a jackknife out of his pocket and began methodically to clean out the grease from underneath his fingernails. Now he looked at his greasy fingernails. Then he gave me that weak smile again, and an almost imperceptible shake of his head, before he walked off.

Al rebuilt the engine that spring while the black car was being lettered in 14-karat gold leaf. "Keating Ford Racing Team" was printed in large block letters along each side of the car. "Mechanic and Engine Builder Al Furnari" was printed in smaller letters on each front fender. "Owner and Driver Pat Jordan" was printed in even smaller letters at the top of each door, just under the windows. "Pegasus" was written in script above each door window on the roof. On the rear of the trunk, visible only from behind, was printed "Mi Segue!"

For all the work Al did on the engine, it ran only marginally better than it did the year before. We won our trophy in D Stock each week easily enough, when something in the car didn't break. A blown head gasket. A blown rear end. A blown transmission shaft. Each Monday after something broke, I would leave school early and drive all over the east looking for exotic race parts for the car. It seemed we were now spending six days a week to prepare the car for a Sunday race that last year had taken us only one Saturday evening. Even my wife, with her infinite patience, was becoming unnerved.

"I feel like such a fool," she said, "riding in that car. Look at it!" I bought a beat-up old station wagon we could use around town while the Mustang was being worked on for days at a time. That failed to appease her. "All that money in the Mustang," she said, "and we can't even drive it now. What's the point?" I didn't know myself by then.

Al and I began to argue at the strip over whose fault it was when something in the car broke. I accused him of experimenting recklessly at the expense of the car's reliability. What I didn't tell him, no matter how hotly we argued, was that I thought the car had gotten away from him. It was too sophisticated a machine now for his limited knowledge. He claimed my driving was at fault. I was shifting at 8000 rpms when I should be shifting at 7600 rpms. To prove his point, he would drive the car on practice runs in the morning. No matter how fast he went, he always claimed it was faster than I had gone. We argued over two-tenths of a second. One Sunday afternoon, we argued so fiercely in the pits that we drew a crowd. Joe was with us. He just put his head down and backed off into the crowd. Soon Joe stopped coming with us.

We didn't race the entire last month of the season because the car was tied up in Al's garage, where he insisted on building a new, even more exotic engine for next season. "We'll move up in class," he said. "We ain't goin' nowhere in D Stock no more." I didn't bother to argue with him. I was just relieved that we didn't have to go to the strip anymore that fall. It was as if the car was his now and I was just along for the ride. I almost forgot about the car over the winter as my wife's belly swelled with our third child. I no longer went to the Greek's.

Al called in February to tell me he had finished the engine. "I'm gonna fire it up tonight for the first time," he said. "I thought you oughtta know." I drove over to the garage in my ratty old wagon. I was stunned by what Al had done to the Mustang. He had stripped out the rear seats and the carpet and the heating ducts in the dashboard to make the car lighter.

"Jesus Christ, Al! What the hell did you do to my car?"

He hitched up his pants and gave his shoulders a little tilt. "I'm running C Modified Sports this season," he said. "I need every tenth I can get."

I just shook my head as Al got into the driver's seat. He put his hands on the steering wheel as if he was going to drive somewhere. I saw, in my mind's eye, Joe sitting behind the wheel of the Mustang when we towed it to the strip. Joe, who wasn't around anymore. Al brought me back when he started the engine. The noise rattled the windows in the garage. Al had taken off the muffler system too, so that the engine now breathed through open exhaust headers, just like an out-and-out race car. I realized immediately I could no longer drive the car much on the street. Still, the engine sounded so strong, with its lopey, rumbling idle, that for an instant, I forgot about everything. I saw myself driving the car before vast, cheering crowds.

"Sounds strong, Al," I said. He smiled up at me from the driver's seat. He shut off the engine, got out, and checked under the hood one final time before leaving. I told him I wanted to take the car home with me. He insisted I leave it at the garage. I told him I didn't like leaving it here at night, with no one to watch it. It was a valuable piece of property that a lot of midnight auto racers would love to get their hands on. "They'd chop it up in pieces and have 'em all sold before we even knew it was gone," I said. He told me I was crazy. "What about Salerno?" I said. "He stole the whole goddamned Yankee Peddler and parked it in front of his house overnight! And that's a Funny Car!" But he wouldn't give in until, for the first time ever, I pulled rank on him. "It's my goddamned car!" I said. "And I'm driving it home."

I rumbled through the city's darkened side streets, hoping that no cops would stop me. When I was almost home, I came to a stoplight. It was well after midnight and the streets were deserted. I brought the rpms up to 6000. When the light turned green, I popped the clutch. The rear tires spun and burned and then caught and the front end of the car lifted a foot off the ground. I panicked and backed off the accelerator. The front end hit the ground with a jolt. Jesus, I thought, it's a goddamned monster! I drove slowly the rest of the way home. When I pulled into our narrow driveway between our house and our neighbor's, the grumbling exhaust echoed like thunder off both houses. My wife opened her bedroom window and looked out. Our neighbor did the same. They looked down. Then they looked across at one another and both slammed their windows at the same time.

That night my wife and I had a terrible argument over the Mustang. I slept downstairs on the sofa.

My wife went into labor on a cold, windy night in the spring. I went outside to warm up the station wagon but it wouldn't start. I told her we'd have to take the Mustang. She looked at me. "You're kidding?" she said. I shook my head, no. We drove slowly through the city streets in a black Mustang with gold-leaf lettering all over it. Cold air blew in from the empty heater duct up my wife's legs. She held her big stomach in both hands and glared across at me. "We'll be there in no time," I said. I smiled at her, but she didn't smile back. "I just got to drive slow," I added. "The engine's cold, I don't want to ruin it."

"Slow!" she snapped. "It's a goddamned race car! You've got to drive it *slow?*"

I didn't bother to explain to her how race engines have to be warmed up a long time before they can be run fast. Besides, she was probably delirious with contractions. She wouldn't understand anyway.

Her water broke before we got to the hospital. It froze to her leg.

I rumbled up to the emergency entrance and stopped. I left the engine running to blow out excess exhaust smoke, which might foul up the spark plugs. Three nurses, hugging themselves in sweaters, hurried out the door to get my wife into a wheelchair. When they saw the car they stopped and stared. They walked around it to my side. They leaned their heads down and began asking me questions.

"Is it yours?"

"Far out!"

"Do you run at Dover?"

"I'd love to go for a ride in it one day."

My wife sat in her seat, holding her stomach and groaning loudly. The nurses couldn't hear her over the sound of the car's exhaust.

We had a son that night. I drove home alone at three o'clock in the morning. I was too excited to sleep, so I drove to the Greek's to see if any of the guys were there. Even though the Greek's was closed, there were still a few cars parked back in the darkness. I parked alongside an Oldsmobile 442, with two guys in it. They had heard about the Mystery Mustang, they said. Everybody had. I asked them if they wanted to race on the parkway. They said no, it wouldn't even be a contest. Their car was literally stock. "You'll blow us away," the driver said.

"Just for the hell of it," I said. "No money. I want to see how the new engine is running." Finally, they agreed. We drove up to the same spot where I had beaten that 427 Vette what seemed like centuries ago. We staged, side by side, on the darkened highway. I popped the clutch, felt the wheels spin, then heard something clank in the rear end as my car died at the starting line. The 442 took off down the highway. The Mustang was barely drivable. The rear end clanked and rattled as I coaxed the car back home.

Al called me the next day. Word had already spread throughout the city that the Mystery Mustang wasn't such a mystery anymore. Two kids in a stock 442 had blown it away last night on the parkway. I told Al that the only thing that had been blown away was the Mustang's rear end. But still he was furious. He screamed at me. How could I be so stupid as to race the car on the street, like a kid, for chrissakes! And then to blow the rear end on top of it! I had embarrassed him. I had caused him to lose face. I remembered my father telling me that the fear of "losing face," was an Italian-American's curse. It forced us to do foolish things that had always separated us from real Americans. As long as an Italian-American feared losing face, he would remain an Italian, not become an American, my father said. It was what separated me from Al. I had already lost face once with my baseball career. Like virginity, it seems, once face is lost it doesn't seem so important anymore. To me it didn't, anyway. I tried to explain this to Al. But he didn't understand.

"I'm not like yous," he said. "I don't unnerstand da tings yous do. Dat car. Dat's a toy for yous. Dat's no toy for me!"

I didn't hear from Al again after that. I guess he couldn't even bear to look at the Mustang anymore. It was like it had died on him, or maybe done something to him so disgraceful that he couldn't bear to be reminded of it. Weeks passed. The car sat in the garage collecting dust. Every so often I would go outside and start it up, just so the battery wouldn't die. The rear end was still broken, so I couldn't drive it anywhere. The growling exhaust rattled the garage windows and shook the walls. I sat in the driver's seat and remembered the car's early days at Dover Drag Strip. The beautiful Sunday-morning drives. The race against that 427 Vette. Al and Joe. Finally, one day, I told my wife I was going to sell the car. She didn't seem surprised, only relieved. I put an ad in the newspaper. It read simply: "The Mystery Mustang for Sale." A lot of kids came around. Teenagers who worked in gas stations and didn't have two nickels to rub together, much less the price of the car. They just wanted to gawk at it, the "kill" stickers covering the rear window, the gold-leaf lettering that was beginning to peel, the roar of the engine. They pleaded with me, "Can I just sit in the driver's seat? For a minute?" After a while, it dawned on me that I was wasting my time. I began to offer the car for its parts. Some guy bought the broken rear end. Another bought the transmission. A third bought the carburetors and manifold. A fourth bought the cylinder heads. A fifth bought the pistons and short block. There was nothing left now, just the frame and the tires and an empty black shell of a Mustang. I sold that to a kid who put a stock six-cylinder engine in it. He drove it around town all lettered up in peeling gold leaf. I heard he liked to race cars at stoplights. But after losing so often that he and the car had become a laughingstock, he sold it too.

I heard that Al had bought his own Mustang after a while, a new 390 black Mustang that he planned to race himself. He told all the guys at the Greek's that his Mustang would make everyone forget that my car had ever existed. My feelings were hurt at first when I heard this. But after a while I understood that it was just Al's way of saving face.

I couldn't hide a certain swell of pride when I heard that Al never could make his bigger-engined car go as fast as our little 289.

I didn't see Al again for almost twenty years. Then he stopped by my apartment in Fort Lauderdale one night in the mid-1980s. He looked the same. He still had that shiny, jet-black hair that he combed straight back and that big-nosed face and that little man's swagger. He came into the apartment, hitched up his pants, and looked around, sizing it up as if he was an expert in south Florida decor. "Not bad," he said with a nod. "You got a nice place here, Pat."

We went outside and sat on the deck overlooking the Intracoastal Waterway. Al admired the boats docked along the water. He mentioned the kind of boat he was going to buy at Bahia Mar. I told him I didn't know much about boats, even though I'd lived down there for three years.

"You didn't know much about cars, either," he said with a grin. I laughed.

We drank a few beers and made cautious small talk at first. He told me about his family, his business (he was a wealthy man now), his brother, Joe. We both agreed that Joe was a good kid, at thirty-five. I mentioned how Joe used to sit in the Mustang when we towed it to Dover Plains in the old days. We began to talk about our racing days, cautiously at first; I could see it was still a sore point with Al even after all these years. I reminded him about the time he warned me that

Salerno was planning to steal our Mustang just to find out what Al had done to it to make it go so fast.

"That night," I told him, "I slept in that damned car all night long. My wife swore I was crackin' up." He laughed and shook his head. Then I grew careless. I mentioned a particularly fast time I had turned in a morning practice run at Dover. Al corrected me.

"You wasn't drivin' then," he said. "I was." I just nodded.

Al only stayed an hour or so. Then he got up to leave. I walked him to the door. We shook hands, awkwardly it seemed to me, two grown men who remembered one another only as we had been a long time ago.

TEN

TWO DAYS AFTER I had met his father, Brian and I threw again at St. Thomas. While we were warming up, he said, "Guess what my father said after he met you?"

"What?"

Brian grinned. "He said, 'Pat seems nice, but Bri, there's no adult supervision there.'" We both laughed.

After we finished throwing we sat in the grass, talking, while I took off my spikes.

"How's it going?" I said.

"Oh, Pat! I had a great day yesterday." He was smiling. "I took my SATs, then went to the beach with my friends. We had a cookout that night. I drank a few beers and met this really nice girl."

"Another one? What's that make, four?"

"Yeh. But she's only a sophomore. I'm just gonna keep my eye on her."

"What? Use her in long relief this year? Maybe spot start her next year?"

"Absolutely. By the time she's a senior, she'll be my ace." We both laughed.

"You know, Bri, I could never do that." He looked at me, confused. "Enjoy the moment. I was always looking ahead for bigger satisfactions. I missed a lot of great days when I was a kid."

"Oh, I don't wanna miss any of it. My life is fun."

I thought of his father. I didn't want to interfere. But Brian was my friend. If I knew something maybe he didn't, I should share it with him. I said, "You know, you've got to have patience with your father. He means well. He just wants a lot for you."

He looked down at the grass. "I know," he said. "But I can't talk to him." He looked up angrily. "I sometimes just want to say 'Fuck you!' "

We came to the same place by a different route. I thought my way through to things I know. Brian knew things intuitively, the way young, innocent kids do. But sometimes they need to have someone verify what they know when what they know is painful. Their painful intuitions make them feel guilty and cloud their perceptions with what my father once called "the most destructive of human emotions," guilt.

"My brother was a little like your father," I said. "He was so serious about my career. He wanted it so badly for me, you know."

Brian nodded. Then he said, "That's the way it is with old people. They forget to have fun when they do young things." He smiled at me. "Not like us, eh, Pat?" We laughed.

"You ever see that movie, *Some Kind of Wonderful?*" I said.

"You mean the one where the father wants his son to go to business college and the kid wants to be an artist?"

"Yeh. Maybe you should rent it some day. Watch it with your father."

Brian just nodded. We got up and walked across centerfield to our cars. Brian got in his car and started the engine. I leaned over through his open window and handed him some money.

"What's this for? Heh, Pat, I don't want money for catching you." He looked hurt, like I was redefining our relationship in a way that pained him.

"It's not for that. You should be paying me for showing you good stuff you might learn to hit someday." He smiled. "Take your father out to dinner on me for Father's Day. But don't tell him where you got the cash."

"Aw, Pat, I can't . . ." He tried not to take the money the way kids do who are used to taking money from adults. I threw the bills into his car.

"Thanks, Pat," he said, and drove off.

*   *   *

I had been calling Mike Veeck once a month to keep him informed about my progress. "I'm throwing good, Mike," I told him in late May. "I get the ball over, I'll get a few guys out."

But he seemed less enthusiastic now. I asked him how Charlie Sheen was throwing.

"Oh, he's not gonna do it," he said.

After I hung up I was confused. A few days later I read in the paper that the St. Paul Saints had signed a woman, Ila Borders, to pitch for them this summer. So that was it. Mike didn't have the heart to tell me he couldn't have two novelties on his team at the same time. An old man and a broad. Too much even for the son of Bill Veeck. A year ago, this might have given me an excuse to pack it in. Heh, it wasn't *my* fault. I tried, didn't I? But it only made me angry. All those months of work, for *nothing!* I would not accept it. Nothing was going to stop me from stepping on a mound and pitching this summer.

I called Miles Wolfe, the president of the Northern League, and told him my problem. I had met Miles once when I was researching a story on the all-female Colorado Silver Bullets baseball team when they played an exhibition game against the Northern League All-Stars. I introduced myself before the game and asked Miles some questions.

Miles was one of those nerdy-looking baseball people with glasses whom people constantly misread. He looked like one of those baseball functionaries, farm directors, general managers, vice presidents, whose only interest in the game is as a business. But that was not Miles. He loved baseball as passionately as any player. I asked him a few questions that first day I'd met him, before he interrupted me. "I always wanted to meet you," he said. "I loved *A False Spring.*"

Now, over the phone, I told him how important it was for me to pitch this one last time.

"Don't worry," he said. "If Veeck won't pitch you, I'll find a team in the league that will. But there's something else you should think about."

"What?"

"There's another independent league, the Northeast League. They've got a team in Waterbury, Connecticut, the Spirit. You're from Connecticut, aren't you? Maybe it would be more fun for you to go back home to pitch? I know the Waterbury owner, Bob Wirsz. I'll call him for you."

As soon as I hung up with Miles, I felt that old fear coming back. The pressure to be me. I didn't mind pitching in St. Paul in front of people who had never known me. But in Waterbury, I'd be pitching in front of people who remembered my youthful successes. They had been burdened with them for years until they could finally delight in my failure. They would want to see me fail again. Make a fool of myself. I had fled Connecticut because as long as I lived there, I'd always be remembered for my most distant failure rather than my most recent successes as a writer. I'd written hundreds of magazine articles and nine books. After the first book I wrote in 1972, the *Bridgeport Post Telegram* carried a headline over a story about me that read: "Reject of the Diamond Writes Book."

There was another problem. My brother. Seventy now. But once he found out I'd be pitching in Waterbury he'd insist on coming to see me. We'd been estranged, on and off, over the years in part because he could never see me as anything other than that young boy he used to coach. Even in my fifties, he still called me "the kid." He still lectured me on how to live my life in such a condescending way he never failed to rouse my anger, make me act again like that hot-tempered kid storming around the pitcher's mound. I played into his hands with that anger. I became the hot-tempered kid again, so now the focus was not on his condescension but on my childish temper.

Was that what I was doing with Brian? I thought. Telling him how to live his life? Interfering in his life in a way I always hated when my brother did it to me? But there was a difference: I didn't tell Brian what to choose. I tried to tell him *how* to choose. I wanted to show him the process of choice, not the ends of choice.

Once my brother found out about my pitching, he'd want to be a part of it, the way he used to be. I'd have to listen to his instructions on how to pitch. I was beginning to lose my temper even as I thought about this. I wanted to do it alone, by myself, *for* myself, without his help. Jesus, it was all getting so fucking complicated! All these things fucking up the simple thing I wanted to do.

* * *

I had been estranged from my brother for years in my midthirties, when I saw him one day on the sidewalk in the town where we both lived. A towering man, 6′ 4″, 225 pounds, with a horsy face and beady eyes. He wore a gray worsted suit from the racks of J. Press Clothiers in New Haven, a rep tie, and wing-tip cordovans. He was standing perfectly still on the sidewalk, a stiff, unbending man capable only of breaking. He was staring up into a blinding sun, without blinking, as if defying God to strike him blind.

I blurted out, "Brother! What the hell are you doing?"

Still staring into the sun, he smiled and said, "It's good discipline." Finally, he looked down at me. "Brother," he said, and opened his arms. He hugged me to him and kissed me on the cheek. The men in my family always kissed one another. My father, in his late eighties today, still greets me with a kiss on the lips.

I smelled my brother's stale smell, the smell I remembered from childhood when we slept in the same bed. I scratched his back while he told me endless stories about Jimmy and the Ghost until I fell asleep. When I woke the next morning, I would ask how the story ended. He'd say, "Wait until tonight." But the story never ended.

I could feel the tears welling up in my eyes as we hugged on the sidewalk that day. My brother gripped my shoulders in his big strong hands and held me at arm's length, as if I was as light as a child.

"What's wrong, Brother? Why are you crying?"

"I love you, Brother," I said.

He smiled that ethereal smile of his. "Yes, Brother," he said. "That's always been the problem, hasn't it?"

I knew what he meant. "You wanna see my new office, George?"

He checked his watch, always the busy lawyer. "Only for a few minutes."

He followed me to my office on the third floor of an old Victorian house. I had quit my teaching job at an all-girls high school years before to try to become a writer. I had worked first out of an attic room in my house where I lived with my wife and five young children. Then I took the office downtown in the hope that it might inspire me to work harder, and because it was a refuge from a failing marriage.

I sat at my desk looking down at Main Street. My brother sat in the director's chair underneath the big orange "?" I had painted on the wall.

"So, how's the writing going, Brother?" he said.

"Not so hot." I told him there was no money coming in.

"How's the wife holding up?"

"The same. She's silent a lot." He nodded. "I'm thinking of leaving for a while," I said. "A little sabbatical."

He shook his head. "You can't run away from life's responsibilities," he said. I stared out the window at the traffic down below. "You know what your problem is, Brother?"

"No," I said.

He smiled his long-suffering smile. "You refuse to accept life's answer, Brother."

I nodded. "I know. It's just . . ." I could see the orange question mark directly behind his head. "I don't even know the fucking question, Brother."

We have rarely called each other by our given names. We have called each other mostly "Brother" all these years. It is only a half truth. My brother is not our father's natural son. Our mother was married briefly when she was a teenager and then divorced after she had a son. When my father married her years later, he promised to raise her son as his own. And he did. He was such a good father to my brother, better even than a natural father could have been, that for years when I was a boy it never dawned on me that my brother was only my half brother, even though we had different last names. I was ten when I learned the truth. At the time, my brother had some small fame as a high-school basketball coach. Each week his name would appear in our local newspaper after yet another of his team's triumphs. One day I brought one of those stories to school to show my friends.

"That's my brother," I said. My friends didn't believe me.

"He has a different name," they said.

I insisted, but they only laughed at me. I grew red-faced with anger and leapt at them all. I fought them on the playground at recess. I was sent home by the principal with my knees scraped and my nose bloodied.

When I told my father what the fight had been about, he told me the truth about my brother. He said he had not changed my brother's last name to his own because my brother's natural father was a wealthy man. My father wanted to make sure my brother shared in that wealth when his natural father died.

Because of his profession, my father knew he'd never be able to give my brother the things he wanted for him. Respectability. Legitimacy. A career that would make an Italian-American father proud. He thought that if my brother kept his natural father's last name, my brother would be entitled to his natural father's inheritance.

By the time my brother was ready to go to college, my father had no money. So he journeyed alone to upstate Massachusetts to talk to my brother's natural father, who hadn't seen his son in years. My father stood before that wealthy man, fingering his fedora hat in his hands, humbled, not my father's natural pose, and pleaded with my brother's father for the money to send his son to college. After he got the money, my father returned home. I heard him in the kitchen with my mother, cursing the day my brother's father was ever born.

My brother was so grateful for such acts from my father, for my father's very real love for him, that when he got married he wrote my father a letter. He told him not to worry. Even though he had a wife now, that didn't mean he'd neglect his brother. And he didn't. He always found time to come by our house at lunchtime to have a catch with me on the sidewalk while my parents sat on the cement porch steps and applauded my pitches. By the time I was twelve, George realized I had an extraordinary pitching talent. He began to "work" with me seriously to make sure I had a big league career. He took over my upbringing in other ways too, since my father was too busy gambling to raise a second son. It was always George who had long, serious talks with me when I misbehaved in school. I was the class clown.

When my father thought I was old enough, at thirty, to understand all this, he showed me my brother's letter. It was a sign of my brother's love for me, he said, with tears in his eyes. My flash of anger shocked my father. I tried to explain to him that this bargain they made, my brother's attempt to repay Dad for the natural affection he always showed him, made me only a piece of barter between them.

My father looked at me. "Why are you so jealous of my special relationship with George?"

I wasn't jealous. But he was right, it was a "special relationship."

*   *   *

When my parents were in their seventies, I used to stop by their small apartment for lunch. I was a grown man in my thirties now. But to them, and my brother, I would always be a little boy. My father and brother called me "the kid."

I entered their little apartment that smelled of sweet red peppers in olive oil and grated Pecorino cheese and steaming bowls of *pasta e fagioli*. My mother, a tiny, dark-skinned, birdlike woman with steel-gray hair, met me at the door. She was like most Italian women her age, more masculine than feminine, with a certain hardness she prided herself on. When I asked her once why my brother was so much older than I, she said, matter-of-factly, "Because you were an accident. There were no abortions in my day."

My mother stopped me in the doorway with a finger raised to her lips for silence.

"Dad's working," she whispered. My father stood by the wall phone in the kitchen, nodding into the receiver at the voice of his bookie. He was a distinguished-looking man with a ring of gray hair around his bald head. He had pale, blue-gray eyes and a prominent lower lip. He was dressed as he always was, in a navy blazer, rep tie, and gray flannel slacks.

Our little lunches began as they always did. My father and I sat at the tiny kitchen table while my mother hovered over us, urging us to *mangiare*. I asked my father to tell me yet another story about his gambling exploits. The time he'd met Arnold Rothstein, the man who fixed the 1919 Black Sox World Series. The time the French Canadian held a knife to his throat over a gambling debt my father refused to pay.

"What'd you say, Dad?" I said.

"I told him, 'Go ahead. See if you got the balls.' "

"Jesus!"

My father was an orphan who never knew his real father. He lived the first fifteen years of his life in an orphanage and then was out on the city streets, living by his wits. He turned to gambling for his livelihood, and to reaffirm his worth, his legitimacy, in the face of his father's rejection. When he married my mother, he was three years her junior. All the men in my family married women older than themselves. My father did it, he said, because "I wanted a wife and a mother."

My father supported my mother and her young son by hustling pool through upstate New York and into Canada. When my brother was fifteen and I was a baby, my father took him on one of his hustling trips. My brother was a tall, homely, gangly boy. He stood off in the shadows of some little country pool bar and watched as Dad hustled farmers and hardware salesmen and local hustlers. Dad always won, my brother told me years later. "Dad was the best," my brother said.

The losers flung their crumpled bills on the green felt table. My brother emerged from the shadows, scooped up the bills, and pocketed them. Later that night, my father and brother went back to their seedy hotel room with only a wrought-iron bed and a slowly churning overhead fan and a metal-legged washstand. Dad ordered up steaks for them from the bellman. Then he poured himself a scotch and soda. My brother sat cross-legged on the bed. He straightened out each of the crumpled bills and stacked them in neat piles.

How I wished I had been with my father and brother on those trips! I would have beamed to see my father shoot pool then! But I was only a baby. By the time I was a teenager, Dad no longer hustled pool. He preferred, instead, to make his living betting on baseball, basketball, and football games. I remember one afternoon in my thirties when I came to their apartment for lunch. My father was in bed with the flu, a thermometer stuck in his mouth. My mother was on the telephone in the kitchen. Wide-eyed and harried, she signaled me to silence with a finger to her lips. Spread out on the counter was a napkin on which she was writing out the evening betting line from my father's bookie. My father, groaning in bed, called out, "Flo, get the line on Frisco!" My mother, scribbling as fast as she could, the napkin bunching up, took her responsibility *so* seriously.

It wasn't much fun for me, in my thirties, to sit in my parents' kitchen and watch my father book bets over the phone. So I always asked about his pool-hustling trips with George. He played me off.

"That was long ago," he would say with a backhand toss of his hand. "I never made that much anyway."

The only stories my father liked to tell me when I became a man were about my brother. They were all designed to show how good my brother was ("A saint," my father said), how much he loved me, how I owed him the utmost loyalty and gratitude. I never needed to be told such things when I was a boy, or as a man, either. But my father was obsessed that I should love my brother, which, in a way, insulted us both. He made what was a natural instinct in me, my brotherly affection for George, an unnatural burden. On us both. The *endless* stories of my brother's sacrifice for me! How he had changed my diapers! How he had worked at night washing toilets to buy me a birthday present! How he had understood why I poured Pepsi Cola in his car's gas tank when I, a child of seven, heard my brother say he had run out of gas! How he had interceded for me when Ma and Dad wanted to spank me for throwing the cat out of the third-floor window because I had heard them saying that cats always landed on their feet! How he used to take me for Sunday walks in my baby carriage! Housewives stopped him to exclaim over the "adorable little girl with the golden curls." My brother returned home in tears. He insisted my mother let him take me straight to a barber shop.

"He was always trying to make a man of you," my father said. "Even then."

My father was right, of course. My brother *was* always trying to make a man of me. He pointed out my every deficiency as a sign of weakness. As a twelve-year-old, I was soft, pudgy, cherubic looking. My brother, at twenty-seven, was tall and lean and hard. He told me that being fat was a sign I lacked character, resolve, discipline. Years later, I had taken up bodybuilding and become a muscular thirty-year-old. My brother, in his forties, had begun to get fat. He told me that my obsession with my body was unmanly. "A woman's vanity," he said.

In my teens, I was the star of my brother's high-school basketball team. He insisted I call him "Coach" during the season, never "Brother." He called me by my last name in front of the other players. He belittled me constantly during practice. At the same time, he devised elaborate plays for me to get off my soft, feathery, jump shot. When I scored with that beautiful shot during games, it was always because of the brilliance of his plays—for *me*, his brother—never my own talent. In this way, he not only shared in my talent, he created it, controlled it.

I sprained my ankle before an important game in my junior year. I told my brother I didn't think I could play. He accused me of "dogging it." He looked at me with disgust. "Show some guts," he said. So I played on a painfully sprained ankle and scored thirty points by a sheer act of will. Still, we lost. After the game, he accused me of being selfish for playing hurt "just so you could score your points."

It was a game my brother played with me. He made manhood so elusive to me. It shifted with his whims I was never privy to. Which was the point. I would never be a man, in his eyes or mine, as long as he kept shifting its definition.

When I was about to marry at nineteen, he summoned me to his office for little talks—long monologues, really, by him. He sat behind his lawyer's desk in his J. Press suit. I sat before him like a supplicant, hunched forward, listening to his rambling monologues. He told me that sex was only for procreation, never pleasure, because then it would give women power over men. Men had to rule their families, he said. With that rule came responsibilities. He had to make as much money as possible for his family, or else he was not a real man.

"But what about happiness?" I said. "Shouldn't a man do a job he loves first?" He waved the back of his hand at me in disgust. "It isn't a man's place in life to be happy," he said. "It's to be responsible."

Even then, I had begun to disagree with my brother. I was beginning to have my own ideas on what it meant to be a man. I began to argue now with my brother, whom I worshiped so, during our little lunches at the diner near his lawyer's office. I would get flushed in the face, stammering, while he sat calmly in front of me, dismissing my childish thoughts. Our lunches always ended in the same way now, with me standing up, shouting "You're fucking crazy!" and storming out. He always called me an hour later. The conciliatory older brother with the soothing voice.

"You can't fight me, Brother," he'd say. "You can't fight good." I'd slam down the receiver in frustration.

Over the years, I began to realize that he created these little scenarios on purpose to anger me. It was his way of fulfilling the role Dad had prescribed for him. It was his way of reaffirming his legitimacy over me. The older, wiser, compassionate brother trying to make a man of the immature, hot-tempered, younger brother. He *was* always trying to make a man of me. But only up to that point, never beyond, at which I would become independent of him.

It was a crushing blow to my father when his two sons began to drift apart. He saw it as my fault. "After all your brother's done for you!" he said. My father always turned our disagreements into moral issues that revealed a certain lack in me. When I grew bored with the ponderous tweeds and flannels of J. Press, which I had affected in imitation of my brother, I began to dress in jeans and sneakers and workshirts. "Like a boy!" my father said. "Look at your hair, for chrissakes!"

My father was most crushed by my decision not to become a lawyer and join my brother's firm. A fantasy of his. I would become a junior partner. Then, when I matured, I'd be an equal partner with my brother.

"You don't get it, Dad," I said. "I'll always be a junior partner."

He responded only with contempt. "A writer!" he said. "What kind of work is that for a man?"

I didn't have the heart to tell my father that it was my brother who talked me out of the law. That I had always felt he never really wanted me to be his partner. He hated the law, he said. It was stifling. Just meaningless paper-pushing.

"Then why did you become a lawyer?" I said.

He smiled his ethereal smile, turned up the palms of his hands to heaven as if presenting an offering, and said, "For Dad."

"Fuck Dad! Quit and do something you love."

Still smiling, he just shook his head at my simplistic ignorance. "There's more to it than that, Brother," he said.

I sold my first magazine story when I was thirty. When I got a copy of that magazine, I rushed to my brother's office to show him. I entered by the back door as he had instructed me ever since I had grown my scruffy beard. "I don't want my clients to think I'm representing criminals," he had said, only half kidding.

"I'm busy now, Brother," he said from behind his desk.

I showed him the magazine with my byline. He looked at it without interest. Then a pained smile spread over his face as if he had somehow been defeated. He tossed the magazine among the papers on his desk.

"I told you I don't have time," he said.

I felt tears welling up in my eyes, then anger. "How could you?"

He looked at me with that smile of his and said, "Why do you always have to be better than me, Brother?"

We didn't speak much after that for years. My brother tried, at first, to wear down my resolve by the sheer force of his will. But after I had slammed down the receiver enough times on the sound of his maddeningly soothing voice, he simply stopped calling. He was relieved, it seemed to me, that he no longer had to fulfill the little charade of our brotherhood after all those years. God, how he must have hated always being the loving brother! How he must have hated the terrible pressure that I, unwittingly, had burdened him with. How he must have hated—no, I will never believe that—how he must have *resented* me!

I began to understand all these things over the years of our estrangement. That understanding gradually wore away my anger. In my forties, we began to talk again. Gingerly at first. Then the way we always had at our little lunches. My brother, in his sixties now, expounding. Me, in my early forties, listening. Two men who have finally made their uneasy peace. I no longer got flushed in the face. No longer stood up in midlunch and stormed off. I just sat there, listening, nodding, loving my brother by giving him what he needed. My acquiescence. When I did speak, it was only to tell him about my problems so that he could slip as effortlessly into his role over me as he did into those J. Press suits. It was the only role he could ever play with me, I knew now.

My father was pleased by our reconciliation. But still he was hard on me, harder than he could ever be on my brother, as if to punish me for all those years of anguish he suffered during our estrangement. When he found out I had been having affairs while I was married, he shook his head in disgust. "A real womanizer, eh!" he said, with satisfaction. Like most gamblers, my father couldn't countenance the other vices.

"If it had been my brother," I said, "could you have called *him* a womanizer?"

My father looked truly pained. "I couldn't do that," he said. "It would hurt him." After a long pause, he said with a smile, "Why have you always been jealous of our special relationship?"

"I'm not jealous. I just think it's sick."

But it wasn't sick. It was perfectly understandable. My father was harder on me than on my brother because I was his natural son. His only blood relation in all the world. My brother had been rejected by his real father. My father knew how that felt. Alone. Unwanted. Adrift in life. He was determined that my brother would never feel that way too, even if it had to be at my expense. It was their common bond that shaped or misshaped their lives. In the process, it excluded me. So what? I was my father's natural son. I was supposed to know these things if I was ever to become a man. I was supposed to know that despite everything, these two men loved me. Everything else I felt was the self-pity of someone who would never be a man. A pampered boy who would never realize how blessed he was to have not one, but two fathers.

ELEVEN

A FEW DAYS AFTER I talked to Miles Wolfe I got a call from Bob Wirsz, the Waterbury Spirit owner. He was circumspect over the phone. "I'll pitch you," he said. "But I don't want this to be a joke."

"It's no joke, Bob. I've been throwing five months now. I'm throwing good. I get the ball over, I won't embarrass you."

He agreed to let me start a game on July 29. I told him I'd be in New Rochelle, New York, covering a golf tournament in early July.

"I'll drive up to Waterbury," I said, "and throw on the side for you and your manager. If I don't look good, don't pitch me."

A few days after Wirsz called, a friend from my college days, John Hennessey, called me. We'd kept in touch only intermittently since I'd moved to Fort Lauderdale in 1983. He told me he was friends with Wirsz. When Wirsz found out that John knew me, he told him, "I hope this Jordan doesn't make a joke of this."

"What'd you tell him, John?" I said over the phone.

"What'd I tell him? What do ya think, P.J.? I told him, 'Bob, trust me. Pat Jordan will never make a fool of himself on the mound.'"

I continued throwing with Brian into June. I was throwing the ball better than ever. I'd cut my fliers down to one in ten fastballs. My fastball was consistently around the plate but still not consistently a strike. But my slider was sharp. I could throw it for a strike almost at will. But now I feared I was deceiving myself. Maybe Mark was right. I needed to pitch to batters to see if I really was a pitcher again. I had recaptured a semblance of my talent, but had I regained that killer instinct I had as a young pitcher who thought he was unhittable? The thought of pitching again in Connecticut had brought back all my old fears. Would I be found lacking? Would I make a fool of myself? I hadn't worried about these things when I thought I was going to pitch in St. Paul.

I came to the park to throw with Brian one afternoon. He snapped at me, "Take that fucking cigar outta your mouth." I threw it on the ground. "Now let's work. You only got a coupla weeks."

It was an unbearably hot, sunny day. I started to sweat as soon as I began to throw. Within minutes, I was throwing full speed.

"Let's do a coupla innings," Brian said.

I worked the first batter to a 3–2 count, then walked him on a slider just low and away. "That was a fucking strike, Brian," I said.

"Not today it isn't."

I was already breathing heavily. I got 2–2 on the next batter and then reared back and threw a fastball. Brian caught it, inside and at the knees to a righthanded batter.

"Fucking ay!" He smiled. "Strike three."

I smiled. "A good one, Bri?"

"That was the best fastball you've ever thrown."

"Ever?"

"To me, anyway. I'll bet it was ninety."

I smiled. "You serious? You're not shitting me?"

"Come on. You got two more outs."

I walked the next batter on a 3–2 fastball that just missed the outside corner. I put my hands on my hips and glared at Brian. He fired the ball back to me. "Stop begging," he said.

I was breathing heavily and drenched with sweat in the heat. I felt weak, almost exhausted, with two runners on base and only one out. I started off the third batter with a slider for a strike. I threw two more sliders that were low and away. I stood on the mound, gasping for breath, with the ball in my hand. I began my motion and threw a fastball down the middle.

"Strike two," Brian said. "Just hope he was taking on that pitch."

"I suppose you woulda ripped it, you little shit."

Brian pointed to the leftfield scoreboard. "Bounced it right off the scoreboard for a double and two RBIs."

"Fuck you!" He crouched down for my next pitch. I threw another fastball low and on the outside corner to a righthanded batter.

"He's outta there!" I yelled.

"I'm the friggin' umpire," Brian said. Then he smiled. "Good pitch. Maybe eighty-eight."

But I had nothing left. I walked the next batter on four pitches to load the bases. After the last pitch, a wild fastball high that Brian had to leap for, my shoulders slumped.

"That's it, Bri. I've had it. I'm beat."

Brian walked halfway out to the mound. "No way," he said. "Bases loaded. Two outs. You're not gettin' off the friggin' mound till you get the third out." He fired the ball back to me.

He pissed me off. The little shit! Who'd he think he was? His father. I had all I could do to keep from throwing the ball at the back of his head as he walked back to the plate. He turned around and got into his crouch. He gave me a big target.

"Come on," he said. "Show me what you got."

I threw a good fastball waist high, inside to a righthander.

"Strike!" He threw the ball back to me. "Again."

I threw another fastball that nicked the low outside corner.

"Strike two." He fired the ball back to me. "Again."

"Slider," I said.

"No. Another fastball. Right here." He held the glove waist high and inside to a righthander. "Make him swing through it."

I began my motion, reared back, and threw as hard as I could. I could hear the ball ripping through the air. It hit Brian's glove with a loud *crack*.

He bounced out of his crouch, grinning. "Fucking ay!" he said. "Even I couldn't hit that one."

I collapsed. I sat down on the mound, exhausted. I was panting for breath when he walked out to the mound. "You're throwin' *good*," he said.

"You sure?"

"Jeez, Pat! I'm tellin' you."

"I don't know, Bri. I still haven't faced a batter yet. How do I know?"

"Because I *told* you." Poor Brian. Even he, of infinite patience, was losing it with me. But I wasn't sure he was right. I thought I was throwing good. But I didn't trust him. He was only a kid who liked me too much. Besides, he didn't have the killer instinct himself. He was only faking it with me. It was his only weakness as an athlete, but his best attribute as a human being. He was a good kid.

I needed *my* sense of indomitability to overcome the pressure I'd face in Waterbury. All those fans who remembered me. My brother. What if I failed him again? He never did understand my failure in the minor leagues. He never saw my failure, as I had. Its roots. He remembered me only as I had been, when he coached me. Unhittable. I went away on a cloud of success and came home a leaf blown by the wind.

It wasn't enough to have fun with Brian. Having fun was an excuse to fail. I needed this other thing I had once, and lost. This thing that every great athlete had and never lost. Will.

*   *   *

I was standing under the shade of a palm tree on a hot South Florida morning in early July. I saw her walking toward me under the blazing sun, across the parking lot of Florida Atlantic University. She was dressed, as always, in a man's polo shirt, baggy khaki shorts, and flip-flops. She looked shorter than I remembered, maybe 5' 8." But then she had always appeared to me to be of mythic proportions when she was an athlete. Now, at fifty-six, she didn't look so mythic. She looked like an older woman gone fleshy with age. She seemed broader than she was tall, broad shoulders, broad hips, thick, shapeless legs. Once those legs were so muscular that they could push her off a pitching rubber with such power that the muscles in her thighs trembled. Batters trembled.

She came closer, her head hung slightly, her eyes staring down at the pavement. She moved in that loose-limbed, shoulder-shifting way of an athlete perpetually limbering up for some as yet unspecified contest. Any contest. It did not matter.

When she was almost to me, she looked up. Her plain, small-featured face was creased from the sun and age. Her small, narrowed blue eyes were still suspicious. Her thin lips still unsmiling. Her short reddish hair still parted to one side.

I stepped out from the shade of the palm tree. She looked at me, a man of fifty-six, with a white beard. "You got old," she said, and smiled. It was the first time I ever saw her smile. She was always so grim, with those thin lips. She was wearing lipstick.

"Ah, Joanie!" I said. "It's been a long time."

"Thirty-eight years."

When I signed my $50,000 bonus contract with the Braves I immediately quit my part-time job as a sporting-goods salesman for the Arctic Sports Shop in Bridgeport. The owner called me a week before I was to start my professional career in the Class D Nebraska State League.

"We're going to have a media day for you, Pat," he said. He was a short, bald, excitable little man. Spittle formed on his lips when he talked. "Just the two best pitchers in the country."

After I hung up, it occurred to me that he had said, "two best pitchers in the country." It must have been a slip of the tongue I thought then, at eighteen. There was no young pitcher as good as me.

I arrived at the sport shop in the afternoon. The owner came toward me in that funny, sideways way of walking he had, like he was sliding on ice. He pumped my hand in congratulations for my bonus contract. Then he began introducing me to the sportswriters there. I noticed he had hung red, white, and blue bunting from the ceiling. He had also set up a card table with coffee and punch and doughnuts. The older men he introduced me to all stared at me with that lustful look of older men staring at the infinite possibilities of youth they no longer possessed. It embarrassed me. I excused myself and went over to the wall stacked high with baseball gloves.

I had often worked alone at the shop late at night. When there were no customers, I would go over to that rack of gloves, take one and a baseball, and then, in that deserted store, I would begin pitching in pantomime, another no-hitter. But this day, there was someone else at the rack of gloves. A blockily built girl in a pink, linen, shirt-waist dress fluffed out with crinolines. She already had on a glove and was pounding a baseball into it in the same way I did when I was alone in the shop. I heard the owner's sliding footsteps behind me.

"Pat," he said, smiling. "I want you to meet Joan Joyce, the other best pitcher in the country. She's just signed with the Raybestos Brakettes."

The girl looked at me with small, suspicious eyes and thin, unsmiling lips. I stared back. Two young hotshot jocks checking out the competition. Finally, she stuck out her hand. I looked at it. Grudgingly, I shook it. A girl! I was humiliated. The thought has occurred to me over the years that maybe Joanie was humiliated too. I am certain she always thought of herself as the best young pitcher in the country then too.

After I left baseball, the phrase I always use, I was too busy with my ordinary life for sports. Yet once a week I drove to Stratford, Connecticut, the home of the Raybestos Brakettes, to watch Joanie pitch. By then she was the greatest female fastpitch softball pitcher in the world.

Why did I go when I didn't have the stomach to see other men my age pitch in the Senior City League? All they did was remind me of my lost promise. But Joanie, somehow I equated my career with hers. We were joined at the hip, at least once, when we were both the best young pitchers in the country in 1959.

It is difficult to describe just how great Joan Joyce was as a softball pitcher. Even her records, after twenty-six years of pitching, do not do her justice. She herself described her games as "boring." All those strikeouts, no-hitters, perfect games. She was 42–0 one year, with 38 shutouts. She lost only 42 games in twenty-six years, while winning almost 800. She averaged 16 strikeouts every 7 innings, pitched 103 no-hitters, 33 perfect games, and led the Brakettes to 12 national amateur championships in eighteen years. During that span she was described by an umpire who stood behind the plate during many of her performances as one of the three greatest fastpitch softball players in the world. He added, "And the other two are men."

Watching Joanie pitch was not like watching a *girl* pitch. I never had the sense that Joanie was doing well something foreign to her sex. That she had mastered an essentially masculine activity, which, no matter how well she had mastered it, never let me forget that she was still a girl doing a man's thing. She was no pale mimicry of a male athlete the way the women playing in the Women's National Basketball Association are, moving and jumping as if wading through water. Joanie transcended her sex. She was just a pitcher.

She had a 114-mph fastball that never went in a straight line. It rose, or sank, or tailed in or away. She fired it from her hip, with a slingshot motion. Her pitcher's arm shot back behind her, then shot forward, the ball brushing her right thigh. As soon as she released the ball her momentum carried her forward to her left. She had to make little hops on her left foot to retain her balance. The big ball approached the plate as a blur. It was already in the catcher's glove when the batter swung. It was pitiful watching Joanie pitch against other women. No matter how well *they* had mastered a man's game, they never let me forget they were *girls* playing a man's game. For those women, softball was a learned activity. They thought about what they did on the field. I could see it. Joanie pitched on instinct. It was just part of her nature. She *was* a pitcher.

Her games *were* boring to watch. For others, maybe, but never me, and certainly never for Joanie. "My games are boring to everyone but me," she once said. "I set up challenges for myself, a pitch in a certain spot, a no-hitter, a perfect game." The year after she was 42–0, she developed a changeup, not because she needed it but merely as an intellectual exercise.

"I can lose," she once said, "but only by luck." That was another thing about Joanie that I could identify with. She talked about herself and her talent so objectively, without false, feminine humility. She was merely stating a fact she saw no reason to sugarcoat. When a local sportswriter once suggested to me that I owed my high-school success to my coach and my teammates, I just looked at him. "Are you kidding?" I said. "Eighteen strikeouts a game I owe to *them?*"

Joanie's pitching never bored me because I could read her pitcher's mind as she worked. Two fastballs on the outside corner of the plate. And then, with the batter leaning across the plate, she'd fire a rising fastball up and in on their hands. They'd swing feebly, the ball above their head in the catcher's mitt before they even *began* their swing. No one could touch her. The only games she ever lost *were* by luck. I remember a tournament game she lost in the 20th inning, 1–0, on a walk, a bloop single, and a sacrifice fly. She had struck out 36.

During her career, Joanie occasionally pitched against men's teams in exhibitions. She did only marginally less well than she did against women. Maybe a strikeout an inning instead of two. She once struck out Hank Aaron in an exhibition. Another time she pitched to Ted Williams, the greatest hitter who ever lived, the year he retired from baseball in 1961. After ten futile minutes swinging at Joanie's pitches, Williams threw down his bat in disgust. "I can't hit her," he said.

"He missed every one," said Joanie. "You know, he tried to bait me before I pitched to him. He told my coach he didn't like the high tight pitch. I said, "Come on. Ted Williams? He's got the best eyes in baseball!' I threw him nothing but drops."

Joan Joyce was not a graceful athlete. She could not run fast or jump high. She had little of the all-around athletic talent of an Olympic athlete like Jackie Joyner Kersee. She was always a blue-collar athlete. What other female athletes achieved through grace and style and fluidity, Joan achieved through brute force, hard work, instinct, and an indomitable will. "I *hate* to lose!" she said in her fifties. When she competed in the Women's Superstars competition in 19TK, she found herself among a host of more famous female athletes who viewed the competition as only partly a "real" competition and partly an opportunity to finally meet other athletes they'd only heard about. The competitors went to dinner together. They sat around in each other's rooms telling tales. They laughed with each other. Joanie did not laugh, nor did she speak to her other competitors. The only time she joined them in their pursuits was when they all rented mopeds and went for a leisurely ride. Joanie tried to outrace every one of them from stoplight to stoplight. For Joanie, there was no sisterhood among competitors.

Joanie mastered her sport to a degree no other female athlete ever mastered her sport. She is the only woman athlete *ever* who could have moved on to a man's team in her sport and been almost as successful. No other female golfer, no tennis player, no sprinter, no other female athlete could ever compete as successfully against men as Joanie could. That's why she was the greatest female athlete who ever lived.

Joanie and I sat at an outdoor table next to the FAU swimming pool. Mothers watched their small children take lessons in the water. Joanie did not notice them. She lit a cigarette. She has smoked since she was thirteen.

"But I never drank a beer until I quit softball," she said.

"Why not?" I said.

She looked at me as if I should understand. "Because I was an athlete," she said. "I always was, since I was nine."

"Why did you like sports so much?"

Again she looked at me. "It's all I knew. I mean, what else would a kid want to do? I was just like any other kid. I wanted to be an athlete or a cop or a carpenter." It did not occur to Joanie that not every little girl growing up in Waterbury, Connecticut, a blue-collar factory town, wanted to be an athlete or a cop or a carpenter.

"Across the street from where we lived when I was twelve," she said, "a construction crew was preparing to build a house. I went there every day to help the carpenter, an old guy about seventy. He let me carry the wood and the cinder blocks at first, and then he let me help put on the roof, the tile in the bathroom, everything. It was the most fun I ever had. He said he'd hire me in a minute if he could." She smiled. "Eventually my parents bought that house I built. They still live there."

She came to softball through her father, Joe, who played on the Waterbury Bombers fastpitch team. He'd take her and her younger brother, Joe Jr., to all his games. At nine, Joanie would warm up that night's pitcher. "The players always worked with me," she said, "teaching me things. They were tough, shot-and-a-beer guys, but I never had any problems with them. They treated me just like any other athlete. You know, I've never gotten any negative reaction from men. Maybe it's because I had so much talent." She has a basketball in her office that was signed by John Havlicek and Dave Cowens. Cowens wrote, "To Joan, a gifted athlete and a great lady."

When Joanie was twelve, she played on the boys' Little League team as a catcher. In her first game, she hit two doubles and a single. She was almost as great a hitter as she was a pitcher. She had the second most career hits of any Brakette; the most career doubles, the most career triples. But before her second game the league passed a rule prohibiting girls from playing with the boys. It was the only time Joanie ever experienced sex discrimination in sports.

"I just switched over to softball," she said, "and basketball." In the winter, she would shovel off snow from the outside basketball courts near her home and practice shooting by herself. She made the Crosby High School varsity girls' basketball team as a freshman. She was so good that her coach limited the amount of points she could score to twelve before she pulled Joanie from the lineup. She never got to play more than a few minutes each game. (As an AAU basketball player in her twenties, Joanie once scored 67 points in a tournament game.)

"When I went to class after a game," she said, "the men's coaches always asked how I'd done the night before. They always supported me. We had this mailman, his name was Tony Marinaro, he was a softball pitcher. He used to stop at my house every afternoon on his rounds to pitch with me. He told me he wanted me to pitch for the Brakettes. I'd never even heard of them then."

During her career with the Brakettes, Joanie supported herself first by teaching and coaching in high school, and then with her Joan Joyce's All-Star Travel Agency. When she took a job as the Bethel High School women's volleyball coach in the 1970s, she was told the men's coaches were horrible to the women's coaches. They often refused to let them use the gym for practice. On Joanie's first day, she went up to the men's basketball coach and told him she needed the gym that day for volleyball practice. He said, "Certainly." She had expected to have to do battle with him. When she asked him why he didn't give her a hard time, he said, "But you're different, Joan. What *you* do and what *they* did is different."

"They respected me, I guess," she said. What they respected, what most men respected about Joanie, was not only her talent but her attitude about sports. ("I *hate* to lose!") Joanie was a woman ahead of her time. Many of her contemporary female athletes approached sports as an exercise, as something to have fun with, to *try* to do their best at. "Trying" was the operative word among women athletes of Joanie's day. They "tried hard" and then congratulated the winner. But "trying" was never enough for Joanie. She never liked congratulating the winner.

When her softball career was winding down in the late 70s, Joan decided to take up another sport, golf. She moved to south Florida and spent two years learning to play a game she had only played once in her life before. She was thirty-five. By thirty-seven, she was a professional on the women's tour.

"I did okay," she said, taking a drag on her cigarette. "I made enough money to survive. I mean, you put the ball down and you hit it! What's so hard about that? The ball isn't *moving*."

She further supported herself by teaching golf until she got her present job coaching golf and softball at FAU in 1994. The young women athletes she works with now confuse her.

"They have no clue," she said. "They have better conditioning, better equipment, more advantages like scholarships, money, and recognition, and better coaching, like myself. But they don't have the attitude. They don't want it as bad. When my girls softball team lost a doubleheader this year, they weren't even *upset!* They wanted to know where we were going to *eat!* I screamed, " 'We lost two and you wanna *eat?'* " Joanie shook her head in disbelief. She calmed herself and went on. "I was good because I never tried to prove I was as good as the guys. I never had any goals in sports except to strike out every batter I faced. I worked at being as good an athlete as I could. If I wasn't good, I worked harder. I guess you could say I had the same attitude as men. I remember pitching a nineteen-inning game once. The umpires wanted to call it, zero–zero, because they thought the girls were getting tired. I said, " 'What? You want me to pitch nineteen innings and come away with *nothing!* ' "

I stood up to leave. I looked down at Joanie and hesitated. Finally, I decided to tell her.

"I'm pitching again, Joanie." I waited for her to laugh at me, a man of fifty-six, "pitching again." But she didn't. Nor did she ask me why. She knew why. I was a pitcher, wasn't I? Like her. She just stared at me and waited for me to go on.

"I'm gonna pitch for the Waterbury Spirit." I smiled. "Your old hometown, Joanie."

"Are you in shape?" A pitcher's question.

"I think so. I've been throwing three times a week for the past six months."

"How you throwing?" Another pitcher's question.

"Pretty good. My fastball's in the mideighties. I got a nice slider too."

She shook her head. "That can be a dangerous pitch."

"Yeh. But I can throw it for a strike whenever I want. I like to keep it on lefties. You know, jam the shit outta them."

She smiled. "Batters don't like that tight pitch, do they?"

"No. A lot of pitchers are afraid to come inside."

"But you've got to." She shrugged. "You just can't miss, get that slider out over the plate"—she touched her fingertips to her thin painted lips—"you can kiss it goodbye."

I sat back down and lit a cigar. I leaned across the table, closer to Joanie. We exhaled smoke at each other. The smoke hovered around our faces, the tanned, creased faces of two old pitchers sitting in the Florida sun.

"It's like with fastballs," I said. "They say good batters murder fastballs."

"Yeh. Like all fastballs are equal." She laughed, remembering *her* fastball. I remembered mine. Jim Hicks on one knee.

"I'm having trouble throwing it for a strike now," I said. "I know if I can get it over I can get guys out."

"Don't worry about it," she said. "You get on the mound, it'll all come back. You never lose it."

TWELVE

I RENTED A CAR at LaGuardia and headed straight for Waterbury, two and a half hours away. It was early Wednesday afternoon in the second week of July. Wirsz expected me in Waterbury by 5 P.M. to throw on the sidelines for him and his manager before that night's game.

I lit a cigar as I passed Shea Stadium, heading for the Whitestone Bridge. I felt good, excited, nervous, the way I always felt before I was going to pitch. It was a good nervousness I learned to control even when I was in Little League. I kept it bottled up during the day, like a mysterious potion boiling inside me. I'd go downtown to Bridgeport to buy stamps for my collection to keep my mind off pitching. Then I'd go to the movies. I'd sit in the darkened theater for three hours, lost in Buck Rogers serials, Abbott and Costello movies, Roy Rogers, and Hopalong Cassidy movies. At four o'clock I'd be outside in the blinding late-afternoon sunlight that made me squint. Now I remembered my pitching again. I felt the nervousness coming back. When I got home I'd go straight to my room to calm myself. I'd put the stamps I'd bought in my albums, carefully, neatly, for another hour until it was time to put on my uniform. I felt the nervousness coming back, trying to escape the bottle, so I never ate dinner before my 6 P.M. games. By the time I took the mound I was ready to explode. *Now* I let loose all that nervousness that became an almost maniacal energy and pitched yet another no-hitter.

As I passed through the Whitestone Bridge toll I thought how good it would feel to be in a uniform again. I wondered what the Waterbury Spirit uniforms looked like. My team. I wondered who my teammates were. Even after thirty-five years, I knew that once I put on that uniform they would be my teammates even if it was only for this one game. I wanted to do right by them. My teammates. They were tied for first place. I didn't want to give up five runs in the first inning and put them in a hole before they even came to bat. I didn't expect to strike out the side. But I had to be respectable.

They were the same kind of players who had gravitated to the Northern League. One of them was even an ex-major leaguer, Dave Fleming. He had won seventeen games for Seattle in the early 1990s and now was trying to come back from rotator-cuff surgery. Comeback? Like me?

I wondered how they'd see me when I walked into the locker room. Probably not the way I see myself. It was still hard for me to see myself the way others did. An old man with a white beard, smoking a cigar, dressed in ridiculous Hawaiian shirts. I looked down at the shirt I was wearing. Aqua blue with pink flamingos. I was wearing shorts and flip-flops. A cool dude from Paradise. Living on spongecake. Sipping margaritas. I assumed everyone saw the me I saw. I would never escape my solipsism. It was exhausting being me. My *obsessive* kindnesses. They were meant only incidentally to please others, and primarily to assuage my own pathological guilt. To prove I was not the man *I* knew I was. Which was why I understood Bubba, and Hoshi was a mystery to me. I could never understand Hoshi's pure selflessness no matter how much I aspired to it. I was, after all, Bubba. But that is an insult to Bubba. He is never as solipsistic as I am. My kindnesses were always mere acts meant to reflect on myself. That's how I became a writer. When I first started working on that newspaper in my early twenties, I had no intention of becoming a writer. It was just a job that allowed me to do my homework late at night until I graduated from college and then could get a real job.

One afternoon, driving home from college, I picked up a hitchhiker. He was a tall, rugged college freshman named Ed McCarthy. I had heard about his high-school football successes at my former alma mater, Fairfield Prep. I asked him where he was going to school now. He said Yale. I asked about his football. He seemed embarrassed to talk about himself. He changed the subject and asked about my writing for the newspaper. I had just begun to publish bylined articles on local high-school sports events. I talked about my stories until I dropped him off.

A few days later, Ed was killed in a car accident. The obituary on the front page of our newspaper described him as the greatest quarterback prospect Yale had ever had. He was destined for greatness at Yale. An NFL future had been predicted for him. I went over to my editor with the obituary and told him about my ride with Ed.

"Can I write a column about it?" I said.

"Go ahead," he said. "Let's see what you can do."

When the column was printed, readers called and wrote to the paper to compliment me on such a fitting tribute for such a fine young man. I had written about how humble Ed had been about his talent and, conversely, how self-obsessed I had been about mine. Some of those readers asked to speak to me. They told me how moved they were by what I'd written. A day later, I went to Ed McCarthy's wake. The funeral parlor was filled with grieving friends and relatives. I walked down the aisle, past those grieving people, and knelt down in front of Ed's coffin. I looked at him, with his chalky-white skin. He did not look like the rugged young man I had picked up in my car. He looked like a wax figure from a museum.

I blessed myself and said a prayer for Ed's soul. I should have been praying for mine. I prayed, mere words, because I was distracted. I could feel the eyes of everyone behind me boring into me. *Who is this young man? Oh, that's Pat Jordan. The writer who wrote such a wonderful story about Ed.* I felt diffused with pleasure that filled me up, like a drug. I felt a great power in me. It was not unlike the power I once had on a pitcher's mound. I felt that power return to me. I could make people notice me again, only now there was a difference. The power I had as a pitcher was always one-dimensional. People noticed my talent but not *me*. That power was purer, in a way, than the power I now felt, kneeling there, mouthing the words of prayer. The power I now felt as a writer was twofold. I could make people notice my talent as a writer, *and* deceive them into reading into that talent a host of human attributes—compassion, sensitivity, selflessness—I knew I did not have. I could create any false me I wanted to with my new talent. The grieving, compassionate young man at another man's wake. Only I knew that I was kneeling there to draw attention from the young man in the coffin to the young man praying for his soul.

Even now, exposing my fraud these many years later, I am deceiving my readers into believing that any man who could reveal his utter baseness with such honesty (the most facile virtue, and my greatest), must be a better man than the one he is revealing. Not so. I am what I am, not what I write.

*　*　*

I knew that when I entered my teammates' locker room I'd see players no differently than I saw myself. But what would they see? What would they think? Would they look at me with disdain as an old man making a joke of their game? I had to put them at ease before they saw me throw. I remembered a line from *Bull Durham*. I'd toss it off at them as I entered the locker room. A wise-guy line. Let them think this was no big thing for me. That I was cocky, like most pitchers, not a scared old man.

I passed the first Westport exit and remembered how it had been when I was younger, a man of thirty-seven, and first dating Susan. We used to meet at Bunyan's, a singles' bar in Westport, in the early 1980s. The bar was always crowded with men and women in their thirties, on the make. Susan and I were still in the early stages of a courtship that was almost entirely sexual. We couldn't keep our hands off one another, even in that crowded bar.

One night, as a joke, I threw Susan over my shoulders and carried her like a sack of potatoes through the bar. The drunken men and women cheered me as I carried Susan into the manager's office and closed the door. I dropped her down on the manager's desk.

"We'll wait a few minutes," I said. "Let them think we screwed. Then we'll go back out."

She looked at me with wide, glassy eyes. "Why waste the time?" she said, peeling off her panties. "Let's do it." She pulled me down on top of her as she lay down on the desk.

I was smiling to myself at the memory of that night, when we were young—younger, anyway—when I saw the Fairfield exit. Mill Plain Road. My brother's house. I'd have to call him sooner or later. Jesus, he was like a black cloud.

I lit another cigar as I came to the exit that led to the house where I was raised and where I raised my family. I was only a boy of four when I moved into that house, and I was a man of forty-four when I left it. My parents still lived only a few blocks away from that house in an apartment. My mother was ninety now, my father eighty-seven. I hadn't seen them in five years. It had been that long since I finally made my peace with my father and his gambling.

*   *   *

I told my father a magazine would pay for us to go gambling at the Foxwoods Casino near Ledyard, Connecticut. He didn't act thrilled. He knew I'd never been much enamored of his gambling. I never saw it like my brother did, as Dad's personal idiosyncrasy that made him so amusing, a character out of Damon Runyon. I saw it as a debilitating vice that almost destroyed us all.

We left Bridgeport for Ledyard, a two-hour ride, in a driving snowstorm at five o'clock on a Saturday morning—Dad and I going to gamble together for the first time in our lives. He was eighty-two, an old man by some standards, but as young, vigorous, and quick-witted as always. I hated to admit it, but it was gambling that kept him young.

"We've got three hundred dollars to gamble with," I said.

"Well, then we'll go right down the line like Maggie Kline."

I looked across at him. "Now what the hell does that mean?"

"It's a Prohibition expression." He smiled. "It means we'll shoot it all."

Jeez, I thought. The old man will never change. Just a few weeks ago he'd shot pool with his sixteen-year-old great-grandson. It inspired him to go to a pool hall in Bridgeport to hustle up a game. He found a black guy named James. Well dressed, Dad said, whatever that meant.

"He was a pretty good shooter," Dad said. "So I made him spot me the eight and nine in nine-ball. He said, 'You may be an old man, but you might make me stand up and take notice. How do I know you ain't hustlin' me?' '' Dad just lowered his head, fingering the fedora in his pudgy hands, trying to look as pitiful and harmless as he could. James bought it. "I guess I'll take a chance," he said.

Dad let him win five dollars. "The setup," Dad said. "Next time we'll play for more money." I couldn't help but laugh. The old man was still hustling. That's what he loved about gambling—the hustle.

He began hustling pool when he was discharged from the orphanage at fifteen. He played nine-ball for $100 a game. A fifteen-year-old kid. But he was so good at it, the balls dropping with a thudding monotony, game after game. I should know. I spent most of my adult life trying to beat him at his game. But I never could, except once.

My parents had visited us in Florida when they were in their late seventies. They had only been with us for two days when I had my first argument with Dad. We had been arguing constantly, it seemed, for over forty years. That's why I had invited them to come visit Susan and me. To make my peace, finally, with the old man. But it wouldn't be easy.

After the argument, I called my brother back in Connecticut. "Jeez," I said, "the old man's still a pain in the ass."

"Why can't you just get along with him?" my brother said.

"I'm trying! I'm trying! But he drives me nuts!"

"Forget it, already. Listen, why don't you take the old man out? Just you and him. Go shoot some pool. You know how you used to love to shoot pool with him."

"All right."

I took Dad out to a bar–pool hall out on Dixie Highway, near the body shops and the auto-parts stores. A redneck sort of place just over the railroad tracks. I parked in a gravel lot between a pickup truck that looked like it had been repainted with a brush and an orange Chevelle Super Sport with racing slicks and rusted mag wheels. I heard country and western music through the open door. It was dark inside. It smelled of urine and baby powder and stale beer. I went over to the barmaid, who was talking to a fat, bearded.guy with a clip of keys hanging from the belt loop of his oil-stained jeans. She seemed deliberately not to notice me and Dad. I waited at the bar. Dad stood by the door, a small, tentative old man fingering his hat in his hands. Finally, the barmaid came over to me. I asked for a rack of balls.

She gestured with her head toward Dad. "For you and pops, huh?" She had teased hair like straw, dyed black.

"Yeh," I said with a smile. "The old man shoots a pretty mean stick."

"I'll bet, honey." She handed me the balls. "Take your pick." She gestured toward the six deserted Brunswick tables.

My father and I went over to one of the tables and turned on the conical light over it. Dad ran the flat of his hand over the green felt. He shook his head. We got two pool cues from racks along the walls. Dad laid his cuestick flat on the table and rolled it over the felt. It wobbled. He got another. That one wobbled too. He got another and another until finally he got one that didn't wobble. I racked the balls.

"A game of straight, Dad?" I said. He nodded. I played a safety. The cueball stopped at one end of the table, and only one ball broke free from the rack at the other end. I'd left him a long, straight-in shot. It was a tough shot, but it could be made. Dad went over to the barmaid and said something. She handed him a can of Johnson's baby powder. He sprinkled it on his hands and returned to the table. He examined the balls quickly, bent low over the cueball, and sighted his shot.

He had short, fat fingers. Not a pool shooter's hands. My mother called them "sausage fingers." Like she threw in the spaghetti sauce, she said. I watched Dad grip the stick. He still had that firm lefthander's bridge, even at seventy-six, and that smooth stroke that I always tried to copy, but never could. Dad shot and missed. The cueball broke into the rack and scattered the balls. I had a dozen easy shots to choose from. I remembered what Dad had told me once. "The eyes go before the stroke," he had said. "When you play an old man, always leave him long." That was almost twenty years ago. I was a pretty fair shooter then. I had picked up the game during all that dead time I had in the minor leagues. But I could never beat Dad. We would play for hours. I would get sweaty and hot-tempered while he, cool-eyed, with that maddeningly methodical stroke, pocketed ball after ball without missing. The other players stood around and watched my father shoot. I was both proud of Dad's talent and furious that I could not beat him. More than anything then, I wanted to beat him in pool. My father's game. Like Bubba with his father, Nero.

After only a few racks it became obvious that Dad's eyes were gone. I had built up a big lead, playing hard and ruthless. The way Dad had played me when I was in college. He never let up on me. Never gave me a break, the way some fathers do. I wouldn't have had it any other way. The thought of seeing him deliberately miss a shot so that I could win would have made me sick. It was a good lesson. But it never really took. I could play Dad hard and ruthless for a while. But it was an act I could never sustain. I didn't feel it. The hardness.

I stepped back from the pool table and blinked. I shook my head to clear it. I was ahead by over twenty balls. Dad was standing there, leaning on his stick, an old man with a gray fringe of hair at his temples, waiting for me to shoot. I leaned over the table, took an almost impossible shot, and missed. The balls scattered over the green felt.

"What the hell's a matter with you?" he said. "You know better than that." I shrugged, shook my head as if disgusted with myself. Dad leaned over the table and ran out the rack. I racked the balls again. "That's what happens when you get careless."

I missed my next shot by hitting the object ball just hard enough to make it pop back out of the pocket after it had dropped in. "You've got a touch like a blacksmith," Dad said.

I lost the game to my father by three balls. I threw my arm over the old man's shoulders and said, "Dad, you're still the best."

"You shoulda beat me," he said. "You got careless." He looked up at me and shook his head as if truly sad. "As usual."

I returned the balls to the barmaid and paid the bill. She smiled at me. "The old man took you to the cleaners, huh?" she said.

I looked around for Dad. He was over by the door, out of earshot. "I let him win," I said.

"Sure you did. Sure you did."

I smiled.

That night my parents and my wife and I ate dinner on the deck outside our apartment that overlooked the Intracoastal Waterway. It was a warm, soft, Florida night in February. My wife had lit candles enclosed in glass. The sky was the color of purple plums, dotted here and there with white stars. A breeze blew upon the water while we ate. Boats rocked in the water. I raised a glass of red wine and said, "A toast! To Mom and Dad!" Their faces were illuminated by the flickering lights of the candles. We all clicked our glasses over the table heaped with food. Me. My wife. My mother. My father.

"Who won, Son?" my mother said. I looked at her as we all began to eat. "In pool," she added. "Did you beat Dad?"

I smiled. "Are you kidding, Ma? You know I can't beat the old man."

Dad stopped eating. "He got careless, Florence," he said. "He had me beat and then he began taking these crazy shots."

"Oh," she said. "You mean Patty let you win." My father looked at her and then looked at me.

"You sunuvabitch!" he said to me. "You *did* let me win."

"Come on, Dad. I've been trying to beat you for years. You think I finally get you on the ropes I'm gonna go in the tank?" I shook my head.

"You sunuvabitch!" he said. He was furious. Not that I'd let him win. But that he didn't pick up that I was letting him win. I had outhustled him.

* * *

We drove past New Haven toward Ledyard, the snow thick on the highway now. I could feel the car drifting on me. I slowed to 40 mph. It was starting to worry me. But Dad didn't seem to notice. He was talking.

"I gambled because of the excitement," he said. "Gambling was a shortcut for me. Illegal gambling was the most exciting. Even if the only game in town was fixed, I had to play. That was the kick. Not winning, but the possibility of loss. Hell, for a gambler, is a game he *can't* lose. The money I won, well"—he made a backhand toss of his hand—"I lived good. But mostly I gave it away."

When he was younger, he gave it to his cronies, never letting them pay for a meal or a drink. When he was older, he gave it to me. Now he gives it to his grandchildren. It's a lesson I learned about money from the old man. My father is a smart man. More than that: He's one of those brilliant self-educated men who spend their lives trying to make up for a lack of education. He still reads Plato and Socrates and Kafka and especially Dostoyevsky. *The Gambler* is his favorite book, because it perfectly captures a gambler's masochism. "Gamblers love to lose," he said. "The more they lose, the more of a man they think they are."

My father's lack of education has always frustrated him. "It's the one thing I miss the most," he said. "Sometimes people would use a word I didn't know, and I'd run to the dictionary and look it up. I tried to fake it. As a kid, I dressed collegiate, but I wasn't thinking collegiate. I was thinking wise guy."

I remembered a few old pictures I'd seen of my father in his twenties. He wore a double-breasted Chesterfield topcoat, a regimental striped tie, and brown and white spectator shoes. He looked like a dandy out of an F. Scott Fitzgerald novel. Not the Jordan Baker crowd, with their easy inherited wealth and comfortable, preppy way of dressing. More like Gatsby, the parvenu. Trying so desperately, and pathetically, to look as if he'd gone to Princeton and then on to a seat on the New York Stock Exchange, but overdoing it.

Since my father had no legitimate outlet for his intelligence, he turned that intelligence to gambling. It was the secret of his success. He always found an edge. "The percentages are in your favor when you know something the other guy doesn't," he said. Sometimes what Dad knew was the percentages of a winning poker hand, and sometimes what he knew was that the dice were loaded or that he was dealing cards from the bottom of the deck.

"It's not how well you gamble," Dad went on, "but how many mistakes your opponent makes. That's why I don't like to gamble at casinos. You can't beat the 'iron,' the house winning percentage. The casinos win because they don't make mistakes. You can't outwit a casino like you can a guy in a private game."

He knew his opponents. He read them—their angers, their frustrations, the insecurities that made them bet stupidly, something he never did. In a way, reading people is something I inherited from him. It's how I make my living now as a writer. Yet I have never gambled—because of my father. When I told him this, he laughed. "A freelance writer all your life," he said, "and you say you never gamble."

* * *

Twenty miles from Ledyard, the snow was falling so heavily that dozens of cars had drifted off the Thruway. State police directed traffic, and tow trucks pulled cars out of snowdrifts. I was hunched over the steering wheel like an old man myself, driving barely 30 miles per hour. But Dad was still talking, oblivious to the snow.

He said he'd already been to Foxwoods a few times because "It's my style. It's not like Vegas or Atlantic City, where people expect a show, girls, liquor, a steak. It's for hard-core gamblers who can't help themselves."

As for the other vices, women and liquor, he said, well nobody much cared about them at Foxwoods. The gamblers at Foxwoods were his kind of gamblers, he said, because they had room in their lives for only one vice. "There are drinkers, womanizers, and gamblers," he said, "and if you're gonna do it right, you have room for only one vice."

* * *

Ledyard is a typical New England village of 15,600, with a big white Congregational church on its green and a reputation, before Foxwoods, of having the largest oak tree in New England, which died a decade ago. It's off the Thruway, along a narrow two-lane blacktop that rolls past snow-covered woods and old clapboard-sided colonial homes.

"Turn here," Dad said. I'd almost missed the casino because it was set back off the road in a little valley surrounded by hills thick with fir trees. We reached the parking lot at 9:00 A.M. It was already filled with cars, most of them piled high with snow, as if they'd been here all night.

Inside, at first glance, the casino looked like a shopping mall. It was painted pale purple, green, and beige. There was a towering rock waterfall in the lobby, a gift shop that sold Native American crafts that looked as if they had been made in Taiwan, and a deserted bar. There was a dining room to the right of the waterfall, with only a few people eating there, and behind it a cafeteria. It was only when I looked to the left and right of the waterfall that I realized it was a casino. To the right were hundreds of slot machines and beyond them a huge bingo hall. To the left were the gaming tables, already packed with gamblers.

Dad checked our coats and gave me a tour. He took me first to the slots. Most of the players were women, mechanically pulling the iron levers. As their winnings hit the metal tray with a clatter, they fed more money into the machines.

"Here's where the profit is," Dad said. "The casino can regulate the percentage of payoffs. Most of the games, roulette and craps, earn the casinos between five and six percent, but the slots are higher. If a casino eliminated the slots, it would have a tough go."

I approached an unoccupied slot machine to look at it. A woman with teased, frosted hair, wearing a bowling-league jacket, stretched her arm across the machine like a school crossing guard. "That's for my husband," she said. "He's been playing all morning. He just went to the john."

"Oh, I'm sorry," I said. Dad just shook his head and led me past the waterfall to the gaming tables that stretched as far as the eye could see. Blackjack. Chuck-a-luck. Craps. Baccarat. Roulette. "The poker games are downstairs," Dad said. Waitresses dressed in skimpy outfits were circulating among the gamblers, offering them free drinks as long as they gambled. They wore short skirts and shiny, orthopedic-looking hose. Most of their high-heeled pumps were too big for them, so they had stuffed wads of paper in the backs. Nobody paid them any attention. "They don't look like much compared to Vegas and Atlantic City," Dad said.

He led me over to the crap tables, his game. There was a lot of shouting after each roll of the dice. A good-looking blond guy with a beard was making a great production of shaking the dice in his hand, exhorting them "Come on, baby," before flinging them across the green felt. His pretty girlfriend was massaging his neck in between throws, but he didn't seem to notice. Some of the men looked as if they had been playing all night. They leaned on the table as if for support. The air was thick with cigarette smoke.

Dad said, "You know, you could put six police dogs in a room filled with smoke, and they'd be dead in twelve hours. But crapshooters"— he shook his head—"could stay alive for days."

One of the pit bosses stopped play to check the dice. He was a burly man in his late twenties, dressed in a double-breasted suit too big for him. He held the dice up to the light. Dad said, "He doesn't know what the hell he's doing." He called to the pit boss, "What are you checking for?"

The pit boss smiled. "Too many people been winning with these."

The baccarat tables were in a small room behind the crap tables. Baccarat is a card game favored mostly by Europeans in places like Monte Carlo. The gamblers here, however, were mostly Asians. In fact, I noticed that almost a quarter of the gamblers at Foxwoods were Asians.

"They're the best," Dad said. "They're control gamblers. They'll come with five hundred dollars, and if they lose it, they'll quit. If they win, they'll break the bank. They'll knock the casino right through the ceiling."

One of the Asians playing baccarat was a fresh-faced girl who looked no older than nineteen. She had short lustrous black hair, big round eyeglasses, and a brightly colored ski parka. She looked like a Wellesley student, except for the cigarette dangling from her lips and the fact that she was betting $100 chips on every hand. Throughout the day, I would come back to the baccarat table and she would still be there.

Alongside the baccarat table were the high-stakes blackjack tables. A lean, grizzled man wearing a black trucker's cap was betting $1500 a hand and losing every one as we watched. A well-dressed Asian woman beside him was also losing heavily. She kept glaring at me and Dad standing behind her. Finally, Dad said, "We'd better go. We're bothering her."

"We're not doing anything," I said.

"It doesn't matter. She's a player, and she's entitled. Any whim she has, the casino will accommodate." He paused. "Until she busts out, and then she won't exist."

We went downstairs to the high-stakes poker room. Most of the players were men, unshaven, looking as if they had been playing for days on end. Dad went over to one of the casino managers and asked a question. He came back disgusted. "No one here knows anything," he said. "If you asked them how to get out of this place, they couldn't tell you."

We stood behind a game and watched. The men were silent, intent, calculating. Dad whispered to me. "They play against each other. The house gets a fee every half hour."

One of the players, a man named Scott, had a little fan in front of him to blow away the other players' cigarette smoke. Scott was losing, so he changed chairs for luck. He looked like a young college professor with his reddish beard and wire-rimmed spectacles. A voice over the loudspeaker announced a call for Mr. Scott. He jumped up, hurried to a nearby phone, and answered it. He listened for a moment, glancing anxiously back toward the game, then shouted into the receiver, "I'll be home when I'm home!" He hung up and hurried back to his seat. Dad looked at him and said, "Degenerates! It's the only outlet they have."

I sat down at one of the empty poker tables. The chair was plush. Dad stood over me, smiling. "That chair comfortable?" he asked. I nodded. He said, "They're the most expensive you can buy. They fit your back so you can sit for hours. The casino doesn't care if you drop dead while you're playing."

We went back upstairs. I asked Dad if he wanted to shoot craps now. He put his head down as if embarrassed. "I don't have to," he said.

"Go ahead. I want to watch you."

"If you insist. If it'll help your story." I gave him $180 to start out with. He went over to a table, bought $100 in chips, and began to play. I moved back, away from his line of vision to watch. He was just another old man, bald, with a little friar's tuft of hair around his ears. Nobody noticed him. He began to win. A chip here, a chip there. His eyes were quick and alert as he calculated the odds after each throw. He stretched his neck the way an athlete does in the heat of competition. He didn't look so old now.

The shooter shook the dice in his hands, whispered to them, and fired them across the table. Dad lost. I felt a sinking in my stomach. The dice were handed to Dad. He picked them up, turned his head away, and flung them backhanded, as if with disdain. He won. Someone shouted, "You're on a roll, old man!" Dad flung the dice again and won. "All right! All right!" the players shouted. They noticed him now. Not an old man, but a winner, ageless. My old man, competing in his sport the way I used to compete in mine. It was funny, I thought at the time, I can't pitch anymore, and sometimes that thought makes me feel old. But Dad can still gamble—which, in a way, makes him younger than me.

He tossed again and lost. My heart sank. He tossed again and won. The chips began to pile up in front of him. I got excited, rooting for him the way he rooted for me all those years that he sat in the stands watching me pitch. For the first time I knew how he must have felt, how unbearable it must have been to see me lose, how joyous it was to see me win.

But I didn't have his stomach. I couldn't take the pressure. I drifted away toward the blackjack tables. The exhilaration of watching Dad gamble made me want to gamble too. So I sat down, bought some chips, and began to play. I lost a hand. Then another. I looked across the room for Dad. I could see his tufts of hair, hear the shouts from the table as he flung the dice.

The dealer dealt another hand and I won. I won again. And again. Hours passed. I was so lost in the game that I was barely conscious, every so often, of a voice beside me. "Can I get you a drink, sir?" I glanced up to see a smiling waitress. "Something to eat?" she said. I shook my head no, annoyed at her interruption, and went back to my game. By the time I was ahead $375, I had completely forgotten about my old man. He was right: It was addictive. Then I began to lose. My pile of chips shrank. I began to sweat.

I heard a voice behind me. "I hope you bust out." I turned around. It was Dad.

"Just in time," I lied. "I was ready to quit anyway."

"How'd you do?" he asked.

I counted my chips. I had won $100.

"Too bad," he said.

"What, you afraid I'm gonna get hooked on gambling like you?" I asked. He just shook his head. "Pops, it's not my idea of fun to drive four hours in a snowstorm and sweat all day just to go home with a hundred dollars. What do you think, I'm crazy like you?"

He smiled. "You know, sometimes I had such bad luck I hoped I wouldn't wake up in the morning. I had no more doors to knock on to get money. I had tapped out everyone."

"By the way," I said. "How'd you do?"

"I was up big for a while. I finished a hundred ahead."

We cashed in our chips and headed for the door. It was late afternoon. I threw my arm over the old man's shoulder. He looked up at me and said, "Was I helpful, Son?"

"The best, Dad. You make a great reporter."

He smiled shyly, thrilled that he could use his intelligence in a way that he respected. "I had a wonderful day," he said.

Then I remembered something. "You know, Dad, watching you shoot craps, I realized how it must have been for you watching me pitch."

He looked up at me, startled, as if I'd said something outrageously stupid. "What? Are you crazy?" he said. "You watched *nothing!* I watched a *thunderbolt!* I watched a *talent!*"

* * *

I was driving through the Naugatuck Valley toward Waterbury. Down below the highway, I could see all the old red-brick abandoned factories with their broken windows. Rusted metal machinery was turning orange by the side of the river that ran past the factories.

I reached Waterbury at 4 P.M. I turned off the exit toward Municipal Stadium. It was set down below a little rise. I drove down into the dirt parking lot behind the outfield fence. I lit one more cigar, then got out, got my bag from the trunk, and walked toward an opening in the fence. I could hear the sounds of bats against balls, the smack of a ball in a catcher's mitt, the shouts of infielders. I walked through an opening in the fence and found myself on the rightfield foul line. I could see my teammates taking batting practice up ahead. Closer to me, in the rightfield bullpen, I saw two pitchers warming up under the watchful eyes of other pitchers and the pitching coach. They were all wearing just shorts and lavender T-shirts that had "Waterbury Spirit" written on them.

As I walked past the pitchers, they stopped throwing and stared at what they saw. An old man with a white beard, smoking a cigar, wearing shorts and a pale-blue Hawaiian shirt dotted with pink flamingos.

One of my teammates called out, "Heh, Jimmy Buffett! You lost?"

I smiled and called back, "I'm the player to be named later." They looked confused. Maybe they hadn't seen *Bull Durham.*

I found my manager, Stan, in his office in the locker room. He was a short, pudgy man in his late thirties. He was hunched over his desk, writing out that night's lineup card. A little fan on his desk rearranged the hot, sticky air in his tiny office. I waited for him to notice me. But he didn't look up. I reminded myself to call him "Skip" or "Skipper," so he'd know I once played professionally. Only amateurs called their manager "Coach."

Finally I said, "Hi, Skip. I'm Pat Jordan." He looked up without interest. I smiled, reached out my hand to shake his. He let me shake his hand. "I'm supposed to pitch for you July 29," I said. "Didn't Bob Wirsz tell you?"

"Oh, yeah. I heard something about it."

"I was gonna throw for you and Bob today." I smiled. "Put your minds at ease, Skip."

"Sure." He went back to writing out his lineup card. "Go change. I'll get you a catcher."

I changed into my shorts and spikes in the hot, damp locker room that smelled of sweat and analgesic balm. No one else was there. No one seemed to care that I was there. Why should they? This was a big deal for me, not them. If Wirsz wanted to let an old man indulge his fantasy, so what? It didn't mean anything to *their* careers. That's all they cared about. They had their own hopes and dreams and fears, and no interest in mine, just as I had no interest in theirs. I'd forgotten this about baseball. Every player lived in his own world. The team, yes. But me first. We all thought that way, but few admitted it like I did.

I went back outside to the bullpen. Stan was waiting for me with a catcher in full gear. Did he think I was that wild? Maybe he thought I threw that hard? I began to soft toss with the catcher in the late afternoon heat. The other pitchers sat on the bullpen bench and watched in silence. A girl sat with them. Short dark hair, cute, maybe twenty-six. Jeez, I thought, concentrate on throwing. I began to sweat in the sun. I peeled off my T-shirt and tossed it in the grass. The pitchers weren't making jokes about Jimmy Buffett now. They could see I threw like a pitcher. I looked like a pitcher. I was in shape, tanned, even muscular. That's why I'd stripped off my T-shirt. Maybe for the girl too. Jeez, I could never stop fantasizing, making up scenarios in my head that had no basis in reality. Concentrate, goddammit!

The catcher was crouched behind home plate now. I was throwing hard. I was no longer just an old man with a white beard now. I was a fellow pitcher. It confused the pitchers watching me. I had stepped onto their turf. I was nervous as I threw. Not the good nervousness, the bottled-up energy waiting to explode. But the bad nervousness that made me too self-conscious. Everyone watching. What were they seeing?

I was conscious of the way I caught the ball from my catcher, the way I put my foot on the rubber, the way I pumped, kicked, reared back, felt the old fear rising, and delivered. I was out of sync. I was thinking a split second too late about all the parts of my motion that had once been just a fluid piece when I was throwing with Brian. Bits and pieces swirled around my mind. I couldn't put them together, in order. I landed too soon on my left leg. My upper body was already forward, my energy spent, while my arm trailed behind, too late. I was flinging the ball with my arm, not throwing it with my arm *and* body.

My fastball hit the catcher's mitt without that sharp *pop* I'd come to expect with Brian. My slider broke too soon. A lazy break, not sharp. I could see the big loose spin on the ball, revealing a slider's white dot, instead of that tight spin I had had with Brian that made that dot all but disappear. Still, it *was* a slider.

My catcher seemed not to notice how I was throwing. Nor did the pitchers watching. Nor Skip. Nor the girl. Forget about the girl! I was throwing better than they had expected an old man to throw. I wasn't a *joke.* But I wasn't here to throw better than a fifty-six-year-old writer. I expected to throw like a minor league pitcher.

I stopped throwing after fifteen minutes. I stood there panting, exhausted in the heat, and waited for someone to say something. Anything. My catcher just walked toward home plate to take batting practice. Skip nodded and walked back to his office. The pitchers on the bench just stared at me. The girl stared at me too.

I turned to go back to the locker room when I noticed a man behind me. He must have been watching me all this time. He was short, bald, dressed in navy slacks and a pale blue dress shirt open at the collar. He looked like every minor league baseball owner I had ever known.

"Hi, Pat," he said, reaching out a hand to shake mine. "I'm Bob Wirsz."

"Hi, Bob. You watching long?"

"Long enough." I waited for him to say something else. I stood there, smiling, waiting. Finally he said, "I'd like to get a few photos of you in uniform. Run them in the papers before you pitch."

"Sure, Bob. Anything you want."

Wirsz and I went back into the locker room, where he found me a clean cream-colored uniform. I put it on. It had lilac piping on the shirt and pants and lilac script across the chest, "Waterbury Spirit." The stockings were lilac too. I pulled up the pants legs to the knees to expose the stockings, as was the custom of players in the 1960s. Then I remembered that players today wore their pants long, almost to their shoes, to conceal their stockings. I pulled the pants legs down to my shoes so I would look like my teammates, not an old man from another era. I should have shaved my white beard too, I thought. I will before the game.

I went back to the bullpen, where Wirsz was waiting for me with a little camera. He snapped a few pictures of me in my uniform, then called over two pitchers to pose with me. They stood on either side of me, two kids with goatees, maybe twenty-five, looking confused. I tried to make small talk with them, just as Warren Spahn had tried to make small talk with me in 1959, when I posed with him at Milwaukee County Stadium for publicity photos after I had signed my bonus contract at eighteen.

"Those pictures run in the papers," I said. "You think there might be a coupla groupies hangin' around my hotel?" I smiled at them, waiting for them to smile. Nothing. Wirsz kept snapping pictures. Finally I said, "Maybe a coupla old ladies with aluminum walkers, wanna ball that night's starting pitcher?" Still nothing.

Wirsz dismissed the two pitchers and called over the girl with dark hair. She wore a white polo shirt, very loose, to hide her breasts, and baggy khaki shorts. Wirsz introduced her to me as the team's trainer. I shook her hand as he snapped our picture.

"So," I said, smiling at her. "You like old men, honey?" She looked at me and rolled her eyes to the pale blue sky.

*   *   *

I sat on the edge of the bed in a hotel room in New Rochelle, New York, staring at the accusing telephone. Finally, I dialed my brother's number. I knew it by heart, after all these years, even though I often didn't call him for over a year. I heard his disinterested voice on the other end of the line.

"Hello."

"Bro. It's me."

"Who is this?"

"It's your brother, for chrissakes!"

"Patty. What's the occasion?"

"No occasion," I said. "I just wanted to talk to you."

"What's wrong?"

"Jesus! Does something always have to be wrong? I just wanted to talk to you."

"About what?" He was always maddening. Get to the point. No time for small talk. So I told him. I told him I was pitching again. I told him about the Waterbury Spirit. July 29. My comeback.

"I hope you're throwing like I taught you. Not like when the Braves got hold of you."

He wasn't even surprised. It was as if he'd expected it all these years. That I'd try to get it right finally. After I had quit. He was always merciless with me. My brother. He never let up.

"I'm throwing good, George. Really."

"We'll see. Meet me at the house. We'll go throw again. Like we used to." It was exactly what I'd expected him to say. And what I dreaded. No matter how well I was throwing with Brian, no matter how many scouts sat behind the home-plate screen and nodded at my devastating slider, it was only my brother's approval that I craved, and his disapproval that I feared. He had always been the most important person in my life. As a boy I worshiped George, my older brother by fourteen years. I loved him more than anyone when I was a boy. In many ways, I still did.

The next morning I drove to my brother's house. He lived in an old white-clapboard colonial on a hill surrounded by a stream and a small lake. A moat to protect him from the world. The house had a plaque on the front door. "Josiah Perry, 1688." Inside, it was dark and old, as if it had not been touched in centuries. There were faux paintings of Abraham Lincoln and George Washington in gilt frames on the walls. It was less a home than a monument to the life my brother, the successful lawyer, had made for his family.

I pulled up the driveway and parked in front of the red barn where he used to keep his oldest daughter's jumping horses. When she was a teenager she used to jump at shows in Madison Square Garden. She wore a black hard cap with a little bill, a tight-fitting red riding jacket, wheat-colored jodhpurs, and long patent-leather black boots. She was one of the only jumpers in those shows whose last name ended with a vowel.

My brother's gold Mercedes Benz sedan and his wife's gold BMW with the "Milly II" license plate were parked in front of the barn. I got out and walked down the long flagstone walk to the kitchen door and went inside. Mildred was cooking spaghetti sauce at the stove. My brother was sitting at the kitchen table. He wore a bulky satin jogging suit to hide his expanding waistline.

"Patty!" Mildred said, smiling. "George, it's your brother."

George looked up from the table and smiled. "Brother. You got old. When did your beard turn white?"

"About when you turned seventy," I said.

"Seventy! I'm only sixty. Same age as you." We both laughed. I went over and gave my brother a kiss on the cheek and sat down across from him. He looked the same, except for the gray in his short bristly hair. He never seemed to age. I lit a cigar.

"Jesus, Brother," he said, waving his hand in front of his face. "You're gonna smell up the house with that stinky thing."

"It'll be a reminder I was here, Bro. Now you owe me one. When you gonna visit us in Fort Lauderdale?"

"All those dogs," he said. "You'll have to get rid of them before I come."

"You kidding? My dogs are my life, Bro. The only things that love me without judging me."

"But *I* love you, Brother." He grinned.

"Yeh. But you judge me, Brother. And I always come up short."

"Well, you're just not perfect. I've always tried to make you perfect, Brother."

"Like you."

"Of course."

"You going to stay for lunch, Patty?" Mildred said.

"No. I don't have time, Mil. I'm just gonna throw with George, then I got to get back to Florida."

"For his wife's cooking," George said, smiling. "What's that Irish wife of yours know how to make? Boiled potatoes?"

"Chef Boyardee out of the can," I said. George shook his head. "But she gives great head, Bro."

Mildred laughed. "You never change, Patty. Thank God!"

I started to tell my brother about my throwing. He interrupted. "Mil, I told you, don't put too much garlic in the sauce."

"George, I know what I'm doing," Mildred said.

"You always put in too much garlic."

"You always say that."

"You always do it."

"Mil," I said, "did you hear the one about the Italian mother stirring the spaghetti sauce on her daughter's wedding night?"

"No, Patty." She looked over at me, smiling. Mildred was still beautiful, in her early seventies. She had had hair as black as a raven's wings when she was younger. Now she dyed out the gray.

"Milly," I said. "How come my hair is white and George's is gray and you don't have a single gray hair?"

"Just lucky, I guess." She had brilliant blue eyes and a straight nose that made her look more classically Greek than Italian. When Mildred had begun dating George I was only a child. He told her stories about me, the Pepsi in the gas tank, the cat out the window. She was terrified to meet this little monster. When she finally did, I was asleep in my bed. She stared at me. "That can't be him!" she said. "He looks like an angel!"

When Mildred and George got married, I was a child of five in short pants, standing on the church steps with a smile on my face, now that there would be some softness in my family. I already loved Mildred for all the softness and beauty and patience and femininity she had that my mother lacked. Mildred was not hard on me like my parents were. I was raised in that rare Italian family that did not worship children. My parents' constant refrain to me, when I babbled excitedly, was simply "Patty, go to your room." Mildred sat for hours with me and taught me how to draw. She taught me how to add and subtract with flash cards. She was the only one in my family who understood a side of me that might be called "sensitive" today. When I was a child, it was called, derisively, "feminine." I showed that side only to Mildred.

"So, this guinea mother is stirring the sauce," I went on, "when her daughter comes home from the wedding with her bridegroom. The daughter's gonna have her wedding night in the bedroom above the kitchen where the mother's stirring the sauce. But the daughter's scared. She's a virgin. The mother tells her not to worry, it's her duty now, and she sends her up to bed with her husband. Suddenly the mother hears a scream. The daughter comes running down to the kitchen.

" 'Momma, Momma, he took off his shirt and he's got hair all over his chest!'

"The mother, stirring the sauce, reassured her that all men had hair on their chest and sent her back upstairs to do her duty. Again there was a scream, and the daughter came running downstairs.

" 'Momma, Momma, he took off his pants and he's got hair all over his legs.'

"The mother, still stirring the sauce, reassured her daughter that all men had hair on their legs and sent her back upstairs. When the new husband took off his shoes and socks, his young wife saw that he had five toes on one foot and only two and a half toes on the other foot. She screamed again and ran downstairs to her mother.

" 'Momma, Momma, it was horrible! He's only got a foot and a half.'

"The mother handed her daughter the spoon and said, 'Here, you stir the sauce. I'll go upstairs.' "

Mildred shrieked with laughter. "Patty! You're incorrigible!"

My brother just smiled his weary smile. "Brother. Barbara's coming in a little while. Not around her, okay?"

"Jesus, George! She's fourty fucking years old." His third youngest daughter.

Mildred glanced at me with that resigned look of hers when she saw me getting angry with my brother.

George patiently tried to explain. "She's a little skittish after the divorce, Brother. She's dating again too. But don't mention it."

My brother always affected a sexual prudishness around me. It had less to do with his nature than the role he felt obligated to play with me. When I was fifteen I used to play basketball with men ten years older than myself at the North End Boys Club. The Globe and Porky were tough, inner-city men already out of college. They taught me how to hook my arm inside the arm of an opposing player under the basket to prevent him from jumping for a rebound. They also taught me how to swear. "Fuck" was my favorite word. One day my brother came to play with us. He had played basketball at Georgetown University. He was only a few years older than the Globe and Porky, but their game had already passed him by. They ran fast breaks, dribbled behind their backs, and took long, feathery-light jumpshots. My brother played a game from the 1940s. Stiff, unbending. Crisp bounce passes. Two-handed set shots. I played Porky's and the Globe's game.

After the game we all took a shower together in the big open shower room. Porky started telling George about the opposing college player who told him once, before their game, that he was going to "shut me down," said Pork. "Imagine, Moose! [My brother's nickname. He did look like a moose.] The fucking cocksucker. I scored fifty-six. Nobody stops the fucking Pork."

George glanced at me, his kid brother. Then, very seriously, he said, "Not in front of the kid, Pork."

The Globe and Porky stared at him. The kid? Who said "fuck" every other word? They both laughed.

I started again to tell George about my pitching. "I picked up a nice slider, George."

"What happened to the overhand curveball I taught you?"

"I can't do it now. It's just a big, slow, sloppy break."

He shook his head. "You used to have a great overhand curveball. Nobody could hit it."

"I was eighteen, Brother. For chrissakes. What do you expect now?" Mildred glanced at me. "Wait till you see the slider, Bro," I said. "It comes up to the plate like a fastball and then . . ."

George got up from the table and left the kitchen.

"Where the fuck you going?" I said.

"I have to make a call."

"Jesus, George. I was *talking!* You're so fucking rude."

He peeked his head back into the kitchen. He was smiling. "Rude, Brother?" he said in a girlish voice. "Pardon me, Brother. You're so sensitive."

When George returned from his call, Barbara was standing in the kitchen with her teenage daughter, Samantha. Barbara was thin and beautiful, like Mildred had been—still was—only she had a halo of kinky blond curls instead of her mother's straight black silky hair. I saw a photograph of Mildred once when she was eighteen. She wore an organza prom dress and looked like Ava Gardner.

"Sam, honey!" George said to his granddaughter. "Give Beep a kiss." Samantha hesitated. She was embarrassed in front of me, a stranger. "Please, Sam!" George begged. Finally she kissed him on the cheek. "Isn't she beautiful?" George said. Samantha blushed. "Barb, give your Uncle Patty a kiss."

Barbara gave me a peck on the cheek. Then she stepped back, with a thin smile, and said, "So, Uncle Patty. What's the occasion?"

I said, with a thin smile, "So, Barb. How's sex after forty?"

My brother and I drove to the park in his Mercedes. He was quiet, distracted, like a tired old man. He had gotten old. Not physically but mentally. He had spent all his energy trying to impose his order on the world. I remember the time I tried to help him carry a wingchair up the narrow attic hallway of his house. The chair wouldn't fit through the hallway, but George kept trying to jam it through. Finally I measured the chair and the hallway. The chair was forty inches wide. The hallway was thirty-six inches wide. I put my end of the chair down.

"No way, Bro. It ain't gonna fit."

He looked at me with sweat pouring from his forehead. "It'll fit," he said. "I'll make it fit."

When I left he was still struggling with the chair. I called him a few days later. "I got the chair up," he said. "As usual, you quit too soon."

"How'd you do it?" I said.

"I sawed the legs off."

Over the years, the world had exhausted my brother. He got tired of sawing the legs off things that didn't fit. So he stopped trying. He had lost the energy, and the will, to control things. So he just made his world smaller and smaller and smaller until he was left, as he was now, an old man sitting at the kitchen table hectoring his wife over the sauce and begging his granddaughter for kisses. He lost himself in an orgy of familial affection he could control.

My brother's life and mine always seemed to be moving in opposite directions. Somewhere along the way we passed each other, like two trains at an intersection, one heading south, the other north. In his forties, he'd had a lot of men friends. Men he'd grown up with, played sports with, and now were fellow coaches. Some of his friends were Jesuit priests, since George had always been a devout Catholic. He was going to be a priest when he was in high school, my parents told me, until he met Mildred.

When I was thirty, I would often enter my brother's house at night to find him and his friends and a gaggle of Jesuit priests sitting in the living room, sipping wine and discussing some arcane point of Catholic theology. I would sit down at the edge of the group and listen. I was a struggling freelance writer then who'd just begun to travel. I had no time for friends, nor the Church and its mind-numbing certitudes. One night I was sitting there, listening, when the talk turned to writers. Someone mentioned Hemingway, my favorite author at the time. I spoke up and said Hemingway had redefined twentieth-century writing. I was quickly dismissed.

"A Godless man," said a priest. "He committed suicide, the sin of pride."

Another priest turned to me. He was a thin, pale, delicate man with an affected English accent. He taught the classics at the college I had gone to. He was obviously gay, but no one ever mentioned that then. He looked at me with a sardonic smile. I had long hair and I affected workshirts and jeans and cowboy boots now, which my parents saw as a rebuke to George's J. Press clothes. The priest said, "So, you like Hemingway, Patrick. I would have thought Mickey Spillane was more your style."

I smiled at him. "Oh yes, Father. I love Spillane. And his wife too. She's the big busty blonde who always poses for his book covers. She's quite a babe . . . if you like that kinda thing, Father."

Over the years George lost his Catholicism, and his priests, and finally his friends. He settled for the certitude of his family, his wife and six children, his eleven grandchildren. I had moved to Florida by then. I had lost my family. My ex-wife and five children no longer spoke to me. It was partly because of something in my own nature and partly because of Erwin.

I was responsible for Erwin's death. I was responsible too for keeping him alive. And yet he was a man I never knew. I never met him, nor talked to him. He sent me a letter once, and a week later a note. That was it, the only communication I ever had with him. Or, rather, he with me, because I never responded to either his letter or note. The former was too infuriating, and the latter was too painful. In his note he enclosed copies of Father's Day cards my children had sent him. They were addressed to "The Big E"—his nickname, I guess—and after the verse they were signed "Love" and my children's names. The verses weren't especially emotional or warm—they were pretty nondescript, in fact—but still, they were Father's Day cards my children sent to Erwin and not to me. Erwin was my ex-wife's lover, or boyfriend, or significant other, or maybe even her secret husband, which was only part of the problem.

My ex-wife met Erwin in the hospital in Connecticut where she worked seven years after our divorce. Erwin was a patient there. He had diabetes. He had just had a toe amputated, and my ex-wife was his physical therapist. Even then, approaching fifty, she was a beautiful woman with pale, almost translucent skin, high Slavic cheekbones, and pale blue eyes. Erwin was immediately smitten with my ex-wife, who had always been at her best nursing people, our children, me, through physical discomforts. She had infinite patience with all the paraphernalia of such discomforts. The vaporizer in the bathroom at 2 A.M. when one of our children had the croup. The cold washcloths soaked in ice water and applied to our children's backs when they had a high fever. The soup she made me when I had a cold. She never panicked in those situations, something I always did, but rather calmed and diminished them. She only panicked once in all the twenty-four years of our marriage, when my youngest daughter, seven at the time, fell off her bike and broke her arm so badly she almost lost it. When my wife rolled up my daughter's shirtsleeve and saw a bone almost sticking out through the skin, she grabbed the hair on her head with both hands and ran screaming from the room. I, for once, did not panic. I gathered my daughter up in my arms, carried her out to the car, and rushed her to the hospital just in time to save her arm.

Erwin was a tall, thin, good-looking, gray-haired man in his early sixties. "A real tough guy, Dad," my children told me. "You'd like him." He was very rich, they said. He owned a house in Stamford, Connecticut, and another in Florida. He owned two cars. He owned all the concession stands at Shea Stadium, where the Mets played. They also told me about the tragedy in his life: His only child, a son, had been killed in a car accident when he was nineteen.

I know all this, like I know most things about Erwin and my ex-wife, from a great distance (they lived in Connecticut for six months and in Florida, three hours from my home in Fort Lauderdale, for six months), and in bits and pieces I picked up from my children, and my parents, who also liked Erwin. In that first year that Erwin and my ex-wife began dating, my children seemed to delight in telling me about him. "He's a tough guy" and "He's good for Ma," things like that. Maybe they were just thrilled their mother had finally "found someone," as they said, or maybe they were trying to let me know in their way that someone appreciated their mother even if I didn't. A none-too-subtle rebuke for my divorcing their mother. I let it pass. Then, over the years, my children became reticent about Erwin and their mother. My few questions about them were answered with a shrug. "I don't know, Dad." Finally they lapsed into total silence, not only about Erwin and their mother, but to me. They stopped visiting me and calling me. By then, of course, I had found out a few things of my own about Erwin.

He didn't own a house in Stamford. He lived in a rented room at the Stamford YMCA. His "house" in Florida was a modest condominium, heavily mortgaged. His two cars were aging Chryslers with vanity plates: "NO COUTH" and "UNCOUTH." Erwin didn't own all the concessions at Shea Stadium, he just worked in one, selling hot dogs and beer during Mets games. By the time I learned all this, Erwin had moved into my ex-wife's house, the house where I was raised and which I had bought from my parents when we married. I was still paying the mortgage on that house, in addition to alimony, which was supposed to stop when my ex-wife remarried or cohabitated with a man for six months. Which I know now is what precipitated my children's silence.

Erwin moved quickly to usurp my place in my ex-wife's life. We had remained friends after the divorce, and often she would call me with problems about her latest boyfriend. She even visited Susan and me in Florida for a week. But that was before she met Erwin. After Erwin, her calls ceased. Erwin also moved quickly to usurp my place with my children. He bought them things, slipped them a twenty every now and then, and even took my two sons to Shea with him to work at his concession stand. My mother, in her eighties, called me once and said, "Oh, Erwin's a wonderful father to the kids." I snapped at her, "Thanks, Ma, that's just what I need to hear," and hung up.

I tried to control my jealousy over Erwin's taking my place with the children. I explained it away with his tragedy. He must be starved to have a family of his own, I thought. So I did nothing to stand in his way. I told my children I was glad they liked him, and that he was good to them and their mother, and left it at that. But there were times, usually at 3 A.M., when I was lying in bed counting the blades of our overhead fan, when my anger would bubble to the surface. My wife, sleeping beside me, could feel my hot anger in her sleep. She would wake and, more than once, admonish me "to have the courage of your suffering."

Erwin, however, couldn't leave it at that. It wasn't enough for him to supplant me with my family. He had to obliterate their memory of me too. Maybe he'd heard stories from my children that I was "a tough guy." Maybe he felt burdened by my past, my four years as a professional baseball player. Maybe he felt burdened by my manhood in a way I didn't feel about his. Who knows? I just know that in Florida I felt a very palpable hatred from him, as if, in his mind's eye, he and I were engaged in some terrible battle to the death. And, as it turns out, we were. As long as that battle was being fought, it kept Erwin alive.

Things changed. When I was a few days late with my alimony check, now my ex-wife would scrawl me a note. "Own up to your obligations, or else!" Always the same words. Not my ex-wife's words. She didn't talk like that. (Now, in *my* mind's eye, I could see Erwin standing over her, pacing, furious, while she wrote and he dictated.) When I started annulment proceedings so that Susan and I could be married in the Catholic Church and go to Mass again, the Miami diocese sent a questionnaire to my ex-wife. She refused to accept it at first, and then, finally, she did. She scrawled another note to me. She said she'd be happy to fill out the questionnaire if I'd increase her alimony payments. When I showed that note to my priest, he said, "What kind of woman did you marry?"

"She was a sweet woman," I said. "But I don't know her now."

Finally, four of my five children stopped calling me, except, on rare occasions, to ask me for money. When I refused my twenty-year-old son's request to give him $600 for "architect school" ("There is no such school," I blurted out), he said to me, "Now I know why everyone here wishes you were dead." I was stunned. Who wished I was dead? Why?

Only my second daughter continued to call. Inadvertently, she'd drop a comment or two about her mother and Erwin. He was in the hospital again. Another toe had to be amputated. They stopped by to visit her on the way down to Florida for the winter. She met them at a downtown hotel. "It was the strangest thing, Dad," she said. "They were registered as Mr. and Mrs."

They'd been living together now for over two years. I had been waiting for them to get married, but always, it seemed, just before they were going to, Erwin would get sick again and be hospitalized. I felt sorry for him, which is why I made no attempt to terminate the alimony even though I had proof my ex-wife had been cohabitating with him for six months. Then something happened that brought to the surface all my jealousy I'd been fighting to keep repressed. My youngest daughter, twenty-five at the time, the one who had almost lost her arm, announced that she was getting married. I heard about this the way I heard about all things now concerning my family: in bits and pieces from the only daughter who was still talking to me. I was happy for my daughter who was getting married. I hoped marriage would soften her hardness, which had surfaced immediately after her broken arm. She had always been such a sweet girl until then. But after her arm healed, it was still noticeably crooked at the elbow. It affected her.

I had a momentary hope that I would have a rapprochement with her. That she would call me, finally, to ask me to give her away. But she didn't. She asked Erwin to give her away. To walk down the aisle with her, arm in arm. When my second-oldest daughter told me this over the phone, I screamed out, "She wouldn't have that arm if it wasn't for me!" I was so angry that I immediately drafted a letter to my ex-wife and sent it to Florida where she was living with Erwin. I wrote that she had broken the terms of our divorce by cohabiting with Erwin. That's when I got Erwin's letter.

In the letter, he referred to me as "asshole" and my second wife as "the bimbo slut." He threatened to drag me into court for nonpayment of alimony, which I found strange. Who was this man to make these demands on me? A man I barely knew. He ended the letter with these words: "Own up to your responsibilities. You've already lost the respect of four of your five kids. Quit while you're ahead." And then he revealed what I already knew. He wrote, "I've lived by my wits and cunning for a long time. I'm the master of dirty tricks. When provoked, you don't want to fuck with me." There it was. The gauntlet thrown down between two twentieth-century warriors. The new lover and the ex-husband. A battle to the death. He finished me off, in his mind's eye, a week later with a note and copies of my children's Father's Day cards to him.

Nothing much came of Erwin's threat. Just a few letters from his lawyer, threatening me if I did not pay the alimony. I did nothing, said nothing, just waited. I was an Italian-American, and I had learned early at my mother's knee. Say nothing, do nothing, never give yourself away in battle until absolutely necessary. Finally, even the lawyer's letters stopped. I assumed either they didn't have enough money to pursue it, or their lawyer told them they didn't have a case, or maybe Erwin got sick again.

Almost a year passed when my second daughter called me. She was crying. "Erwin died, Dad," she said. "Last night in Florida."

"Jeez, I'm sorry," I said. "The poor guy."

And then she told me that Erwin was broke. He didn't have enough money for medicine, or to go to the hospital. "The bagel shop went bankrupt," she said.

"What bagel shop?" I said.

"The one Erwin started in Florida," she said. "Ma worked as his waitress."

When I hung up, I felt guilty. What if I had continued sending the alimony? Would Erwin have been able to stay alive? And then I thought of my ex-wife in a waitress's uniform, at fifty-two, bringing bagels and eggs to Florida retirees. The image depressed me out of my mind.

It took me a few days to realize that that call was meant to make me feel guilty. That it was all about money, and nothing about grief, lost love, emptiness. What did my ex-wife feel when Erwin died? How did he die? Quietly, in his sleep, beside her in bed? Or awake, lying on the sofa wracked with pain? Did my ex-wife comfort him in the way she was good at? Or did she panic, run fleeing from the room for help? I'll never know these things. Nor will I ever know what kind of man Erwin really was. Was he really good to my ex-wife and children? Did he love them, or was he just using them in his battle with me? Did they love him, or were they just using him to hurt me? All of this has been kept from me, and I can only know what I feel about Erwin and me. I know his hatred toward me kept him alive for four years. And when he had lost his battle, in his mind's eye, anyway, he had nothing more to live for, so he died. I know also that in his dying he left behind irrevocable damage to us all, the living.

Over the years, I have learned to have "the courage of my suffering," as Susan put it. I resigned myself to the loss of my children. I had my friends now. The Usual Suspects. Sol, the marijuana smuggler. George and Alberto, two fags. Phil, the strip-club owner, and his girlfriend, Chelsea. Peter, the lawyer, an orphan like my father. Ronnie and Her Bee-ness. We were all from someplace else. We'd all fled to Fort Lauderdale, Paradise, for the same reason. We were suffocating in our past lives. Sol was trying to escape a contract on his life in Brooklyn. George and Alberto were trying to escape the stigma of their homosexuality. Phil was trying to escape a domineering mother. Chelsea was trying to escape a low-rent past. Ronnie was trying to escape the insecurity of a small-town childhood. Mary Beth was trying to escape a stuffy mother and a blissed-out father. Susan was trying to escape her guilt over having left her children with her ex-husband. I was trying to escape myself. But it followed me.

We had nothing in common, it seemed, on the surface. Mary Beth said we were all "expatriates." But we did have one thing in common. We had all decided at some point in our lives that love was more important than blood. An Italian heresy. Yet, without love, there is no blood.

On the day of our wedding, Sol was serving the last months of his two-year sentence for marijuana smuggling at a halfway house where he was supposed to "reacclimate" himself (Sol's word) back into society. He was let out only for work in the morning and for our wedding. I picked him up and drove him to the church. Fifty of our friends were already there, sitting in the pews, chattering loudly, to the annoyance of the priest. When Susan and I entered the church and walked up the aisle, our friends cheered as if at a football game. After the ceremony, when we walked back down the aisle to the sounds of "Dixie" and then "Long Tall Sally" coming from the organist, they cheered again at the game's final result. I was fifty. Susan was fifty-two. We had been legally married in 1984, and now, after my annulment from my first marriage, we were remarried in the Catholic Church.

*　*　*

The day before I flew to New Rochelle and then drove to Waterbury to throw for Bob Wirsz, my father called me.

"What's up, Pop?"

"It's George," he said. "I'm worried about him."

"Why?"

"He's got no one to talk to but women and children."

"His choice, Dad. That's the way he set it up."

"For chrissakes! He's your brother."

"So . . . what am I supposed to do?"

"He needs a man to talk to. Spend some time with him. For me."

"All right, Dad."

So I called my brother. Now here we were, in his Mercedes, going to throw again like we used to. It was my responsibility to bring him back to the company of men. It was the least I could do for the man who had made a man of me.

We pulled up in front of the park where I had pitched in high school. The field was nothing but clumps of dirt and overgrown weeds. A construction crew was digging up the dirt around the park for a building. We got out of the car and went to the dugout so I could put on my spikes. Two construction workers, in their twenties, were eating lunch there.

"Heh, guys," I said as I put on my spikes. They just glanced at us but said nothing. One of them whispered to the other, who grinned. They looked at me, an old man lacing up baseball spikes, and snickered.

"What the fuck's so funny?" I said.

"Nothing," one of them said. They went back to their lunch.

I walked out to the mound where I had struck out all those batters in high school forty years ago. The dirt was packed down hard like cement. I began soft tossing with my brother a few feet away. He caught the ball stiffly, as he always had, but not like an old man of seventy. George had never lost the physicality of his youth. He was always so strong, stronger than me. He taught me how to shake hands firmly, like a man, when I was a boy. He made a game of it when I became a teenager, a young man, an adult, even now. "Come on," he'd say, "shake your brother's hand." I squeezed as hard as I could. But when he began to squeeze back, his hand like a steel vice around mine, I'd yelp in pain.

When George was twenty, he stood by the side of the railroad tracks at the station in Bridgeport, waiting for the train that would take him back to Georgetown University in Washington, D.C. The platform was crowded with waiting passengers, and others, the kind of seedy denizens who hung around such places looking for a soft touch. My brother felt a hand slip into his back pocket. He whirled around, with his cocked fist, and punched the pickpocket in the nose. Blood spurted everywhere as the pickpocket fell, stunned, to the platform. My brother was instantly shamed by his quick, violent reaction. He helped the pickpocket up. He tried to stanch the flow of blood with his handkerchief. Finally, he gave the pickpocket all the money in his wallet.

I waited for George to begin coaching me as he had when I was a boy.

After every pitch, he would have something to say. "You're not bending your back enough." Or "You're not throwing straight overhand." But this day, he had nothing to say. We threw silently in the afternoon sun while the two construction workers watched us.

When I was loose, George moved back behind home plate. I stood on the mound. "Get down in a crouch," I said.

"I can't, Brother. Bad back."

So I threw to him standing up, stiffly. I threw a few half-speed fastballs and a few decent sliders. He seemed not to notice. He caught them without interest, his mind someplace else, lost in his slough of despondency. Or maybe not. Maybe my brother was making a concerted effort this day not to coach me, not to preach to me after every pitch about the things I was doing wrong. It used to upset me so, when I was a boy. So many things I did wrong. I thought I could never correct them all and please my brother. Suddenly, I heard a voice call out from the dugout.

"You guys gettin' ready for an old-timers' game or sumthin'?"

I caught the ball from George and turned on the construction workers in a fury. "Old-timers, my ass!" I snapped. "*You* grab a bat, fuckhead! I'll show you old-timers!"

The two workers looked stunned. Too stunned even to be angry at an old man who'd just cursed them. I turned back to my brother to throw again. He was smiling at me. Finally, he spoke.

"You still haven't lost it, Brother."

Thirteen

I THREW WITH Brian a few days after I returned from Waterbury. I met him at the park near his house. He greeted me with his big smile and said, "How'd it go in Waterbury?"

"I threw all right. Not great. Not like with you, coach."

He laughed, then said, "How'd it go with your brother?"

I wasn't sure what to say. "Not bad," I said. "The same. Maybe a little better."

"I know what you mean." Brian had a brother too. He was fourteen, a tall, languid, silent boy who spent too much time, Brian thought, playing video games and watching TV. "I try to get him to play ball and stuff, but it's hard," Brian said. "I don't want to rub his nose in my sports stuff. I don't want to push him and be a dominating older brother."

"You got to deceive him," I said. "Find ways to do things with him without letting him know why."

"Yeh, but it's not so easy. He's smarter than me."

"You and me both, huh, Brian? Two dumb jocks without a brain in our heads."

He laughed. "You dumb too, Pat? Jeez, I never would have known. You talk so much."

"Fuck you, Brian." We both laughed.

I began throwing under the hot, humid South Florida sun that always comforted me. I loved the humidity. It was like a protective blanket around me. I quickly worked up a sweat. It felt good to be back throwing a baseball with Brian, the simplicity of it, in contrast to the complexity of my visit with George. He wore me out. I had to think so hard for ways to drag him out of his lethargy. When he seemed to have no interest in my pitching, I tried shock therapy. "Fuck" every other word. Dirty jokes. Feigned anger at two poor working stiffs sitting in the dugout. It was hard work trying to be a good brother to George. Not like baseball. Baseball was simple. My life was simple. Orderly. My dogs. My wife. My friends. My writing. Now my baseball. For so long, my life was discordant like experimental music, cymbals clashing, drums banging, horns blowing. It confused me. *I* confused me. Then I began to write. I began to make a harmonious order out of all those discordant sounds. I began to understand my self, my life. I simplified my life, gave it order, which freed me. My old man was right. "Read the Greeks, for chrissakes!" he said. Order calmed me in the same way that the order of the pack calms my dogs. Except for Bubba. He fights the order of the pack. He tries to impose *his* order on the pack, just as my brother tried to impose his order on the world by sawing off the legs of chairs that didn't fit. But instead of imposing order, Bubba disrupts the order of the pack. Then he's abject in his apology when he realizes the chaos he's caused. I remember one early morning at our cabin in the western North Carolina mountains. Bubba had been fighting with Nero for days. I beat him with a stick. I fired a shotgun close to his ears to terrify him. Finally, he stopped. Then we got ready to return to Fort Lauderdale at 4:30 A.M. It was black outside as I began to pack our Ford Explorer with our bags. Finally it was time to go. I put all the dogs in the back cargo space. Susan walked ahead of me to open the gate, let me drive through, then close the gate and get in herself.

I saw Susan up ahead, in the headlights' glare, holding open the gate in darkness. I opened the driver's side door. Bubba was sitting in the driver's seat like a king. I grabbed him by his collar to pull him out of the car and lead him around back to the tailgate to throw him in with the other dogs. But Bubba must have feared I was pulling him out of the car to leave him behind because of his fights with Nero. He stiffened, wild-eyed, and pulled away from me. He leapt over the front seats into the midst of the pack and immediately lay down now, with pleading eyes, as if to say, "See! I'll be good. I promise."

But it's not a question of Bubba being good. He's just being what God made him. Which is why we love him for what he is—a noble, primitive beast—and not for what he gives us. He gives us less pleasure and affection than any of the other dogs. Yet he demands the most attention from us, when he wants attention. He insists on being petted when he wants to be petted. He sticks his dog nose under my elbow and noses my elbow into the air. I pet him. I scratch the small of his back in front of his tail. He lets me. I go to hug him. He bolts away and runs outside to chase a possum. We love him for the very reasons that make him so impossible. The purity of his nature. He is natural, irrepressible selfishness. Susan says Bubba's unrestrained exuberance reminds her of what I must have been as a boy. He's a wolf cohabiting with humans and half-human dogs. He doesn't fit. We don't fit with him. We can't give him what he needs to become the great dog that is his nature. Our other dogs have accommodated themselves to our orderly life. They have given up that part of their instinct to hunt for that other part of their instinct to be loved. Bubba tried, but he wants less to be loved than he does to be a great hunter. And we have reduced him to waiting for possums to fall off a fence. To chasing salamanders in the lariope. It frustrates him. So he takes it out on Nero. He has begun to fight again with his father. I fear Bubba will not be with us much longer. The thought that some day I might have to give up Bubba to a new home has filled me with a despair so profound that I have not been able to write a word for one week. My heart is broken at the thought of the inevitable. The loss of Bubba. The disruption into the order of all our lives. I hope against hope that Bubba will overcome his nature, as I have mine. Yet, even as I pray for this, I know, in the deepest place in my heart, that it is a prayer that cannot be answered. Bubba will never change. His nature is too pure. I console myself with the thought that God must want something else for Bubba, for me, for Susan, for us all. Who am I to question God? But I do question Him. Why? Why? Why?

After Brian and I finished throwing we sat in the shade of the dugout and waited for his father and his younger brother, Jarrod. Mark wanted Brian to take 300 swings today in the batting cage. Brian showed me his hands. They were callused and scabbed from all the batting practice Mark made Brian take. Brian just shook his head in disgust. I tried to get his mind off his problems with his father. I told him about Bubba. Brian listened. Then he asked me how I could love something so totally that didn't love me back.

"He can't," I said. "It's his nature to love only himself. You have no control over who you love, Brian."

"But you'll still have the other dogs."

"It doesn't matter. I don't love Bubba one-sixth of the pack. I love him and all the dogs 100 percent each. The loss of any one of them will be devastating. The remaining dogs can't make up for it."

"Then don't give him up."

"Sooner or later, I'm afraid I'll have to. It'll be best for Bubba, and Nero, and the others. Bubba needs to be himself. We're all holding him back."

"What about you? What do you need?"

"It doesn't matter. You love something, you're compelled to do what's best for them, not you. Even if it hurts them and you both."

Mark pulled up in his van with Jarrod. They got out and carried bats and balls over to the dugout. I said hi to Mark. He introduced me to Jarrod. A tall, slender youth with a knowing, sideways way of looking at you that let you know he was more silently interior than Brian.

"Jarrod wants to be a veterinarian," Brian said.

"We were just talking about dogs," I said.

"What about?" Jarrod said.

I began to tell him. Mark listened for a minute, then glanced at his watch. "We've only got thirty minutes, Brian," Mark said. "Let's get to work."

Brian gave him a disgusted look. Jarrod said, "Wait, Dad. I want to hear."

I told Jarrod Bubba's story while Mark fidgeted. When I finished, Jarrod said, "How will the other dogs react when Bubba's gone?"

"I don't know," I said. "I'd like to ask Nero about it. Maybe he'd say 'It's okay. He's a good kid. Keep him. I can take a beating every now and then.' Or maybe he'd say 'I can't take it anymore. Bubba makes me a nervous wreck.' But he can't tell me. I can only guess what's right.'"

"Come on, guys. Let's go," Mark said.

Jarrod smiled as he picked up the bats. "So this is what you and Brian talk about?"

Brian said, "Life Extension 105."

I watched them walk toward the batting cage. Mark, his shoulders hunched, plodding off to work. It's the only way he knows. He was like those Old World guineas my mother and father taught me never to be. Heavy, ponderous, without light in their life. It wasn't their fault. They weren't raised in a gambler's family.

That night Susan called Dawn LaBasco and invited the family to dinner. They all arrived at our door with a gift of ambrosia Dawn had made. It was a southern dessert of fruit mixed with Jell-O and whipped cream. Dawn was a southern girl. A sweet, pale, blond woman with the reticent nature of her younger son.

Our dogs greeted them effusively at the gate. Jarrod went outside to the deck to play with the dogs. Brian went to the Florida room to watch TV. Dawn stood in the kitchen with Susan as she cooked. Mark and I sat at the dining-room table. We drank beer and talked. I could hear Dawn's soft, insistent voice behind me.

"So, Brian had a bad game last week?" I said to Mark.

He shook his head, unsmiling. "Terrible."

"He says you were pissed at him."

Mark looked up from his beer with a pained expression. "Aw, it's not just that. There's more to it than that. I'm worried about him."

"Why? He's a good kid."

"That's it. Everybody likes him. They give him breaks. I'm afraid he's just gonna slide by on his charm."

"Well, the Air Force Academy will take care of that," I said. Brian had decided to accept a scholarship to the Air Force Academy. "They won't give a shit about his charm."

Mark was quiet for a minute. I saw, outside the living-room window, Jarrod on the deck floor, roughhousing with Bubba and Blue. I heard the sounds of a baseball game on TV in the Florida room. I heard Dawn's soft, insistent voice in the kitchen behind me.

Finally, Mark said, "I don't know about the Air Force Academy. It's so far away. I want him to be close to home. Florida at Gainesville, so I can see him play. I've never missed one of his or Jarrod's games."

"Well, maybe he'll like it out there in Colorado Springs."

Mark shook his head. "I don't know what I'll do if I can't see him play. That's all I live for, his and Jarrod's games."

Susan and Dawn put the food on the table. Mark called in his sons. They sat down at the table. Mark looked at Brian. "Did you do the lawn today, like I told you?" Brian glanced at me, embarrassed. He nodded. "It better be done right." Brian put his head down. We ate in silence.

When the LaBascos left, I asked Susan what Dawn was talking to her about. "Breast cancer," Susan said. "I told her it was a loss of will. She agreed." Then, angrily, Susan said, "That father! He's impossible!"

"No. He's all right. He's just limited in a family that isn't."

I threw with Brian a week before I was to pitch in Waterbury. I warmed quickly in the humid July heat. Brian was crouched behind home plate as I threw hard from the mound. The red clay was damp and slippery from last night's rain. After every pitch I had to dig out the clay stuck between my cleats with a stick. But I was throwing good.

"That's the best fastball you've ever thrown to me," Brian said. The ball was hitting the deep pocket in his glove with a resounding *crack*. "I should have brought my sponge." He took his hand out of the glove and shook off the hot pain, the same gesture my brother used to make when I was twelve. I knew he wasn't just trying to pump me up, because when I wasn't throwing hard he was able to catch the ball in the web of the glove where it made a soft sound, like a ball thrown into a bale of hay, and saved his hand. Now I was throwing so hard he didn't have time to adjust the glove and catch the ball in the web. *Crack!*

I remembered some lines from Hemingway's short story "The Battler." Nick Adams meets a punch-drunk fighter named Ad, who tells Nick, "I'm crazy. Listen, you ever been crazy?"

"No," Nick said. "How does it get you?"

"I don't know," Ad said. "When you got it you don't know about it."

That's the way it was with pitching, only in reverse. When it's going bad, you *do* know why. You're conscious of every single flaw in your motion. Your flaws are like points on a graph. See! There, I'm reaching back too far with my arm. And there! I'm not raising my left leg high enough. And there! I'm rushing with my body. See! My throwing arm's lagging behind.

But when it's going good, you don't know why. There are no flaws in your motion, so you can't break it down to points on a graph. It's just one beautiful, fluid line drawing without any points. It's all of a piece. Effortless. The harder I threw with Brian this day, the less effort I felt. When I was throwing badly it was like trying to walk through a strong wind. Every step is a struggle. But today, it was as if I'd found an airless pocket in that wind that allowed me to throw without effort, as in a dream.

I began to pitch to imaginary batters. Brian called balls and strikes. Fastball down the middle. "Strike one!" Slider outside corner. "Strike two!" Fastball up and in. "Ball one! Good waste pitch." Slider down the middle, then sharply off the plate at the last second. "Strike three! Unhittable!" Brian leapt out of his crouch, smiling.

"What do you think, Bri?" I said.

"You're gonna do fine. You're throwing the best you ever have with me."

"Just a few more," I said. I began my motion, pump, kick, remembered I had forgotten to dig the clay out of my spikes, followed through, my left foot slipping in the mud, twisting my knee sharply to the left. I instantly felt the pain. I hopped on one leg off the mound, holding my sprained knee.

"What happened, Pat? You all right?"

"Jeez, I twisted my knee," I said. I tried to put pressure on it. It felt sore, but there was no sharp pain that would indicate a serious injury. "Lemme just throw a few more, Bri. See how it feels."

I threw a few half-speed fastballs but had to stop because of the pain when I landed with all my body weight on my left leg.

"That's it for the day," I said.

"You sure? You gonna be all right?"

"It's nothing. I'll go home and ice it. It'll be fine."

I limped into the house. The dogs came running, leaping on me with their dog smiles and tails wagging. "Down guys, down!" I pushed them away. They backed off, their feelings hurt. "I'm sorry, guys." I bent over and petted each one until they were reassured they'd done nothing wrong.

The house was empty. Susan was still at the beach. I got some ice from the refrigerator, wrapped it in a wet towel, and sat down at the dining-room table. I put the icepack on my knee, which was already swollen. Great. I don't get hurt for six fucking months. Now a week before I pitch I sprain my knee. It didn't matter, though. I'd have to pitch next week no matter how much pain I felt. If I didn't, if I tried to postpone it, everyone in Waterbury would think I was just an old man who couldn't cut it. If I had been twenty, with a sprained knee, they'd just think I had an athlete's injury.

The ice had melted into a little puddle on the hardwood floor. I got up and went to the refrigerator for more ice. I reached up for the ice with my right hand and felt a sharp pain in my shoulder. I rotated my shoulder to feel where the pain was. It was a pinpoint deep inside my arm where it meets the shoulder. I must have hurt it when I slipped off the mound. Christ! Just what I needed. A pinched nerve. Then I remembered the Los Angeles Lakers trainer. He tapped me on the shoulder with a smug smile. "Rotator cuff," he said, "I guarantee it." Fuck him! I won't let it be that. I won't.

I was sitting at the table, icing my knee, when Susan came in from the beach. She was wearing her bikini bathing suit with the thong bottom that exposed her small, tight ass. Not bad for an old broad, I thought, as I always did when I saw her in that bikini.

"Get any play today, baby?" I said.

"The usual," she said. "Some pink tourist trying to camcord my ass when I was lying on my stomach. I caught him and screamed at him so everyone on the beach could hear. He was so humiliated he slunk off."

"That's my girl."

She noticed me icing my knee. "What happened? Did you hurt yourself?"

"Just a sprain, I think." She bent over to examine my swollen knee. Over her back I could see the bare cheeks of her ass in her thong.

She straightened up and caught me staring at her ass. She put her hands on her hips. "I thought your knee was sprained."

"It is."

"Well, it couldn't be that bad."

I shrugged. "You took my mind off it for an instant."

She reached both hands behind her back and unhooked her bra top. "Let's see if we can't keep your mind off it for more than an instant, baby."

Boiled potatoes instead of homemade spaghetti sauce was a small price to pay, I thought, as she helped me, limping, into the bedroom.

When I got out of bed the next morning, my swollen knee was locked stiff. I could barely bend it. I limped into the kitchen to make my Cuban coffee, then let the dogs out the back door to hunt the possum.

I was smoking my first cigar of the morning, reading the newspaper, when Susan came onto the back porch.

"How's your knee?" she said.

"Not so hot," I said. "I can't bend it."

She knelt down and looked at it. "It's awful swollen. Maybe you should put some heat on it now."

"What is it? Twenty-four hours after a sprain you go from cold to hot?"

"I think so. If it doesn't work you can call Bob Wirsz and postpone your game."

"That's not an option, babe."

"Why not?"

"I can't even let them know I'm hurt. They'll think I'm stalling or getting cold feet, or just an old man who can't cut it physically."

Susan grinned at me. "You weren't an old man yesterday." She smiled, dreamily. "You certainly did—how did you put it—'cut it' yesterday."

"Yeh, but I didn't sprain *that*."

"No. But it was swollen." We both laughed. Then she said, "I guess

I'm going to have to baby my jock husband for the rest of the week, huh? Be a good little dutiful baseball player's wife.''

"Dutiful wife? Jeez, babe! I don't think I can stand it.''

"Oh, no! It'll be good for me, sweetheart. See, I'm already slipping into it. A new role. We actresses love playing against type. Let's see . . .'' She put a long finger to her chin as if thinking. "I'll have to learn to say 'Yes, honey' to all your commands. Look up at you with limpid, cow eyes. Live my entire life around hubby's career. 'Oh, yes, we hurt our knee throwing yesterday, but we'll be ready for the big game.' How's that?''

"Good. I think I know that broad. I've interviewed her enough times over the last thirty years.''

"Yes. I'm becoming her as we speak, sweetheart.'' She flashed me her syrupy, 8-by-10 glossy smile. "How's that?''

"Good.''

"A baseball wife always smiles.'' She assumed the deep voice of a male sportswriter. "Tell me, Mrs. Jordan. Don't you think your husband's a little long in the tooth to pitch a baseball game? Maybe pre-Alzheimer's?'' She smiled her big-eyed, syrupy smile and said in a girlish voice, "Oh, no! We can still cut it. We threw smoke yesterday.''

"There's one other thing.''

"What's that, sweetheart?''

"A good baseball wife never does anything without asking her hubby's permission.''

"Hmmm. That'll be a hard one.'' She flashed her smile and assumed her girlish voice. "Honey! Can we have another teensy-weensy double Stolichnaya? Pretty please?''

"There's still one more thing.''

"Jesus, babe. You're pushing it.''

"You'll have to cook. I mean, for real. Things with more than one ingredient.''

A sore subject, Susan's cooking. She once cooked a turkey in a paper bag because she read somewhere that that made it more tender. It still wasn't done after ten hours, so she served it rare to our friends for Thanksgiving dinner.

"I didn't know turkey was supposta be pink," Sol said.

I glared at him. "You wanna piss her off? Just eat it."

When she served the biscuits they were burned on the outside. They were the kind of Pillsbury instant biscuits that came in cardboard cylinders you had to whack against the kitchen counter. They popped out already made. All Susan had to do was bake them in the oven at 375 degrees for 12 minutes.

Sol looked at his burned biscuit but said nothing. Ronnie split his open to butter it. The insides were runny and leaked down his plate. Before I could warn him to silence he said, "Amazing, Susan! Overcooked on the outside, undercooked on the inside."

Phil said, "I thought they were foolproof."

Susan's cooking became a standing joke among our friends. Whenever we invited them to dinner, they'd say, "Is Susan gonna cook? Biscuits?" Sol always stopped at McDonald's first. "Just in case," he said.

Susan glared at me now. Not the dutiful baseball wife now. "Yes, I'll cook for you. *Sweetheart*. And not biscuits either. Whatever you want."

"Homemade spaghetti sauce?"

I told her about George and Mildred. My brother's slough of despondency. Susan had met Mil only a few times. But they hit it off right away. Susan stood at the stove in Mil's kitchen and asked her questions about cooking. Susan even took notes. When we got home, she stuck the notes in one of the dozens of cookbooks she never looked at. "The point is to use the recipes to *cook* things," I said.

"I'm building up to it," she said.

Mil waited until she was alone with Susan before she asked her questions too. They were mostly about our life in Fort Lauderdale. She was fascinated by our friends, especially Phil and Chelsea and the Booby Trap. Susan described what went on there. Naked girls dancing for men on top of plastic boxes under blue- and rose-colored lights.

"And you're not embarrassed to go there?" Mil said.

"Not usually," Susan said. "I do it for Pat. He likes to meet his friends there." She told Mildred about Sol and Phil and Chelsea and Peter. "He won't go unless I go with him. I try not to pay attention to the girls. I talk to Chelsea mostly." Susan sighed. "But sometimes . . ."

"Sometimes, what?"

Susan explained. She told Mil about the time we drove to our cabin in the western North Carolina mountains. We always stopped halfway between Fort Lauderdale and North Carolina to eat at a country kitchen south of Macon, Georgia, on I-75. On this particular trip, we were looking forward to a rich country dinner when we noticed, for the first time, a lot of new billboards along the highway. They were painted pink and baby blue, with pictures of beautiful girls on them. They were advertisements for "Club Exstasy, Nude Entertainment."

"Something new," Susan said, without interest. The signs began to appear more frequently as we approached the exit to the country kitchen. But we were famished, so we forgot about the billboards. We fantasized about our dinner. Fried chicken. Candied yams. Fried okra. Peach cobbler. I pulled off the highway into the parking lot of the country kitchen. It had been repainted pink and baby blue, and there was now a big sign on the roof that read: "Club Exstasy, Nude Entertainment."

Susan stared at the sign glumly and shook her head. She muttered to herself, "Sometimes pussy's just not enough."

Mildred thought Susan was, as she put it, "a sketch." George thought Susan was a sketch too, only a sketch he didn't want to color in. He had met Susan only a few times more than Mil had. He tried to keep her at arm's length. "I just can't seem to warm up to her," he told me one day. Of course not, I thought. Susan wasn't exactly a dutiful Italian wife who deferred to her husband. It wasn't that George didn't like Susan. He just didn't understand her. Sometimes I would catch him looking at her as if she was some new species of extraterrestrial life. That snapping alien that tormented Sigourney Weaver. Whenever George phoned our house and Susan answered, he'd say "Hello! Is this Patty's wife? Is Patty there?" Susan would hand me the phone, whispering, "I don't think he even knows my name. Maybe he doesn't want to."

One day George phoned when I was in the bathtub. Susan called in to me, "Babe, it's your brother."

I called back, "Tell him I'm in the fucking tub."

I heard her voice: "George, he's in the fucking tub."

I was still laughing when she hung up. I called out, "Did he laugh?"

She poked her head around the bathroom door. "He laughed. But it was a strange laugh. Sort of strangled. Like he was trying to stop himself."

"That's my brother."

"I don't think he knows what to make of me."

"*I* don't know what to make of you."

The funny thing was, Susan was more George's ally in our oft-strained relationship than she was mine. Whenever I got angry with him over some slight, it was Susan who tried to get me out of it. She did it always with the same refrain. "But your brother loves you," she said.

"How do you know?"

"I just do."

For the rest of the week Susan was a dutiful baseball wife. She pored over Italian cookbooks, her brows furrowed. Then, in a panic, she called my mother before she began cooking. I heard her whispering to my mother over the phone in the kitchen. "Are you sure, Mother?" Susan said. "Just follow the directions?"

I had to laugh. My mother and Susan. The hated Irisher and the tough old guinea mother-in-law. Sisters now. But thirteen years ago . . .

* * *

"Ryan!" my mother said into the telephone when I told her my new wife's maiden name. "What kind of name is that for an Italian wife?"

Which was why she and my father, both in their late seventies, hotfooted it down to Florida shortly after we were married. To check out my Irish wife.

My mother hated to fly, and even more, she hated to leave the safety of the neighborhood. Pacelli's Bakery. Sorrento Importing Company.

Frank's Market. She had no curiosity about Florida, which, in her mind, was a foreign land of cowboys, yentas, South Americans, WASPS, and, worse, Irish.

Susan recognized her immediately at the airport. "There!" she said. "I told you." My mother was wearing the mink coat my father had bought her for Christmas.

"It's eighty-three degrees," I said. "How did you know?"

"A woman can always find an excuse to wear her mink."

They came toward us, a scared old couple not used to flying. I hadn't seen them in more than a year. They looked so much older to me— small, shrunken, hesitant, barely resembling the fierce Italian couple who had raised me. My father wore his hat and his topcoat. My mother clutched his arm with one hand while in the other she held a paper bag filled with Genoa salami, provolone cheese, and roasted sweet peppers in olive oil. I introduced my parents to Susan. My father kissed her. My mother greeted her politely. She must still be disoriented from the flight, I thought.

Susan gushed over my mother's coat. My mother pulled it tightly to herself and said, "It was so cold on the plane." Susan smiled at me.

They settled in the backseat of my old Alfa and we left the airport. I turned on the air-conditioning. My mother shivered. "Oh no, Patty!" she said. "It's too cold." I was about to say something when Susan laid her hand on my arm.

We were immediately caught in bumper-to-bumper tourist-season traffic heading toward the beach. There was construction going on all around us. Dust swirled in the heat. I opened the window to a blast of hot air and the sound of jackhammers. I inched the car along and then stopped at a light. One of the hookers who usually work Federal Highway came up to my window. She smiled at me.

"Wanna party, hon?" she said.

I motioned to my parents in the backseat. "You got a group rate, sweetheart?"

She stuck her head in the car and then pulled it back out. "Sorry, hon." She moved to the next car.

"Who was that, Son?" my mother said.

"Just a hooker, Ma."

"A what?"

"*Puttana,*" my father said.

My mother nodded. She looked back at the girl. "Poor thing," she said. "It's so hot."

Susan smiled at me just as we heard the screech of tires and first one crash, then another, and then we felt the impact. Everyone was jolted forward a bit, but no one was hurt. The beginning of a perfect day, I thought as I got out to inspect the damage. It was just a dented rear bumper.

The guy who had hit me was standing in the street, waving his arms and screaming at his wife. She screamed back. They were both in their sixties, fat, slovenly people with swollen ankles and unlaced shoes. I went over to their battered old Comet and tried to calm them down.

"Relax," I said. "It's no big deal."

"Look at it! Look at it!" the guy screamed, gesturing toward the crumpled hood of his car. A greenish liquid was leaking out of the engine. "It's ruined! And it's all her fault! I told her to stop nagging!"

"Don't worry," I said. "Your insurance will cover it."

"Insurance!" he screamed. "Insurance! What insurance?"

"Oh, jeez!" Just what I needed, I thought, and went back to my car. My mother was poking Susan in the back.

"Tell him, dear," she said. "Go ahead."

Susan looked guiltily at me. Her eyes flitted toward my mother and back to me. "I think I hurt my neck."

"You're kidding!" I said.

"Whiplash!" my mother screamed. "You can sue him."

Susan turned toward the backseat and said, "Really, Mother. I'm fine. It's nothing."

My mother glared at her as if, as she had expected, my Irish wife had betrayed her as soon as possible. I tried to intercede.

"Besides, Ma, the guy's got no insurance."

"No insurance! What kind of a place is this?"

We drove the rest of the way in silence. My mother brooded in the backseat. It took us almost an hour in the heat and traffic to make the ten-mile trip back to our apartment.

My mother feigned enthusiasm for our place in a way designed specifically to let us know she did not approve. "It's so . . . so . . . Florida," she said. She was not used to glass-and-chrome furniture and framed Art Deco prints. Her apartment back in Connecticut was filled with heavy, thickly brocaded Mediterranean furniture that was so precious to her she wouldn't let anyone sit on it. The pictures on her walls were faded sepia photographs of men and women from another time, another place. They had round, dark-skinned faces. The women had luxuriant black curls and the men slicked-back hair and high-buttoned collars. Her parents and her grandparents from Italy.

"Pink walls?" she said.

"That's coral," I said. "It's a Florida color, Ma."

I showed her our only bedroom, where she and my father would sleep while Susan and I slept out on the deck.

"It's a double bed," she said. She glared at my father, who, embarrassed, was fingering his hat. "Well, I hope the old man doesn't get any ideas," she said. "I'm an old woman, for goodness sake." It was then I remembered that even while I was growing up, they slept in separate beds.

After we put their bags away, my mother took out all the food she had brought us, under the assumption that my Irish wife was, naturally, not feeding me properly. Then, mapping out her territory as quickly as possible, she began puttering around the kitchen.

"I'll cook a good Italian supper tonight," she said. She fixed Susan with that withering stare of hers that I had been dreading. She stared at this tall, thin, very Irish-looking woman who was wearing a T-shirt, satin shorts, and, of all things, sneakers, as if she were seeing her for the first time. Susan's face turned red.

My mother put her hands on her hips, a tiny, fierce woman who was about to begin the fight. "I have to buy some things," she said to Susan. "I don't suppose *you* would know if there's an Italian importing store in this city, would you?"

Susan looked quickly at me and then back at my mother. I closed my eyes and exhaled a great breath.

My father and I stayed at the apartment while my mother and Susan went shopping at Fernando's International Food Market out on Federal Highway. Susan followed my mother up and down the aisles of the store. My mother carried a shopping basket in the crook of her arm, like a bent, aged, steely-haired Little Red Riding Hood. She examined a jar of red peppers in olive oil through her bifocals. She explained to Susan that the color of the oil was too pale, not green enough. The price was too dear. Susan nodded. Other shoppers stared at them, this incongruous couple. My mother and my wife, a Florida woman in satin shorts and sneakers.

My mother stopped at the delicatessen counter. She looked at salamis, the cheeses, the stuffed peppers.

"I always make them myself," my mother said, pointing to the peppers. "I never buy breadcrumbs. I toast my own bread and grate it."

"I see, Mother," Susan said. My mother explained how to mix the ingredients for the stuffing.

"The raisins are the secret," she said. "My mother taught me." Susan nodded again. The deli man spoke to my mother in Italian. She looked at him, a young man with a florid face and slicked-back black hair. He smiled and spoke again in a Neapolitan dialect. My mother looked confused. It was years since she had spoken much Italian. Now her mind was a cobweb of a few bastardized words and phrases. Susan came to her rescue. She and I had spent four months living in Florence the year before, and she had learned the language quickly. When she got back to the States, she took a course in Italian.

"He says he has some very fresh bread for the *signora*," Susan said to my mother. She looked at Susan, dumbfounded. "Do you want some bread, Mother?" My mother just shook her head no, as if embarrassed. Susan spoke to the man again in Italian. He nodded and smiled.

They went up and down the aisles again. My mother made a great production of looking for homemade pasta, white beans, and tomato paste, but it was obvious that she was shaken. Susan thought it was only because my mother had never expected a deli man in Florida to speak in her native tongue.

Susan tried to assuage her embarrassment. "There are a lot of Italians in Florida, Mother. You know, the weather reminds them of southern Italy and Sicily, and then, of course, there's the ocean, which reminds them of the Mediterranean. The lifestyle too is much easier here, less hectic. It reminds Pat and me a lot of Italy."

My mother waved the back of her hand at Susan, as if to say, no, that's not what bothered me. Then my mother said, "Your Italian. You speak it beautifully. How did you learn?" Susan told her about living in Italy and how much she loved it and then about her Italian course here. My mother nodded. She was silent for a while as she put things in her basket.

"You know, I have always been ashamed of my Italian," my mother said. "It was really always just a bastard Italian, the kind Italian-Americans speak. I could tell your accent was much purer." Then she began to tell Susan about her childhood, the homemade wine her mother sold, the Irish cops who demanded a kickback and who mimicked the strange language my mother's people spoke. "That was how I got so prejudiced against the Irish," she said. "They made fun of our Italian, so we tried to add American words to it until it became a language that wasn't Italian and wasn't English. Dad and I rarely spoke Italian in the house. We didn't want Patty to learn it and have the same trouble we did."

"But that was long ago, Mother. Things are different now."

"I know. I know. But I'm an old woman. Stuck in my ways. I can't change. I'll always be prejudiced against the Irish."

"I understand, Mother. That's all right."

"I even told Patty he could never marry an Irish girl. But he never listened to me anyway. Now look. You, an Irisher." She stopped a moment and looked up at Susan. "I don't suppose you have any Italian blood in you, do you?"

"I'm afraid not. A little German and English. But mostly Irish." My mother looked defeated. Then Susan added, "And a tiny bit of Spanish somewhere."

"Oh, don't tell me!" my mother shrieked. "God forbid! They cut up their men with knives! Just like the Italians!" She let out a shrill, cackling laugh. Then she said, "Do you know why Italian mothers never want their sons to marry an Irish girl?"

"No, Mother, why?"

"Because when an Italian husband strikes his Irish wife, the first thing she does is call the police. And it's always an Irish cop who comes to the door. What does he see?" Susan shook her head. "He sees this poor pudding-faced Irish girl with blueberries for eyes, holding a hand to her cheek, and her Italian husband in the background. Now, who do you think he's gonna hit with his nightstick?"

Susan couldn't keep from laughing out loud. When she finally stopped, she said, "And what does a good Italian wife do, Mother?"

"Oh, they never call the cops. They wait until their husband is asleep, and then they stick the kitchen knife in his heart. Just like the Spanish!" My mother let out another high-pitched cackle, and her eyes filled with tears of laughter.

My mother and Susan were still laughing when they got home with their groceries. The two women went straight to the kitchen and began to cook supper. They chattered back and forth while my father and I looked first at them, then at each other, and then back at them. Susan wrote down all the directions my mother gave her while she was preparing the food.

We ate dinner out on the deck, under the stars. Jim, our landlord, and his wife, Jane, joined us. Susan lit candles enclosed in glass. A breeze blew up the Intracoastal Waterway. Susan and my mother laid out the food. Sweet red peppers stuffed with raisins. Italian bread torn in chunks and served in a wicker basket. A jar of hot-pepper flakes. Steaming bowls of *pasta e fagioli*. Bottles of Chianti Classico.

Susan and I talked about our stay in Italy, a place my mother and father had never seen. They were born here only a few years after their parents had come over. The only Italy they knew was the Italian neighborhood where they had been raised and from which they had not strayed in more than seventy-five years. And now here they were, on a deck in Florida with their new Irish daughter-in-law, who was telling them about their parents' native land. Susan told them about the gypsies who begged on the steps of Florence's Duomo; about the teenagers and shopgirls who rode to work on Vespas that sounded like swarms of wasps; about the *carabinieri,* unsmiling young men in military uniforms, with snub-nosed machine guns, and how they were quick to toss their machine guns on the seat of their car whenever they were talking (with a smile now) to a pretty girl; and, finally, she told them about the transsexual prostitutes with their perfect breasts and mannish voices and the sound of their high-heeled shoes clattering on the cobblestoned streets as they ran from the *polizia.*

My mother cackled with laughter. *"Puttana frigida!"* she said.

Suddenly my father stood up in the darkness, his face illuminated by flickering candlelight. He raised his wineglass and proposed a toast. "To our new daughter-in-law," he said. We all raised our glasses and clicked them over the table.

My mother turned to Jim and Jane and said in a stage whisper, "My daughter-in-law, she's Spanish, you know."

*   *   *

Now my mother's Spanish daughter-in-law was spending all her waking hours in the kitchen. Sweat dripped from her brow as she chopped and diced, like *The Madwoman of Chaillot,* or maybe Carrie Snodgress in *Diary of a Mad Housewife.*

She made chicken Abruzzi and chicken Florentine and *pasta arrabiatto* and homemade Tuscan bread. Flour dusted the kitchen walls. Black olives and bits of cherry tomatos were ground into the floor. Escarole leaves were burned and stuck to the stove. I sat at the dining-room table quaking with fear. She brought the plates of steaming food to the table and put them down in front of me. She stood there, hands on hips, defying me to complain. I looked up at her as I put the fork to my lips. "Mmm. Delicioso!"

"Really?" she said.

"Really." She smiled.

Susan cooked and cleaned and fed the dogs and Francis. I lay around the house for five days, waiting for my knee to heal. I didn't tell her about the pain in my shoulder because I didn't want to worry her. She knew how much this game meant to me, after all these years. It meant a lot to her too, to see me finally do the one thing I loved to do when I was a boy.

But my knee wasn't getting any better. The pain in my shoulder was still there too. I hadn't thrown in five days. I didn't know if the pain would go away once I began throwing or get worse.

On Friday, I went to the Sports Authority to buy a knee brace with a metal hinge. While I was there, it occurred to me to get a jock strap too, with a metal cup. Jeez, I hadn't worn a jock and a cup in thirty-five years. I laughed to myself, remembering the first time I had taken Susan to a major league spring-training game in Fort Lauderdale. She was mesmerized as batter after batter stepped up to the plate in their tight uniform pants over their big metal cup. She moved forward to the edge of her seat and stared in rapture. Finally, in the third inning, she said, "God, babe! I didn't realize all baseball players were hung like horses."

"They aren't. They're all wearing the same size cup. Who knows what little thing is floating around in there."

"Bummer."

When I got home I tried on the knee brace. It fit so tightly I could barely bend my leg, even if it wasn't swollen. I tried to go through my pitching motion in the living room. I could only raise my left leg about six inches off the floor. When I landed on my left foot, however, the pain was lessened, but not by much. I could still pitch, I thought. I had to.

On Sunday morning I called Bob Wirsz to tell him about my knee, but not the pain in my shoulder.

"So you can't pitch," he said.

"No, Bob. It's getting better. I'll pitch. I just thought maybe your trainer could tell me how to bring down the swelling."

"I'll have her call you." A few minutes later the team's girl trainer called me. I told her what had happened, the swelling, the stiffness.

"When you try to bend it," she said, "do you hear a clicking noise?"

"No."

"Good. What you do is go get some Aleve. Take one every four hours. And ice the shit out of the knee."

"I've been putting heat on it."

"Wrong. Ice it at least a half hour at a time, twice a day."

I got some ice from the refrigerator, wrapped it in a wet towel, and sat down on the sofa in the porch. The dogs lay around me. I could see Susan in the kitchen, cooking. Still! Jesus! I can't wait for this to be over. I clicked on the TV to a Braves game. Greg Maddux was pitching. I tied the icepack to my knee with an Ace bandage and lay down.

Maddux was his usual maddeningly machinelike self. Every pitch had a purpose. Every pitch went where he wanted it to go. Mostly low and away to righthanded batters. I slipped into my old habit and began thinking along with Maddux on every pitch. Fastball off the plate and then tailing back in for a strike. Slider starting on the outside corner, then breaking off the plate for a swinging strike two. Now up and in with a fastball, I thought. Straighten him up. But no. Maddux continued to work away from the batter until he grounded out to short. He was such a machine. He seemed conditioned to do only one thing. Low and away every pitch. He couldn't get out of himself, break his pattern. Maybe he was afraid if he did, he'd lose the delicate balance he'd created over the years. He was a craftsman, not an artist. It dawned on me that he must be fearful. That if he changed anything, he might lose his success. Like my wife's daughter, the actress Meg Ryan. She had worked so hard to create a screen persona of herself as Meg Ryan, the ditzy, loveable comedian, that now she was trapped into playing only those roles because they pleased her fans. This had begun to frustrate her. She wanted to stretch herself as an actress. But she also wanted to keep the fans that loved adorable Meg Ryan. So she made a Sophie's choice that was ultimately frustrating. She refused to give up her painstakingly crafted persona. She hoarded her success that did not please her anymore because the other thing, the unknown, was too fearful. It *was* a fearful thing to break the pattern. I remembered a poem by Amy Lowell. It was about a woman trapped in the social conventions of her day that ultimately led to her great tragedy. When she realizes this, she says:

I walk down the patterned garden paths
In my stiff, brocaded gown.
With my powdered hair and jeweled fan,
I too am a rare
Pattern . . .

Christ! What are patterns for?

I remembered another line from somewhere, too: It is more fearsome to run from your fears than to stand and face them. I remembered too what my father's gambling had taught me: Even if the game if fixed, and you know you're going to lose, you have to play the game if it's the only one in town. After all, it's never victory that excites a gambler but, rather, the possibility of loss. Hell, for a gambler, is a game he can never lose. Some people, like my wife's daughter, are so terrified of loss, they choose not to play the game. They want power, not freedom. I learned as a gambler's son that life always comes down to a choice between freedom and power, and you can never have both.

I was watching Maddux throw in the bullpen in West Palm Beach during spring training last year. It was the first week of training and *still* he threw every pitch to his catcher's glove. Chipper Jones walked by and stopped to watch. Maddux paused in his stretch, slightly hunched forward, his upper body curling in, his brows furrowed with a kind of ocular bloc I'd never had, never would have. Then he delivered, the catcher turning to say something to a fan, the ball hitting his outstretched glove without him even looking at it. Chipper Jones muttered out loud, "Still having trouble with your location, eh, Maddux?"

Maddux threw every pitch like that, with total concentration, as if nothing else in the world mattered, or existed, except his intent to throw every pitch exactly where he wanted to. I marveled at his will, his ocular bloc, because nothing in my life was that important. *No one thing* in my life was that important because *every thing* in my life was important. I did not have the nature to break down the things in my life—my wife, my dogs, my friends, my writing, my pitching—to their proper importance. Sometimes it was more important to me to play with my dogs than to write. Sometimes it was more important to me to laugh and drink with my friends at dinner than to pitch that afternoon. And sometimes it was even more important for me to pitch than it was to please Susan by going to the beach with her. I loved everything in my life. I refused to let one thing dictate my life. That's why I became a writer. My job encompasses all of life.

I remembered years ago, when I interviewed Tom Seaver. He was the most like myself of any athlete I ever met, except in one regard. He was able to force himself to do what I either never could or refused to. Tom told me that when he woke every morning during baseball season, the first thing he did was check the box scores in the *New York Times* to see who got two hits the night before, so he'd know how to pitch them.

"I might want to read the theater review first," he said, "but I never do. I force myself to read the box scores."

I felt sorry for Tom. He deliberately made his life smaller rather than bigger. It was a way I could never be.

This pitching, then, was just one more thing that made my life bigger. If it didn't, if it diminished my life, then it wasn't worth it. If I couldn't do it as simply one more thing in my life, rather than the most important thing, I would stop it. It wasn't the end result that mattered. Three strikeouts in one inning wasn't the point. The whole experience of the last six months—Brian, Susan, my brother—that was the point.

I heard Susan's voice from the kitchen. "Dinner's ready, babe!"

I got up and walked to the dining-room table. Susan looked down at my knee. "You're not limping anymore," she said.

I looked down at my knee. I tried to bend it. It bent without pain, only a little stiffness.

FOURTEEN

ON MONDAY, July 28, we flew to Hartford late in the afternoon. Just as the plane was about to land I felt a searing pain, like an electric shock, shoot through my brain. It was the most blinding pain I had ever felt. I cried out so loudly that the other passengers turned and stared at me as both palms slapped over my forehead. It felt like my head was going to explode. Tears flooded my eyes as I winced in pain, bent over in my seat, and rocked back and forth.

Susan screamed, *"Babe!* What's happening?" She tried to comfort me but she could do nothing except put her arm around me and hold me until the pain finally subsided.

"God!" I said, wiping the tears away. "It felt like a stroke."

"Are you all right?" she said. She was breathing heavily, her eyes wide in fear.

"Yes, it's gone."

The black woman in the seat across from me said to Susan, "Is he all right?"

"Yes. Thank you." Susan exhaled a great breath. She looked at me. "It must have been psychosomatic. You have to relax, babe. There's nothing to worry about." She smiled. "Just think of this as Patty's Big Adventure."

We rented a car and drove south to Waterbury. I was quiet, a little spacey, my mind lost in Patty's Big Adventure. Where would it take me?

Susan chattered away beside me: partly to take my mind off the attack I'd had, partly because she was so excited for me, and partly because she was trying to hide her own worry too. Not only for me, but for our dogs, especially the puppies, Blue and Bubba. This was the first time she had gone on a trip with me since the puppies were born, almost three years ago. They had never been left without at least one of us.

Before the puppies were born, Susan used to go with me on all my assignments. Sometimes she helped me out with my interviews. While I talked to Tommy John about his slider over dinner, Susan talked to his wife in hushed tones. Tommy looked over, annoyed that they were not giving his monologue about his slider their rapt attention. Or maybe he was just afraid that his wife would share an intimacy with Susan that would find its way into print. He was right to be worried: Susan was my beard.

When we got back to our hotel room after dinner with the Johns, Susan said, "Can you believe it? She has to ask his permission to have another strawberry daiquiri."

"You never know," I said. "A lot of baseball wives tipple when their husband's on the road. Besides, a baseball player's wife knows her place." I grinned at her. "You oughta take a hint, sweetheart."

She looked at me with raised eyebrows. "Not in this life. Sweetheart."

Usually, though, Susan just stayed in our hotel room while I interviewed my subjects. Most of them were men, actors and athletes. Susan disturbed them. Partly because of the way she looked: a tall, leanly muscled older blonde with short spiky hair like spring grass. She dressed in tight spandex dresses and a stripper's four-inch pumps. "Why not?" she said. "Geriatrics need sex objects too." But mostly she disturbed such men for the same reason she disturbed my brother: They didn't know what to make of her. More than once some egocentric actor or athlete would say something so outrageous—"My life is bigger than ordinary people's"—that I would instantly cringe.

"Bullshit!" Susan would snap.

So I left her in the hotel room a lot. She spent the hours ordering room service to check out the silver plate. If the silver plate was hefty enough, she'd steal it. Sometimes without telling me. One night we were flying back from L.A. Susan put her bags on the X-ray conveyor belt at LAX. The bags jangled as they passed through the X-ray machine. "Hold it!" snapped the female security guard watching the monitor. She made Susan open her bag. The guard reached in and pulled out a handful of silver plate knives and forks. She had to check with her supervisor to see if they'd be classified as concealed weapons before she finally let them through.

At dinner with our friends, our table was set with mismatched silver plate with different initials on them. S for Sheraton. H for Hilton. Never R for Ramada Inn. One night Sol held up his fork with an S on it and said, "A family heirloom, Susan?"

"My initial." She smiled sweetly.

Sol held up a knife with an H on it. "Who's H?"

Susan said, "My former husband, Harry."

One time in L.A., I was out all day on an interview. Susan must have finally gotten bored with room service because when I returned to the hotel room I found her lounging on the bed in her silk negligee. She looked up at me with lascivious eyes and said, "I've been waiting for you, baby." The television was on. A movie. A naked blonde with a tattoo on her ass—a rose, naturally—was kneeling on all fours between the legs of a particularly hairy guy lying on a bed. The blonde's big ass filled the screen. Her legs were spread, so the cameraman behind her could shoot through her legs to her head, which was bobbing up and down on the guy's prodigious joint.

"An interesting shot, don't you think?" Susan said. "I got it from room service. Better than silver plate." But those days were gone forever after the puppies were born. Maybe we had just gotten old? Or maybe Susan's maternal instinct had taken over? The puppies had been born in our bedroom and had never spent a moment away from Susan. We both agreed it was a sacrifice we wanted to make for them. So Susan stopped traveling with me, until now.

We had boarded all six dogs in a kennel before we left. Susan gave the girl at the kennel strict instructions. "Bubba and Blue stay in a run with their mother," she said, sternly, like the school mistress she'd once been. "The older dogs, Hoshi, Kiri, and Nero, stay together." The girl led the dogs away from us to the runs in back. I followed the girl to make sure she separated the dogs properly. When I returned to Susan in the lobby, she had tears in her eyes. We were becoming like the old people we used to laugh at. They retired from the Northeast to Florida to spend their days tending a lone orange tree in their backyards (in our case, mango, avocado, and key lime trees) and lavishing all their affection on their dogs as a substitute for their adult children who never visited them. Our children had turned their backs on us too. We swore we'd never do that to our parents. We agreed that her cold, distant father (her beloved mother had died of cancer) and my hot, overbearing parents would come to live with us when they became infirm. But who would take care of us when we became infirm? Who would take care of our dogs when we died? It was a common worry of old people in Florida.

It's funny. All your life you look at old people and wonder why they live the lives they do. Then, as you become old, you see yourself living the same lives.

In our late fifties, we lived our lives in a Twilight Zone. We were both young and old. With one hand, we held on to our fading youth, bikini thongs and pitching baseballs. With the other we reached out to beckoning old age. We did not fear losing the former or embracing the latter. Getting old was the natural order. We were just trying to extend the limits of youth at the expense of our old age. We refused to be old before our time, but we refused too to hold on to a youth that had passed us by. Susan made me promise that when I looked at her body in her bikini thong and saw the sagging flesh of a foolish old woman, I would tell her. And I made a promise to myself that I would give up pitching the moment twenty-four-year-old batters proved to me that I could not get them out. We both knew that the days of our youth were closing fast. That with each passing year we were becoming more old than young. The balance was shifting. I realized this for the first time the day I got into a fight on Fort Lauderdale beach. It was the first fight I had gotten into in almost forty years. I was fifty-three.

*　　*　　*

It was a beautiful Sunday morning in Fort Lauderdale. The sun was hot, the blue sky clear, and a faint, insistent breeze was blowing in from the Atlantic Ocean across the beach. My wife and I were pedaling our bicycles on the sidewalk alongside the beach, as we often did on such Sunday mornings. We liked to pedal alongside the beach in our bathing suits, watching the tourists and locals bake in the sun, until we were tired. Then we would stop at a little liquor store on the corner, buy two cans of Lite beer, and go sit on the wall lining the beach and watch the people and cars pass by. Sometimes we brought along the Sunday papers to read. Usually I smoked a cigar with my beer.

On this particular Sunday in April, the beach was packed with sunbathers smelling of coconut oil. The sidewalk was crowded too, with strollers and other bikers and rollerbladers, and even a father on rollerblades pushing his baby daughter ahead of him in a carriage. My wife moved ahead of me on her bike to clear a path for us by squeezing the little rubber-knobbed horn on her handlebars. It made a funny little *toot-toot* sound, and when people heard it behind them, they invariably smiled as they made way for us to pass. "Thank you," my wife would say.

We were halfway up the beach when I saw a rollerblader skating backwards, heading right toward us. He was a big guy, with a bodybuilder's muscles, in his late twenties. His perfectly tanned skin in his bikini bathing suit was glistening in the sun with oil. His glistening, ominous presence momentarily disoriented me. And then I realized he was skating backwards without even looking back over his shoulder, as if the entire sidewalk was his own personal rink. He was weaving left and right and left, so that his presence endangered everyone on the sidewalk. My wife didn't see him until too late. He skated right at her and brushed her bike. She wobbled on it a bit, then regained control, as he, oblivious, skated toward me now. I shouted out, "Asshole! Watch where you're going!"

For the first time now, he looked over his shoulder, swerved to miss me, and then stopped. He studied me for a minute, an older guy with a white beard, but not that old, still threatening in his way, or else why would he have called out like that? Then he made his decision and skated back toward me. When he pulled alongside of me, he said, "Who are you calling 'asshole'?"

"You," I said. "You almost ran into my wife."

He must have expected me to back down from what I had called him. When I didn't, it confused him. He decided to try to stare me down to intimidate me. He was so intent on glaring at me as he skated a little ahead of me that he still didn't notice my wife. He skated into her. She tumbled to the sidewalk, her bike falling on top of her. She cried out in pain, and at that moment I felt myself leaving my bike, my body in the air, everything slowing down, silent, like in an old movie. I hit him in the chest with my right shoulder, and he fell backwards onto the sidewalk with me on top of him. I heard my wife screaming, "No, Patty! No!" as I grappled with the rollerblader on the sidewalk in full view of passing cars and strollers. We rolled over and over, each of us searching for an advantage. Finally, I managed to get him in a headlock with my left arm. I pulled back my right hand into a fist and was ready to punch him. But he was so lathered with oil that he managed to slither out of my headlock like a snake. He leapt to his feet in front of me. He had the advantage now, and I braced myself for his attack. He turned and skated off as fast as he could, calling back over his shoulder, "You're fucking crazy!"

My wife helped me up. "Are you all right?" I said.

"Yes. Just a skinned knee. What about you?"

I was shaking, weak-kneed, not with rage but with a spent physicality I had not known in years. It had all happened so fast I hadn't had time to think. I had just reacted with a pure, visceral rage. Then I felt the pain in my left arm.

"I think I hurt my arm," I said. We both looked at it. My left bicep had rolled up into a tight ball high up my arm. I knew instinctively that I had ripped the tendon that connected the bicep to my inner elbow. "Wait here," I said, and I went across the street. I got some ice from a waiter at a restaurant and returned to my wife. She was sitting on the wall, trying to compose herself. I sat beside her and iced my bicep to keep the swelling down. The pain was now a dull ache. I was still shaking. I began to feel light-headed, dizzy, and nauseous.

"You look pale," my wife said. "Do you think you can make it home?"

"In a few minutes," I said. We sat there for a long time, staring out at the passing cars, neither of us speaking. The ice had numbed the pain now, and I felt well enough to pedal back home. "Let's go," I said.

I had only pedaled a few yards when the sidewalk began to shimmer and move ahead of me. I felt like I was going to pass out. I stopped and sat on my bike until the nausea and dizziness passed, then tried again.

It took us almost an hour to pedal back home. I had to stop at every block to keep myself from passing out. When we finally made it home, I lay down on the sofa in the sunroom. My wife brought me more ice for my arm. We both looked at it. The bicep was still shriveled into a tight ball.

"Well," she said. "At least it's not your pitching arm."

We both laughed. Then she added, seriously, "That's the first time in my life a man ever fought for me." She was fifty-five.

I let my bicep heal as it was, shriveled into a small ball, a reminder.

*   *   *

We checked into the Ramada Inn in downtown Waterbury. "No silver plate," Susan said. I picked up a local newspaper and we went to our room. There was a huge Jacuzzi next to the bed. "There's a first time for everything," I said.

I sat on the edge of the bed and flipped to the sports section of the newspaper while Susan put our clothes away. When I checked into a hotel on an assignment, I never put my clothes in dresser drawers. I just pulled out fresh clothes from my bag each day and stuffed the worn ones in a laundry bag. It was my way of making my stay impermanent. But Susan, like most women, could not countenance impermanence. So she quickly made our hotel room our home.

There was a photograph of me in a Spirit uniform on the front page of the sports section alongside a story that mentioned I was going to pitch tomorrow night. The famous author returning to the scene of his failure. The rest of the article focused more on my writing over the last thirty years than it did my brief three years in the minor leagues. Why not? I thought. To most people I was a writer, not a pitcher.

I showed Susan the article. She looked at my picture and said, "I'll have to keep an eye on you, baby. Watch the groupies hanging around the lobby trying to score with tomorrow night's pitcher."

"Just look for the chicks with the aluminum walkers."

She went into the bathroom to arrange our toiletries. I undressed, took out my knee brace and metal cup, and tried them on. My knee was stiff in the brace, but I felt no pain. The metal cup felt awkward between my legs. It chafed against my thighs. I rotated my shoulder. I could still feel the deep pinpoint of pain where my shoulder met my arm. Maybe it would go away when I warmed up. I began my pitching motion in front of the mirror just as Susan came out of the bathroom. She looked at me, naked, in my knee brace and metal cup.

"Kinky," she said. "Where are your black socks and garter belt?" She smiled and tossed a head fake at the Jacuzzi. "Want to try it out?" We both stripped naked and bent over the Jacuzzi to try to figure out how it worked. We weren't sure whether the water had to be above or below the jets. We turned on the water, waited until it was an inch below the jets, then turned on the jets. The jets sprayed water everywhere, soaking us, the rug, the bed, the plate-glass window across the room that looked down over the parking lot.

"Jesus!" Susan said, turning off the jets. She began sopping up all the water with towels. She stripped off the soaked bedsheets and tossed them in a pile in the bathroom. She stood naked before the plate-glass window, wiping off the water with a towel. She was like a woman possessed, terrified someone might enter and see what a mess her room was.

"Don't worry about it," I said. "Housekeeping will clean it up."

"Are you crazy? I can't let anyone see this!"

The phone rang. Susan stopped wiping and stared at it. "It's probably the manager throwing us out already," she said.

I picked up the phone. "Paddy wagon!"

"Heh, Ronnie! What's happening?" Susan looked relieved and went back to the window.

"I'm downstairs in the lobby with Bee."

"What?"

"You didn't think we'd miss Patty's Big Adventure, did you?"

I looked over at Susan, smiling now. She'd known all along that Bee and Ronnie were going to surprise me by coming to watch me pitch. Ronnie had even brought his cameras to take pictures of my big night.

"Give us an hour to check into our room," Ronnie said. "Then we'll go out to dinner, pound some brewskis."

We found an Italian steakhouse on the outskirts of town. It was a dark-wooded, comforting, upscale restaurant. We sat at a booth in the bar and ordered drinks. Ronnie glanced at the drinkers at the bar. Wise guys like Sol, studying the *Racing Form*. Their women, aging blondes with lacquered hair, sat beside them, ignored, smoking cigarettes.

"A real guido joint," said Ronnie.

"With their painted up Pleasure Boats," I said. We all laughed as the waitress brought our drinks.

Ronnie raised his bottle of Heineken over the table. We all clicked glasses as Ronnie said, "To Patty's Big Adventure."

We ordered steak Milanaise and steak Florentine and steak Siciliano with mounds of garlic-mashed potatoes. We all swapped food, eating off each other's plate, talking and laughing and drinking, until finally we staggered back to the hotel at midnight.

We made plans to drive with Bee to Fairfield the following morning to show her Susan's and my old haunts, maybe stop in to say hello to my parents, but mostly to keep my mind off my pitching. Ronnie would stay behind to check out the stadium for the best place to set up his cameras to take the kind of award-winning shots he was famous for. It was a habit we'd both acquired over the years, showing up early for an assignment or, in my case, an interview. I always drove to my interview an hour early in case I got lost. When I found the house or hotel where the interview would take place, I'd relax, drive around for a while, check out the sights. I went over my questions in my mind. I reminded myself to always ask the most innocuous questions first, to put my subject at ease. Sometimes I asked the same question three and four times, but with slight variations. The answers to those four questions would really be the answer to the one question I wanted answered but was afraid the subject might balk at. I picked around the edges of my subject without ever going to the heart of the matter. All the little bits and pieces would eventually form the heart of what I wanted to know, like the pieces to a puzzle. Only rarely did I ever ask "the nut question." And then I only asked it as I had one foot out the door, like Columbo.

"Oh, and by the way," I said to Steve Carlton as I stepped outside the door of his concrete, bunkerlike house in the woods of Durango, Colorado. "Why did you bury all those guns around the house?"

Steve looked at me with his small, terrified, birdlike eyes and said, "For the revolution, that's why."

I always showed up at my subject's door fifteen minutes early to catch them off guard. When I was assigned a story on Andy Garcia for GQ, I prowled around the streets of Little Italy in New York at eight o'clock in the morning while cameramen were setting up their first shot of the day for *The Godfather, Part III*. I talked to the cameramen and the grips and the extras. I asked them what kind of guy Garcia was. When the movie's publicist caught me talking to an extra an hour before I was supposed to be there, he threw me off the set. Garcia refused to talk to me after that. That told me something about a man who presented himself to the press and his fans as just "a regular guy." Unfortunately, I wasn't able to use that little bit. The editor of GQ, Art Cooper, took the assignment away from me and handed it over to a woman writer who was more interested in Garcia's dark, Latin good looks. Garcia found her adulation less disturbing than my surreptitious probing. "We need Garcia on the cover," was Cooper's explanation.

Another time I showed up twenty minutes early to Wilt Chamberlain's house. He appeared at the door wearing only a towel.

"I'm sorry," he said. "I was in the shower."

"That's all right, Wilt. I'm early." He was a huge man, over seven feet tall, with a small head.

"Come on in," he said. "Can I get you something?"

"No, that's all right."

"I wished I'd known," he said with a pained look. "I wanted to put on the lights around the pool for you."

Which told me a little something about Wilt. He liked to direct things, make sure everything was just so. It was only a tiny bit of information. One of those small pieces I needed to fill in the bigger picture. But it's why I always showed up early. To flesh out the picture. To find the truth. It was all part of the game between interviewer and subject. Hide and seek. They wanted me to know only what they wanted me to know. I wanted to know more. Everything. Which was why I talked a lot about myself. I told my subjects the most intimate details of my life. My divorce. My fears. Anything that would connect with them. It was only fair. How could I ask them an intimate question about themselves if I wasn't willing to share my own intimacies? But there were more surreptitious reasons. I wanted them to forget this was an interview and think it was just a conversation between two like-minded people. See! We had something in common! We shared what we had in common. They told me about their divorce, their fears. Then, when the story appeared in print, they were shocked that their intimacies had been revealed. It never dawned on them that they were telling their intimacies to millions of readers, and I was telling mine only to them. It was one of the first things I told young writers whenever I spoke at colleges or magazines. "You have to learn to talk a lot about yourself," I say. "You talk and talk, and somewhere along the way, you connect."

Susan and I went up to our room to bed. I turned on the TV to watch movies. She rolled away from me in bed and put a pillow over her head. She hated the TV on when she was trying to sleep. It reminded her of her former husband, a local basketball player of some renown.

"I spent fourteen years in bed," she said, "listening to Bob Wolfe, and then Marv Albert, calling the Knicks games. I heard 'Yessss!' in my sleep until I was ready to go mad."

But this night she said nothing as I watched movies I didn't see. My mind wandered to my pitching tomorrow night. Alone in that bed, with Susan sleeping, I began to feel the fear coming in great waves, like an endless pack of ravenous predators looking for something to devour. I tried to fight it, but I couldn't. No matter how intellectually I rationalized fear, my fear, Maddux's fear, Meg Ryan's fear, it did no good. Fear could be intellectualized only when it came to someone else. When it came to you, like the hyenas in the night at the edge of the tent line in *The Snows of Kilimanjaro,* it was beyond rationalization. That fear was visceral. It took root deep inside you and defied logic. I felt it clawing at my breast. I saw myself on the mound making a fool of myself. Sweat pouring off my forehead. Helpless, as batter after batter ripped my "devastating slider" off the outfield wall. Or worse. One wild pitch after another. Walk after walk. The fans growing restless, then angry, then derisive, laughing, finally, at this pathetic old man who dared think *he* could recapture, not even what he once had, but what he never had even in his youth: Success. I could see Susan in the stands, crying for my humiliation, bewildered too, by all the derision around her being heaped on her husband. She had never seen baseball fans turn on a player before. She had never experienced it as an actress. Theatergoers didn't boo and hiss at bad plays. They clapped politely after the first act and left. People who never played sports can never understand what it's like to be booed. No one boos IBM executives. There is no public humiliation for a failed IBM executive. Just a brief chat in the president's office and then severance pay. Once you've been booed on a playing field, it changes you. Nothing in life is ever so fearful to you again. You become inured to the fear of the ordinary failures of daily life. I wasn't afraid of failing as a writer. If I did, it would be a private failure. But I was going to pitch again. I was going to put myself in jeopardy of a very public failure. Nothing ever inured you to the fear of that failure.

It must have been about 2 A.M. when Susan rolled over toward me. She was still half asleep as she slid down the bed, eased herself over between my legs, and began to emulate the blonde with the rose tattoo on her ass. For an instant, I was annoyed. I was trying to concentrate on the fear. But the fear was backing off, silently, into the night.

I woke the next morning with the sunlight through the windows in my eyes. Susan was already dressed in her shorts and T-shirt.

"Sleep well?" she said, smiling.

"Not bad."

We left for Fairfield, an hour south, at 9 A.M. I drove. "The man always drives," said Susan to Bee, sitting in the backseat. "The man always makes the drinks too. And cuts the meat."

"What does the woman do?" said Bee.

"What Suzie did last night," I said. "What she's good at."

We all laughed as we drove through the Naugatuck Valley in the bright morning sunlight. When we came to the Merritt Parkway I instinctively turned east toward the exit that led to my parents' house, where I was raised, and where I raised my own family. My parents were now living in an apartment only a few miles away from that house.

"Are your children still living at your old house?" Bee said.

"No," I said. "I don't know where they are."

We drove in silence for a while. I came to the exit that led to my old house. I pulled off the parkway. I'd spent forty years there. I hadn't seen it since I left sixteen years ago. It was a tract Dutch colonial with a 50-by-100 lot. There was a Japanese maple tree in the front yard. Its tiny, burgundy-colored leaves spread over the yard like an umbrella, killing the grass. A driveway led in back to a garage. I had put a basketball backboard and basket on the garage when my children were young.

I slowed the car as we came to the house. It was painted a pale rose instead of the gray I remembered. The maple tree was gone. Grass had grown. The garage at the end of the driveway was gone. The backboard and basket were gone. My ex-wife and children were gone. My parents and my brother were gone. I was gone. Someone else lived there now.

"This is it," I said. I stopped the car across the street close to the woods where I used to play as a boy. The woods were gone. A rolling, manicured lawn led to a stucco and dark-wood Elizabethan mansion where the woods had been.

We looked at my old house. It was like all the other houses on the street. It had always been like all the other houses, except to me. "It's not the same," I said.

"It never is," Susan said.

Bee looked at the Elizabethan mansion. "Who lives there?"

"I don't know," I said.

"It's beautiful," Susan said. Susan and Bee talked about the mansion while I stared at my old house.

I saw ghosts. They were not hazy images seen through the gossamer mist of years past. They were clearly defined, stark, real, alive.

I saw a man with curly black hair and a black beard sitting on the concrete front-porch steps. He wore a black athletic jacket with the word "Braves" scripted in red across the chest. He was reading a book. A woman appeared at the screen door behind him. She had translucent white skin and pale blue eyes. He turned and looked up at her with a sad, forced smile. She reached a languid hand through the half-open screen door and beckoned him inside like a seductive spirit. He stood, and was gone.

I saw down the long driveway the same man again, only younger now, without the beard. He was dribbling a basketball between a flock of children. They reached out with tiny hands, slapped at the ball, hung on his arms like dangling fruit, until he let the basketball bounce away from him. The children scrambled after the ball, struggled over it until he intervened. He lifted each child in turn on his shoulders and held them high over his head so they could drop the ball through the basket.

I saw the same man as a young boy now. He stood on the sidewalk with a glove and baseball. He wound up like a pitcher and threw the ball to a tall homely man. The homely man caught the ball, pulled his hand out of his glove, and shook it. The boy smiled and turned toward the front porch. A short, dark, older couple, sitting on the porch, clapped their hands, but I could not hear the sound.

I saw the same boy, even younger now, standing in the darkness on the front steps. He was calling someone who did not come. He called again and again and again. His face was contorted with fear. Finally a dog came running out of the woods, across the street, up the front steps to the boy. The boy bent down, hugged the dog, and was gone.

"Lady was the first thing I ever loved more than myself," I said out loud.

Susan and Bee looked at me. "Who was Lady?" Susan said.

"My dog. A collie. She followed me everywhere when I was a kid."

"How long did you have her?" Bee said.

"Ten years."

"What happened?" Susan said.

"I went away to play baseball when I was eighteen. She died while I was gone."

"What'd she die of?" said Bee.

"My parents said she died of a broken heart." I laughed. "Maybe they were right. She was like Hoshi, you know. She knew things dogs know. She knew I wasn't a little boy anymore. I didn't need a dog anymore. I had a car and a girlfriend and my baseball career. So she let me go."

I shifted the car into gear and drove away from my past. I remembered what my father had taught me. "You can't live in the past," he said. "It ruins your life." Everlasting regret, I thought. My old man and Tennessee Williams. I laughed out loud. An odd couple.

"What's so funny, babe?" Susan said.

"Nothing."

We drove up the hill that led to my parents' apartment only a few miles from my old house. Susan remembered. "Babe, let's go visit your parents," she said.

"I'd love to meet them," Bee said.

I looked in the rearview mirror at Bee. "You sure?"

"It'd be fun," Bee said. Then, to Susan, Bee said, "Do you get along with Pat's mother?"

Susan and I looked at each other. Then I said to Bee, "You really want to know?" I told Bee about my mother's visit to Fort Lauderdale when she found out I was marrying "the hated Irisher."

Bee was still laughing when I pulled into the parking lot in my parents' apartment complex. I parked between my father's old, battered, powder-blue Volkswagen Beetle and my mother's new Honda Accord. My mother bought the Honda a year ago when she turned eighty-nine. The salesman gave her a five-year payment plan. The car would be paid off when she turned ninety-four.

"When I die, Patty," she told me, "it'll be yours."

"Ma," I said, "you're gonna dance on all our graves."

She laughed. Then, in her pitiful voice, she moaned her constant refrain: "Oh, Patty! I don't feel like I used to."

"Ma. You're a hundred fucking years old! *I* don't feel like I used to." She shrieked with laughter.

They lived on the third floor of a modest, three-story, brick building. We walked up the narrow stairs. I knocked on the door. My mother's shrill voice called out, "Who is it?"

I winked at Bee. "It's me, Ma. Your favorite son."

My mother called out, "Dad! It's George!" She opened the door. When she saw me, she called out again, "Pat! It's Patty, my baby!"

I bent over to kiss my mother. She was heavier than I remembered. More stooped, with mottled skin and swollen ankles. I introduced her to Mary Beth. "This is my new wife, Ma. I got rid of the old Irisher."

She flung the back of her hand at me. "She's too young for you," she said. "Where's my lovely daughter-in-law?" Susan stepped out from behind me. "Give Mother a kiss," my mother said. Susan bent over and kissed her on the cheek. My mother said to Mary Beth, "She's Spanish, you know."

I glanced at Bee and shook my head. "I told ya."

We went inside. Dad got up from a chair in the living room and came over to kiss me, as he always did, on the lips. Then he kissed Susan and shook Mary Beth's hand. He tried to be charming to Mary Beth in that exaggerated, courtly way of men who are in awe of women because they do not really know them.

We looked around the apartment. It was the same as I remembered. The rich, brocaded Mediterranean furniture. The big, sepia-tinted photograph of my mother as a girl of fourteen alongside a photograph of my father at twenty. I pointed them out to Mary Beth.

"See, even Ma was pretty once." Then I pointed to the photograph of my father in his sharp, camel-haired sports jacket. "Curly was bald even then."

My mother said, "Thank God Patty has all his hair. Isn't it beautiful?" I looked at Mary Beth. She didn't know what to say. My mother said, "Oh, he was always such a beautiful boy. Until he grew that horrible beard. When are you going to shave off that beard? It makes you look old."

"I am old, Ma."

"No you're not. You're just a boy."

My parents led us through their tiny kitchen where I used to sit and listen to Dad book games on the telephone. They had set up a bookshelf in the kitchen with all my books lined up. They had pictures of all my dogs on the shelves too. We stepped outside to their little porch overlooking the woods in the backyard. We sat down on wicker chairs in a tight circle. My mother scurried back to the kitchen. "Dad, come help me." They returned with trays of fruit and cheese and glasses of red wine. Susan went to pull a bunch of grapes off the bigger bunch.

"Oh, no, dear," my mother said. "Use this." She handed Susan a little grape scissors.

My father was charming Mary Beth. He told her stories about me as a little boy. How he used to take me every Saturday morning to the Waldorf Cafeteria in downtown Bridgeport when I was six. I wore a quilted snowsuit and sat at a Formica table with aluminum legs eating pancakes by myself. I was surrounded by rheumy old men who smelled. They stared blankly into their cups of black coffee. The big plate-glass window that looked out on the sidewalk and the street was streaked with dirt. Still, I could see my father standing on the sidewalk with my "uncles." They were dressed alike in double-breasted, camel-haired overcoats and felt Fedora hats. I watched them stamp their feet in the cold and blow into their hands while they waited for their bookie to pull up in his car for his morning payoffs.

I'd forgotten about the Waldorf Cafeteria.

My mother was telling Mary Beth and Susan now about our dinners every Friday night at the Ocean Sea Grill. They used to dress me, a child of eight, in a little suit and tie. My mother wore her best pale chiffon orchid dress with the floppy matching hat. My father wore his navy blazer, rep tie, and gray slacks. The maître d' who greeted us at the door wore a tuxedo and a frilly white shirt. He had slicked-back black, wavy hair. His name was Tommy Rotundo. He looked like those second-rate guinea crooners from the 1950s. My father reached into his pants pocket and withdrew a ten-dollar bill folded neatly to the size of a commemorative stamp. He shook the maître d's hand with his hand that had the bill in it. When he withdrew his hand the bill had miraculously disappeared. The maitre d' put his hand in his pocket now and led us to the best table in the restaurant. We slid into a burgundy leather banquette against the wall. We could see everyone in the restaurant and everyone could see us. My mother put a cigarette into her mother-of-pearl cigarette holder. My father lit it for her. She held the holder limp-wristed, beside her head, very ladylike. Her other hand cupped her elbow. My father ordered Manhattans for us all. Mine was a coke with a maraschino cherry in a pyramid-shaped Manhattan glass.

I always ordered a two-pound Maine lobster. My parents smiled at me as I cracked open the claws, expertly, with lobster pliers and then extracted the white meat with my thin lobster fork. I dipped the meat in melted butter and put it to my mouth. A waiter hovered over me with a child's lobster bib. My father shook his head no. "He doesn't need it."

Men and women entered the restaurant through the front door. They were dressed more garishly than my parents. They'd come from the vaudeville theater across the street. Baggy-pants comics. Soft-shoe men. Strippers. Club fighters with smashed noses and scar tissue over their eyelids. They all stopped at my parents' table to pay homage to my father. They greeted my mother first, very formally, with respect. They called her "Mrs. Jordan." She acknowledged them with a slight wave of her cigarette holder. She was a respectable wife who was nothing like their wives and mistresses, or the wives and mistresses of my "uncles."

"How's it going, Patsy?" the men said to my father.

He nodded. "Good. I got a nice line on Brooklyn." They talked in hushed voices for a few minutes. My mother posed with her cigarette holder. I cracked open my lobster claw with my pliers. I ate in silence while I watched and listened. Before the men left, they told my mother I was "a fine little man." It was a refrain I remember hearing from my earliest childhood.

I was a child of four, quaking in short pants, when my mother's mother used to summon me in her commanding voice. She was a fat, bossy woman her children called "the General," but never to her face. She held me firmly at arm's length and studied me for that sign of manhood that all those tough Italian women in my family prized so highly. Finally, she said, *"Bella. L'uomo."* Then I was dismissed.

"Patty was always a little man," my mother said to Bee. "He never gave us any trouble."

"I forgot about the Ocean Sea Grill, Ma," I said.

"You only remember the bad things," my father said.

"Maybe you're right, Dad." Susan and Bee looked embarrassed. I tried to change the subject. "Ma, tell Bee about Paul Berger."

"Oh, he was such a bully," she said. "He was fourteen and Patty was only twelve. He used to pick on Patty terrible."

One day Paul Berger pushed me to the ground. I ran home crying and told my mother. "Stop crying like a baby," she said. She pushed me back outside. "Don't come back until you get even," she said and slammed the door. I hid behind a tree, my heart pounding with fear. When Paul walked by I jumped on his back. He fell on the sidewalk, bloodying his nose. I jumped off him and ran home. I pounded on the door but my mother wouldn't let me in until I assured her I'd gotten my revenge. I was telling her in the kitchen what I'd done when we heard a knock on the door. My mother opened it. Paul stood there, crying, blood leaking from his nose. He told her what I'd done to him. I heard her say, "Don't you worry. I'll punish him right now. Wait here." She closed the door and came over to me. She whispered, "When I clap my hands, Patty, make believe you're crying." She began to clap her hands. "Take that!" she snapped, while I faked terrible sobs. After Paul had left, satisfied, my mother and I laughed in the kitchen.

"He was always a little man," my mother said again.

"But he was too sensitive," my father said.

"He was innocent," my mother said.

"Not now, Ma," I said.

She pursed her lips and shook her head. "Still," she said.

I told them about my pitching tonight in Waterbury. They already knew about it from George.

"Don't get hurt, Patty," my mother said. "You're too old now."

"I thought you said I was still a little boy," I said.

"Only to Dad and me," she said.

"How's the writing going, Son?" my father asked.

"Okay," I said. "I've been trying to sell a novel based on my *Playboy* stories. Nobody's biting."

"Why not?"

"They want me to write it all first. I can't take the time. I gotta meet my nut, Pop." He nodded. He understood the nut. He had taught me what it was. A man's obligation to his family. Pay the bills first. I said, "It pisses me off I can't just take the time to write it. This fucking guy who wrote *Cold Mountain* took off seven years to write his book."

"How'd he live?" my father said.

"His wife worked," I said.

"Disgusting," my mother said. "Living off a woman."

"I know, Ma. None of my wives ever worked."

Susan said, "You sound like Henry VIII."

"You'll get it done," my father said. "Don't worry."

"I know, Pop. But it's just so fucking unfair."

The old man glared at me. "What'd I teach you?" he snapped. "Only a fool or a child expects perfect justice. Remember the car accident?"

I was sixteen. My parents let me use their car to visit my girlfriend every night. One night I came to an intersection with no stop sign. The cross street had the stop signs. I went through the intersection and a car came speeding through the stop sign and smashed into my passenger-side door. No one was hurt. When I got home that night, with the side of my parents' car all smashed in, I tried to plead my case with my father.

"But it wasn't my fault, Dad! The other guy went through the stop sign."

He lashed out at me. "It *was* your fault," he said. "You should have known."

"Known what?"

"The other guy *always* runs the stop sign. You should expect that." It was a lesson I never forgot. "There are no such things as 'accidents,'" he told me. "'Accidents' are always your fault."

Now, on my parents' porch, forty years later, I said, "Yeh, Pop. I remember the accident. You were right. You're always right." I looked across at him. An old man with a brush mustache and a friar's tuft of white hair around his bald head. And no blood relatives in the world, except for me, his son. He knew a lot about justice. If there was justice in this world he would have had a mother and a father. He would have had someone to tell *him* the other guy always ran the stop sign. He learned that on his own, the hard way, and passed it on to his son. From the day he was born, he has always had to be his own *consigliere.* He had no one to tell what he thought, what he felt, what he feared, what he was. He never had the luxury I had, to be obsessively self-absorbed. He didn't have the time to rationalize decisions, like Hamlet and me. He had to rely on his instincts, think on his feet. "I had to make it up as I went along," he once told me. "Sometimes it worked out. Sometimes it didn't."

Then he met Florence Dimenna, four years older than himself. With a young son. At twenty-one, he had an instant family. Even more than that. "I wanted a wife *and* a mother," he said. They have been together sixty-five years. They don't argue anymore, as they did when I was a child. They dote on each other now that they are frail. It's almost cloying. All those "Dad's the greatest" and "Mom's the greatest." They have rewritten history, like the Communists. Their arguments were never as fierce as I remembered. Dad's gambling was never a debilitating vice. It was just a personal idiosyncrasy we can all laugh at now. Maybe they're right. Maybe everything I remember from my childhood has been imagined. Embellished by a "too sensitive" boy. And even if what I remember is true, so what? It's in the past. They have made their peace now after a great war. They're allies now, against time, waiting.

My mother and father are an inspiration to me. In their own way, they are a great love story. Over the last ten years, they have become like young lovers again. I called from Fort Lauderdale once, recently, to talk to Dad. I heard Ma giggling like a girl. "What the hell's going on?" I said.

"Mom is sitting on my lap," my father said.

"Jesus, Dad! Do you have a hard-on?"

"It still works," he said.

I heard Ma's shrill voice in the background. "Dad can still get it up."

The thought that my parents, ninety-one and eighty-eight, were still having sex didn't surprise me. What did surprise me was four years earlier, when Dad told me he and Ma had stopped having sex. He'd called me in Fort Lauderdale to ask about Stella, who had just had her puppies. He loved hearing about our dogs.

"How'd it happen?" he said.

"How do you think? Nero nailed her outside behind the barbecue grill. I shoulda known something was up when he came into the house smoking a cigarette."

I waited for him to laugh, but all he said was, "Your mother and I have stopped having sex."

That was it. He just dropped it, matter-of-factly, an afterthought, like he was telling me he dropped a C-note shooting craps. Just a little tidbit of information from the home front Pops thought his fifty-two-year-old sonny boy might like to hear. His eighty-five-year-old parents had stopped screwing.

"Well," I said. "Yes. And how are things otherwise, Pop?"

"Oh, fine. And you and Susan?"

What'd he want me to say? Oh, we don't fuck much anymore either. Maybe that would cheer him up. Or maybe it would depress him. Maybe he really wanted to hear, Oh, we're still fucking like rabbits, Pop! But then I had this insane fear he'd ask, How often? Any interesting positions? And I'd have to say, Well, actually, Susan likes it best when I bend her over the dishwasher. Something about the vibrations. I had to stop myself. I was losing it.

"We're fine," I said. "Susan got our house historically designated."

"That's nice."

Was he disappointed? Maybe it wasn't too late. I could still cheer him up. Of course, she had to give the guy at the historical society a blowjob. Jesus! I had to get off the phone!

"Well, Pop. I gotta go now."

"So long, Son. Good talking to you."

*   *   *

My parents began to teach me about sex, in an offhanded way, when I was a young boy.

I was seven when we got our first TV set, a round-screened, black-and-white Zenith. I lay on the floor, my head propped up on pillows, while my parents sat on the sofa behind me. We all watched Bob Hope's comedy special. Hope stood alone onstage looking out at the audience with his leering smile.

"Did you hear the one about the little girl who swallowed a safety pin when she was eight?" said Hope. He paused. Flashed his leering smile. Then said, "She didn't feel a prick until she was eighteen." I can still hear my parents' laughter behind me while I tried to figure out what they were laughing about.

When I was twelve, my Little League games were played at a park down the street from Woodfield, "Home for Unwed Mothers." Sometimes I would be on the mound in the middle of yet another no-hitter when I would be distracted. I'd see a teenage girl walking past the park toward Woodfield. They all looked the same. Young, not even sixteen, with a sweet, innocent face and a big belly they held in their hands as they walked.

One night my parents and I were driving home from a game. I said, "Are those girls from Woodfield bad girls, Ma?"

My mother glanced at my father in the front seat, then turned to me in the back. "Don't ever say that," she said sternly. "Those are good girls."

"Then why are they having babies so young?" I said.

"Because only good girls get caught," she said. "Bad girls know how to protect themselves."

I was fourteen when I became sexually active. In the mid-1950s that was a relative term. It didn't mean much more than spin-the-bottle parties, a rare open-mouthed French kiss, and maybe a hand over a breast encased in a bullet bra made of cast iron and stuffed more with cotton than flesh. Most of the boys my age gravitated toward the pretty blond girls still wearing camisoles instead of bras. Girls with names like Faith, Hope, and Charity. I, however, was more advanced for my age. I'd rather spend my time at the park near my house than at spin-the-bottle parties in the basements of my friends' homes, where everyone gawked at you when you had to kiss a Faith, Hope, or Charity. It was there I met Carmine, a year older than myself.

Carmine wasn't very pretty. She was cross-eyed behind her thick-lensed eyeglasses with the horned rims. She even had a faint mustache above her full upper lip. But she had breasts. Big, firm breasts straining beneath the tight blouses she wore. She would lead me by the hand into the woods, away from the other kids playing baseball or on the swings. When we were far enough into the woods, she would lay down in the leaves, pulling me down on top of her. She taught me how to French kiss. She put my hand over her breasts. She didn't even stop me when I put my hand inside her bra and felt her breasts, not so hard as they looked, softer, spongy-liquidy sacks with hard, erect nipples. She'd clamp her legs around the small of my back and press her crotch against my crotch. We'd "dry hump," a noxious 1950s term, until I ejaculated in my pants and she had an orgasm too. Her crossed eyes grew wider and wider until she exhaled a great breath and a smile spread across her homely face, which, flushed with sex, did not look so homely now.

We didn't know that some of the other boys had begun to spy on us in the woods in the late afternoon. I found this out when she called my house one night. She was crying uncontrollably.

"What's the matter?" I said. She told me the other boys had begun to spread rumors about her, that she was a "dirty" girl (another noxious 1950s term). The rumors had gotten back to her parents, who thought she was pregnant. "But we didn't really *do* anything!" I said.

"I know!" she said. "But they think we did. Please, Patty. Do something!"

I told her I'd straighten out those boys in school the next day. Just as I hung up, I heard the click of the phone downstairs. Then my mother's voice. "Patty! Get down here!"

I stood before my mother, expecting her wrath. But I should have known better. "Have you been doing anything with that girl that could get her in trouble?" she said, seriously, but without anger. I shook my head no. She said, "Good. She's too young to get in trouble. You could ruin her life." She expected me to know what she was talking about. I did. Before I left, she said one more thing, the first and only real sex talk I had ever had from her. She said, "Now that you're dating girls, make sure you don't buy them a hamburger and expect them to let you squeeze it out of them afterward."

Like most fathers, mine wasn't much given to talking about sex as openly as my mother when I was a teenager. In fact, I can remember only one sex talk he ever gave me. It was as brief and elliptical as my mother's. I was fifteen, a freshman in high school. Every morning my mother made my father drive me to school. Often, he had been out gambling until the early hours of the morning the night before. He was in no mood to get up early to take me to school. But he did it, grudgingly, out of fear of my mother's wrath. This one day, they'd had their usual argument over breakfast. As we drove to school I sat in silent fear of disturbing my father. He glared straight ahead at the road. He cursed stop signs and other drivers. Finally he turned to me and said, "You know what the strongest thing in the world is, kid?"

"No, Dad."

"One hair from a lady's pussy." I looked at him, confused. "You know why?" he said. I shook my head. "Because it'll make men do things nothing else in this world can." I flashed back to that night when I was twelve and I heard them having sex. I knew what he meant.

It has occurred to me, over the past few years, that my father was just being melodramatic when he told me he and Ma had stopped having sex in their late eighties. They'd probably just had an argument, and Ma was punishing him, the only way she could, by withholding sex. Two days later, I am sure, the argument was forgotten and they resumed their sex life.

* * *

Susan and Bee and I got up to leave my parents' back porch. They walked us to the front door. We all kissed goodbye. My father kissed me on the lips. I looked at him a moment, then said, "Dad. Everything I am I owe to you and Ma."

He brushed aside my compliment with a backhand toss. "Some things, maybe," he said. "But you made your own life, Son. I'm proud of you."

We walked down the narrow stairway. I heard my father's voice echo in the hallway: "Go visit your brother. He'll want to see you."

"Sure, Dad," I lied.

We drove east on Park Avenue toward I-95 and Fairfield. It was a broad street with a wide esplanade. We passed stately old mansions with Greek columns that had begun to decay. Some of the homes were boarded up. Others had been turned into lawyers' and dentists' offices. My parents used to drive me down Park Avenue every time they took me, a young teenager, to the North End Boys Club in the Italian ghetto where they had lived and I had spent the first four years of my life.

"Your parents are so sweet," Mary Beth said from the backseat.

"Now," I said. "But not always."

"The first time I went to their apartment," Susan said, "they were still fighting. Almost eighteen years ago. Pat took me to the apartment for dinner. His parents got into a vicious argument, over nothing. I had never seen anything like that. Terrible curses. I went to the bathroom and threw up."

I laughed. "And that was nothing. Nothing like I remembered."

"Thank God they never had girls," Susan said.

"Well, they certainly knew how to raise boys," Mary Beth said.

FIFTEEN

I DROVE TO FAIRFIELD to show Bee our old haunts. The town center with its studiously re-created Main Street from 1700's. Red brick sidewalks. Street lamps. The white Federal town hall. The white Federal houses that lined Reef Road all the way to the beach and Long Island Sound. They all looked alike. White. Black shutters. Twelve-over-twelve windows. American flags. Little plaques beside the front door commemorating each house's first owner since 1639. The British burned all the houses in the Revolutionary War. They anchored their frigates off the beach, marched up Beach Road, and burned everything. After the war the townspeople rebuilt the houses exactly as they had been, right down to the plaques.

Just before we reached the beach, I turned right. Susan pointed out the modest ranch house where she had grown up. Her father had sold it a few years ago and moved to a condo. There were children's toys in the front yard.

"How do you get along with her father?" Bee asked.

"Okay, now," I said. "At first he wasn't too crazy about Susan being the mistress of a married man."

"I was dating this corporate type my father liked," said Susan. "A vice president of Otis Elevator."

I laughed. "Remember the day I came to your house to take you to the Naut?" Susan smiled. "It was in the middle of summer. I was wearing shorts and a black T-shirt with a drawing of Dracula on the front and the words 'He comes at night.' I knocked on the screen door. I saw Susan's father coming toward me through the living room. I said, 'Hi, Mr. Duggan.' He just looked at me as if I wasn't there, turned around in midstride, and left the room."

We drove along the beach. We showed Bee the jetty of rocks that led out into the Sound for a quarter mile.

"Our first date was on those rocks," Susan said. "Patty was at the very last rock. When I saw him I got so excited."

"She ran over the rocks to me," I said. "We barely knew each other."

"We lay on the rocks and talked for eight hours," Susan said. "Then we went to the Naut for Bloody Marys."

"What's the Naut?"

I pointed to a bar along the beach. The Sea Grape Inn. "That used to be the Naut," I said. "Now it's a touristy bar for New Yorkers who rent beach houses for the summer."

"It didn't look like that when it was the Naut," Susan said.

We were driving up Reef Road toward the center of town again. I said to Bee, "Susan and I spent a lot of days and nights in the Naut when we first started dating." I told her about Bernie, Babe, and Billy, the bartender.

"Billy seemed like such a bitter guy," Bee said.

"A disillusioned Romantic," I said.

"He visited me in the hospital when I had my mastectomy," Susan said. "He brought me a rose. This big, hulking, one-eyed guy in his best suit. He was so sweet. He began to cry. Patty had to take him out into the hall."

"He stopped crying there," I said. "He got furious. He began to curse that 'bearded bastard' who deserved his own crucifixion for what he'd done to Susan. Imagine, cursing Jesus Christ like that! He scared me. I'd never seen such hatred."

I turned right onto the Post Road, past my brother's law office. I said nothing and pointed out to Bee the three-story Victorian house where I used to have my office on the third floor.

"Susan and I used to ball on the floor," I said. Bee laughed. Susan looked embarrassed. "The first time she gave me a blowjob, she looked up at me and said, 'I was told I was very good.' I said, 'Whoever told you that, baby, never got much head.'" We all laughed.

"There," Susan said. "That's the hair salon where I used to get my hair cut." She pointed to another Victorian house alongside my old office. Moda di Capelli. "My hair was turning gray. Pat insisted I let Joe bleach it blonde."

"Joe was an old friend of mine," I said. "I'd known him since he was a kid."

"Aren't you going to visit your brother?" Susan said. I was driving through Fairfield Center toward I-95 and Waterbury at noon.

"And ruin a good day?" I said.

"Your father asked you to," she said. Bee was silent in the backseat. "At least call him. . . . You've got your cellphone."

"Jesus, babe! It's *my* fucking day! Why spoil it?"

I looked across at her. She wouldn't look at me. "Suit yourself," she said.

Bee was still silent in the backseat. Finally, she spoke up. "Don't you get along with your brother?"

Susan turned to look at Bee. "His brother loves him," she said.

"That's not the fucking point!" I said. "He's just impossible."

"How?" said Bee.

"He treats me like a child."

"You're acting like one," Susan said. I glared at her. She glared right back.

I tried to explain. I told Bee how I had written about my brother and myself in *A False Spring*. When the book came out, George read it and summoned me to his office. He had the book laid out on his desk. The pages were all marked up, passages underlined, notations in the margins, question marks, like a college student's textbook. He leaned forward, his elbows on his desk, like a professor about to criticize a student's term paper.

"He explained to me all the places where I got it wrong," I said to Bee. "I said, 'But that's how I remember it, George.' He just shook his head in that maddeningly patient way of his in the face of my foolishness. 'But that's not the way it was, Brother,' he said. I lost my temper, the way only he could make me lose it. I stood up, red-faced, and snapped, 'Then why don't you write the fucking book!' I said. 'All you've ever done is criticize me. My pitching, my writing, my whole fucking life! *You* go out on the mound and strike out nineteen batters! *You* sit down for a year and write a book! *You* go face to face with failure for once in your life, Brother! See how it feels.' He just smiled that ethereal smile of his at my foolish childish temper and shook his head. 'I'm just trying to help you, Brother. That's all.' "

"Those were cruel things to say to George," Susan said.

"But they were true," I said.

"That's not a good enough reason," Susan said. "The truth can hurt."

"That's not *my* problem," I said.

"Maybe it should be," Susan said.

I knew what she meant. It was how I'd begun to lose my children long before Erwin appeared. I had always thought it was my fatherly responsibility to tell them the truth about themselves. I thought I was helping them by pointing out their deficiencies that, I thought, would lead to their future failures. They thought I was wishing those failures on them. But I wasn't! That's not how *I* saw it in *my* mind.

My oldest daughter was so overcome with emotion on her wedding day that she almost fainted at the altar. An altar boy had to bring her a chair. She sat throughout the rest of the ceremony. Afterward, I told her she had to control her emotions. "You're so self-indulgent," I said. "Think of others, for chrissakes!"

My second-oldest daughter was a sweet, amiable, conciliatory girl who was always trying to smooth over conflicts. I told her this was "cowardly," her way of avoiding hard decisions she had to make in her life.

My oldest son always felt burdened by his father's successes. No-hitters. Books. "Oh, you're Pat Jordan's son!" So he retired from the field. He drifted from one meaningless job to the next, and from one girlfriend to another. I told him he was afraid of failure. He had to confront that fear to live a meaningful life. "Or else," I said, "you'll be living over a gas station, greasing cars at forty."

When my youngest daughter broke her arm so severely that she almost lost it, the radial nerve that controlled her wrist was stretched. The surgeon said it might grow back if she exercised it. I would sit with her on our front porch with a small can of peas. I put the small can in her hand and told her to try to lift it with her wrist. I made a game of it. "You're lifting weights like Daddy," I said. The nerve came back, but she was never the same girl again. That broken arm hardened her. I told her her selfishness would make her life pinched and meager when she got older.

I was living in Florida with Susan when my youngest son was a junior in high school. He called me twice a week to tell me how many batters he'd struck out in his latest high-school game. Seventeen. Eighteen. Nineteen. "More even than your old man," I said. "Great, Bobby!" I eventually found out from his mother that he hadn't even tried out for his high-school team, much less been its star pitcher. I called him up and told him to stop living in a dream world. He said, between his tears, "Now I know why everybody hates you and wishes you were dead."

It's best for them all, I guess, not to be burdened with my merciless truth. Merciless truth never bothered me. Just the opposite. I sought it out. I welcomed it. It freed me. But it burdened my children. *I* burdened my children. So they turned away from me, with Erwin's help, so they could live their lives in peace, with their own truth, not mine, just as my brother and I have turned from each other to live our own truths. Sooner or later, it seems, everyone close to me turns away from me for reasons I still do not understand.

Even Claire turned away from me. Then she came back to me, and to Susan, her mother, in our cabin in the mountains of western North Carolina. I remember that day so clearly, as if it is now.

*   *   *

She looks the same. She says she's gained weight, but I can't see it. I remember her the way she was when she lived near us in Florida seven months ago, before she left to live in Atlanta where, she says, she lost a lot of weight, and then gained it all back again. But we didn't see her or talk to her during those seven months, so the Claire who came back to us looks just like the Claire who left us.

She seems the same too. Maybe just a bit mellower, removed from me. During the day she lies around the cabin up here in the mountains, too uninterested even to play socks with the dogs. She used to love to play socks. She'd roll an old sock into a ball, toss it from the kitchen to the living room, and watch our three dogs retrieve it. They'd bark and yip and fight over the sock until each one had a piece of it in its mouth before they'd all bring it back to her in tandem. Claire would laugh, "My honeys!" and try to tug the sock away from them.

But she doesn't play socks anymore. She no longer laughs outrageously, either. She feels "blah," she says. She just wants to go back to Florida to get control of her life, she says. A job, an apartment, a dog, friends, maybe even a boyfriend. She wants to work out at the gym, jog on the beach, bicycle through the park where all the wild parrots shriek from the palm trees.

Claire insists we play Trivial Pursuit every night. "The way we always do," she says. Drinks first in the kitchen while I cook dinner. Susan has vodka on the rocks. I have bourbon and branch water in a tin cup. Claire has wine. We talk. Claire listens, mostly. I try to make her laugh.

After dinner, Claire and her mother wash the dishes while I start the fire in the Franklin stove in the living room. Claire insists on the fire even if it's not that cold outside. "We always have a fire," she says. She uses the present tense, as if to imply there was no past, no past that was different from the way it always was, between us, anyway.

Claire and Susan sit on the living-room floor with their glasses of wine and cigarettes. They lay out the Trivial Pursuit on the coffee table while I lie down on the sofa with my tin cup. Claire calls the dogs to her. "Honeys!" she says. Hoshi, Kiri, and Stella lie around her, but she soon forgets about them. Claire gives me the pink pie, the way she always did, our joke, and then we start. Claire waits for me to cheat so she and Susan can catch me. Sometimes I forget to cheat, or the heat from the fire makes me too drowsy, and the game just plods along without any life. Then I see Claire's black eyebrows knitting together, and I feel selfish. So I cheat outrageously right in front of their eyes. Claire cries out, "Pat! You cheater!" And then her face comes to life and she adds, "Oh, you never change." But Claire has changed.

It happened in Atlanta shortly after she left us to join a rock and roll band. I tried to talk her out of it. I told her she had a good job as a newspaper reporter, her own car, her own apartment on the Intracoastal, her friends, her life, us. But she kept hearing stories about this band, how it needed a "girl singer" with her voice (she has a Judy Collins voice, only stronger, less fragile), to become really successful. I tried to explain to her about the "quiet life," how it was better for some people. She snapped at me. "You don't think I can accomplish anything!"

Finally I told her that I thought she wanted to be a singer rather than a journalist because it would be easier for her. "I hate that!" she snapped. "You always telling me what I'm like!" We did not hear from her for seven months.

The rest is history. When Atlanta didn't work out for her, she blamed me for what happened, as if I'd wished it on her by predicting it. A friend of hers told me, "She says you're a bully who's always tried to control her life."

I cried a lot over the next few weeks. Susan kept in touch with Claire through her ex-husband, Claire's father. He told us how she wanted to be near him now, so she went to live with him in New England. I was glad for him and Claire, but I was jealous too. A stepfather has no rights in the final analysis. I could do nothing but sit and wait.

Then Claire started to call again, to speak to her mother mostly. After one call, her mother said, "Claire says she misses Florida."

"Let me talk to her," I said. I told her to forget the past and do what she wanted. If she wanted to live in Florida, she could live with us until she got her own apartment. She jumped at the opportunity. We were in the mountains of North Carolina at the time, so she drove there first, before driving down with us to Florida.

That's where we are now. In the cabin in the mountains. Claire, her mother, me, and the dogs. We take each day as it comes. She doesn't show me much affection anymore. Not the way she used to. I wonder if it'll always be like this. Maybe I'll never get back the Claire I once knew. It doesn't matter. I want Claire to be only the Claire she wants to be. Whatever that is. In the meantime, I wait.

*　*　*

I heard Susan talking to me in the car as we drove through Fairfield.

"He thought he was helping you," she was saying.

"Who?" I said.

"Your brother. Babe, where are you?"

"I'm sorry. I was just thinking about pitching tonight."

"I was saying that George thought he was helping you in his own way. It's just not your way. It doesn't always have to be your way, babe." I exhaled a breath. She said, "He really does love you, Patty."

"You're both fucking merciless," I said. I dialed my brother's number that I knew by heart. Susan smiled. Mil answered.

"Patty! Where are you?" I told her. She laughed. "You're like a bad penny. You always turn up. Are you coming for lunch?"

"I don't think so, Mil. I don't have time."

"Don't be ridiculous, Patty. Of course you do. Your brother will want to see you. I'll start lunch."

*　*　*

George and Bee and I sat on the white wrought-iron chairs in my brother's screened-in porch. Sunlight slanted through the screens and fanned across the flagstone floor on a warm afternoon. I could hear Susan and Mil talking in the kitchen as Mil prepared lunch.

"You don't brown the garlic first?" Susan said.

"Never," Mil said. "Just sauté it enough to give the oil a little flavor. . . . I always use whole cloves. I never chop the garlic."

George looked at Bee with a sardonic grin. "Did you ever eat Susan's cooking?"

Bee smiled, wide-eyed. "Susan's a very good cook."

"Sisterhood," I said.

Bee blushed. "Except for biscuits."

I heard Susan in the kitchen. "You don't simmer the sauce for hours?"

"It's not necessary," Mil said. "Just bring it to a boil and let it cook for ten minutes. That way the ingredients stay fresh."

George called out to Mil. "Not too much garlic, hon!"

"*George!*" Mil said.

"Just follow Susan's recipe, Mil," I said.

George groaned. "Oh, no!"

Susan stuck her head into the porch. "Thanks, George."

George looked at her to see if she was angry or kidding. Susan was the only woman I ever knew who could cause George trepidation. Finally, he smiled. "I was only kidding, Susan. I trust my sister-in-law. My brother doesn't look undernourished."

"Boiled potatoes are very nutritious," I said. Susan shook her head and went back to the kitchen. I turned to Bee and said, "So, what do ya think? Me and my brother. Two peas in a pod?"

Bee couldn't stop herself from laughing. "Like Siamese twins," George said. "Except I'm the handsome one." Bee looked at George's long, small-eyed, horsy face and suppressed another laugh.

"Yeh, Cary Grant," I said. "In a purple satin sweatsuit. You were right after all, Bro. I did get it wrong in my book. I should have described you as a handsomer Cary Grant."

My brother shook his head, no. "A homelier Walter Matthau," he said. "You were always the pretty brother." Then to Bee, he said, "That's why Patty was always Ma's favorite."

"Bullshit!" I said. "*I* don't go to Ma's for lunch every Tuesday for those little tunafish sandwiches she makes you. Does she cut the crust off for her sonny boy?"

George smiled. "Always. Then she stands behind me and scratches my head for hours."

"I think I'm gonna retch," I said. Then to Bee, I said, "George was always the good brother. Ma and Dad said he was a saint."

"It's tough being a saint," George said.

"It's tough being pretty too," I said.

"I'd like to try it just for a day," George said.

Mil called out from the kitchen. "Patty looked like an angel when he was a child. But what a monster. . . . George used to tell me all these horrible stories about Patty. The time he cracked Patty Federicci over the head with a cut-glass ashtray and blood spurted everywhere. And the time he threw himself on the department-store floor, crying and kicking his feet, because his mother wouldn't buy him a toy."

"I got the toy, Mil," I said.

Mil appeared in the porch doorway, smiling, wiping her hands on a dishtowel. "I was afraid to meet this little monster," she said. "When I finally did, he was fast asleep in his bed. He had golden curls and the smile of an angel. I said, 'George, this can't be *him!*'"

"Patty was such a terror," George said, "Ma had to hire a bodyguard for him when he was a child." He looked across at me. "Remember Patricia?"

I'd forgotten Patricia. She was a girl from the orphanage my father had hired as my babysitter when I was five. She was a tough, raw-boned, city girl of about sixteen with bleached-blond hair and acne. She wore jeans rolled up to her knees and a black leather jacket. She looked so different from the suburban girls of my neighborhood that the older boys in the neighborhood used to taunt her. They called her a "hood" and a "delinquent." She stood it as long as she could. When they called her a "bastard," her face got red with rage and she went after them. They ran off, laughing at her. One day, Gunnar Warmie made the mistake of not running off. He turned and confronted her.

"A girl!" he said. "Whatdaya think you're gonna do?" Gunnar was nineteen, a professional boxer. His face was already lumpy with scar tissue and a broken nose.

I looked up from the front lawn where I'd been playing. I saw Patricia cock her fist low at her waist. I saw the fist swinging up in a slow-motion arc until the full force of it caught Gunnar on the jaw. He dropped to the ground as if he'd been shot. Patricia stood over him. She held her shaking fist close to his face.

That night, Gunnar's parents called my mother. They threatened to call the police if they ever saw Patricia at our house again. Gunnar's jaw was broken, they said. He could only sip through a straw. I never saw Patricia again.

George was telling Bee what a great pitcher I had been. "My brother was the greatest from the first moment he stepped on a mound."

"My brother taught me everything," I said.

"But you had the arm, Brother. Remember the time we took Tony to Yankee Stadium?"

Tony was my brother's grandson. He was a talented college shortstop at Stanford. A year ago, I met him for the first time. I was working on a story for the *New York Times Magazine* on my old minor league catcher, Joe Torre, who was then the Yankee manager. I brought George and Tony to the stadium with me to meet Joe. When I introduced Tony to Joe, Joe said to him, "Did you ever see your uncle pitch?" Tony shook his head. Joe said, "What an arm he had."

"But no head to go with it," I said, smiling.

Joe just shrugged. "We were all young then."

Tony was inadvertently the cause of one of my estrangements from my brother four years ago. When Susan and I finished restoring our old Key West bungalow in Fort Lauderdale, we wanted to invite my parents down to see it. They had given us the $20,000 down payment we had needed to buy it. I wanted to show them what I considered to be partly theirs. Dad said he'd love to come, but Ma was too halt to make the trip. He had to find a nurse to take care of her while he was gone. He'd ask George about a nurse. He called me back a few days later to say that George didn't think it was a good idea to leave Ma with a stranger. I called my brother to ask him why.

"You haven't seen Ma in a few years," my brother said. "She's gotten old. It's selfish of you to expect Dad to leave her."

"I didn't know," I said, and forgot about it. A week later I called my parents to see how they were. A woman's voice answered. She said she was Ma's nurse.

"Where's my father?" I said.

"He flew to Omaha with your brother," the nurse said. "To see his great-grandson play baseball."

When Dad returned from Omaha, I told him he'd hurt my feelings.

He repeated his old refrain: "Why are you still jealous of my special relationship with your brother?"

I let it drop. I stopped calling my brother for almost a year. He never noticed. Now, on his porch, the mention of his grandson's name brought back my anger. I forced it back down and said, "So, Brother. How's Tony doing at Stanford?"

"He's leading the team in home runs," he said. "He should be a first-round draft choice this year."

"Great."

Susan and Mil began bringing in the food from the kitchen. Salad. Spaghetti with shrimp marinara. Roasted pork with garlic. Garlic bread. George went down to his wine cellar and came back with a bottle of wine. He uncorked the wine and sniffed the cork. "A good year," he said. He poured everyone some wine.

I poked at my spaghetti as if looking for bugs. "Susan doesn't put so much garlic in her sauce, Mil."

"See, Mil?" George said. "I told you."

"Thanks, Patty," Mil said. "You always were a rotten kid." She laughed.

"Mildred, don't you listen to them," Susan said. "It's wonderful."

"Delicious," Bee said. George and I looked at each other and rolled our eyes to the ceiling.

George raised his wineglass over the table. "To my brother's pitching tonight," he said. Everyone touched glasses over the table.

"To Patty," Mil said.

"What time is the game?" George said.

"Seven-thirty," I said.

"Want me to come?" George said.

"It's a long drive, Brother," I said. "It's no big thing."

"But I want to," he said.

"You don't have to," I said.

"Whatever you want, brother."

We ate in silence for a while. Finally, Mil said, "Are you nervous, Patty?"

"A little."

"You shouldn't be," Mil said. "You don't have to prove anything. You're a writer now, not a pitcher."

"Not when I get on the mound, Mil. No excuses then."

"My brother was always a pitcher," George said. "He was the best. He'll do okay. Just remember what I taught you, Brother."

I looked at my brother. When I was a boy of ten, he used to take his lunch breaks from his law practice at my house. He'd drive up in his red Volkswagen convertible. I'd be waiting for him on the front porch with my ball and gloves. He'd step out of that tiny car, a tall, gangly, homely man dressed in a plaid J. Press sports jacket, rep tie, Gant oxford-blue button-down-collar shirt, and wing-tipped cordovan shoes. He'd take off his jacket and throw it in the car. Then he'd roll up the sleeves of his shirt and we'd have our catch on the sidewalk. Those catches were what I lived for when I was a boy. I would sit there, waiting, my heart pounding in my breast, until my brother arrived. I could not calm myself until he stepped out of his car and began to roll up the sleeves of his shirt, methodically, soothing me, until they were past his elbows.

When I got my $50,000 bonus from the Braves, I offered to buy my brother a new car. He wouldn't let me. He asked only that I pay off Dad's mortgage on the house. Which I did. I should have forced my brother to accept a new car from me. But I was only a teenager. I was in awe of him. It never dawned on me to do anything except what he asked.

My brother invested my bonus money in second mortgages. He wouldn't let me spend any of it, except on a new car, a Chrysler 300, which I traded for an Oldsmobile Starfire in 1962. One day, three years after I'd signed with the Braves, he asked if he could borrow my Starfire. "I have to take a long trip," he said. "Where?" I said. "I'll tell you when I get back," he said. He returned a week later. Then he told me. He had invested my money with a man, he discovered, who was a swindler. The man had gotten dozens of second mortgages from banks and individual investors like me on the same piece of property. When George found out, he went to the man's house. He grabbed him by the throat and told him that he either paid me back my mortgage money, with interest, or else he'd beat the shit out of him and then turn him into the police. The man agreed to pay George my money if George promised not to turn him in. George agreed. The money was in a bank in North Carolina. George forced the man to go with him, in my Olds Starfire, to that bank, where the man withdrew the $23,000 he owed me, in cash.

When the man's fraud was finally discovered, my brother was questioned by the police. They wanted to know why his client, of all the investors defrauded, was the only one to get his money back, plus interest. "It was my brother's money," George said. "I don't give a shit about anyone else."

Now, sitting on my brother's porch in sunlight, I realized how crazed my brother must have been, thirty-seven years ago, to get my money back. Money that *he* had invested for me. Money I never would have earned if not for all those catches over the years. Money my brother refused to share in. Except once, when he asked me if he could borrow my Starfire thirty-seven years ago. It's the only thing he ever asked of me.

"Yes, Brother," I said. "How could I forget what you taught me?"

After lunch, Susan and Bee helped Mil clear away the dishes. I said to George, "We have to go now."

"You sure you don't want me to be there, Brother?"

I saw Susan in the doorway. She looked at me. Finally, I said, "If you really want to, Brother."

My brother's homely face broke into a big smile. "Are you kidding? Pass up a chance to see my little brother pitch again?" He reached out his big hand, clamped it on my knee, and squeezed hard until it hurt, just like he always did when I was a boy.

George and I went into the kitchen. George said to Mil, "I'm going to Patty's game tonight."

"Me too," Mil said. "I wouldn't miss it for the world."

We all kissed goodbye. Susan, Bee, and I walked outside into the bright sunshine. Mildred stood in the doorway, smiling. I thought I heard her speak, in a dreamy, lilting voice, as if to herself. "What a nice Tuesday," she said.

Sixteen

WE DROPPED BEE off at the Ramada Inn at 3 P.M. Susan and I drove to Municipal Stadium. My teammates were lying in the rightfield grass, stretching their muscles. I went to the clubhouse to change into my uniform. Susan went to sit in the rightfield stands. "I don't want to miss any of it," she said.

The clubhouse was deserted. I stripped naked and put on my uniform as I always had. Jockstrap and metal cup first. Thin white sanitary stockings. Lavender stirruped stockings. Knee brace. I flexed my knee. It was stiff but not sore. I rotated my right shoulder. The tiny pinprick of pain was still there. Maybe it would go away when I warmed up. I put on my Spirit T-shirt and my uniform blouse over it. Then my pants. I fastened the bottom of my pants legs a few inches below my knees, exposing my lavender stockings, the way I always had thirty-five years ago. Then I remembered my teammates. I pulled the bottoms of my pants legs down to a few inches above my ankles. I laced up my spikes and sat there, on a low, three-legged stool in a hot, damp, musty-smelling locker room. I took a cigar out of my shoulder bag and lit it.

"Nice touch," said a voice. I looked up to see Ronnie snapping my picture. "Put on your shades too."

"How long you been here?" I said.

"Ten minutes. I got some good shots of you dressing."

"Jeez, Ronnie. I musta been in dreamland."

"Go ahead. Put on the shades. And put a ball in your hand." I did as I was told. Ronnie began snapping pictures of me in my uniform, wearing shades, smoking a cigar, a glove in one hand, a baseball in the other. I remembered the picture he'd taken at my fifty-six birthday party. An old man with a white beard. It wasn't too late to shave it. I didn't want to call attention to myself. I didn't want to be the famous old man writer indulging himself with a whim. I remembered one day three years ago, in Anaheim, California. The Yankees were playing the Angels. I stood behind the batting cage watching batting practice. I looked to my right. There was Billy Crystal, the actor, in a Yankee uniform. He had a batting glove half hanging, just so, out of his back pocket. Crystal never did take batting practice, or infield, or anything. He just wandered around the sidelines looking like a tiny actor playing a ballplayer. This day, I wasn't a writer. I was a ballplayer, like my teammates. That's how I saw myself and that's how I wanted everyone else to see me. But my white beard was a giveaway. I would shave it. Then I remembered what Susan had said.

"I love your beard. It's you. Why would you want to be someone different?"

Ronnie followed me outside. I put my cigar on the bullpen bench and joined my teammates stretching in rightfield. They acknowledged me with a few nods but said nothing. I lay down in the grass and mimicked their stretching, only not so strenuously. I heard Ronnie snapping my picture behind me. I saw Susan watching me from the rightfield stands. She was wearing a tight black sweater and tight jeans. I heard my teammates talking about her as they stretched.

"Who's the older chick with the blond hair?"

"I don't know. Not bad though."

"Aw, you wouldn't know what to do with her."

Yeh? I'd like to try."

I said, "Once you boys have an older chick, you'll never go back to young stuff."

They laughed. One of them said, "Why's that, old man?"

"Because they're grateful," I said. "They always leave a little mint on your pillow in the morning. And a note written in lilac ink."

"I'll bet I'd make her grateful," said a player.

"Man, I'd wear her ass out," said another.

"You're wasting your time," I said. "I think she saw tonight's starting pitcher's picture in the paper this morning. Now she's only got eyes for me."

My teammates hooted and laughed at me. "In your dreams, grandpa."

"Watch me," I said. I got up and walked over to Susan. She stood at the railing looking down at me.

"Watch yourself stretching," she said. "You don't want to pull a muscle."

"I'm just faking it," I said. "How 'bout a kiss?" She leaned over the railing and kissed me on the lips. My teammates hooted and cheered behind me.

"What's that all about?" Susan said.

"I'll tell you later."

I walked back to my teammates. Susan called out, "Break a leg, baby!"

I lay down in the grass again. One of my teammates said, "Aw right!" Another said, "The old man's still got some moves."

I tossed off one of my old lines. "Yeh. This old man's turned down more pussy than any of you will ever see." They all laughed. Nothing changes, I thought. A ballplayer's trinity: pussy, beer, and steak.

I remembered my first year in baseball in the Nebraska State League. I was sitting in the visiting team's dugout in North Platte, talking to the North Platte Indians catcher Duke Simms. He was telling me how he'd had a huge steak last night, a dozen beers, and then fucked a stewardess all night long. Almost fifteen years later, I was a reporter for *Sports Illustrated,* working on a story on the Cleveland Indians pitcher Sam McDowell. I was sitting in the Indians' dugout in Cleveland, talking to Sam. I heard a voice I recognized coming from the end of the bench. It was Duke Simms, now the Indian catcher. He was telling a teammate how he'd had a huge steak last night, a dozen beers, and then fucked a stewardess all night long.

After their stretching, my teammates went onto the field for batting practice. I got my cigar from the dugout bench and went up in the stands to sit with Susan. A few players walked past me below. They smiled and gave me the thumbs-up sign.

Susan looked at me. "Oh, I get it now," she said. "You told them you could score with the old broad."

"They thought you were hot."

She shook her head. "Too hot for them. My children are ten years older than them, for goodness sake."

"Don't remind me."

Bob Wirsz came walking down the aisle toward us. I introduced him to Susan. He looked at me puffing on my cigar in my Spirit uniform.

"Do you think that looks good?" he said. "For the fans, I mean."

I looked around the deserted stadium. "Let's hope we get some fans," I said.

"It should be a decent house," he said. "We've been averaging seven hundred a game."

"Did you promote it much?" I said.

"Enough," he said, with a weak smile. So. He hadn't promoted my pitching tonight. He was probably afraid I'd embarrass him.

"You know what you shoulda done, Bob?"

"What?"

"Advertised in the papers. Every fan who's older than tonight's starting pitcher gets free food and beer all night long."

He smiled. "Yeh. I should have."

"And not tell them who was pitching. Probably woulda filled the house with people expecting free beer and food." He pursed his lips and shook his head at a lost opportunity. "What time is the game, anyway? Seven-thirty?"

"No. Seven o'clock."

"Jeez. What time is it now?"

"Five."

I turned to Susan. "Babe? You got the cellphone?" She took it out of her purse and handed it to me. I called my brother's number. Their answering machine clicked on with my brother's droning, disinterested voice. I waited for the beep, then said, "George, the game's at seven, not seven-thirty. I hope you get this."

I asked Wirsz to make sure my brother had his tickets at the gate. He went off to check on them. Susan and I sat in the sun, watching batting practice. I explained to her what was happening on the field. Why the pitcher threw from behind a half screen so he wouldn't get hit by a line drive.

"What about you?" she said. "You won't have a screen."

I hadn't thought about that. About getting hit with a line drive. Fielding a bunt. Throwing over to first base to hold a runner. Covering home on a play at the plate. Jesus, I hope there won't be many of those.

"It's something you never worry about," I said. "Until it happens."

"What if it does happen?" she said. "What if someone does hit the ball at you?"

"You just react. It's all reflex. The ball comes toward you, you put your glove up. It's not something you forget."

"Like riding a bicycle," she said.

"Like fucking too." I looked around to make sure no one was watching, then put my hand between her legs. She pulled it away.

"Behave yourself," she said in her school-mistress tone. "You're supposed to be an athlete."

"Athletes fuck."

"After the game," she said. "If you do well." She assumed her ballplayer's wife's girlish voice. "Otherwise, sweetheart, I'm cutting you off."

"Then no drinkee with dinner."

She looked around, grabbed my hand, and put it between her legs. "You win, sweetheart." We both laughed.

A few fans began straggling into the stadium. The concessionaires opened their booths behind the bullpen bench. I could smell cooking hot dogs and hamburgers and Polish sausages and onions. I yelled down to one of the concessionaires. "What time is it, guy?"

He looked at his watch. "Five-thirty."

"It's time for my rubdown from the trainer," I said to Susan. "Remember? I told you about her?"

"Don't get a hard-on, baby."

I went into the clubhouse again. My manager, Stan Hough, was filling out his lineup card at his desk. His little fan was close to his face, rearranging the warm, humid air. He looked up and nodded at me, but said nothing.

The trainer's room was next to his tiny office. The girl was waiting for me. "Take your shirt off," she said, "and get on the table."

I lay on my stomach while she kneaded the muscles in my back and neck. I told her about the pain deep in my arm near my shoulder. "They all have that," she said. She began working on my arm with her strong fingers. She dug her thumbs deep into the muscle, trying to find the pain. It was so deep she couldn't reach it. Still, the massage was relaxing me. It was the first time I'd ever had one. I felt drained of energy and worry.

Finally, she slapped my back and said, "That's it." I sat up too quickly. My head was spinning.

"Wow!" I said. "I feel spacey."

"Maybe it's all those cigars," she said.

I put my shirt back on and went into the manager's office. He looked up from a computer on his desk. "Did Bob tell you?" he said. "The other team's manager wanted to see you throw in the bullpen before the game. He wants to make sure this is no joke."

"No problem," I said.

He turned on his computer. "Look at this," he said. The computer gave a rundown of every batter I'd face tonight. What pitches they'd hit off of other Spirit pitchers. Low fastballs. High sliders. I watched all the dizzying information flash before me.

"I don't know whether I'll need all that," I said. "I don't want to get confused."

"Sure," he said. He clicked off the computer. "Let's just go over the batters anyway." He told me the team I'd face tonight, the Adirondack Lumberjacks, was the best hitting team in the league. "We're both tied for first place," he said. "We don't want to fall too far behind tonight. You know what I mean?" I nodded. I could tell Stan wasn't too thrilled about me pitching tonight in this crucial game. This was a real game for everyone involved, including me.

"The first and third hitters are free swingers," he said. "They like to jack up on fastballs when the pitcher falls behind in the count." I nodded. "The second hitter takes a lot of pitches." I nodded again.

"The fourth hitter is a good fastball hitter." He went on talking about the fifth, sixth, seventh, eighth, and ninth hitters, but I didn't hear him. I was scheduled to pitch only one inning. If the eighth batter got up in the first inning I'd be long gone. My relief pitcher would be Dave Fleming, a stylish lefty who'd once won seventeen games with the Seattle Mariners in the early 1990s. Now he was trying to come back after rotator-cuff surgery.

After we had finished going over the hitters, Stan shook my hand. "Good luck," he said. "Don't worry. We'll be behind you."

I thanked him and went outside to get a coke from the concessions stand. There were dozens of people milling around the stand now. When I emerged from the clubhouse in my uniform, they all turned to look at me. They stared at me. A little blond girl came up to me with an autograph book. She asked me to sign it.

"Sure, honey," I said. I felt foolish. Did she know who I was? Or maybe she didn't care. I was in a uniform. That was enough for her.

Two men with beards came up to me. They were in their late forties.

"We're great fans of your work," one man said.

"We've read *A False Spring* dozens of times," said the other. He held out a worn copy of my book. "Would you sign it for us?"

"Of course."

The other man said, "Do you know what my favorite passage is?" I shook my head. "When you describe your career as a box of unnumbered slides." He thought a minute, trying to remember. "You write, 'My career was no well made movie, rising action, climax, denouement. It was a box of unnumbered slides.'"

I smiled at him. "I wish I had more readers like you," I said.

The other man said, "Do you mind if I ask you a question?"

"Shoot."

"Why are you doing this? Is it for a book?"

"No," I said. Which was the truth. The book would come much later.

The man who'd read the passage said, "You want to finally put those slides in order, huh?"

"Something like that," I said. But even that wasn't the entire truth. I looked at the two men, holding their copy of *A False Spring*, and said, "I don't really know why. I just never felt complete without baseball."

They both nodded, then each shook my hand and wished me luck. I walked over to the bullpen bench and sat down. I could see the two men looking at their copy of my book where I'd signed it. They were smiling and nodding, as if over a precious object. The book had sold modestly well when it was first published, and then, over the years, a strange thing had happened. It became a cult classic. It was reprinted regularly, four times over the next twenty-three years. Men would call me up from strange places in the middle of the day. Kansas City. Peoria. Spokane. Macon. "Is this really you?" they'd say over the phone. "I just had to tell you how your book changed my life." They all said the same thing. My book had helped them deal with their own failures. I was, to them, the guru of failure. Not a bad legacy, I thought after each call.

Women called too. In their forties. They had just had a divorce. They were throwing out their husband's belongings when they came across his copy of *A False Spring*. They hated the book. It was a reminder of their husband, who had urged them to read it. They refused. A baseball book? Now, with him gone, the book in their hand, ready for the garbage, but no one around to see them, they sat down and began to read. When they finished they called me up. "Now I know why he wanted me to read it," they told me. "I would have understood him better." The funny thing was, even as they told me this, I could still sense their anger at me, that book, and their husbands.

George Plimpton once interviewed me for a novel he was writing about a mythical pitcher, Sid Finch, who could throw a fastball 200 mph. He sat on the deck of our apartment overlooking the Intracoastal Waterway. Sailboats rocked in their moorings. A soft breeze rustled the big leaves of the palm trees at twilight. George and I and Susan sat in deck chairs and sipped drinks. George and I talked at first about our days together at *Sports Illustrated* in the 1970s. He profiled heroes. I profiled failures.

George was the guru of success, who wrote eloquently about Hank

Aaron's mystical grace that allowed him to break Babe Ruth's career home-run record. I had pitched against Hank Aaron one spring training. I walked him on four pitches. The story of my career.

"Hank was no mystery, George," I said. "He had quick wrists, that's all. He could wait on a curveball longer than most. He swung after it broke, not before. It was God's grace, not Hank's."

I wrote about Bo Belinsky, the playboy pitcher famous for his late-night drinking binges and all the beautiful women he dated—Mamie Van Doren, Jo Collins, Ann-Margret—before it was acceptable in sports (see Joe Namath) to be a playboy athlete. Bo retired from a career that never fulfilled its potential in 1970. He was living in a whore house high in the Hollywood Hills when I interviewed him. We sat on a white sofa, drinking vodka on the rocks at 10:30 A.M. Women in bikinis moved languidly about the house, the swimming pool, and then upstairs with strange men. Mostly, Bo and I talked about failure. Why had we failed? What did it mean? What was in us that caused our failure? What did we learn from it? "It was just in the cards," Bo said. "A leopard can't change his spots, can he? You can shave all the fur off the poor bastard and he's still got his spots."

Which was why I always preferred to write about failures rather than successes. Successful people pulled up short. "I try not to think too much when I'm pitching good," Tom Seaver once told me. Failures go all the way. They're always picking at the scab of their failure despite the pain. Successes, like Aaron and Seaver, see no point in such self-inflicted pain. They don't want to know why they're successful. They just want to ride it. Thinking about it might jinx it.

Finally, George took out a notebook and a pen. He asked me to put into words for him what it felt like to throw an unhittable fastball.

"I already did, George. Did you read *A False Spring*?"

"Of course," he said in his patrician accent. He was wearing a wrinkled summer suit and tie in the Fort Lauderdale heat. His white hair fell boyishly across his brow. He had sagging, pale, mottled skin, small, peering blue eyes, and a sharp nose above thin lips. A pale, eager bird. So quick and eager to please. "A won-derful book!" he said. "*Won*-derful!" He paused a moment, then said softly, without his patrician accent, "I would have given up everything I've ever written if I could have written that book."

But that did not please me. I said, "I know, George."

* * *

I heard a voice behind me on the bullpen bench. "Brother!" I turned to see my brother smiling at me.

"Heh, Bro! I'm glad you got my message."

"What message?"

"That the game was at seven, not seven-thirty."

"We were already on our way," he said. He came over and hugged me. I smelled my brother's musty smell. He looked at me in my uniform. The first time he'd seen me in a uniform in thirty-eight years. "You still look like a pitcher," he said.

"With a white beard," I said.

"Look who's here," he said. Mil and Dad were standing behind him. Dad was looking at me strangely, as if he didn't recognize me in my uniform.

"Curly!" I said. "What a surprise!" He came over to me and kissed me on the lips.

"Mom's mad at me," he said.

"What'd you do now?"

"We didn't ask her to come tonight. George didn't think she'd be up to it."

"She's even mad at me," George said, smiling.

"Can you imagine that, Patty?" Mil said.

"No, Mil. I can't."

"Are you nervous?" Mil said.

"Not really," I said. "I've been filling up my time with all those meaningless baseball things you do before a game. It keeps your mind off it."

"There's nothing to be nervous about," my brother said. "Just go out and have fun." He grinned. "And strike out everyone, or else." We all laughed.

"It's not too late, Bro. Maybe I can get another bonus. Smaller, though."

"I'll handle the negotiations," he said. "Like I did before."

I saw Bob Wirsz walking toward me from the first base dugout. The Lumberjack manager was with him. I checked the clock on the scoreboard in rightfield. Six-thirty.

"Time to warm up," I said. "Susan and Bee should be sitting behind the first base dugout by now." They all wished me luck. My brother grabbed my hand and squeezed it, like he did when I was a boy, so hard it hurt.

"Give 'em hell, Brother," he said. I watched them all walk up the stairs to the rightfield stands and down the runway toward their seats behind the first base dugout.

Wirsz introduced me to the Lumberjack manager. I shook his hand. He gave me a disgusted look. Wirsz turned toward the Spirit dugout and signaled for a catcher. A big kid, with an unshaven, melonlike jaw, came sprinting toward us. He was wearing his catching gear, which flapped as he ran. He gave me a big smile and we shook hands. I began to soft toss with him while the Lumberjack manager watched.

My left leg in the knee brace was stiff but not sore. I felt no pain when I landed with my left foot in the dirt. But I couldn't raise my leg as high in my flamingo pose as I could before I hurt it. I felt myself coming down too soon with my left leg. My throwing arm trailed behind, a split second late. The pain was still there in my arm. It lessened as I threw, but not much. It hurt less when I threw from a three-quarter angle, my hand passing a little above my right ear, than it did when I threw straight overhand, the ball above my head. I dropped my arm down on each pitch and threw from a three-quarter angle.

My catcher was crouched behind the plate now. I was throwing harder. I could hear myself grunting with each pitch. I was throwing about 80 percent as hard as when I had thrown with Brian before I hurt my leg. My fastball was in the mid-80s. But I was keeping it low. No fliers.

"Slider," I said. I threw a slider that broke inside to a righthanded batter. I'd let the ball go too soon. I reminded myself to hold on to the next one a split second longer. It broke sharply across the plate to the low outside corner.

My catcher nodded. "Nice pitch." I nodded back and continued to work in the late afternoon sun. I'd forgotten about Wirsz and the Lumberjack manager. I just threw, working up a sweat on a pleasant evening in Waterbury. I felt nervous but resigned. It would all be over soon, one way or another. I didn't expect that much from myself now. I no longer had the exalted expectations of youth. Three strikeouts on nine pitches. Jim Hicks on one knee. I had only the diminished expectations of an adult who lived in the real world. I hoped only that I would give up a few hits, a walk, a run maybe, before I retired my three batters on a ground ball, a pop-up to right, a long fly ball to the warning track in left, and then I could walk off the mound finally and retire that dream from my nights.

I was breathing heavily. I stopped a moment to catch a breath.

"I've seen enough," the Lumberjack manager said. He didn't elaborate. He just turned his back on me and walked back to his team's third base dugout.

I waited for Wirsz to say something. "You've still got fifteen minutes," he said.

"I'll rest awhile," I said. "Then warm up again in a few minutes."

"Suit yourself." Wirsz walked back toward the Spirit dugout. I went over and sat down on the bullpen bench. My catcher came over and sat beside me. I waited for him to say something. Anything.

"You wanna go over the signals?" he said.

"Yeh. It'll be simple. One, fastball. Two, slider. Reverse them with a runner on second."

He nodded, then said, "Don't worry. We've got a good fielding team. We'll help you out. You'll do fine."

He got up and walked back to the dugout. I sat there by myself. I wondered why no one had commented on my pitches. Was I throwing that badly? Maybe they didn't know what to make of me. An old man who looked like a pitcher. I confused them. I was doing something I wasn't supposed to be doing, so they didn't know how to judge me.

I looked toward the first base stands for Susan, Bee, and my family.

But the stadium was filling up now and I couldn't see them. Some of the fans were pointing toward me. Were they laughing? Did they think I was a fool? Did they want me to embarrass myself? Show myself for what I am? An egomaniac who dared think *he* could do what *they,* long ago, resigned themselves to never doing. Grasp at a second chance in old age to redeem the failure of youth. Did they resent me for trying? Did they think my grasping at a second chance was meant to be a rebuke to them? Did they think it was *easy* for me? That I didn't have the same fears they did? Failure. I dreaded, even more than they, making a fool of myself again. But still I had to take the chance. Like my father said, "If it's the only game in town, you got no choice. You gotta play."

I was no J. Alfred Prufrock, nor was meant to be. I did dare disturb the universe. In short, I was afraid, but still I had to ask that woman out. So what if, settling a pillow by her head, she should say, "That is not what I meant at all," then turned to her women friends and laughed at the presumptuous old man with the white beard? I do grow old. I have heard the mermaids singing each to each. But I *do* think that once again they will sing to me.

When I went back to college, after my baseball failure, I took a poetry course on T. S. Eliot. We studied *"The Love Song of* J. Alfred Prufrock." My professor asked the class what Prufrock's fatal flaw was. I said, "He was shy." The professor shook his head and said, "Not at all. He was the ultimate egomaniac. He loved himself so disproportionately that he could not bear to put himself in danger of being hurt. So he never took a chance. Never asked those women out. He settled, instead, for a life of everlasting, self-pitying regret."

My catcher was sprinting toward me again. I got up to throw. My knee was stiff. I threw for five minutes until my knee loosened up. Then I walked toward my dugout for the start of the game. It was dusk. The stadium lights were on. I heard the low hum of the fans' voices as I walked past them. I didn't look up. The sun was setting behind the home plate stands. It blinded me when I reached the dugout. I stepped down into the dugout into cool darkness. My teammates were sitting on the bench, fidgeting with nervous anticipation. I looked at their faces. They were so young. So worried now. Filled with edgy anticipation before they took the field. They had the same fear I did. Would they make fools of themselves? Would they boot the routine double-play ball that let in the winning run in front of all these fans? They looked up at me and smiled. Not knowing grins at an old man. But hopeful smiles at their pitcher. Pleading, almost. Help us. We need you. We need each other. Teammates. I walked down the bench. They raised their hands and slapped my hand with high-fives. "Aw right! Let's get 'em! You can do it! We're behind you! Just help us out!"

"Piecea cake," I said.

"Aw right!"

Suddenly a group of Little League ballplayers in uniform was ushered onto the field near our dugout. They stood around in awe of us. The public-address announcer began to call out the name of each Spirit player by position. When he called shortstop, two Little Leaguers trotted out to shortstop with our starting shortstop. Two Little Leaguers trotted out to each position with every Spirit player. There were only two Little Leaguers left now. The announcer called out my name as the starting pitcher. I signaled the Little Leaguers to follow me out to the mound. They looked at me, confused, and shook their heads. They looked around for the Spirit starting pitcher.

"It's me," I said. "Come on." They wouldn't budge. I grabbed each of them by their little hands and half dragged, half led them out to the mound with me. They stood there, blinking into the lights, looking around, waiting for the Spirit starting pitcher.

The fans stood for the National Anthem. I faced the centerfield flagpole and placed my cap over my heart. The two Little Leaguers did the same. The fans began to applaud and cheer as the Anthem ended. All the Little Leaguers trotted off the field. The umpire stepped in front of my catcher and threw me the ball. The ball moved in and out of a blinding light. I turned my head away and reached up my glove to catch it. Immediately, my manager trotted out to the mound.

"What's the matter?" I said. I had the insane fear that he had just seen something in me that convinced him he should take me off the mound before I even threw a pitch.

"Nothing," he said. "I'm just trying to stall until the sun drops behind the stands. It's fuckin' merciless at this time of day."

The umpire signaled him off the field. He ignored him. "Make him throw me out before the game even begins," Stan said. He grinned. "A fucking first, huh?"

Finally, the umpire walked out to the mound. "Stan! What's going on? We gonna play this game or what?"

"Yeh, yeh, yeh." Stan gave me a little pat on the behind. "Go get 'em," he said, and trotted off.

I began my windup. I reminded myself to do all the things I had worked on for seven months. I threw my first warmup pitch high. The umpire was leaning over my catcher's shoulder to get a look at my pitches. The first batter was standing a few feet from the batter's box, studying my pitches too. I threw a few fastballs, then a few sliders. My catcher caught the eighth pitch, stepped in front of the plate, and threw the ball to second base. My infielders tossed the ball around until it ended up with the third baseman. He stepped toward me, tossed me the ball, and said, "It's all yours."

*   *   *

For the first time in all those years that I had the dream, I saw the ball actually leaving my hand. I saw it all, in perfect silence and slow motion. My body lunging forward to my left. My head jerking to my left. I lost sight of the ball as my left foot landed in the dirt and then my right foot. I turned my head back toward the plate. I saw the ball spinning in and out of shadows and a blinding light. I saw the catcher's big round mitt. The umpire hunched over the catcher's left shoulder. The batter striding toward the ball. The ball emerging from the blinding light, crossing the plate high and inside, the batter pulling back his head, the ball hitting the catcher's mitt with a *pop* I could hear now, the umpire turning his head away, calling out so clearly, "Ball!"

I heard everything now, as everything returned to normal speed. I heard my teammates' meaningless chatter behind me, the fans' cheers and shouts of encouragement, my own labored breathing. The catcher stepped in front of the plate to throw me the ball. The umpire straightened up and stretched his neck. The batter stepped out of the box, knocked dirt off his spikes with his bat, and then stepped back in. It was all so real. I wanted to laugh out loud. My catcher threw the ball back to me. The blinding light was beginning to fade. I caught the ball with a *thwack*. It was all so simple. A game of catch. I felt suddenly calm. There was nothing to it. Joanie had been right. It all came back to me. Without thought. I wasn't thinking about my motion, the fans, my brother, my fears, the tiny point of pain in my shoulder, my stiff knee. I was thinking only about throwing my next pitch. I was a pitcher again. I felt like such a fool. All those years of recriminations. Over what? Nothing. There was nothing cosmic about what I was doing. There was nothing to fear. That fear had only been in my mind. Milton was right: "The mind is its own place, and in itself can make a heaven of hell, a hell of heaven."

I toed the rubber for my next pitch. The noise around me receded now as I concentrated on my catcher's sign. Fastball. I nodded, pumped, and threw a fastball low and off the plate by inches. The batter held back his bat at the last second. The umpire turned his head away again. "Ball two!" A nice pitch, I thought. Close.

I caught the ball from my catcher. The blinding light was gone now, sunken behind the home-plate stands. I concentrated on my next pitch. My catcher stuck one finger between his legs. I remembered what Brian had said: "Use your slider as your out pitch." And Stan too: "The first hitter likes to swing when he's ahead on the count." I shook my head, no. My catcher stuck two fingers between his legs. I nodded, began my delivery, kicked, and threw a hard slider at the batter's waist. I saw him striding toward the ball, his bat whipping around, the ball suddenly darting down and away from his bat. His fierce swing died as he reached weakly for the ball with his bat. The ball hit the end of his bat and dribbled past me to my right. I stared at it in disbelief. I turned to follow it. My shortstop was charging the ball before it died on the infield grass. He was black! He scooped up the ball on a dead run, bent low to the grass, and, still charging, flipped the ball underhanded toward first base. I saw the first baseman stretch toward the ball. He caught it a split second before the runner crossed the bag. The first base umpire made a pumping motion with his fist, as if curling a weight toward his shoulder, and then turned his back on the field.

The runner made a U-turn in short rightfield and trotted back to his dugout. I could hear the fans cheering. Someone shouted out my name. "Patty! Attawaytogo!" The ball moved around the infield until it came to the third baseman. He stepped toward me, flipped me the ball, and said, "One down. Two to go."

I walked the second batter on four pitches. Three fastballs just off the plate and a slider low and away that could have been called a strike. The runner trotted toward first base. I caught the ball from my catcher and turned my back on him. I looked toward centerfield and rubbed up the ball. I waited for the fear to return, as it always had in the minor leagues, when I walked a batter. I waited. Nothing. I turned back toward the plate to get my sign. I stood sideways to the plate in my stretch position, facing third base. I peered down at my catcher, nodded, came to a stop in my stretch, and glanced over my shoulder at the runner taking a lead. I looked back at the plate and threw a perfect fastball on the low outside corner to the righthanded batter. "Strike one!"

The batter was taking a pitch after the walk, I thought. Now he'll be swinging. I came to my stretch again, glanced over my shoulder at the runner, then turned and threw a flat high slider for a ball. I let the ball go too soon, I thought. I have to hold on to it a split second longer.

My catcher signaled slider. I shook him off. I threw a low inside fastball that the batter had to hop back from. Ball two.

The runner might be going on this next pitch, I thought. Two balls, one strike. A good pitch to try to steal second. The batter would have to swing at any pitch close to the plate to protect the runner. I remembered Stan telling me the third batter liked to swing when he was ahead on the count. I came to my stretch, glanced over at the runner, then back to the plate. I whirled toward first and threw the ball. The runner dove back to the bag. I saw the ball sailing high over the first baseman's head toward the first base stands. The first baseman leapt in the air, his long glove shooting up, and snatched the ball. He came back down with the ball, walked a few feet toward me, and made a calming gesture with his hands, as if patting down the air. I nodded. He tossed me the ball.

I turned back to the batter. Fuck the guy at first, I thought. Concentrate. I got my sign, came to a pause in my stretch, didn't bother looking at the runner, reminded myself to hold on to the ball longer, and threw a hard slider at the batter's hips. He swung hard just as the ball darted down and away from his bat. The ball hit the end of his bat and dribbled down the first base line with a little cueball spin and stopped. I stared at it, frozen. My first baseman waited a split second for me to field the ball. When he saw I made no move for the ball he ran in, picked it up, and tagged the batter running to first. The runner on first had moved to second.

"Two down," my first baseman said. "One to go." He tossed me the ball.

The fourth batter was a big righthanded hitter with a two-day growth of beard. He was the Lumberjacks' leading home-run hitter. I started him off with a slider low and away, off the plate for ball one. I didn't even bother holding the runner close to second now; I was intent only on getting this batter out. I heard a voice behind me. I turned. It was the second base umpire. He was young, maybe twenty-five, with a pink face. He looked at me so seriously and said, "Pat, you're not coming to a complete stop in your stretch. I'll have to call a balk next time."

I smiled at him. "What do you expect?" I said. "I haven't had a runner on base in thirty-five years." He just nodded seriously and assumed his spread-legged umpire's stance between second base and the mound.

I turned back to the batter. He's probably guessing slider, I thought. I got my sign from my catcher, reminded myself to pause in my stretch, and threw a fastball down the middle of the plate. The batter watched the ball cross the plate all the way into my catcher's glove. Strike one.

My catcher threw the ball back to me. The big hitter pointed the head of his bat at me as if daring me to throw another fastball. He's guessing slider again! I knew it, as surely as I knew anything in my life. I wanted to laugh. It was so easy. My catcher flashed me the sign. I shook him off. He gave me another. I nodded. I came to my stretch, glanced at the runner on second, then threw to the plate. The batter lunged toward the ball, his bat whipping around, then stopping in midswing because my high inside fastball was already past him in my catcher's glove. The umpire signaled a ball. My catcher leapt out of his crouch and pointed at the second base umpire. The second base umpire raised his fist to indicate the batter had swung. The home-plate umpire changed his call to a strike. One ball, two strikes.

I stood on the mound with the ball in my hand. I watched the batter take his practice swings. He tried to glare at me. But the confusion in his eyes betrayed him. He was helpless. We both knew it. I smiled at him. He blinked, once, twice. He raised a hand to call timeout and stepped out of the box. He fidgeted. He tugged his shirt, rotated his shoulders, adjusted his metal cup. Then he stepped back into the box. He held one hand in front of the umpire's face to keep his timeout as he dug his spikes into the dirt like a bull preparing to charge. Finally, he held his bat high behind his head and waited for the fastball we both knew was coming.

I remembered Jim Hicks on one knee. "Jim Hicks murders fastballs," my fellow pitcher said. "He murders your fastballs," I said, "but the sunuvabitch won't murder mine." I threw Jim Hicks nothing but 95-mph fastballs every time I faced him in 1960. He swung through them all with such force that he fell to one knee. He pushed himself up with his bat, like an old man. I struck out Jim Hicks four times in one game. I threw him nothing but 95-mph fastballs. He swung through them all, fell to one knee, then pushed himself up with his bat like an old man. After his fourth strikeout to end the game, he just stood there at the plate and stared at me on the mound. He pointed his bat at me and yelled, "Don't you worry, boy. Jim Hicks gonna get you yet." I yelled back, "You keep tryin', Jim." We both laughed. But he did. Get me, that is. The next time I faced him he hit a home run off my 95-mph fastball that beat me, 3–2.

Now, thirty-five years later, I was going to do it again. Jim Hicks on one knee. I got my sign from my catcher. I came to a pause in my stretch. I didn't bother glancing at the runner on second. I stared at the batter, my catcher's big round mitt, and then I threw the ball. I followed the ball with my eyes as it headed, waist-high, toward the middle of the plate. I could see the batter almost smile at the ball as he began his vicious swing. I saw his big bat whipping around toward the ball just before it crossed the plate. The meat of his bat was aimed directly at the heart of the ball. The batter's eyes were fixed on that point a few inches in front of the plate where the ball and bat would meet. In his mind's eye, he could already feel the impact of his bat against that ball. The faint tingle that went through his fingers and up his arms the moment that bat made contact with the ball with an echoing *thunk!* The bat was there now where it would meet the ball. The batter saw it, the bat flat against the ball, distorting the ball, flattening it on one side before it sprang back into shape and sailed into the darkness. He squeezed his hands even more tightly around the bat at the moment of impact, waited for that pleasurable tingle in his hands and arms, that echoing sound.

But he felt nothing. He heard nothing except his own grunting. He saw nothing except his bat whipping past where the ball had been and was no longer. It had vanished! Poof! Like magic! He blinked, once, twice. It was still gone! It had to be there! So he kept swinging, waiting for the vanished ball to reappear, to hit his bat. But his bat just kept whipping past the vanished ball and beyond with such uninterrupted force that it caused him to lose his balance. He fell to the ground on one knee. He steadied himself with his bat against the dirt. He looked behind him for the ball. He saw it in my catcher's mitt. My catcher held the ball in his mitt for a split second, a few inches off the ground on the far outside corner of the plate. The batter's shoulders sagged, his head dropped. He pushed himself up from the dirt with his bat, like an old man.

Seventeen

SUSAN WAS SITTING beside George behind the first base dugout when I struck out that last batter on a slider. She said I looked dazed and uncomprehending on the mound. "Like a lost little boy," she said. "I felt sorry for you."

But I didn't feel dazed and lost. I didn't feel any of the things I had expected to feel at this moment. I just stood there on the mound, thinking, Is that all?

My teammates had already run in from the field, patted me on the back—"Way to go, Pat!"—and continued on toward the dugout. I turned to follow them. All the fans were standing, cheering. I saw Susan, Mildred, my father, Ronnie, Bee. I saw my brother. He was pumping his fists in the air and shouting. "Atta boy, Patty! I knew you could do it, Brother!" As I crossed the first base line I saw my brother turn to Susan and say something.

I stepped down into the darkened dugout. As I walked down the dugout my teammates raised their hands and slapped my hand. "Good job, man! Awright! You held them for us!" There were no jokes about "the old man."

I walked to the end of the dugout and onto the field toward the clubhouse behind the rightfield foul line. Fans shouted congratulations as I passed them. Halfway down the rightfield line I turned through an open space toward the clubhouse. Wirsz was waiting there for me with a camera crew from a local television station. The reporter stuck a microphone in my face and asked me questions. Was I surprised I pitched so well? I said no. I knew I was throwing good. He smiled. Wasn't I afraid I'd get hurt, at my age? I said no, I didn't think of that. What was I trying to prove? Nothing. I just wanted to pitch. I told him how I set up the last batter with fastballs so I could strike him out with a slider.

"It was a great slider," I said. He nodded, without interest.

After the interview, Wirsz told me he had researched the baseball records and discovered I was the third-oldest pitcher ever to pitch in a professional game. He was disappointed. He'd hoped I was the oldest. He was also disappointed that there were no national TV stations or newspapers covering my pitching. But he hadn't called them. He was afraid they'd come and I'd embarrass him. Now he regretted his mistake. I waited for him to say something about my pitching. When he didn't, I said, "I'm gonna take a shower now, Bob."

"I'll meet you in the stands," he said. "I want the public-address announcer to introduce you to the fans for applause."

"Sure, Bob."

The clubhouse was deserted. I sat down on a stool and took off my spikes and uniform. I had to struggle to get off the knee brace. I'd forgotten about my knee and the pain in my shoulder when I was on the mound. I rotated my shoulder now. The pain was still there. I flexed my knee. It was still stiff. I took a cigar out of my bag and lit it. Then I went into the shower room and turned on the water. It took awhile before the water got hot. I soaped myself up and let the hot water run over me while I smoked my cigar.

"Oh, Jesus! You scared me!" I said. The female trainer was standing in the doorway looking at me.

"Sorry," she said. "I just wanted to know if you wanted me to ice your arm."

"No, thanks. It was only an inning." She nodded and left.

I dried myself off in the shower and tied the towel around my waist before I stepped out into the clubhouse. I looked around for the trainer. She was gone. I went to my locker and got dressed quickly. I had brought my good jeans, my pink and blue Hawaiian shirt, and my blue suede loafers. Clothes from Paradise. But I felt foolish in them now. I didn't want to call attention to myself in the stands.

I went back outside to the open area between the stands and rightfield foul line. It was dark now. The field was patchily illuminated by the stadium lights. I found a small dark space where the lights didn't hit and watched the game. My team was leading, 5–2, in the third inning. Dave Fleming, the ex-major leaguer who had relieved me, had given up two runs. I watched him throw. He was a stylish lefty with a big, lazy curveball and a soft fastball he tried to make sink. I compared myself to him. I had a better fastball. The second fastball I had thrown the last batter must have been about 88 mph, or else he would have been able to get around on it and crush it. My slider was unhittable, like Brian had said. I smiled, thinking of Brian. I couldn't wait to tell him.

I stayed there in the darkness for a while. No one noticed me. The fans' attention was on the game. I felt nothing. I waited. Still nothing. I walked up the concrete steps toward the stands behind the first base dugout. I could see Susan, George, Mil, Dad, Ronnie, and Bee waiting for me. I saw John Hennessey, my friend from college, and his wife, Marianne. I saw Bob Wirsz.

Ronnie, Bee, Susan, and I ate dinner at the same Italian restaurant we had eaten at the night before. The food wasn't as good. We had less fun. Before we left, Ronnie told me he had been standing by the Lumberjacks' dugout when I warmed up to start the game. "They said guys like you, with soft stuff, gave them trouble."

"If it was so fucking soft," I said, "why didn't their cleanup hitter crush that high fastball?" Ronnie looked at me, startled. We paid the bill and went back to the hotel.

That night in bed, I turned to Susan before she drifted off to sleep.

"What did my brother say to you?" I said. "After I struck out the last batter?"

"He said, 'That's my brother. He never quit at anything in his life.' " We fell asleep. For the first time in thirty-five years, I didn't have the dream.

We flew home the next morning. Susan read *USA Today* during the flight. "Babe, look at this," she said. She handed me the sports section. In the left-hand column of the first page there was a two-paragraph story about my pitching. The tone of that short story was humorous. The old man chasing youth.

"Everybody will pick up on it now," I said. It had never dawned on me that my pitching would be news. I had spent thirty years writing about other people's newsworthy activities. Now I know how they felt. Me? I remembered the housewife in Oklahoma City who had shot an intruder who was going to kill her children. When I told her over the phone I wanted to write a story about her for *Reader's Digest,* she said, "Why me?"

"Because you're a hero," I said. But she didn't think of herself as a hero any more than I thought of myself as a newsworthy novelty. I was just a pitcher, like any other minor league pitcher. I had pitched a nice inning. So what? Fleming had gotten the win. Why not write about him?

I was right. When we got home I got calls from radio and TV stations and newspapers. All their questions were the same: Why did I do it? What was I trying to prove? I tried to explain about my fastball and my slider, but no one seemed interested. They were interested only in the novelty of it. I felt like one of those female boxers no one really took seriously. *I* didn't take them seriously. But what if they took themselves seriously? And no one listened?

A sportswriter from the *Fort Lauderdale Sun-Sentinel* interviewed me over the phone for his column. He laughed when I told him I was throwing my fastball 85 mph.

"How do you know?" he said.

"I just know. My slider was devastating."

"Sure it was."

"I could have gotten them out for four or five innings if my knee wasn't stiff."

"Sure."

The headline over his column read "The Old Man and the Slider." He quoted Brian saying I reminded him of Hemingway's *The Old Man and the Sea* when he first met me. Most of the column was devoted to my being a writer and a failed pitcher years ago, who was chasing lost youth. The tone was faintly mocking. They used a photograph of me taken during the game. An old man with a white beard, his features distorted with the effort of throwing a pitch. But I didn't think of myself as that old man. The old man in that picture wasn't me. He was an old man making a fool of himself. Secretly, everyone was laughing at him.

Only he wasn't laughing at himself. He was taking it all so seriously. He thought he was just pitching.

I called Brian. "I already heard," he said. "I read about it."

"I was throwing pretty good, Bri."

"You don't have to tell me. I know you were throwing good."

"Nobody believes me. They keep talking about how old I am."

"Fuck 'em. We know how good you're throwing."

But that wasn't enough for me. "Bri, I want to start throwing again. Can you catch me?"

"Are you kidding? No problem."

"I want to pitch again next summer. Once a week for the whole season. See how long I can go each game. I want to do it for real, Brian."

When I got off the phone with Brian, Susan was sitting at the dining-room table, looking at me. "You didn't tell me," she said.

"I wasn't hiding it," I said. "I didn't think you'd mind."

"I don't. Except you'll be gone all summer."

"No I won't. I'll have Wirsz fly me up the day of each game and fly me back the next morning."

"I won't be able to go. I don't want to leave the dogs at the kennel every week. I'll have to stay home alone to watch them." I knew what she meant. Every time I left the house to go away on an assignment, we both worried about Bubba fighting with Nero. I was the alpha male in the pack. When I was gone, Bubba felt there was a void in the pack he had to fill. He did it by challenging his father. Most of Bubba's fights with his father happened when I was gone. That's why I called Susan six and seven times a day. My first words to her were always the same: "How are the dogs? Is Bubba behaving?"

"Please, babe," I said. "It's something I have to do."

She nodded, then smiled. "If you have to."

I began throwing again, twice a week with Brian during the late summer. We worked on a circle changeup and an overhand slider that broke straight down.

"You'll need two extra pitches if you expect to last a whole game," Brian said.

By September, my overhand slider was even more devastating than my flat slider. It approached the plate like a fastball, with tight spin, then darted straight down so quickly Brian had trouble catching it.

"Man!" he said one Sunday afternoon. "I thought I had quick hands. I know it's gonna break, but still I can't catch it." I smiled at him from the mound. I felt like I'd found a new toy. The circle change, however, was a different story. I'd throw one or two that approached the plate and then just died as if it had hit a headwind. But then I'd throw three or four more that sailed over Brian's head.

"You gotta be more consistent," he said. We worked on the change. It was the most difficult pitch to master because you had to throw it as hard as a fastball, even while you knew that it was a changeup.

"You're pulling back on it," Brian said. "Just throw it."

I began telling anyone who called me and asked about my inning at Waterbury that I was going to pitch the full season next summer. Everyone wondered why. They said I'd already proved my point. What point? I wasn't trying to prove any point. I was just trying to be a pitcher again. So I did it and became a novelty. A footnote. I was on the fucking Internet as the third-oldest pitcher ever to pitch in professional baseball! Jesus! I wanted to erase that footnote from the Internet. I wanted to pitch for the entire summer in such a way that the fans would forget it. I would make them talk about me as if I was just any other minor league pitcher. "Jordan's starting tonight. What is he, five-and-five on the year? He's having trouble with his circle change or else he'd be seven-and-three."

In early September I called Wirsz and told him what I wanted to do.

"You think you can pitch a whole game?" he said.

"I'll go as long as I can."

"I don't know. How will you know if you can't?"

"The batters will let me know, Bob."

He was silent for a moment, then said, "If you think you can do it, I'll pitch you until you can't get anyone out."

In late September, Brian invited me and Susan to one of his high-school football games. He was the team's wide receiver, one of the best in the county. He was small, quick, and tough, and he had those great hands. But he was too small, I told him. "You're a fucking baseball player," I said. "What are you gonna do with football in college? You're a fucking midget!"

"Fuck you! I'm a little under six feet." He laughed. "Maybe a little more under."

"You could get hurt, Brian."

"Naw. No way."

Mark insisted we get to the game an hour early so we could join him and Dawn and some of the other parents at their tailgate party in the school parking lot. We sat around his van on aluminum deck chairs, drinking beer. Suddenly Mark stood up. "Time to go," he said. Everyone hurried after him as he walked quickly toward the stadium.

We sat in the stands among the students and parents and watched Brian, number 10, warm up on the field. He looked so small among his much bigger teammates. A young girl in a tight sweater walked down the aisle past us. Mark elbowed me in the ribs. "I wish I was back in high school again, don't you?"

"Tonight, maybe."

On the second play of the game, Brian slanted across the field, caught a high pass with his fingertips on the dead run, and was hit hard by the opposing team's linebacker. He was momentarily suspended horizontally in midair, then landed hard on his right shoulder. He didn't get up right away. His team's coach and trainer ran onto the field. They hovered over Brian for a few minutes, then helped him up. The fans applauded as he hobbled off the field. His right shoulder hung down limply. The team doctor examined him on the sidelines as play resumed. Then the doctor turned toward the stands, looking for Mark. He waved Mark down to the sidelines.

Susan and I followed Mark. We had to stand behind a chain-link fence while Mark went onto the field. While he conferred with the doctor I called out to Brian. He turned, saw me, put his head down, and turned back to the field.

Mark came toward us, smiling. "Broken collarbone," he said. "Looks like you lost your catcher."

Susan was livid on the drive home. "What the fuck was he smiling about?" she said. "His son just broke his collarbone."

"That's part of the game," I said. "Mark thinks it's macho. Like a war wound."

"It's sick."

"What about 'The show must go on'?" I said.

"That's different. You do it because you have to, for the audience. Not because you think it makes you a man."

I went back to throwing by myself against the screen at Holiday Park. I threw three times a week for the next four months while waiting for Brian's shoulder to heal. It was frustrating without a catcher. I had no target to shoot for. No feedback. I couldn't tell if my slider was breaking down hard at the last second or not. I stopped throwing the circle change. It was distracting me from my other pitches.

Over the winter, I called my brother every other week. We talked about my pitching at first, and then, when there was nothing more to say about it, we struggled for other things to talk about. I reminded him he'd said he was going to visit us in January.

"Only if I can bring my own cook," he said. We both laughed. January came and went.

"He said he would come," I said to Susan one night.

"You know he's never going to come. Why don't you put it out of your mind?"

I did. But still I called him.

Brian's shoulder finally healed in February. We began throwing again every Sunday afternoon. He couldn't catch me during the week because he had his high-school games and practices. By March, I was throwing harder than at any time in the last year. "At least ninety," Brian said. "And your overhand slider is unhittable. Man, I can't wait to see you pitch this summer." I had told Brian I would fly him out to Waterbury with me for my first game, June 10. "Maybe pound some Budweisers and chase some pussy after the game," I said. He laughed. "Of course, I gotta ask Susan for permission first," I said.

I hadn't had the dream since the night I pitched in Waterbury. I kept waiting for it to come back, maybe in a new form, but it never did. There was nothing to dream about anymore, I decided.

In late March, I had to fly to Tampa to interview the Cuban defector pitcher Orlando Hernandez, known as El Duque, who had been signed by the Yankees for $6.6 million. He was still in extended spring training at the Yankees' minor league camp. Brian would be in Tampa at the same time. His high-school team was in a tournament only a mile from the Yankees' camp. I made plans before I left to watch one of his games and then take him and Mark out to dinner at Bern's Steak House.

The night before I left, I packed my bags. Susan watched me stuff my spikes and glove in the bag. I grinned. "Maybe the Yankees will let me throw a few," I said.

We went to bed early that night. The older dogs slept around us on their rugs on the floor. Nero, Bubba, and Blue jumped onto the bed and began elbowing each other for a spot to sleep. Bubba growled at Nero. I sat up and snapped at him. "Cut it out, goddamn it!" I grabbed Bubba by the scruff of his neck and threw him off the bed. He looked up at me with his wrinkled brow, in abject sorrow for the instinct he could not control. "That's all right, Bub," I said. I patted the bed. "Come on." He hopped back on, squeezed himself into a little corner of the bed, and went to sleep.

I spent the next day in Tampa following El Duque around the Yankees' camp. I watched him practice covering first base with the other pitchers. I watched him do calisthenics in the outfield. I watched him throw batting practice. He had a nice, effortless arm motion. His 92-mph fastball seemed to pick up speed as it approached the plate. His slider, however, was just a small curveball, a little wrinkle with no bite to it like mine. I turned to the Yankee vice president of player personnel, Mark Newman, and said, "You can't teach that fastball."

"I know," he said. "It explodes at the last minute."

"His slider isn't much, though. It's more half-ass curve than a sharp slider."

Mark nodded. "We're hoping it'll come around."

At the end of the day, I went into a Yankee conference room to interview El Duque through an interpreter, another Latin player. We sat around a big mahogany conference table: I started off by telling El Duque I had pitched in the minor leagues last summer.

The translator translated my English into Spanish for El Duque. When he finished, El Duque looked at me without smiling. He said, in Spanish, "How old were you?"

"How old do I look?"

"Forever."

"Thanks. I was fifty-six."

He nodded, then said, "How hard were you throwing?"

"Eighty-five, eighty-six." He pursed his lips and nodded again. I said, "How hard are you throwing?"

"Eighty-four."

"Jeez! I shoulda got your $6.6 million."

He stabbed his hand into his pants pocket, withdrew an imaginary $6.6 million, and handed it to me. We both laughed.

The interview was over late in the afternoon. Brian's game was just beginning. I didn't have time to call Susan, so I rushed over to the field where Brian was playing. Mark was waiting for me in the stands behind home plate. I sat down beside him. "How'd he do so far?" I said.

Mark shook his head. "He struck out in his first at-bat. He hasn't been swinging the bat right since he got hurt."

"You guys set for dinner tonight?" I said.

"Sure. If Brian's coach lets him go."

"We'll go to Bern's. Have a big steak." Mark nodded. I started thinking about how I'd pay for dinner. I had five $100 bills with me. But I didn't want to throw $100 bills on the table in front of Brian and his father. Like I was this cool dude and Mark was just a working stiff. But the only credit card I had was a gold American Express card. Maybe that would look just as bad. I berated myself back and forth over how I should pay the bill. I decided to break the C-notes into twenties at the hotel before we went to dinner. Then I remembered I hadn't called Susan all day, I had been so busy. I took out my cellphone and dialed our number just as Brian's team ran onto the field. Brian, at shortstop, saw me. He smiled and waved. I waved back. The phone rang for a long time. I was just ready to hang up when a breathless voice said, "Hello?"

"Suzie?" I said.

"No. This is Mary Beth."

"Her Bee-ness! His Pee-ness here. Where's the old girl?"

Bee was silent for a moment. Then she said in a studied, calm voice, "There's been a problem. Bubba and Nero had a bad fight. The paramedics are here. Susan's hands got bit badly when she tried to separate them. She managed to lock Bubba in the guest room, but Nero's hurt. He's bleeding from the head and shaking. He's hiding under your desk in the office. He snarls at anyone who tries to get near him. The paramedics are trying to stop Susan's bleeding now before we go to the emergency room."

I saw it all, in that instant. The life we had known and loved these past years was over. "Let me talk to her."

Susan got on the phone. She was breathing heavily. Before I could ask her if she was all right, she said, "Babe! You've got to get home! Something has to be done!" I heard muffled voices. "I have to go now," she said. Then she began to cry. "It was so savage! I thought Bubba was going to kill Nero. He had Nero's head in his mouth." Then she was gone.

When I got home the next morning, Bee opened the door. She had stayed overnight to help Susan. The dogs, except Bubba, came running to me. Nero's head and right ear were shaved. He looked like he was wearing a yarmulke, except for the stitches and bloody scabs. Bubba was locked in a cage in the kitchen. He looked up at me with his sad brown eyes and wrinkled brow. He wagged his tail for forgiveness. Susan was sitting up in bed, her hands swollen and bandaged like a fighter's. I sat down on the edge of the bed.

"What happened, babe?" I said. She told me.

Susan was frying chicken in the kitchen when she heard the low, menacing growl we always knew meant trouble. She looked into the dining room just as Bubba leapt at Nero with his teeth slashing. She screamed, "No, Bubba! No!" and ran to them. They were both reared up on their hind legs slashing their teeth at one another. Susan reached in her hands to separate them. She didn't even feel the bites until afterward. Finally, she managed to grab Bubba by the ruff of his neck and yank him in the air. His jaws were clamped so tightly around Nero's head that Nero was lifted in the air too. With one hand, Susan managed to pry Bubba's teeth from around Nero's head.

When she finally separated them, she got Nero into my office and Bubba into the guest room. "Bubba was so agitated," she said. "His eyes were glassy, like he loved it."

She called Bee and then the paramedics, and waited. Bee got there first, then the paramedics. Bubba barked so viciously at the paramedics that they were afraid to enter the house. When they finally did, they treated Susan's hands at the chair in her front-room office. Then Susan went into my office to check on Nero. She got down on all fours and tried to coax Nero out from under my desk. He snarled at her. "His head was twisted to one side," Susan said. "I thought his neck was broken. There was blood everywhere, on the floor, the walls. It looked like there had been a murder."

Bee took Susan to the emergency room to get her hands treated and bandaged. Then they went back home, coaxed Nero out from under the desk, and took him to our vet to be stitched up. The vet said his neck wasn't broken. They got back home at midnight. Bee helped Susan wipe up all the blood on the floor and the walls. Then they went to sleep.

We kept Bubba separated from the other male dogs for the next ten days. We let him outside to pee only with Stella and Kiri. The other male dogs, even Nero, looked confused when Susan held them by their collars as I dragged Bubba past them by his collar until he was outside. As far as all the dogs were concerned, the fight had been forgotten. Even Nero didn't growl at Bubba when I dragged him past him. He'd already forgiven his son.

We kept Bubba in the cage in the kitchen when he was in the house. The other dogs walked by him and stared in confusion. Bubba growled at them, then looked up at us pitifully, pleading for forgiveness. "I'm sorry! I'm sorry! I'm sorry!" But what he had done wasn't funny now. It was too late for forgiveness. Susan was adamant. Bubba had to go.

"I'm afraid to be alone with him now," she said. "Look what he did to me and Nero." She held up her bandaged hands. "Look what he's done to all of us," she said. "We live our whole lives around him. He has to go."

I tried to plead Bubba's case. I said I'd make sure he was always separated from Nero. "What about when you're gone?" she said. "I'm the one who's home with them when you're gone. I'm the one who saw the fight. I'm the one who loved Bubba more than the others." She began to sob.

Bubba was always her dog, just as Hoshi was mine. She had raised him since the night he was born. She loved his gruff, aloof, macho-ness that made him Bubba. She had thought he'd grow out of his hatred for Nero. Now that she knew he hadn't, and never would, she knew he had to go. "He'll start on Blue and Hoshi next," she said. "You know how he is. He won't stop until he dominates everyone, including me and you."

We called the Shiba Inu Rescue Network in Maryland. We told the woman on the other end of the line that we had a three-and-a-half-year-old male for adoption. We told her everything about Bubba. We told her how smart he was, how loving he was with people, what a great hunter and watchdog he was, how hyper he was, but in such a funny and loveable way. Finally, we told her about his fights with Nero. "I don't understand it," I said, between my tears. "Bubba's such a great dog in every way except that."

The woman said, "He's trying to tell you something. You should have listened."

"What?"

"He's not a pack dog like most Shibas. He wants to be in a one-dog family."

I remembered the moment Bubba was born. His first instinct was to crawl as far away from his own mother as possible. He slept there by himself, while Blue had to sleep as close to his mother as he could get. I should have known then. He would never change his nature. It was unfair to even ask him to.

We waited in our silent house for the person to call who would take Bubba from us. I tried to work at my desk, but for the first time ever, I couldn't. I didn't have the heart even to go throw with Brian. Besides, Susan wouldn't let me leave her alone with Bubba, not even in his cage. I walked from room to room, hour after hour, crying hysterically at my loss, at Susan's loss, at our loss of Bubba and the comfortable order I had worked so hard to maintain all these years. I felt adrift on a dead sea. Lost in a desert. Will-less for the first time since I left baseball. I didn't want to see our friends, or talk to them, or my family, or my editors. Whenever anyone called, I tried to talk to them and then broke down in hysterical sobs and hung up. I couldn't sleep. I paced the darkened rooms at 2 A.M. I went outside and sat on the deck. I saw, in my mind's eye, Bubba, Blue, and Nero racing around the fence after the possum in a way they never would again. I couldn't stop crying. I couldn't go to the gym. I tried to watch television. The images swam before my eyes. I began to pour my bourbon in my yellow tin cup earlier and earlier each day, until one day I looked up at the clock and saw it was 11:45 A.M.

I glared at Bubba in his cage and screamed at him. "Why? Why? Why?" But he didn't know why. My heart broke for him. I pushed the other dogs out of the house and let Bubba out of his cage. I got down on the floor with him and tried to pet him. He let me pet him for a few seconds, then yanked his head away and ran to the porch door. He waited for me to let him out with the other dogs. The other dogs stared at him through the screen door and waited for him to join them. When he didn't, they looked up at me. Why? When I finally let him outside, I held tight to his collar, ushered the other dogs in past him, then pushed him outside, alone. Blue now scratched at the screen door and cried to get outside with his brother. But Bubba didn't notice him. He was pacing along the perimeter of the fence, looking for the possum.

The other dogs looked at me, wagged their tails, and jumped up on me for affection. I petted them each for a few seconds, then walked away. They slunk down. Hoshi went into my office and lay down under my desk. The others went to different rooms to lay down. Even in his leaving, Bubba dominated our house.

Susan and I sat at the dining-room table and ate in silence. Whenever we tried to talk about Bubba we both broke down sobbing, gasping. Our hearts were broken.

A woman called. She said her name was Olivia Lodato. She lived in Carson City, Nevada. She had heard about Bubba on the Internet. She spoke hesitantly, choosing her words carefully, like a prospective adoptive mother. Her beloved hunting dog had died this past Christmas. It had broken her heart. She couldn't even bear to think about getting another dog for months, until now.

"He sounds like the perfect dog for me," she said. "He'll be the only dog in the house. With a declawed cat. I'm used to big, gruff dogs. I live alone. I want a watchdog and . . ." She paused, as if afraid to say what she wanted to say next.

"What else?" I said.

"I'm a hunter," she said. "I hunt small birds called chuckers. It would be wonderful if he was a hunting dog too."

I told her about the possum. She was thrilled. Then I said, "Bubba's a very strong-willed dog. How old are you?"

She hesitated, then said, "I am fifty-one."

"Are you vigorous enough to handle such a dog?"

She said, very precisely, "I am five-feet, six-inches tall and I weight one-hundred-and-twenty-two pounds and I go hunting in the woods with my brother every weekend. My mother is seventy-two. She's a bow hunter."

We sent her a photograph of Bubba standing in the snow in the mountains of North Carolina. She called us the moment she got it at work. Her voice was breaking. "He's so beautiful!" she said. "My hands are shaking. Do you think there's a chance, even a slim one, that you might let me have him?"

"There's a chance," I said, and broke into tears. "I have to go."

Susan and I tried to talk about the woman at dinner that night."

"She seems perfect," Susan said.

"I can't believe our good luck," I said. "She's everything we could have hoped for."

"It'll be best for all of us," Susan said. "Bubba, Olivia, our other dogs, you and me."

I began to sob and gasp. "Not for me! Never for me!"

We told Olivia everything we could about Bubba, his good points and bad. She loved them all. Like Susan, she was drawn to macho, strong-willed dogs. I was hoping I would tell her something that would turn her against Bubba. But every bad thing I told her seemed to delight her even more. She giggled over his mischievous idiosyncrasies, the way he nosed your arm up in the air when he demanded to be petted.

At five o'clock in the morning on April 8, 1998, Susan and I put Bubba into his traveling crate, carried him outside in the darkness, and loaded him into the back of our Explorer. The other dogs woke and ran to the gate. They began to bark. Stella howled her mother's howl whenever one of her puppies was in danger.

We got to the Delta Dash cargo terminal in ten minutes. We paid $225 to make sure Bubba got priority treatment on his flight to Carson City. Then we put him in the cargo warehouse among boxes and crates. As we were walking to our car we heard Bubba howl pitfully, beseeching us, in a way we will never forget.

We tracked Bubba's flight to Dallas, and Olivia tracked his connecting flight to Reno. "I bought a ticket to Dallas," she said over the phone, "in case he misses his Reno connection."

We cried all day the day Bubba left. We pulled down the shades and sat in our dark house and cried. Susan swore she'd never get another dog again. Our house was dark and silent except for the sounds of our sobbing. We couldn't control ourselves. Even worse, we couldn't understand it. In between our sobs, we talked and talked about what the loss of Bubba meant to us. It was a disruption of the order in all our lives. It was a reminder to me of my own lost children. Yet another failure. What could I have done differently? For Susan, it was more basic than that. It was a mother's loss of a loved one she had raised since he was born. It was all those things and more. But what? It was the only thing that had ever happened in my life that I could not understand. It was proof to us both that God existed.

Blue was lost without his brother. He cried and whimpered incessantly. He sniffed the cage where Bubba had been. He had no personality without Bubba. Hoshi sat and watched us cry with his sympathetic eyes. Kiri slept, her way of dealing with all disruption. Stella went about her day as she always had. She knew her son would go off on his own one day. But Nero was inconsolable over the loss of his son. He refused to eat. He went under Susan's desk and wouldn't come out. The mailman knocked on our front door. None of the dogs barked. They just lay around the house with their eyes opened.

Only Francis still chattered madly in his cage. "Merry Christmas. Fuck you. What a guy. Hoshi, Nero, Kiri. No, no, no, Bubba!"

Susan and I didn't leave the house for days. We were afraid we'd meet a friend and break down, crying. Finally, two of our friends invited us over to their house for dinner. We went early in the evening. We sat outside at dusk on lawn chairs and tried to talk about other things. Finally, as always, our talk turned to Bubba. He's happier now, we said. Olivia is happy. We gave her a gift that changed her life. We gave Bubba a gift too. We gave him back to himself. We freed him to be what was in his nature.

"But it's *so* hard," I said, tears welling up in my eyes. "It's such a loss for us all. I don't know if we'll ever get over it." I began to sob uncontrollably. My friends looked at me strangely. I stood up. "I'm sorry. I have to go."

Susan stayed for another hour. When she got home I saw the look on her face. "What happened?" I said.

"They couldn't believe it," she said of our friends. "They said, 'He's crying over a *dog!*' They said it four times. 'A dog! A dog! A dog! A dog!'"

I have a quotation pinned to the wall over my desk. It's from a sixteenth-century English lord. He said, "He cannot be a gentleman which loveth not a dog."

I remembered the time I was in New Orleans, years ago, interviewing David Duke, the handsome, KKK darling of New Orleans society. We went to a cocktail party with him on St. Charles Avenue in an old, antebellum mansion. I could hear the streetcars pass by outside in the darkness. Suddenly a woman rushed into the parlor, crying hysterically. "It's my dog!" she screamed. "He's been killed by a car! Everybody get out!"

I left, laughing at the woman's grief. Over a dog? But I understood it now. It was *her* grief! Now it was my grief. I didn't expect my friends to share it, feel it, or even understand it. All they had to know was that it was *mine!*

We have never seen those friends again.

Bubba has been with Olivia for two months as I write this. She says she's having a love affair with him. "Thank God he's neutered," she said, laughing. "He sleeps with me in my bed."

"He's a slut," I said.

"So am I," she said, giggling. We found out she had lied to us. She was fifty-three, not fifty-one. She was afraid we'd think she was too old to handle Bubba.

"Two years, Olivia! Jesus! At least knock off ten," I said. She sent us photographs of Bubba sleeping on her couch and playing with her. She looked much younger than fifty-one with her long black hair.

At first, we called Olivia every day to check on Bubba's progress. She told us funny stories about him. She was drinking coffee in her easy chair one morning when Bubba nosed her arm in the air, spilling coffee everywhere. "He was sooo sorry," she said, giggling.

She told us how he chased her cat one day and she knew he was going to kill it. "I just hoped he'd do it quickly," she said. But then Bubba came racing back to her with the cat chasing him. "They make such a big deal about not liking each other," she said. "Now I know when I'm gone to work they play. They just want to keep it from me."

She told us how she takes Bubba for a walk every night, around the block. Every time he comes to the neighbor's Great Dane he makes believe he doesn't notice him.

"He's never done a thing wrong in the house," she said one day. "Except last night. My boyfriend slept over. Bubba ate his slipper. I think he was trying to tell me something."

I said, "He has a way of doing that." She giggled like a girl.

"He never leaves my sight," she said. "He always wants to be wherever I am."

"That prick!" I said. "He would never have anything to do with *us.*"

"It's not that," she said. Then she told us. On the third day she had Bubba, she invited fifteen members of her family to dinner to meet him. She went out shopping and left Bubba in her fenced-in backyard. We had told her never to leave Bubba alone in a backyard, no matter how secure she thought it was. When she returned two hours later, Bubba was gone. He had dug a hole under the fence and escaped. He was gone for four days. Olivia was frantic. She called our vet to ask what she should do. He told her, "Don't call the Jordans. They'll be on the next plane to Carson City." Olivia plastered posters with Bubba's picture on them all over town. The local newspaper carried his photo and a story about him. The local TV station ran his photo on the six o'clock news. On the fourth day she got a call from the local dog pound. They had Bubba. A cowboy had lassoed him on the range and brought him in.

"I was shocked he was still alive," she said. "There are coyotes all around. They eat dogs."

"They must have thought twice about trying to make a meal of Bubba," I said.

"My dog could have killed one or two of them," she said. "But not a whole pack."

"Who?" I said.

"Bubba."

Olivia rushed down to the dog pound to pick up Bubba. He was in a cage at the far end of the room when she entered. He saw her and let out his unearthly wolf howl. "His Bubba howl," she said. "He hasn't left my side since."

"It serves you both right," I said.

That night, over dinner, Susan and I laughed over what Olivia called Bubba's Big Adventure. He had disrupted the life of an entire town after only three days. "That's my Bubba," Susan said. We liked to think that Bubba dug his way out of Olivia's yard to get home to us, but we know that's not true. He dug his way out to find Olivia. They are devoted to one another. Olivia said, "I love him more than any living thing in this world." Bubba is so protective of her that everyone who tries to enter her house has to stop at the door and wait until Bubba sniffs them, then looks up at Olivia. "It's all right, Bubba."

Her daughter brought her 80-pound husky to meet Bubba at Olivia's house. Bubba was nervous at this intrusion into his and Olivia's world, but he behaved himself with the husky at Olivia's insistence. But the husky didn't behave. He lunged at Bubba. Bubba sank his teeth into the husky's shoulder and wouldn't let go. Blood spurted everywhere. After the dogs were finally separated, and her daughter and the husky had left, Olivia called us.

"Now I've seen what you mean," she said. Then, coldly, she said, "My dog beat the shit out of that bigger dog."

She began to teach Bubba how to hunt. She keeps dead birds in her freezer. When it's time to hunt, she puts Bubba in a back room, goes outside, and hides the birds in the grass. Then she lets Bubba out. He races immediately to the birds, picks them up in his mouth, brings them to Olivia, and drops them at her feet. Then he runs back to his room and waits to hunt again.

"He's so smart," she said. "And he's got such a soft mouth. He's going to make a wonderful hunting dog."

After a week, we stopped calling Olivia every day. It was too painful. We called her twice a week for a while, then once a week, then once every two weeks. We haven't called her in three weeks as I write this. Bubba is her dog now. Yet we still call him Bubba Jordan-Lodato. We still cry when we talk about him. I am crying as I write this.

Things change. Susan's hands healed. Nero came out from underneath Susan's desk and began to eat again. We all went back to the routine of our lives, but without enthusiasm. I got up at 4:30 A.M. and opened the porch door to let the dogs chase the possum. None of the dogs came. They slept late. At 3 P.M., Susan and I had our drinks. When the dogs heard the ice cubes tinkle in our glasses, they came running for their biscuits. I made them all sit first. I handed each one their biscuit and then looked down at my hand, confused. I had a sixth biscuit in my hand.

I began throwing with Brian again. But I had no patience. I met him one day at dusk at his high-school field. I had to wait until he finished practice before he could catch me. We went to the bullpen in fading light. I rushed warming up before the light was gone. I threw pitches in the dirt, over his head, and then screamed at him, "For chrissakes, Brian! Catch the fucking ball!"

Two weeks after Bubba left, Susan went shopping. She called me from Borders Bookstore. "I'm looking at a copy of *Dog World*," she said. "There's an ad for Shiba puppies from a breeder in North Carolina."

"Give me the number," I said.

"Babe! Make sure it's a sweet one. Not like Bubba. Please!"

"Don't worry." I called the breeder. She had four male puppies left. I said, "Send me the sweetest-natured one you've got," I FedExed her a check. The next evening, Susan and I went back to the airport, where we'd left Bubba, to pick up our new puppy. Susan looked into his puppy crate and gasped.

"Babe!" she said. "He's the spitting image of Hoshi."

Our friends thought we were gluttons for punishment. "Why six?" they said. "Look what happened with Bubba."

I made a joke out of it. "I had six dog bowls," I said. "Susan wouldn't eat out of the sixth bowl. So . . ."

When the puppy entered the house all the other dogs, except one, growled at him. The puppy ran straight to Hoshi with his ears pinned back and a dog smile on his face. He rolled over onto his back and began licking Hoshi. Hoshi licked him back. He let the puppy crawl all over him, nip his cheeks, his ears, his legs, without a growl. Hoshi, who never played with the other dogs, let the puppy do whatever he wanted to him. Hoshi, with his infinite patience and mystical knowledge, knew what this little puppy meant to us all. When the other dogs saw that Hoshi had accepted the puppy into the pack, they began to accept him too, one by one. Then Hoshi withdrew from the puppy back into his private world.

Blue wanted to play wildly with the puppy at first. We were afraid he'd hurt the little guy, so we kept Blue separated from him for a few days. Finally, Blue calmed down. He let the puppy nip him and chase him around the house. As the puppy got bigger and stronger, Blue played more forcefully with him. The puppy changed Blue. With Bubba, Blue had always been childish, skittish, like one of those teenage boys late to grow pubic hair. Blue became the puppy's big brother. He assumed a certain dignity and selflessness he'd never had, and we'd thought he never would.

Stella treated the puppy like she did her sons. She ignored him until she heard him cry in pain. Then she ran to him, moaning.

Kiri growled at the puppy whenever he walked by her. One time she nipped him on the cheek. The puppy ran, crying. I grabbed Kiri by the scruff of the neck and threw her outside. I beat her with my belt until she cringed. "I will not have it!" I screamed at her. "Do you understand? I don't care if you don't like him, you just can't hurt him."

We were terrified one of our dogs would rip open the puppy's throat. But they weren't Bubba.

Nero wanted nothing to do with the puppy for the longest time. He growled at him constantly. We thought it was because of his bad leg. He was afraid the puppy might hurt him in one of his mad dashes through the house. Also, Nero has a long memory. Maybe he thought his red and white puppy would be a threat to him someday. He was biding his time until the puppy proved himself. Maybe, too, Nero was telling us that for him, no dog can replace his son, Bubba. The puppy isn't much like Bubba. He's cautious and a little timid, but smart and loving, both to our dogs and us. He knows just how far he can go with each dog. He does anything he wants to with Hoshi and Blue. He disregards Stella's angry growls at him. He knows her annoyance is just a mother's sham. He yips and barks at her until she plays with him in a way she never did with her own sons. He does the same with Kiri. He won't let her rest until she rouses herself from her pastoral torpor and chases him through the house. The other day I caught Kiri lying on her back in a languid pose while the puppy licked her face. He still gives Nero a wide berth, although lately Nero has begun to sleep side by side with the puppy under the hot sun in the backyard.

He has begun to bark at strangers. A deep, muffled, throaty sound that reminds me of Bubba. The other dogs hear it, rouse themselves from their lethargy, and bark too.

Sweetness Jordan has been with us for eight weeks now. We did not get him to replace Bubba. Nothing can replace Bubba. We got him to be himself, whatever that is. We got him also to make our lives whole again.

On a Sunday in early May, I went to throw with Brian at the park near his house. Susan came with me. It was a beautiful day. Clear, sunny, hot. A perfect day to throw. Susan sat in the dugout and watched me and Brian warm up. We bantered back and forth as we always did.

"The third-oldest pitcher in minor league history," Brian said. "Jeez, you must be old."

"Fuck you, Brian." I saw Susan smile as we soft tossed. "You gonna play football at the Air Force Academy, Brian? Maybe you can break your other arm?"

"Even with two broken arms I'd still rip that shit of yours."

"In your dreams, Brian. You can't even catch my overhand slider, much less hit it."

Brian was crouched behind home plate now. I was throwing hard, with a good sweat. I cut loose with a fastball. Brian leapt out of his crouch, grinning. He ripped off his catcher's mitt and shook off the hot pain just as my brother used to do when I was a boy throwing on the sidewalk in front of my parents.

"You may be the Old Man and the Sea," he said, "but you can still bring it."

"How fast, Bri?"

"Ninety. You're around ninety almost every pitch."

"Let's pitch an inning," I said.

"Three innings. You've only got a month."

Brian got down in his crouch and flashed me a sign. I began my delivery, kicked, and fired a perfect fastball on the low outside corner of the plate.

"Jeez!" he said. "That one tailed a foot. Strike one."

He gave me a sign again. I shook him off. He came back with another. I threw a fastball that started waist high inside to a righthanded batter and then sailed up and in.

"Strike two!" Brian said. "He had to swing at that one." He grinned. "Even I would have missed that one."

"Even you? Great. I'm throwing hard enough to make a banjo-hitting high-school shortstop miss my fastball."

"Fuck you!" He glanced at Susan. When he saw she was smiling, he smiled too. "Come on, old man. Show me what you've got."

I began my delivery, kicked, and threw an overhand slider waist high down the middle of the plate. Brian went to catch it, then had to twist his glove down at the last instant to catch the ball at his shoetops.

"Un-fucking-hittable!" he said. "Strike three!" He threw the ball back to me. "A perfect sequence," he said. "Let's see if you can do it again." He got down in his crouch and gave me a sign. I stared at it. I kept staring at it. "What's the matter?" Brian said. I felt my eyes welling up with tears again. I forced them back down. "You all right?" Brian said. He was standing now.

"I can't do it anymore," I said. I lobbed him the ball. "I quit," I said. I began to walk off the mound toward Susan.

"What do you mean?" Brian said. "You can't be tired already."

"I'm not tired, Brian. I just quit. I'm not gonna pitch anymore."

"You mean it?"

"I mean it." I went into the dugout and sat beside Susan. She put her arm around me.

"Are you all right, babe?" she said.

I nodded, still fighting back the tears. Brian came into the dugout and sat down with us. I told him about Bubba and the fight and Sweetness. "That's why I can't do it anymore," I said. "Maybe it doesn't make sense to anyone but me. I just don't want to do it anymore. I'm too old."

"You're not old," Brian said. "You're not throwing like you're old."

"But I am old, Brian. I've been deceiving myself. I thought I wasn't old because I didn't feel old. I thought I wasn't old because I can do the physical things you can. But I'm not a kid like you. I don't have the time you do. I don't have the time to be everything I think I can be. I only have the time to be some of them, the important ones."

Brian nodded as if he understood. I think he did.

Susan said, "Are you sure, babe?"

"Positive."

*   *   *

I waited for the dream to come back, as I was sure it would. I lay in bed, fighting off sleep, succumbing, drifting off, and then waking the next morning to realize it hadn't come back. A week passed. Ten days. It was gone. And then one night, when my defenses were down, I had a dream.

I am walking through a woods at dusk. It is autumn. A fading, cold sunlight is slanting through the trees around me. I move in and out of sunlight and shadow. I hear my shoes crunching the dried leaves. I hear my labored breathing. I see my breath before me. I am sweating. My legs feel heavy. I walk between two trees into a small clearing.

I see a dog standing amid the leaves. His back is to me. He is standing perfectly erect, his chest puffed up, his head high. I see from behind him that he has something in his mouth. I call out in a voice I can not hear. He turns, slowly, and faces me. He is holding a small, brown bird between his jaws. He stares at me with his narrow, threatening eyes that do not recognize me. I take a step toward him and call out again in a voice that now I hear.

Bubba!

He turns, and walks off into the woods.

FIVE MONTHS AFTER I stopped throwing, I had my car painted. By then my wife was too embarrassed to ride in it. My 1989 SHO was scratched and dented all over, and its once shiny black paint had faded to a dirty gray-black. I brought it to Kevin at First Class Auto Center in Pompano. Kevin did meticulous work. He was known for painting most of the race cars in South Florida. He told me in his native Boston accent that he'd have my car looking like new. I told him, almost as an afterthought, to paint my five-star mag wheels too.

"What color?" he said.

"Mango orange," I said.

He smiled, shrugged. "Whatever," he said.

"And steam-clean the engine," I said, and left.

Ten days later, Susan dropped me off at First Class to pick up my car. As Kevin led me outside to get my first look at my newly painted car, I said, "How do the wheels look?"

"It's a judgment call," he said.

"What the hell does that mean?"

"It means it's your judgment, not mine."

When I saw the mango-orange wheels I burst out laughing. "Perfect!"

Kevin smiled. "Well, you won't need Lo-jack to trace this car."

I walked around the gleaming black car, looking for painting imperfections, but could find none. "Great job," I said, and went back to his office to pay him.

My car wouldn't start. It coughed and sputtered and then died. I tried it over and over until it finally fired up. It had a sick, lumpy idle I attributed, at first, to its having sat unstarted for almost two weeks. I figured it would smooth out once I drove it. I backed out of his parking lot and headed toward Federal Highway and home. But the car barely moved. It sputtered and coughed with almost no power. I turned it back around and puttered back to Kevin's shop.

When I told him the car would barely run, he went into his shop to talk to the worker who had cleaned the engine. When he returned he looked sick.

"He spilled water on the engine," Kevin said. "There's probably water in the sparkplug holes and on the wires. Leave it overnight. We'll try to dry it out."

When I called Kevin the next morning, he told me there *was* water in the sparkplug holes, but even after he had dried them out, the car still wouldn't run.

"Don't worry," he said. "I'll take care of it." He shipped it on a flatbed truck to my Ford dealer, Maroone Ford, in Fort Lauderdale. I told him to make sure it went directly to Gary James in the service department and no one else. When the car arrived at Maroone, Gary called me. I told him to make sure no one but Brian worked on the car.

"Of course," he said.

Brian was Maroone's top mechanic. He'd done all the work on my car over the last four years, and it was a point of pride with him to keep my car running smoothly. Brian was in his late thirties, a leanly muscled blond guy with a child's eager blue eyes and a guileless smile.

A few days later, I picked up the car from Gary James. It ran beautifully. Before I left, I went back to the mechanics' bay to thank Brian for taking care of my car.

"No problem," he said. "I know how much you like that car." Then he said, "I noticed a baseball glove and spikes in the backseat. Do you play baseball?"

I used to keep my glove and spikes in the trunk when I was throwing with Brian. I didn't want anyone to steal them. But after that last day with Brian, I just tossed them into the backseat and forgot about them.

"Yeah, I used to," I said to the mechanic. Then I told him about my pitching for the Braves years ago, and my one-inning stint with the Waterbury Spirit last summer.

"My son's a pitcher," he said. "He's thirteen. Would you show him a few things?"

"Of course."

I met Brian and his son, Jason, at Holiday Park on a hot, sunny Sunday morning at the same field where I had thrown my first hesitant pitches almost two years before. By instinct, I put on my spikes and took my glove out to the mound where Jason was throwing to his father. I worked with Jason for a few minutes under the hot sun. I told him to raise his left leg higher in midmotion and to drive off the rubber with more force. He tried to do it a few times but couldn't get the hang of it. He flung pitches into the dirt and over his father's head. Finally, Brian stood up from behind home plate.

"Maybe it would help, Pat," he said, "if you showed him how?"

"Good idea, Brian," I said, without thinking.

Brian threw me the ball. Jason stepped back off the mound. I stepped up onto the mound. I put my foot on the rubber, looked down at my catcher, felt the raised seams of the smooth ball in my hand, and then, as I have done so often in my life, and in my dreams, I began to pitch.